Pop Goes the Decade

Pop Goes the Decade

The 2000s

RICHARD A. HALL

GREENWOOD

An Imprint of ABC-CLIO, LLC

Santa Barbara, California • Denver, Colorado

Library of Congress Cataloging-in-Publication Data

Names: Hall, Richard A., author.
Title: Pop goes the decade. The 2000s / Richard A. Hall.
Other titles: 2000s
Description: Santa Barbara : Greenwood, an Imprint of ABC-CLIO, LLC, 2021.
| Series: Pop goes the decade | Includes bibliographical references and
  index.
Identifiers: LCCN 2020034611 (print) | LCCN 2020034612 (ebook) | ISBN
  9781440868122 (hardcover) | ISBN 9781440868139 (ebook)
Subjects: LCSH: Popular culture—United States—History—21st century. |
  United States—Civilization—1970- | United States—Social life and
  customs—1971- | United States—Intellectual life—21st century.
Classification: LCC E169.12 .H3425 2021 (print) | LCC E169.12 (ebook) |
  DDC 306.0973/0905—dc23
LC record available at https://lccn.loc.gov/2020034611
LC ebook record available at https://lccn.loc.gov/2020034612

ISBN: 978-1-4408-6812-2 (print)
      978-1-4408-6813-9 (ebook)

25 24 23 22 21   1 2 3 4 5

This book is also available as an eBook.

Greenwood
An Imprint of ABC-CLIO, LLC

ABC-CLIO, LLC
147 Castilian Drive
Santa Barbara, California 93117
www.abc-clio.com

This book is printed on acid-free paper ∞

Manufactured in the United States of America

This book is dedicated to my five millennial children,
Kyle, Samantha, Jake, Michael, and Lupita,
and my research assistants,
Lupita Hall, Anahi Montelongo, Mireya Montes, Rebekah Rodriguez,
Pamela Wallace, and Samantha Eachus.
These years were yours, and this book is for you!

Contents

Timeline

1999   January 19: BlackBerry releases the 850, an email paging device.

February 12: President Bill Clinton receives a full acquittal on all charges from his 1998 impeachment.

March 31: The first TiVo DVR hits the market.

April 20: Two high school students commit a mass shooting at Columbine High School in Columbine, Colorado, killing twelve students, one teacher, and themselves; this begins a wave of mass shootings in the United States that goes on throughout the early millennium.

May 19: George Lucas releases the long-awaited *Star Wars, Episode I: The Phantom Menace*, featuring the world's first fully CGI character, Jar Jar Binks.

June 1: Napster has its initial release. The free file-sharing service causes controversy regarding the widespread sharing of copyrighted material on the internet.

2000   January 1: The final year of the second millennium—and the twentieth century—begins.

March 4: Sony releases the PlayStation 2.

April 1: The U.S. Census reports the U.S. population has passed 280 million.

July 14: 20th Century Fox releases *X-Men*, directed by Bryan Singer and starring Patrick Stewart and Hugh Jackman, ushering in the modern era of blockbuster superhero films.

October 15: HBO debuts the series *Curb Your Enthusiasm* by writer, producer, and star Larry David, cocreator of the iconic 1990s series *Seinfeld*.

November 7: The 2000 presidential election between Vice President Al Gore (D) and Texas governor George W. Bush (R) results in a dead heat when the election results in Florida prove to be unclear.

November 14: Hand recounts of Florida ballots begins; a battle ensues between the two campaigns, the Bush camp fighting against recounts and the Gore camp pursuing limited hand recounts in a few counties.

November 21: The Florida Supreme Court unanimously supports continued recounts through November 26.

December 12: The U.S. Supreme Court rules in a 7–2 decision to stop the recounts.

December 13: Gore concedes the election to Bush.

2001   January 1: The new/third millennium—and the twenty-first century—officially begins.

January 9: Apple launches iTunes.

January 20: George W. Bush inaugurated as the forty-third president of the United States.

July 11: Napster officially goes offline.

September 11: Nineteen members of the terrorist organization Al-Qaeda hijack four American passenger aircraft, flying two into the Twin Towers of the World Trade Center in New York City and a third into the Pentagon in Washington, DC. The passengers of the fourth plane attempt to retake the aircraft, leading the terrorists to crash the plane into a field in Pennsylvania. Overall, 2,977 people—not including the terrorists—die.

September 12: All professional sporting events except the World Wrestling Federation (WWF) cancel public events out of respect for recent events. WWF chair Vincent K. McMahon thinks that doing so would allow the terrorists to win.

September 20: In a televised speech, President Bush declares what comes to be known as the War on Terror.

September 29: The NBC television series *Saturday Night Live* broadcasts its first show since the terror attacks, making a bold statement to the nation that it is okay to laugh again.

October 3: The NBC television series *The West Wing* airs a special episode titled "Isaac and Ishmael," written by series creator Aaron Sorkin in the weeks since 9/11; the episode addresses White House reactions to terrorism.

October 7: A U.S.-led NATO coalition invades Afghanistan in an attempt to oust the ruling Taliban regime in retaliation against Al-Qaeda for the 9/11 attacks.

October 16: The WB network debuts the television series *Smallville*, starring Tom Welling as a teenage Clark Kent and his journey to become Superman; its ten-season run makes it the most successful superhero series in TV history.

October 23: Apple launches the iPod MP3 player.

October 26: Congress passes the Uniting and Strengthening America by Providing Appropriate Tools Required to Intercept and Obstruct Terrorism Act (USA PATRIOT Act), granting broad surveillance powers to the federal government.

November 4: Comedian Ellen DeGeneres hosts the 2001 Emmy Awards when no one else can be found due to the emotional aftermath of 9/11. DeGeneres has been an outcast professionally since coming out as a lesbian in April 1997; her poise, grace, and respect of the situation shoot her to the top of national popularity.

November 6: FOX television debuts the series 24, starring Kiefer Sutherland as counterterrorist agent Jack Bauer; although controversial for its violence, its popularity—due largely to its post-9/11 timing— ultimately leads the series to a ten-season run.

November 15: Microsoft enters the video game market with the release of the Xbox.

2002   January 28: Verizon launches the first 3G network in the United States.

February 14: Sirius satellite radio launches in four states.

March 4: BlackBerry launches the 5810, its first device to run on a 2G network.

March 24: Halle Berry becomes the first African American woman to win the Academy Award for Best Lead Actress for her work in the film *Monster's Ball* (2001).

May 6: Elon Musk launches Space X (Space Exploration Technologies Corp.).

June 11: FOX television debuts the reality series *American Idol*, with Simon Cowell, Paula Abdul, and Randy Jackson as the judges; it becomes one of the most popular reality singing-competition series of the decade.

November 8: The UN Security Council unanimously passes resolutions giving Iraqi president Saddam Hussein one last chance to comply with all previous UN resolutions regarding alleged possession of weapons of mass destruction.

November 17: Boxing legend Muhammad Ali visits Afghanistan as the official UN messenger of peace.

2003   February 1: The space shuttle *Columbia* explodes on reentry, killing all crew aboard.

March 10: Popular country music group the Dixie Chicks receive harsh condemnation for their remarks against President Bush during a concert in London, England; country music fans in the United States boycott the band for years.

March 20: A U.S.-led coalition invades Iraq in an attempt to oust Iraqi president Saddam Hussein.

April 30: The Human Genome Project concludes its research.

July 15: *Queer Eye for the Straight Guy* debuts on the cable channel Bravo, presenting a team of five gay men who educate straight men on fashion, fine dining, and proper grooming. Beginning the "metrosexual" wave, the original series runs until 2007.

August 29: Skype video chatting service launches.

October 8: Image Comics releases *The Walking Dead #1*, a postapocalyptic zombie narrative by Robert Kirkman and Tony Moore, the popularity of which will result in the wildly popular AMC television series of the same name in 2010.

November 17: Actor Arnold Schwarzenegger is sworn in as governor of California after winning the special election resulting in the recall of the state's former governor.

December 13: U.S. armed forces capture Iraqi president Saddam Hussein.

2004   February 4: Facebook is launched by Mark Zuckerberg in Cambridge, Massachusetts.

May 6: The final episode of *Friends* airs on NBC.

July 22: The 9/11 Commission releases its report detailing the terrorist attacks of 2001.

November 2: George W. Bush wins reelection as president against Democratic nominee Senator John Kerry of Massachusetts.

December 4: Reporters Mark Fainaru-Wada and Lance Williams of the *San Francisco Chronicle* break the story of massive steroid use in Major League Baseball.

2005   February 1: Amazon launches Amazon Prime, originally as a service providing free shipping.

February 14: YouTube is launched by Steve Chen, Chad Hurley, and Jawed Karim in San Mateo, California.

August 23: Hurricane Katrina hits the Gulf Coast as a category five hurricane; the intensity of the storm continues for eight days, leading to 1,833 deaths and approximately $125 billion in damages.

November 22: Microsoft releases the Xbox 360.

2006   March 21: Twitter is launched by Jack Dorsey in San Francisco, California.

March 31: Toshiba releases the first HD DVD discs; the technology fails against Blu-Ray by 2008.

April 23: Spotify audio streaming platform launches from Sweden.

June 20: Sony releases the first Blu-Ray discs; the players follow two months later.

November 13: Google officially purchases YouTube for $1.6 billion in Google stock.

November 17: Sony releases the PlayStation 3.

November 19: Nintendo releases the Wii video gaming system.

December 30: Iraqi president Saddam Hussein is executed in Iraq after being found guilty for atrocities against the Iraqi people.

2007 May 3: BlackBerry launches the Curve, adding a camera to its smartphone.

June 29: Apple releases the first iPhone at a price of $499 for the four gigabyte model and $599 for the eight gigabyte model.

September 24: CBS debuts the series *The Big Bang Theory*, starring Jim Parsons, Kaley Cuoco, and Johnny Galecki, centering on a group of nerdy, pop-culture-obsessed scientists and their attractive female neighbor; the massive success of the series leads it to run for twelve seasons.

November 19: Amazon launches the Kindle e-book reader.

2008 May 2: Marvel Studios makes its debut with the release of *Iron Man*, starring Robert Downey Jr. and directed by Jon Favreau, launching what becomes known as the Marvel Cinematic Universe, one of the most successful film franchises in Hollywood history.

May 20: Paramount Pictures releases *Indiana Jones and the Kingdom of the Crystal Skull*, starring Harrison Ford and directed by Steven Spielberg; it is the fourth film in the series, and the first since 1989.

July 8: Warner Brothers releases *The Dark Knight*, the sequel to the 2005 film *Batman Begins*, both starring Christian Bale and directed by Christopher Nolan; the film quickly becomes the most successful superhero film in history, and actor Heath Ledger receives a posthumous Academy Award for Best Supporting Actor for his role as the Joker.

July 29: Sirius satellite radio merges with XM (officially becoming Sirius/XM in 2011).

September 7: Lending institutions Fannie Mae and Freddie Mac are taken over by the federal government, an early sign of the oncoming Great Recession.

September 15: Wall Street giant Lehman Brothers declares bankruptcy, leading to a massive drop in the stock market.

September 16: The U.S. Federal Reserve takes over American International Group, the nation's largest insurance company.

October 3: Congress passes the Troubled Asset Relief Program (TARP) to bail out the Wall Street banks.

November 4: Senator Barack Obama (D-IL) defeats Senator John McCain (R-AZ) in the presidential election.

2009   January 20: Barrack Obama is inaugurated as the forty-fourth president of the United States, while the country is deep in the Great Recession.

February 19: CNBC financial news channel commentator Rick Santelli calls for a "tea party" (a reference to the 1773 antitax Boston Tea Party) in response to a homeowner bailout program suggested by President Obama; the result is the formation of the radically conservative Taxed Enough Already (TEA) Party.

May 7: Paramount Pictures and director J. J. Abrams release *Star Trek*, a reboot of the iconic science-fiction franchise, with new actors in the established roles for the first time in the franchise's forty-three-year history.

June 29: Samsung launches the Galaxy smartphone.

August 8: Sonia Sotomayor becomes the first Hispanic justice to the U.S. Supreme Court.

September 23: ABC debuts the sitcom *Modern Family*, a story about three related families: one a traditional upper-middle-class white family with three children, the second an older wealthy white man with a much younger Colombian immigrant wife and her young son, and the third a white gay couple with an adopted Vietnamese infant. The popular series legitimizes and normalizes diversity and runs for eleven seasons.

Background and Introduction: America by 2000

As America prepared to exit one century and millennium for the next, they experienced the wild ride that was the 1990s. As that decade dawned, America was still embroiled in the Cold War. Soon, however, in December 1991, the Soviet Union suddenly—and bloodlessly—collapsed, and with a whimper instead of a bang, the decades-long Cold War was over. In the immediate wake of the Cold War, the American economy took a large dip for the first time since the 1970s, but within five years, it rebounded to the largest economic expansion in the country's history. President Bill Clinton won two national elections without ever attaining a majority of the popular vote and became the first president in 130 years—and only the second ever—to be impeached by the House of Representatives. Throughout the decade, America was repeatedly hit by a mysterious organization called Al-Qaeda, under the leadership of the militant Muslim Osama bin Laden. Personal computers took over day-to-day life in the span of only a few years. The internet revolutionized the American economy, politics, and daily life. As the computerized clocks ticked closer to turning from 1999 to 2000, the country held its breath to see if computers understood the change.

This was the decade that Generation X came of age. After spending their childhood in the 1970s learning their values and morals from *Sesame Street* and *Mr. Rogers' Neighborhood* and becoming obsessed with *Star Wars*, Gen X went on to create the MTV generation, spending their teenage years adding considerably to the consumer boom of the 1980s. In the 1990s, Generation X went to college, served their country, got married and divorced, and began having kids of their own. They were the generation that had gone from eight-track players to audio cassette decks to CD players. In the 1990s, they would be the generation that went from VHS to DVD.

They were the grunge rockers and gangsta rappers. They were the first generation that would embrace the internet. They drank and did ecstasy, and by decade's end, they would become obsessed with *Star Wars* all over again. They were avid viewers of *Friends* and *Seinfeld*. They were both narcissistic and politically correct, and they suffered the schizophrenia and neuroses that those programs promoted. It was in the 1990s that Generation X became who they were destined to be—the generation that would take the reigns of America in the twenty-first century. Many of the issues involved in the formation of Generation X were covered in the 2016 National Geographic documentary series *Generation X*, narrated by actor Christian Slater.

In popular culture, television sitcoms took on more and more controversial issues. Lesbian comedian Ellen DeGeneres gambled her career by coming out on national television and spent the next several years all but ostracized for it. The casts of *Seinfeld* and *Friends* held a mirror to how self-absorbed Americans were quickly becoming. The power of MTV, which defined cable television and the music industry in the 1980s, slowly saw a decline that would leave it all but obsolete going into the new millennium. Popular music swung from the grunge rock of Nirvana and Pearl Jam to the upbeat pop hits of Britney Spears and the Spice Girls. In Hollywood, success went from being defined by tens of millions to hundreds of millions of dollars at the box office, and director James Cameron would turn a real-life eighty-five-year-old shipwreck into the most expensive and, conversely, most successful film of all time. Meanwhile, in Great Britain, an unemployed single mother was writing a novel about a boy wizard that was about to completely take over the world. This was the 1990s, and Americans would soon learn that it was actually the calm before the storm.

As the decade came to an end, many Americans began to ponder the question, "When is the millennium?" Many Americans are actually confused about how centuries are numbered. Throughout the 1900s, the century was referred to as the "twentieth century." Those individuals consider it more logical to refer to the 1900s as the "nineteenth century." For most of the century, this oddity was merely pushed aside; but as the millennium came to a close, those Americans were now confused as to when the new millennium would begin. The twentieth century—and all centuries prior to that—were delineated by the last year of that century. The first century AD/CE ended in the year 100. The last year of the twentieth century, therefore, would be the year 2000, making January 1, 2001, the dawn of both a new century (the twenty-first) and a new millennium (the third millennium CE). Overall, though, this small question of calendar counting paled in comparison to the other major issues facing American society in the last decade of the twentieth century.

SOCIETY

The 1990s showed Americans that the ideals, goals, and hopes of the social movements of the 1960s and 1970s remained unfulfilled. Coming into the 1990s, the LGBTQ+ community remained socially ostracized. Sexism and racism remained rampant throughout the country. Though great accomplishments in the decade would go far to address these issues, many of them remain as problematic in American society today than before each movement started.

In the realm of social equality across the spectrum, many issues appear to be never-ending battles, but the struggle to achieve total equality must go on.

LGBTQ+

Coming into the twenty-first century, the biggest social movement in the country was the push for LGBTQ+ rights. Throughout the 1980s, the gay community had been ostracized due to a combination of the radicalization of conservative politics in the Republican Party and the mysterious and deadly HIV/AIDS virus. When AIDS first came onto the American landscape in the late 1970s and early 1980s, victims appeared to be only gay men. For the first couple of years of the 1980s, nightly newscasts called AIDS "the gay cancer." The religious right pointed to that fact to push the idea that AIDS was God's punishment on the gay community for their "lifestyle choices," and many Americans were unable to come to any other conclusion that fit the released facts. As a result, President Ronald Reagan (1911–2004) refused to approve government funding for AIDS research. However, as the decade progressed, Americans learned more about the virus and that, in fact, no one was safe from it.

By 1990, approximately one hundred thousand Americans had died from AIDS. In 1985, gay rights activist Cleve Jones (b. 1954) conceived the idea for the NAMES Project and the AIDS Quilt. For the next two years, Americans from across the country contributed pieces of quilt with names sewn onto them of people who had been lost to AIDS. In 1987, the pieces were brought together in Washington, DC. President Reagan's successor, George H. W. Bush (1924–2018), finally approved government funding for AIDS research, and not too long afterward, breakthroughs were made for drug cocktails that proved to greatly expand the life of those infected with HIV.

Another issue facing the LGBTQ+ community was the right to openly serve in the U.S. armed forces. For decades, applicants to the armed services were asked prior to signing if they were gay or lesbian. An affirmative response equaled immediate disqualification from duty. In the past, presidential orders to racially and ethnically integrate the armed forces in the late 1940s and incorporation of women into the regular armed forces in the early 1970s had both provided massive boons to each corresponding social movement. The issue of LGBTQ+ rights, however, proved to be more difficult. Unlike past social movements, where prejudice was based on "surface" issues, LGBTQ+ rights were perceived to speak to more to long-established social "norms" of sexual "behavior." On December 21, 1993, President Bill Clinton (b. 1946) authorized implementation of the policy that came to be known as Don't Ask/Don't Tell (DADT).

Under this policy, implemented from February 28, 1994, to September 20, 2011, recruits could no longer be asked about their sexual orientation, nor could any future commander or superior officer or noncommissioned officer inquire about a soldier's orientation. At the time, this was viewed as a huge step toward LGBTQ+ rights, but, in hindsight considering how the military handled previous social movements, the policy is perceived more as kicking the can down the road. Though it did not allow LGBTQ+ soldiers, sailors, marines, and air force personnel to serve openly, it did allow them to serve unmolested, in theory. By the time President Barack Obama (b. 1961) discontinued the policy in exchange for full and open service, the gay rights movement had already made huge leaps and bounds, and the community had become more embraced by a larger portion of Americans.

In the late 1980s and early 1990s, AIDS became more demystified, helping to destigmatize the gay community for its perceived connection to the disease. In 1984, thirteen-year-old Ryan White (1971–1990) became infected with HIV from a blood treatment for his hemophilia. White was neither gay nor sexually active. Notable celebrities like Michael Jackson (1958–2009) and Elton John (b. 1947) took up White's cause, bringing his story to the public and working with White to bring national awareness to the inclusivity of the deadly disease. His death from AIDS in 1990 shortly after he graduated high school, was mourned by the entire nation, and it was a significant factor to bringing about government funding for research. In 1991, basketball legend Earvin "Magic" Johnson (b. 1959) announced that he had contracted HIV by way of numerous sexual encounters with many women. These two cases went a long way to educating the general public on HIV/AIDS, helping along the way to destigmatize the gay community.

A huge milestone for the LGBTQ+ movement came later in the decade via popular comedian Ellen DeGeneres (b. 1958). DeGeneres was wildly in the late 1980s and early 1990s and was given her own sitcom, *Ellen* (ABC, 1994–1998). Like stand-up comic Jerry Seinfeld (b. 1954) on the very popular *Seinfeld* (NBC, 1989–1998), Ellen portrayed a slightly fictionalized version of herself. In the spring of 1997, in an interview with TV talk-show host Oprah Winfrey (b. 1954), Ellen came out as lesbian. Shortly thereafter, Ellen's sitcom character also came out as lesbian to her therapist (also played by Winfrey). Although it was one of the highest-rated single television episodes of the decade, having an openly lesbian star and main character made executives at ABC TV and parent company Walt Disney nervous, leading them to dramatically pull back on marketing the show, cancel it after its next season, and severely damage DeGeneres's career.

In the immediate aftermath of the 9/11 attacks in 2001, many professional comedians felt uncomfortable being funny, as the nation's wounds were still so fresh. As a result, no one would accept traditional comedian roles as awards show hosts in the weeks and months following the event. The 2001 Emmy Awards were due to air in November following the attacks. When no one would accept the job of host, organizers turned to DeGeneres, who had mostly been off the national radar since cancellation of her series. As a result of her amazing performance where she brilliantly walked the line of respect and comedy and uplifted the nation from its doldrums, Ellen overnight became a beloved national treasure across the sociopolitical spectrum. In 2003, she launched her own daytime talk show, *The Ellen DeGeneres Show* (Syndication, 2003–present), which remains the highest-rated daytime program on television to the present day.

By the time of Ellen's return, Americans were already becoming more open minded about the issue of the LGBTQ+ community. Popular television series such as the sitcom *Will & Grace* (NBC, 1998–2006; 2018–present) and reality fashion-advice show *Queer Eye for the Straight Guy* (Bravo, 2003–2007), placed openly gay characters—albeit all male—into the homes of Americans across the nation. Seeing gay men as "regular" human beings, with all of the same issues, problems, and foibles as everyone else, went leaps and bounds toward deostracizing the gay community and making issues such as same-sex marriage more palatable to an ever-increasing number of Americans. Finally, in 2015, despite its conservative majority, the U.S. Supreme Court, in a 5–4 decision declared state bans on same-sex marriage unconstitutional in the landmark case *Obergefell v. Hodges* (576US14-556).

THIRD-WAVE FEMINISM

Throughout the 1990s, gay rights and its message of inclusivity became embraced as part of what has become known as third-wave feminism. A key launching point of third-wave feminism was the 1991 congressional testimony of Anita Hill (b. 1956) before the Senate Judiciary Committee during confirmation hearings for Bush appointee Clarence Thomas (b. 1948) for the open position on the Supreme Court. In these televised hearings, Hill recounted numerous instances of office-place sexual harassment on the part of Thomas. Though her heartfelt testimony was compelling, bringing to light the long-standing issue of workplace harassment, a lack of concrete evidence as well as Thomas's own adamant denials failed to prevent his elevation to the high court. Hill's bravery did, however, assist in launching this third wave of the American feminist movement, and sexual harassment would become enjoined with issues such as equal pay, continued protection of abortion rights, and general across-the-board socioeconomic inclusivity to define the feminist movement of the 1990s and early 2000s.

Unlike the more socially active 1970s, popular culture in the 1990s did little to address these issues of mutual respect and inclusivity. One rare instance on television was the late 1990s series *Buffy the Vampire Slayer* (WB, 1997–2001; UPN, 2001–2003). Created by Joss Whedon (b. 1964) and based loosely on his 1992 feature film of the same name, the series starred Sarah Michelle Gellar (b. 1977) as high schooler Buffy Summers, the latest "Chosen One" in a long line of "slayers," young women imbued with enhanced speed, strength, and agility that allow her to protect the world from "vampires, demons, and the forces of darkness" (series opening titles). On this series, only women were chosen to be the slayer. Buffy fights evil with the help of her small cadre of friends, most powerful among them being her best friend, Willow Rosenberg, a lesbian witch, played by Allison Hannigan (b. 1974). Going into the twenty-first century, the number of women and LGBTQ+ heroes and heroines would dramatically increase.

RACISM

Race played a major role in the social fabric of the 1990s. In 1991, Rodney King (1965–2012) was beaten by the Los Angeles police after attempting to evade capture; his ordeal was captured by a local civilian on home video and released to the press and authorities. Just over a year later, after all four officers involved were acquitted, the Black community in Los Angeles broke out into violent riots from April 29 to May 4, 1992. On the first day of the attacks, white truck driver Reginald Denny (b. 1956) was dragged from his truck by Black protesters while stopped at a stop light and severely beaten, nearly to death. In a joint press conference with Denny days later, King uttered the phrase for which he went down in history: "Can't we all just get along?"

In mid-June 1994, football legend O. J. Simpson (b. 1947) was arrested for the murders of his ex-wife, Nicole Brown Simpson (1959–1994), and Ron Goldman (1968–1994), both of whom had been found stabbed to death on the morning of June 12, 1994. The highly hyped and televised murder trial the following year captivated the nation. Though the circumstantial evidence against Simpson was overwhelming, his high-profile defense team—consisting of legendary lawyers Johnnie Cochran (1937–2005), Robert Shapiro (b. 1942), and Alan Dershowitz (b. 1938)—relied heavily on the well-established racism within the Los Angeles Police Department as the key factor in their client's arrest.

Despite the compelling case brought by Los Angeles district attorneys Marcia Clark (b. 1953) and Chris Darden (b. 1956), the jury was not convinced of Simpson's guilt beyond a reasonable doubt, and he was found not guilty on all counts. The case did, however, reignite racial tensions in Los Angeles and brought systemic racism to light in the mainstream media once more. Another member of Simpson's legal team was his longtime friend Robert Kardashian (1944–2003), whose daughters and ex-wife would dominate reality television and American fashion in the twenty-first century with their television series, *Keeping Up with the Kardashians* (E!, 2007–present). The trial has been the subject of dozens of books and documentaries in the decades since, most notably featured in dramatized form as the first season of the television series *American Crime Story* (FX, 2016–present).

Like the women's movement, racial issues on television were not nearly as evident as they had been in the 1970s. The most prominent series to address issues of race in America was the sitcom *The Fresh Prince of Bel-Air* (NBC, 1990–1996). Starring rapper Will "the Fresh Prince" Smith as a teenager of the same name, the show centered on Smith moving from his poor inner-city home of Philadelphia to live with his wealthy aunt and uncle in Bel-Air, California. Established primarily as a standard fish-out-of-water situation comedy, the series frequently addressed the issues of race and systemic racism, as well as the fact that, though some African Americans like the Banks family had attained considerable wealth and social standing, most African Americans across the country still had to deal with the systemic racism in place since the nation's beginning.

In the first two decades of the twenty-first century, the United States would experience an epidemic of mass shootings, mostly at American public schools and universities. This trend began on April 20, 1999, at Columbine High School in Columbine, Colorado. On that day, two of the high school's seniors, heavily armed with various guns, murdered twelve students and one teacher. What Americans initially—and hopefully—viewed as a one-and-done nightmare actually became the first in a seemingly endless spate of violence that would, to date, take hundreds of lives. This caused yet another divide in American society over the arguments of Second Amendment rights versus societal safety, and as America argued, more and more young people died.

POLITICS

As America continued to deal with the ever-changing social landscape, the 1990s also saw some of the most amazing political events and crises in the nation's history. Throughout the decade, the United States transitioned from the decades-long Cold War to the inward-looking Culture Wars that continue to haunt the nation well into the twenty-first century. All the while, several sporadic terrorist attacks against American interests across the globe fore-shadowed the forthcoming event that would bring the world's sole remaining superpower to its knees: 9/11. During the years in between, America would become embroiled in several small military engagements across the globe, see Russia transform from communism to something possibly more dangerous, and witness China emerge as a major player on the world stage; meanwhile, at home, the country would go through its first presidential impeachment in 130 years and only the second in its long history. Through it all, the internet would bring Americans together—and tear them apart—like never before.

The 1990s opened with a new kind of international threat, one really not seen since the Korean conflict of 1950–1953. On August 2, 1990, Iraqi president and dictator Saddam Hussein (1937–2006) ordered his country's invasion of the neighboring coastal country of Kuwait. Tensions had built over the previous decade, due mainly to overwhelming debt that Iraq owed to Kuwait and Kuwait's refusal to join with the rest of the Organization of Petroleum Exporting Countries to cut oil production in order to raise international oil prices. Hussein's aggression did not go unanswered as U.S. president George H. W. Bush coordinated an international coalition to protect neighboring Saudi Arabia and, if Hussein did not voluntarily leave Kuwait, to liberate the small nation.

Operation Desert Shield launched on August 8, 1990, guaranteeing the security of Saudi Arabia. On January 17, 1991, President Bush ordered the beginning of Operation Desert Storm. By the end of February, Iraq had been pushed out of Kuwait and agreed to abide by United Nations resolutions. Although the success of this Persian Gulf War resulted in President Bush enjoying near–90 percent approval ratings in the United States, many criticized him for not pursuing Iraqi forces into Iraq and taking out Hussein's regime. Bush explained that doing so would have destabilized the region and required years of nation building on the part of the United States. The 2003 invasion of Iraq and removal of Hussein by President George W. Bush (b. 1946, and son of the first President Bush) proved that he had been correct.

Another major world event in 1991 was the dissolution of the Union of Soviet Socialist Republics (USSR), or Soviet Union. Since 1947, the United States and USSR had existed in a tense state of Cold War, where both major nuclear powers existed on the brink of possible nuclear war. Throughout the 1980s, the

Soviet Union's economy sank dramatically as the superpower strained its resources in an attempt to keep up with the continuous military buildup of the United States. By November 1991, it was clear that Soviet control of their various republics (including Ukraine, Belarus, Georgia, and Uzbekistan) had severely weakened.

On Christmas Day 1991, Soviet leader Mikhail Gorbachev (b. 1931) resigned, declaring his government dissolved, and handed control of Russia and the Soviet nuclear arsenal to Russian president Boris Yeltsin (1931–2007). The following day, the USSR was declared officially dissolved, independence was granted to the remaining Soviet republics, and communism in Russia was officially over. In February 1992, Yeltsin and U.S. president Bush held a joint press conference in Washington, DC, officially declaring the Cold War over The Soviet Union's permanent seat on the UN Security Council was given to Russia.

Going into the presidential election year of 1992, President Bush's reelection for a second term seemed all but certain. Under Bush's leadership in his first term, international drug lord Panamanian president Manuel Noriega (1934–2017) had been taken into U.S. custody, Hussein had been pushed from Kuwait, and the Cold War had ended. At home, Bush had provided funding for HIV/AIDS research and signed the Americans with Disabilities Act. However, an economic recession beginning in the summer of 1992 caused more conservative Republicans to begin questioning Bush's handling of the U.S. economy; most notably, they criticized his approval of tax increases despite his campaign pledge in 1988 "Read my lips; no new taxes." In response, Texas billionaire H. Ross Perot (b. 1930) launched an independent bid for the presidency, essentially splitting the Republican and conservative vote in November. As a result, the Democratic nominee, Arkansas governor Bill Clinton, won the election with only 43 percent of the popular vote. Perot's independent bid would lead to another upset for Republicans in 1996, once more giving the election to Clinton, who received 49 percent of the popular vote that year.

Another outcome of the 1992 election was the essential birth of what has come to be known as the Culture Wars. Referring to conflict between conservative and liberal elements in society, the term was first coined in the 1991 book *Culture Wars: The Struggle to Define America* by James Hunter (b. 1955), although it is more popularly attributed to conservative commentator Pat Buchanan's (b. 1938) speech at the 1992 Republican National Convention. Although there had been a growing struggle between conservatives and liberals since the 1960s, the fall of our only national "enemy" with the end of the Cold War left Americans looking inward for new "enemies." Despite the term's origin, the Culture Wars since 1992 have continuously and increasingly torn Americans apart, with a brief respite in the couple years immediately following 9/11. Today, everything from health care to immigration, to abortion rights, to gun rights, to LGBTQ+ rights, to the legalization of marijuana, to child vaccinations, to school choice, to race relations, to political correctness, and more continues to divide Americans into seemingly endless battling ideological camps, with no clear end in sight.

The first big fight in the Culture Wars arose during President Clinton's first year in office. Throughout 1993, Clinton sought passage of his plan for universal, government-sponsored health care. This led the more radically conservative wing of the Republican Party to rally in the 1994 midterm elections, winning both houses of Congress for the first time since the 1950s. The new speaker of the House of Representatives, Newt Gingrich (b. 1943), declared the Republican Party's "contract with America," promising to stop the president's universal health care proposal and to cut government spending and taxes. From that point to the present, the Republican Party has become more and more radically conservative on every issue, pushing the liberal wing of the Democratic Party to move further left by 2018.

In 1994, Independent Counsel Kenneth Starr (b. 1946) was appointed to investigate possible criminal activity by President Clinton and First Lady Hillary Rodham Clinton (b. 1947) in an illegal real-estate investment in the late 1970s that came to be known as Whitewater. Although the Clintons' business partners in the venture were convicted, no wrongdoing was discovered connected directly to either of the Clintons. A side investigation by Starr's team, however, did look into allegations of marital infidelity on the part of President Clinton with a White House intern, Monica Lewinsky (b. 1973), that began during the 1995 government shutdowns.

President Clinton was questioned on the matter under oath, and he adamantly denied the allegations. It was soon discovered that he had lied and that he had suggested that others, including Lewinsky and his own personal secretary, do so as well. As a result, on December 18, 1998, President Clinton became only the second president in U.S. history to be impeached. He faced two charges: perjury and obstruction of justice. The Senate failed to achieve the two-thirds vote required for removal from office, handing the president a verdict of not guilty. Though it was popularly portrayed as a strictly political move, some Republicans in the House did vote against impeachment, and five Republican senators voted not guilty on both charges, with an additional five Republicans voting not guilty on perjury. Despite the scandal, President Clinton maintained high approval ratings from the public throughout the remainder his presidency.

The twentieth century drew to a close with a clear foreshadowing of how the next century was going to proceed. In the presidential election of 2000, Republican Texas governor George W. Bush faced off against Democrat Vice President Al Gore. Politically, everything pointed toward a Gore win. Despite his impeachment, President Clinton held high approval ratings, the U.S. economy had just experienced its greatest expansion in its history, and Clinton had just produced the first balanced budget and projected budget surplus since the 1830s. This should have all but ensured that the party in power would stay in power. Only two issues favored the Republican: a sight recession that stoked some fears that the expanding economy—and, in particular, the dot-com bubble—was about to burst and the issue of what the government should do with the projected budget surplus.

The vice president insisted that the surplus should be set aside in what he called a "lockbox," essentially saving the money for a rainy day. The governor felt that if the government was taking more money from the American people than it needed, then the people deserved a refund; in theory, those refunds would boost consumerism, thereby avoiding a deepening of the recession. Then there were the incidents that worked against Vice President Gore. In 1996, President Clinton signed the Defense of Marriage Act, federally defining marriage as between "one man and one woman," hurting the Democrats with LGBTQ+ voters. Also, despite Clinton's continued popularity, Gore distanced himself from his boss during the campaign out of a fear of insulting values voters who may be put off by the president's infidelity. Last was the Elian Gonzalez incident. In 1999, Cuban refugee Elizabeth Rodriguez drowned on her way to seek asylum in the United States. Her six-year-old son, Elian Gonzalez, made it and was staying with relatives in Florida. In the spring of 2000, Clinton ordered Gonzalez returned to his father in Cuba, who was suing for custody. This hurt the Democrats with liberal pro-refugee voters.

On the night of November 7, the networks originally called the election for Bush, with Florida being the deciding state in a dead-heat electoral race. Soon after, however, the Associated Press—the only news outlet that had not yet called the Florida race—reported suspected voting irregularities in some Florida districts, putting the outcome in doubt. The vice president, who had already called Bush to concede the election, withdrew his concession and called for a recount in Florida. The Florida secretary of state, Katherine Harris (b. 1957), resisted the idea of a recount, a controversial stand considering that she also worked for the Bush campaign in Florida.

Both campaigns sent legal teams to Florida, and numerous lawsuits from each began to swamp the state and federal courts. After each recount, Bush remained the winner, albeit by a smaller margin each time, and the Republican argument quickly became that the Democrats wanted to continue recounting until their candidate won. The nation was divided bitterly over the incident. In the controversial decision in *Bush v. Gore* (531US98, 2000), the U.S. Supreme Court decided along strict party lines to order the recounts halted, and the original certified vote count for Bush was declared official, handing Florida—and the election—to Bush.

Up to that point, the major television news outlets—ABC, CBS, NBC, CNN, and FOX News—had been inconsistent in their uses of colors to denote election results state by state, some using blue for Democrats, others using blue for Republicans. Since 2000, all outlets began using specifically assigned colors: red for Republican states and blue for Democrats. This gave rise to the terms "Red" and "Blue" in American politics. These identifying colors remain in use to the present day, further underscoring the divisions in America, eerily similar to the use of the same colors by warring national street gangs the Crips (blue) and Bloods (red). In 2008, HBO aired the television film *Recount*, starring Kevin Spacey as Ron Klain, head of Gore's Florida recount team. By that time, the last year of Bush's administration, Bush's approval ratings were the lowest of any American president since ratings were recorded, and the film claims that the Bush campaign's case against the recount was corruption. As such, the film, as the event itself, represented the dramatic split in the American body politic—a split that would not only deepen but also define the decades that followed.

POPULAR CULTURE

The 1990s were an extremely transitional decade. At the beginning, the 1990s clearly reflected the big-hair, big-spending culture of the previous decade. As the decade proceeded, however, technological advances such as cell phones and the internet paved the way for the very different society of the twenty-first century. This was the decade when Generation X reached adulthood, and pop culture reflected the neurotic narcissism that so defined the children of the 1970s and teenagers of the 1980s. From *Seinfeld* to *Friends* on television, to *Reality Bites* and the films of Kevin Smith in theaters, to the explosive popularity of the World Wrestling Federation (WWF; today known as World Wrestling Entertainment, or WWE), one thing rang clear about the 1990s: Generation X had issues, and what they most wanted to see reflected in popular culture was themselves.

TELEVISION

By 1990, cable television had become a national mainstay, and television programming trudged through the decade very similarly to how it had the decade before. Two of the top programs of the previous decade—the NBC sitcom *The Cosby Show* (NBC, 1984–1992) and the CBS nighttime soap opera *Dallas* (CBS, 1978–1991; TNT, 2012–2014)—were drawing to a close, while animation juggernaut *The Simpsons* (FOX, 1989–present) was just beginning its historic run. Two popular sitcoms from the 1980s carried on well into the 1990s: *Cheers* (NBC, 1982–1993) and *Roseanne* (ABC, 1988–1997; 2018). The two most popular sitcoms of the period also defined the decade: *Seinfeld* (NBC, 1989–1998) and *Friends* (NBC, 1994–2004). Though the ages of the respective casts were more than a decade apart, both shows underscored the same premise: the American ordeal of attempting to merge narcissism with political correctness. The popularity of these series speaks a great deal to how many Americans in the 1990s could relate to this dilemma.

One of the most popular sitcoms of the decade was *Fresh Prince of Bel-Air* (NBC, 1990–1996). This series featured popular late-1980s rapper Will "Fresh Prince" Smith as a young Black man from west Philadelphia who is sent by his single mother to live with her sister's family in Bel-Air, California, to remove the boy from the dangers of the inner city. A traditional fish-out-of-water story, the financially destitute person thrust overnight into high society, the show underscored how socially diverse the Black community had become since the days of the civil rights movement. At the same time, several episodes emphasized how deeply embedded systemic racism still was despite one's social status. Smith proved to be as skilled an actor as he had been a rapper and left the series to become one of the biggest box-office draws in Hollywood for decades to come.

In the category of network drama, standard legal and medical dramas continued to be popular, most notably *Law & Order* (NBC, 1990–2010) and *ER* (NBC, 1994–2009). Both continued well into the twenty-first century, with *Law & Order* spawning numerous spin-off series. The 1990s also attempted to keep the nighttime soap operas alive with the very popular series *Beverly Hills, 90210* (FOX, 1990–2000). Centering on the high school escapades of two midwestern fraternal twins whose parents move them to Beverly Hills, California, this series focused a great deal on the same narcissist–politically correct conundrum as the sitcoms mentioned above but from a more dramatic format. An equally popular spin-off series, *Melrose Place* (FOX, 1992–1999), was essentially a more grown-up *90210*.

The new television network created by Warner Brothers Studios, the WB, took a chance on a different type of teen drama: *Buffy the Vampire Slayer* (WB, 1997–2001; UPN, 2001–2003). Created by Hollywood up-and-comer Joss Whedon and based on his unsuccessful 1992 film of the same name, this series centered on high school student Buffy Summers, the latest in a long line of mysteriously chosen "slayers," protecting the world from "vampires, demons, and the forces of darkness" (Opening Credits, *Buffy the Vampire Slayer*). Although the unavailability of the WB in most markets limited its viewership, the show soon garnered a loyal cult following, becoming one of the most popular series of the decade (and into the next) and spawning its own spin-off series, *Angel* (WB, 1999–2004).

Since the advent of cable television, children's programming had grown by leaps and bounds beyond the weekday afternoon and Saturday morning offerings of the decades prior to cable. The Cartoon Network, which originally aired only reruns of popular Warner Brothers and Hanna-Barbera cartoons of the 1960s and 1970s, began producing original programming that would continue into the 2000s, such as *Dexter's Laboratory*; *Johnny Bravo*; *Ed, Edd n Eddy*; and *The Powerpuff Girls*, to name but a few. In 1991, the popular children's channel Nickelodeon launched the animated series *Rugrats* (1991–1996), which became one of the most popular series in the channel's history. Nickelodeon also delved into gross humor with the animated series *Ren and Stimpy* (1991–1995). The popular music channel MTV continued this trend with their own animated series, *Beavis and Butt-Head* (1993–1997; 2011).

Superheroes became wildly popular on kids' television in the 1990s. In 1993, FOX Kids (the afternoon and Saturday morning programming on the FOX network) launched *Mighty Morphin Power Rangers* (1993–1996). Relying heavily on stock footage from a children's ninja program from Japan, this series centered on five high schoolers who use their ninja skills along with mechanical "zords" to battle the evil forces of Rita Repulsa. The massive popularity of the original series led to numerous spin-offs and three feature films over the course of the next couple decades. FOX Kids also enjoyed considerable success with animated series revolving around longtime comic book superheroes: *Batman: The Animated Series* (1992–1995), *X-Men* (1992–1997), and *Spider-Man* (1994–1998).

As the twenty-first century dawned, one of the most popular children's programs of all time came to an end after a thirty-three-year run. *Mister Rogers'*

Neighborhood, starring the show's creator and Presbyterian minister Fred Rogers (1928–2003), debuted on NET (later changed to PBS) in 1968. For nearly a third of a century, Mister Rogers came into the homes of American children, speaking directly to them through the television screen and openly discussing feelings and emotions such as anxiety, anger, fear, empathy, kindness, and friendship with his large following of "neighbors." Over the decades, he covered topics such as divorce and death, helping children to find ways to deal with these issues in a healthy way. His last original episode aired on August 31, 2001, just eleven days before the most frightening event in American history, which would define the decade to come.

The 1990s could be called the Decade of *Star Trek*. Other than the four feature films from the franchise that were released through the 1990s, the classic sci-fi series dominated television throughout the decade and into the 2000s. By 1987, the classic 1960s original series still had a massive fan following, and reruns continued to garner big ratings in syndication. Paramount had experienced huge box-office success with the first four films of the movie franchise. In 1987, the franchise took a huge risk with a new idea, *Star Trek: The Next Generation* (Syndication, 1987–1994). The impressive response to that series led to its own film franchise in the 1990s, with adventures set on a new *USS Enterprise*, a century after the original series time line. That success led to another spin-off, *Star Trek: Deep Space Nine* (Syndication, 1993–1999), set in the same timeframe as *The Next Generation* but located on a remote space station at the edge of known space. That was followed by *Star Trek: Voyager* (UPN, 1995–2001), with the crew of the titular starship flung across the galaxy, seventy-five light-years from home. Coming into the twenty-first century, the success of those series led to the creation of *Star Trek: Enterprise* (UPN, 2001–2005), set a century before the original 1960s series. By the time that *Enterprise* completed its initial run, it appeared that *Star Trek* may have run its course.

In the late 1990s, on the cable network Comedy Central, two series debuted that would go on to become two of the most popular and important television series of the early twenty-first century: *South Park* and *The Daily Show*. Created by animators Matt Stone (b. 1971) and Trey Parker (b. 1969), *South Park* debuted in 1997 and centered on four third-grade boys in a small Colorado town. What began as silly animated adventures with foul-mouthed protagonists, *South Park* soon began to take on timely sociopolitical issues, becoming some of the most biting satire on television.

A year earlier, Comedy Central had launched *The Daily Show*, a fake news show, originally reporting ridiculous fictional stories and featuring a celebrity guest, hosted by Craig Kilborn (b. 1962). Riding high on the popularity of the show, Kilborn left at the end of 1998. In January 1999, popular comedian Jon Stewart took over the show, slowly moving it away from fake news and celebrity guests to satirical spins on actual news with politicians, authors, and activists as the guest interviewees. The 2000 presidential election and the first Bush term of office gave the show considerable comedic fodder to build a following, but it was their coverage of the 2004 election, dubbed In-Decision 2004, that launched the show and Stewart to iconic status. By 2010, many younger Americans viewed *The Daily Show* as their primary source of news and information. When Stewart retired from the show in 2015 and was replaced by South African comedian Trevor Noah (b. 1984), *The Daily Show* was considered one of the most important sociopolitical commentary shows in television history.

SPORTS

By 1990, one of the most popular names in sports was Bo Jackson (b. 1962). In 1985, he had won the Heisman Trophy for his performance on Auburn University's football team. In 1987, Jackson took on the Herculean task of playing both professional football and baseball, playing for both the Tampa Bay Buccaneers in the National Football League (NFL) and the Kansas City Royals in Major League Baseball (MLB). Due to a 1991 hip injury during an NFL game, Jackson was forced to retire from both sports by the end of the year. By that time, he had become even more popular due to a series of Nike commercials featuring the tagline "Bo knows."

By far the biggest sports celebrity of the 1990s—and one of the biggest of all time—was basketball legend Michael Jordan (b. 1963). Jordan began playing for the Chicago Bulls in 1984, but he achieved legendary status for leading the team to National Champions in 1991, 1992, and 1993 (his and the Bull's first "three-peat"). In 1993, he briefly retired from basketball, taking a turn at Minor League Baseball, but he returned to the court and the Bulls in 1995, leading the team to another three-peat in 1996, 1997, and 1998. In 1999, Jordan retired a second time before returning to play with the new team, the Washington Wizards, which he also co-owned. He played with the Wizards from 2001 to 2003 before retiring a third and final time. By that time, Jordan's name had become synonymous with the Nike Air Jordan brand of shoes, the most popular brand in the company's history.

Jordan was a key member of the 1992 U.S. Olympic men's basketball team, which quickly became known as the Dream Team. After the 1988 Summer Olympic Games, the Olympic Commission decided to drop the amateur requirement for athletes in order to level the playing field with communist countries such as the USSR, who used seasoned professionals. As a result, the U.S. Olympic Commission put together an unstoppable team of some of the greatest names in basketball history for the 1992 games in Barcelona Spain. The team consisted of Jordan, Scottie Pippen (b. 1965), Earvin "Magic" Johnson (b. 1959), Larry Bird (b. 1956), Patrick Ewing (b. 1962), Karl Malone (b. 1963), John Stockton (b. 1962), Chris Mullin (b. 1963), David Robinson (b. 1965), and Charles Barkley (b. 1963). The team easily dominated all opponents, going on to win the gold.

Tragedy once more struck the Olympic Games in 1996. During the Summer Games, held in Atlanta, Georgia, a local man named Eric Rudolph detonated a pipe bomb, injuring more than a hundred spectators. It was soon discovered that he was also responsible for similar attacks at abortion clinics and gay bars in the area. Although not as tragic as the murder of the Israeli team at the 1972 Munich Olympics, the bombing once more marred the international event meant to celebrate peace and sportsmanship with violence. During the games, however, Amy Van Dyken (b. 1973) won four gold medals for swimming, becoming the first American woman to win that many medals at one Olympiad. Shannon Miller (b. 1977) won the gold for gymnastics as part of the legendary Magnificent Seven gymnastics team that year, but it was fellow team member Kerri Strug (b. 1977) who gained the most attention for her near-flawless dismount despite an injured ankle.

Perhaps the biggest story in professional sports in the 1990s, however, was the World Wrestling Federation, owned by Vincent K. McMahon (b. 1945). For decades, professional wrestling had been denigrated as fake" In 1989, McMahon publicly dubbed his organization "sports entertainment," mostly to avoid professional sports taxes and fees. The WWF steadily gained a near monopoly of the industry throughout the 1990s, and in 1997, it launched what has become known as the Attitude Era, with "Stone Cold" Steve Austin (b. 1964), Mick "Mankind" Foley (b. 1965), and Dwayne "the Rock" Johnson (b. 1972).

In 1993, McMahon and company launched the weekly cable series *WWF RAW*, which quickly became the number one show on cable television well into the twenty-first century. On June 28, 1998, during the pay-per-view event *King of the Ring*, Foley faced off against Mark "the Undertaker" Calaway (b. 1965) in a hell in a cell match. That match has become perhaps the most iconic in pro wrestling history. Foley was thrown from the top of the steel cage, roughly thirty feet, into the announcers' table; was choke slammed through the top of the steel cage onto a steel chair within the ring, more than twenty-five feet, causing one of his teeth to break and come out of his nose; and was body slammed onto a pile of thumbtacks, many of which penetrated his back, remaining there for the duration of the match. By 2000, the Rock was recognized nationally as the "Most Electrifying Man in Sports Entertainment" and the "People's Champion."

FILM

By 1990, Generation X had come of age and were ready to add their own distinct perspective on the arts, most notably, movies. This began in 1994 with the release of two films: *Reality Bites* and *Clerks*. *Reality Bites* was written by Helen Childress and directed by Ben Stiller (b. 1965), who also starred alongside Winona Ryder (b. 1971) and Ethan Hawke (b. 1970) as young Gen Xers fresh out of college dealing with the reality of the grown-up world. *Clerks* was the debut film by writer and director Kevin Smith (b. 1970), presenting a fictionalized version of his own experiences as a convenience store clerk in New Jersey. The critical and commercial success of the film would lead to a string of hits by Smith during the 1990s: *Mallrats* (1995), *Chasing Amy* (1997), and *Dogma* (1999). His films are notable for, among other things, making a Hollywood star of Ben Affleck (b. 1972).

The Walt Disney Corporation continued the massive success of their 1989 animated feature, *The Little Mermaid*, with a chain of historic, legendary, and iconic animated films in the 1990s: *Beauty and the Beast* (1991), the first animated film to be nominated for a nonanimated Academy Award; *Aladdin* (1992); and *The Lion King* (1994). Disney also had success with their other animated features: *Pocahontas* (1995), *The Hunchback of Notre Dame* (1996), *Hercules* (1997), *Mulan* (1998), and *Tarzan* (1999). Disney made history by teaming with and eventually acquiring Pixar Studios, an offshoot of George Lucas's Industrial Light and Magic (ILM). In 1995, they released *Toy Story*, the first feature film to be entirely animated by computer-generated imagery (CGI), and one of the most beloved films of all time. Over the decades that followed, Disney/Pixar would release a seemingly endless chain of blockbuster and tear-jerking CGI-animated features.

One of the most critically acclaimed writer and directors of modern times debuted in the 1990s: Quentin Tarantino (b. 1963). Using the money from the sale of his script for the film *True Romance* (1993), Tarantino made his directorial debut with his independent film *Reservoir Dogs* (1992). Hailed by critics and with a considerable cult following, Tarantino was soon green-lit for his first big-budget film, *Pulp Fiction* (1994), which became a massive critical and commercial success. Substantially influenced by the exploitation and blaxploitation films of the early 1970s, Tarantino soon gained a name for himself for his particular gift of writing dialogue. Over the next few years, he wrote and directed portions of the film *Four Rooms* (1995), wrote and starred in the film *From Dusk Till Dawn* (1996), and wrote and directed the film *Jackie Brown* (1997). In the twenty-first century, Tarantino has gone on to produce numerous iconic films, and he is considered largely responsible for the late-in-life success of beloved film actor Samuel L. Jackson (b. 1948).

The two biggest names in comedy films of the 1990s were Jim Carrey (b. 1962) and Adam Sandler (b. 1966). Hot off his success on the sketch comedy television series *In Living Color* (FOX, 1990–1994), Carey has massive box-office success with back-to-back hits *Ace Ventura: Pet Detective*, *The Mask*, and *Dumb and Dumber* (all in 1994); *Batman Forever* and *Ace Ventura: When Nature Calls* (both in 1995); *The Cable Guy* (1996); *Liar Liar* (1997); *The Truman Show* (1998); and *Man on the Moon* (1999). Sandler, meanwhile, already a household name for his years on *Saturday Night Live* (NBC, 1975–present), had his own chain of successes: *Billy Madison* (1995), *Happy Gilmore* (1996), *The Wedding Singer* and *The Waterboy* (both in 1998), and *Big Daddy* (1999). Both continued to have considerable success throughout the 2000s.

In the 1990s, the superhero movie—a mainstay in twenty-first century theaters—experienced a rapid decline. After the massive success of the Tim Burton (b. 1958) film *Batman* (1989), that franchise saw a continual decline in both quality and commercial success. The following films—*Batman Returns* (1992), *Batman Forever* (1995), and *Batman & Robin* (1997)—became increasingly over-the-top and campy and were ridiculed. Another 1997 superhero flick, *Spawn*, directed by Mark A. Z. Dippé, was rivaled only by *Batman & Robin* for just how bad a superhero movie could be. It became increasingly clear that Hollywood special effects had not yet achieved a level that could do justice to comic book fare. As the decade drew to a close, however, the Marvel Comics universe of heroes began to turn the tide with films such as *Blade* (1998) and *X-Men* (2000).

In 1997, writer and director James Cameron (b. 1954) released the most expensive film ever produced to that time, *Titanic*. With a budget at approximately $200 million, *Titanic* starred Kate Winslet (b. 1975) and Leonardo DiCaprio (b. 1974) as star-crossed lovers aboard the legendary doomed ocean liner. The romance between the two fictional leads is set against the backdrop of the actual individuals and events of the actual tragedy, providing the most accurate portrayal of the historic sinking than had ever been committed to film. Cameron's budget gamble paid off, however, with an original box office take of over $1.8 billion, making it the most commercially successful film of all time to that date. It would finally be surpassed in 2009 by the film *Avatar*, also written and directed by Cameron.

Earlier in 1997, to celebrate the twentieth anniversary of the original *Star Wars*, creator George Lucas (b. 1944) released *The Star Wars Trilogy: Special Edition*, with portions of updated CGI effects added to the original 1977–1983 film series. Fans were divided on their reaction to the changes, with some arguing for decades to follow ("Han shot first!"). However, from the profits from the *Special Edition*, Lucas and ILM were able to begin production on the next trilogy of the *Star Wars* saga with *Star Wars, Episode I: The Phantom Menace* (1999). Beginning a new trilogy, all to be written and directed by Lucas, the new series centered on the young Jedi Anakin Skywalker and his slow slide to the dark side and his identity as Darth Vader. Although the film was despised by many older fans of the original films, the younger generation of moviegoers responded favorably, many preferring the prequels to the admittedly dated original films. Despite the mixed reaction, *The Phantom Menace* and its subsequent sequels ensured the continuation of *Star Wars* well into the twenty-first century and revolutionized CGI effects, ushering in the CGI-laden films that would follow for the succeeding decades.

MUSIC

By 1990, MTV reigned supreme as the official word on what was cool in popular rock, pop, and rap music. The two most popular genres of the early part of the decade were grunge rock and gangsta rap. By decade's end, however, the most popular genre had become more traditional bubblegum pop—light, catchy tunes that were easy to dance to and often dealt with issues of young love and romance. As the twenty-first century dawned, MTV's popularity and influence were already showing signs of decline in the new digital age of music. One of the biggest issues in the industry by the early 2000s was file sharing through the online music outlet Napster.

Grunge music was born in the mid-1980s as an offshoot of both punk rock and heavy metal, with a strong emphasis on electric guitar. Lyrics tended to be nihilistic and the term "grunge" came largely from the dirty, unkept appearance of grunge artists. Seattle, Washington, quickly became the unofficial home of the genre. The most popular grunge artists included Nirvana, Pearl Jam, Soundgarden, Stone Temple Pilots, and Alice in Chains. The most commercially successful of these was Nirvana, featuring band leader, lead guitarist, songwriter, and lead singer Kurt Cobain (1967–1994); bassist Krist Novoselic (b. 1965); and, by 1990, drummer Dave Grohl (b. 1969). Their biggest-selling album was *Nevermind* (1991), featuring hits such as "Smells Like Teen Spirit,"

"Come as You Are," and "Drain You." Cobain's 1994 suicide rocked the music world. After Cobain's death, Grohl would go on to create the band Foo Fighters, one of the most popular bands of the next fifteen years.

Gangsta rap was born from the plight of African Americans in the inner cities, which is where the genre of rap originally started. Unlike the more pop rap of 1980s artists RUN-DMC and DJ Jazzy Jeff and the Fresh Prince, gangsta rap had a more violent bend, often speaking to the growing tensions between Black youth and local law enforcement. Popular gangsta rap acts included Ice-T, Public Enemy, NWA and the solo career of member Ice Cube, and Snoop Doggy-Dogg (later simply Snoop Dogg). The rivalry between former friends Tupac "2Pac" Shakur (1971–1996) and Christopher "Notorious B.I.G."/"Biggie Smalls" Wallace (1972–1997) became manifest in the industry as the East Coast–West Coast feud, and both men were killed in drive-by shootings that remain unsolved to this day.

Gangsta rap soon became the soundtrack for the national war between rival street gangs the Crips and the Bloods, whose members were recognizable to each other through the gang colors of blue for the Crips and red for the Bloods. The most iconic song of the genre was "Cop Killer" (1992) by the group Body Count. Although the genre brought national light to the plight of the inner cities and made millionaires of several young Black men, the violence and vulgarity of the lyrics and widely publicized connections to illegal drugs aided in further stigmatizing the Black urban community, deepening racial tensions across the country.

The decade began with the overnight and brief success of the first famous white rapper, Robert "Vanilla Ice" Van Winkle (b. 1967). His 1990 number-one hit, "Ice Ice Baby," ironically became the first hip-hop song to top the pop charts. That was soon followed with a cover of the 1970s hit "Play That Funky Music." "Ice Ice Baby," however, also opened a national discussion on the legality of sampling—taking portions of a previously recorded song and incorporating those portions into a new song by a different artist, often without proper permission or compensation from the original composer. "Ice Ice Baby" by white rapper Vanilla Ice made frequent repetitive use of a portion of the 1981 song "Under Pressure," originally recorded by Queen and David Bowie. In 1999, MTV retired the music video of "Ice Ice Baby," pronouncing it the worst music video in the channel's history. However, more than a decade later, sister music channel VH1 declared it number twenty-nine of the Top 100 Songs of the 1990s (Ali, "Top 100 Songs of the '90s," VH1).

Throughout the decade, numerous female artists achieved iconic status. Jennifer Lopez (b. 1969) began the decade in 1991 as part of the Fly Girls dance troupe on the FOX sketch comedy series *In Living Color*. In 1997, she starred in the feature film *Selena*, as slain pop singer Selena Quintanilla-Pérez (1971–1995). She began her career on the pop charts with her number-one debut single, "If You Had My Love" (1999). In 1994, singer and songwriter Sheryl Crow (b. 1962) had her first chart-topping hit with "All I Wanna Do," from her debut album, *Tuesday Night Music Club*. That would be followed by a self-titled album featuring hits such as "If It Makes You Happy" and "Every Day Is a Winding Road" (both in 1996). By that time, popular singer and songwriter Alanis

Morissette (b. 1974) had already topped the charts with her third studio album, *Jagged Little Pill* (1995), featuring such hits as "You Oughta Know" and "Hand in My Pocket" (both in 1995) and "Ironic," "You Learn," and "Head over Feet" (all in 1996). All three would go on to various degrees of success in the decades that followed.

In the genre of country music, the two biggest names of the 1990s were Garth Brooks and Shania Twain. Brooks (b. 1962) continuously topped charts throughout the decade with hits such as "The Dance," "Friends in Low Places," and "Unanswered Prayers" (all in 1990); "The Thunder Rolls," "Shameless," and "What She's Doin' Now" (all in 1991); and "Longneck Bottle" (1997). Twain (born Eileen Edwards in 1965) had massive success in both Canada and the United States with hits like "Whose Bed Have Your Boots Been Under" and "Any Man of Mine" (both in 1995), "That Don't Impress Me Much" (1998), and "Man! I Feel Like a Woman!" (1999). Throughout the decade, both artists went far in bridging the gap between country and pop music, bringing the traditionally rural genre more mainstream than perhaps anyone prior.

As the decade drew to a close, pop music charts became swamped in what many dubbed bubblegum pop. Similar in many ways to the early rock of the late 1950s, bubblegum pop appealed mostly to the high school crowd, with easily danceable tunes centered on friends, fun, and young love. The British girl band Spice Girls charted international success with their 1996 single, "Wannabe." Many pop artists hit the music scene in the late 1990s by way of the Walt Disney corporation, serving as Mouseketeers in their childhoods in the early part of the decade. Britney Spears (b. 1981) topped charts with the following hits: "Baby One More Time" (1998) and "Sometimes" and "You Drive Me Crazy" (both in 1999). Fellow Mouseketeer Christina Aguilera (b. 1980) had success with "Genie in a Bottle" and "What a Girl Wants" (both in 1999). The massively successful boy band NSYNC had former Mouseketeer Justin Timberlake (b. 1981) as its front man, topping charts with songs such as "Tearin' Up My Heart" (1997) and "Bye Bye Bye" (2000). Spears, Aguilera, and Timberlake would all go on to considerable success well into the new century.

Hispanic artists also hit big as the decade drew to a close. Puerto Rican–born Ricky Martin (b. 1971) had begun his musical career as part of the boy band Menudo in the 1980s. After numerous Spanish-language solo albums in the 1990s, Martin released his self-titled English-language album in 1999 and had a number one hit with "Livin' La Vida Loca." The following year, he would have another hit with "She Bangs." Meanwhile, Columbian-born Shakira Isabel Mebarak Ripoll (b. 1977), more popularly known simply as Shakira, was making her way to massive success around the Spanish-speaking world and would soon hit big in America with her first English-language album, *Laundry Service*, in 2001. Other big Spanish-to-English artists of the period were Jennifer Lopez and Marc Anthony (b. 1968), both of Puerto Rican descent, and Spanish-born Enrique Iglesias (b. 1975). All would have successful chart careers well into the twenty-first century.

The biggest dance craze of the 1990s was the one-hit wonder "Macarena," a Spanish-language dance song released in 1993 by the group Los Del Rio. Formed in Spain in 1962, Los Del Rio consisted of Antonio Romero Monge

(b. 1937) and Rafael Ruiz Perdigones (b. 1939). Appearing on the band's 1993 album *A mi me gusta*, the song tells the tale of a woman who cheats on her boyfriend who is away in the army. Similar to the Hustle of the 1970s, the dance to "Macarena" consisted of a series of specific movements repeated throughout the song. It became a national obsession in the United States in the mid-1990s. In 1997, the American Bluegrass group the GrooveGrass Boyz released a country version of the song, telling the original story of the song with altered lyrics in southern English, often referred to as the "Redneck Macarena."

The 1990s closed with one of the biggest scandals in music history: online file sharing. In 1999, computer software developers Sean Parker (b. 1979) and Shawn Fanning (b. 1980) launched Napster, an online music-streaming service that allowed its members to share digital music files. They were immediately sued by the Recording Industry Association of America later that same year on the basis of copyright infringement. In essence, if people around the globe could freely share music, sales of officially released albums and singles would dramatically fall. In 2001, Napster was forced to shut down operations and pay out millions of dollars to the music industry in settlement against further suits. Despite the record industry's success, however, it was clear that Americans—particularly internet-savvy American youth—were turning more toward digital platforms for their music needs, changing the industry forever and paving the way for future online streaming services such as iTunes and Spotify.

LITERATURE

Coming into the 1990s, the American comic-book industry was enjoying commercial success to a degree it had not seen since World War II. When the stock market crashed in 1987, many began to see comic books as better investments than stocks, leading the two major publishers, DC and Marvel, to capitalize on the trend, flooding the market with new number-one issues to fool new investors. This trend continued through the recession of 1992, but as the overall economy improved after 1993, collectors began leaving the comic book market in droves. Longtime readers saw through the profit motives of story spectacles such as "The Death of Superman" in 1993 and the drawn-out "Clone Saga" in the *Spider-Man* books at Marvel, and recent collectors realized by 1993 that their investments were, in reality, not worth the paper on which they were printed.

The collapse of the collectors' bubble nearly destroyed the entire industry, causing Marvel Comics to declare bankruptcy in late 1996. The declining quality of superhero-based movies only added to the decline of the print arm of the industry. Added to this was the end of the Cold War in 1992. With no more enemies, Americans began to see no need for heroes. As the decade—and the century—drew to a close, it appeared that the comic book industry was soon to be placed on the ash pile of history. However, Americans' need for heroes and the escapism of superhero narratives would soon return on an otherwise-sunny morning in September 2001.

In 1994, Warner Brothers released the film *Interview with the Vampire*, starring Tom Cruise and Brad Pitt. The massive success of the film brought huge attention to the 1976 novel on which it was based, as well as its three sequels, *The Vampire Lestat* (1985), *Queen of the Damned* (1988), and *The Tale of the Body Thief* (1992). Riding the success of the film, author Anne Rice (b. 1941) continued her "Vampire Chronicles" with *Memnoch the Devil* (1995) and *The Vampire Armand* (1998). She would continue with numerous more sequels well into the twenty-first century. In 2018, the online streaming service Netflix announced it had cut a deal with the author to begin an ongoing television series based on the Chronicles.

Little did anyone realize as the decade drew to a close that the biggest event in publishing history was about to begin, from an unknown, unemployed female writer living with her infant daughter in Scotland: Joanne "J. K." Rowling (b. 1965). In 1997, Rowling published her first book, *Harry Potter and the Philosopher's Stone*. The children's book told the tale of an eleven-year-old English orphan living with his emotionally abusive aunt and uncle who discovers that he is, in fact, a wizard and has been accepted into the greatest wizarding school in the world. The book was an instant global phenomenon, launching what would become a seven-book series, eventually turning into eight of the most successful films in history. To date, the books have been translated into eighty languages, selling more than half-a-billion copies. The enduring success of the books and films have led to the creation of a Broadway play, a new film series based in the same universe, and mountains of merchandise. It is the most successful book series in history.

As far as nonfiction, the most successful book of the 1990s was *Men Are from Mars, Women Are from Venus: A Practical Guide for Improving Communication and Getting What You Want in Your Relationship* by John Gray (b. 1951). Originally published in 1992, the book has sold, to date, more than fifteen million copies worldwide. The rather simple premise of the book is that men and women are so completely different in their respective mental wiring that they are proverbially from different planets. The book generally argues that when a man says "this," he really means "that," and vice versa. The assertions and conclusions of the book have, in recent times, fallen out of favor as American society has experienced a queering of monolithic gender stereotypes, essentially making the solutions that the book proffers merely doors opening much more complicated problems. For its time, however, it was highly regarded and hailed for repairing countless relationships.

TECHNOLOGY

In 1993, the company NCSA released Mosaic, the program that gave everyday Americans access to the World Wide Web (or internet, as it came to be known). The Web had been invented in 1989 by an English scientist named Tim Berners-Lee (b. 1955) while working for CERN, a French acronym for European Organization for Nuclear Research, in Switzerland. In 1993, very few Americans had home computers; most home computers in the 1980s had been used for simply gaming or personal financial accounting. Once Mosaic was launched, Americans first used "the Web" for communication: chat rooms and electronic mail (email). In just a couple years, people around the globe began to see the informational opportunities provided by the internet, and the Information Age was born.

Investors on Wall Street soon saw the economic opportunities provided by this new information medium, and the dot-com bubble began. College-age programmers became billionaires overnight, and many lost those billions just as quickly as they'd earned them. In 2000, the bubble burst, as all investment bubbles eventually do, when investors discovered that the value of their gambles had been highly overinflated. When the smoke cleared in 2003, the vast majority of these internet start-ups had failed, cast to the ash heap of history. Others, like online retailers Amazon and eBay, survived and went on to thrive in the decades to come.

Perhaps the most infamous failure in the dot-com crash was the company Pixelon. Founded in 1998, Pixelon promoted the idea of high-quality video-content online (something that is taken for granted today). It was founded by a man named Michael Fenne, a radical Evangelical Christian who was actually a con man by the name of David Kim Stanley. In 1999, Pixelon promoted an online concert, iBash '99, featuring such acts as the Dixie Chicks, Faith Hill, the rock band KISS, legendary crooner Tony Bennett, and rock icons the Who.

However, when the stream went live, most Pixelon users received only error messages, viewing the concert, instead, using Microsoft software. The fiasco raised red flags concerning Fenne, leading to the company's eventual collapse in 2000. Stanley was arrested and served jail time for embezzlement. In 2019, the National Geographic Channel aired a miniseries titled *Valley of the Boom*, which centered considerably on the Pixelon scam (Tsonga 2019).

The concept of a mobile phone had been around in the United States since 1973, when Motorola introduced their handheld portable phones, weighing in at just over four pounds. By the end of the decade, Japan began working with 1G cellular technology. In 1991 a Finland-based company, Radiolinja, launched 2G tech. By 1995, many Americans began buying the first generation of cellular phones, handheld units with a flip-open flap over the speaking end and an extendable antennae. As the decade drew to a close, more and more Americans invested in cell phones, now using the iconic flip phone, where the entire device folded in half for easy carry. Throughout the decade, cell phone use was expensive (in the early days, a consumer could be charged a dollar just for answering the phone), and in the early 2000s, flip phones began to feature texting technology. In today's age of smartphones, it is difficult to imagine just how recently today's technology was introduced.

As the 1990s drew to a close and America was more dependent on the internet and personal computers than ever before, a programming flaw started a wave of anxiety that came to be known as Y2K. This fear stemmed from the discovery that all computers regulated dates by using only the last two digits of years (i.e., a computer identified "1999" as simply "99"). As such, there was the growing concern that when New Year's Eve 1999 clicked over to New

Year's Day 2000, computers would not be able to discern between "2000" and "1900" (or, presumably, "1800," "1500," "1000," and so on).

Programming experts worked diligently to overcome potential issues, while, at the same time, attempting to assure the public that this was not as big a problem as the general public believed. The problem, of course, was that the overwhelming majority of computer users knew absolutely nothing about computer hardware or software, earnestly believing that their computers were going to believe that it was now the year 1000 and put all of society back to the Dark Ages. In hindsight, the idea seems laughable, but it goes to underscore just how little the vast majority of the computer-using public understand about the devices on which their entire lives now revolve.

AMERICA BY 2000

As the millennium dawned—with the country divided over whether the millennium began in 2000 or 2001 (it began in 2001)—Americans were oddly optimistic while simultaneously more divided than at any point since the Civil War (1861–1865). Television and Hollywood were on the brink of new golden ages. Music and literature were becoming increasingly digital, and Americans across the socioeconomic spectrum were becoming more dependent on technology than ever before. However, the American melting pot was beginning to simmer. In a post–Cold War world, with no more enemies to fear, Americans began looking inward for threats. Who American were and what they believed in and stood for became front-page news and sources of division that would only grow in the decades to come. A heated and controversial presidential election was soon followed by the most horrific day in American history, and the United States was about to become embroiled in what has come to be known as a post-9/11 world. America was changing.

FURTHER READING

Ali, Rahsheeda. 2013. "Top 100 Songs of the '90s." VH1, May 23. https://web.archive
.org/web/20120214035830/http://blog.vh1.com/2007-12-13/top-100-songs-of
-the-90s. Retrieved May 15, 2019.

Ashby, LeRoy. 2006. *With Amusement for All: A History of American Popular Culture since 1830*. Lexington: University Press of Kentucky.

Bennett, Jessica. 2019. "This Gen X Mess: The Tech, Music, Style, Books, Trends, Rules, Films and Pills That Made Gen X . . . So So-So." *New York Times*, May 16. https://www.nytimes.com/interactive/2019/05/14/style/generation-xers.html?utm_source=pocket-newtab. Retrieved May 16, 2019.

Berman, William C. 2001. *From the Center to the Edge: The Politics & Policies of the Clinton Presidency*. Lanham, MD: Rowman & Littlefield.

Bodroghkozy, Aniko. 2018. *A Companion to the History of American Broadcasting*. New York: Wiley-Blackwell.

Brands, H. W. 2011. *American Dreams: The United States since 1945*. New York: Penguin.

Castleman, Harry, and Walter J. Podrazik. 2016. *Watching TV: Eight Decades of American Television*. 3rd ed. New York: Syracuse University Press.

Conrad, Dean. 2018. *Space Sirens, Scientists and Princesses: The Portrayal of Women in Science Fiction Cinema.* Jefferson, NC: McFarland.

Coontz, Stephanie. 2016. *The Way We Never Were: American Families and the Nostalgia Trap.* New York: Basic.

Cullen, Jim. 2002. *The Art of Democracy: A Concise History of Popular Culture in the United States.* New ed. New York: Monthly Review.

Danesi, Marcel. 2012. *Popular Culture: Introductory Perspectives.* 2nd ed. Lanham, MD: Rowman & Littlefield.

Farris, Scott. 2012. *Almost President: The Men Who Lost the Race but Changed the Nation.* Guilford, CT: Lyons.

Howe, Sean. 2012. *Marvel Comics: The Untold Story.* New York: Harper Perennial.

Jones, Brian Jay. 2016. *George Lucas: A Life.* New York: Little, Brown and Company.

Kaminski, Michael. 2008. *The Secret History of* Star Wars. Kingston, ON: Legacy.

Kruse, Kevin M., and Julian E. Zelizer. 2019. *Fault Lines: A History of the United States since 1974.* New York: W. W. Norton.

Patterson, James T. 2005. *Restless Giant: The United States from Watergate to* Bush v. Gore. Oxford: Oxford University Press.

Starr, Larry, and Christopher Waterman. 2017. *American Popular Music: From Minstrelsy to MP3.* New York: Oxford University Press.

Toobin, Jeffrey. 2002. *Too Close to Call: The Thirty-Six-Day Battle to Decide the 2000 Election.* New York: Random House.

Tsonga, Taj. 2019. "Remembering the Greatest Con in Silicon Valley History." *Wired,* January. https://www.wired.com/wiredinsider/2019/01/remembering-greatest-con-silicon-valley-history/. Retrieved May 16, 2019.

Tucker, Reed. 2017. *Slugfest: Inside the Epic 50-Year Battle between Marvel and DC.* New York: Da Capo.

TV Guide Editors. 2002. TV Guide: *Fifty Years of Television.* New York: Crown.

Weinstein, Deena. 2015. *Rock'n America: A Social and Cultural History.* Toronto, ON: University of Toronto Press.

Wright, Bradford W. 2003. *Comic Book Nation: The Transformation of Youth Culture in America.* Baltimore, MD: Johns Hopkins University Press.

Exploring Popular Culture

CHAPTER 1

Television

As the millennium dawned, American television looked much like it had for the last decade. Two of the most popular series on television were the sitcom *Friends* and the law drama *Law & Order*. Most Americans still utilized VHS as their primary format for home video entertainment, and Americans still visited their local Blockbuster Video to rent the newest releases from Hollywood. DVD was slowly becoming a more popular format, with Netflix launching in 1997 as an online DVD-rental service. Consumers could visit the Netflix website and choose a DVD to rent. Netflix would then mail the DVD via postal service, and customers could view the DVD and send it back (facing, of course, a fee if they failed to do so).

By 2000, however, television broadcasters were becoming increasingly irritated by the growing pay demands from TV stars, making the continuation of sitcoms and dramas more expensive than some were worth. Enter the reality show. Largely centered on competitions of one sort or another, reality programming required minimal expenditures on sets or crew, and the respective "talent" worked for next to nothing, with the only big payout going to the winner of the competition. Meanwhile, strong ratings continued to bring in equally strong advertising dollars.

With the increasing popularity of animation-centered children's cable channels such as Nickelodeon, Cartoon Network, and the Disney Channel backed up by a nostalgia-obsessed aging Generation X, cartoons began to dominate programming across the cable spectrum to a degree never seen before. Major sporting events continued to be wildly popular, leading sports cable giant ESPN to launch numerous sister channels to allow more televised sports coverage than ever. The near back-to-back events of the 2000 presidential election and 9/11 quickly led to what has come to be known as the Cable News Wars. Longtime cable news juggernaut CNN, or the Cable News Network, now faced stiff competition from MSNBC and, even more so, FOX News. Network news broadcasts became relics of the past as more and more Americans depended on cable news for up-to-the-minute information.

Throughout the 1990s, CNN's coverage appeared to some to be too far left politically. The response had been the creation of FOX News in 1996 by conservative media mogul Rupert Murdoch (b. 1931). The network promised "fair and balanced" news coverage; to many viewers, this banner was meant to promote news without a political leaning. However, FOX News received equal criticism for having a strong conservative bend. When MSNBC emerged as even more liberal than CNN, the original cable news network was forced back to the middle for their audiences. By that time, however, America was already staunchly politically divided, preferring coverage that already met their preconceived ideas on what those events meant politically. This division was only exacerbated by the 2000 election and, even more, by the nightmare of 9/11.

9/11

As the haze of Ground Zero settled, Americans were left in a state of mass grief, filled with fear and uncertainty about the days to come. Just as in the wake of Pearl Harbor on December 7, 1941, and the assassination of President John F. Kennedy on November 22, 1963, Americans needed a hero. Three television series debuting in the fall of 2001 proved timely, as the real-world terrorist attacks of September 11, 2001, left the American populace once more in desperate need of heroic narratives. Up-and-coming writer, director, and producer J. J. Abrams (b. 1966) created the series *Alias* (ABC, 2001–2006), starring Jennifer Garner (b. 1972) as CIA agent Sydney Bristow acting as a double agent to infiltrate the international criminal organization SD-6. Meanwhile, actor Kiefer Sutherland (b. 1966) became a national icon as counterterrorist Agent Jack Bauer on the hugely popular series *24* (FOX, 2001–2010; 2014). What made this series so popular—other than its controversial levels of violence—was that each episode played out in real time (hence, each season being one twenty-four-hour day). After its initial eight-season run, the show returned for a miniseason in 2014. In 2017, FOX gambled with a spin-off series, *24: Legacy*, starring Corey Hawkins (b. 1988), but the lack of Sutherland's Bauer severely affected fan response.

The third of these new hero narratives focused on the original superhero: Superman. The most successful superhero series in television history is the live-action drama series *Smallville* (WB, 2001–2006; CW, 2006–2011). The series, set in the fictional town of Smallville, Kansas, starred Tom Welling (b. 1977) as high schooler Clark Kent. In the first episode (later ret-conned as Clark's freshman year of high school), Clark is already aware that he possesses super strength and speed, but he is, as yet, unaware of his alien origins, which he learns about in the first episode from his adopted father, Jonathan, played by John Schneider (b. 1960).

The series follows Clark through high school and beyond as his superpowers slowly develop and he takes the hero's journey on the road to becoming Superman. Originally set along the monster-of-the-week format of previous cult hit *Buffy*, Clark, over time, is introduced to the myriad of supervillains that make up the *Superman* universe. One of the most intriguing aspects of the series is Clark's friendship with local billionaire Lex Luthor, played to perfection by Michael Rosenbaum (b. 1972). Fans watched with heartbreak as these friends devolve into nemeses, as the hero's long history demands that they must. Collectively, Sydney Bristow, Jack Bauer, and Clark Kent contributed tremendously to the healing that Americans desperately needed in the weeks, months, and years following 9/11.

As the series third season of *The West Wing* (NBC, 1999–2006), a fictional series set around the very liberal fictional President Josiah "Jed" Bartlet, was about to begin, the 9/11 attacks happened. In the immediate aftermath of those events, series creator and head writer Aaron Sorkin (b. 1961) quickly wrote and produced a special episode that would play just weeks after the attacks. The episode was titled "Isaac and Ishmael" and focused on the possibility of a terrorist working inside the White House, placing the building on lockdown, allowing the cast to discuss the issue of international terrorism, and warning against the impulse to react emotionally to such events. The series ended with the end of Bartlet's second term, but as of 2019, NBC was urgently requesting Sorkin to bring the series back. The biggest ratings winners of post-9/11 America, however, were those who kept America updated on the seemingly hourly events unfolding in the weeks and months that followed: the twenty-four-hour news networks.

CABLE NEWS

The year 2000 was the last year of the twentieth century, and it culminated in one of the most divisive U.S. presidential elections in the nation's history. Riding high on the popularity of the incumbent president Bill Clinton (serving 1993–2001) dampened by signs of a possible forthcoming recession, Vice President Al Gore (b. 1948), a moderate Democrat from Tennessee, faced off against Texas governor George W. Bush (b. 1946), a conservative Republican and oldest son of the forty-first president, George H. W. Bush (serving 1989–1993). An extremely tight race was initially called for Bush with a victory in Florida. However, the Florida vote was soon called into question, leading the Gore campaign to call for a recount. The month that followed ripped the country in half before the U.S. Supreme Court finally stopped all recounts and called the election for Bush. At the heart of all of this chaos were the cable news networks.

CNN had been around since the advent of cable television. Launched by media mogul Ted Turner (b. 1938) in 1980, by 2000, CNN labeled itself "the Most Trusted Name in News." MSNBC was launched in 1996 through a joint effort between Microsoft and NBC TV. FOX News was also launched in 1996 by Australian media mogul Rupert Murdoch (b. 1931). The 2000 election drama led to massive ratings boosts for all three news networks. Up to that point, the various cable and network news outlets utilized different colors to represent election results: some used red to signify Democrat victories, while others used red for Republican.

Due to the confusion caused when viewers switched from channel to channel, all news outlets after 2000 agreed to use red for Republican states only and blue for Democrat, with purple signifying swing states that could go either way. This seemingly insignificant choice led to a new labeling phenomenon: red states and blue states. As the 2000s progressed, states and individuals began identifying themselves by their respective colors and viewing the "opposing" colors as the enemy. This proverbially transformed the early 1990s Crips versus Bloods national gang war into an overall political war, utilizing the same gang colors, and the cable news outlets were largely, albeit unintentionally, responsible.

Less than a year after the dust had settled from the election and President Bush began his term of office, the cable news outlets received their next ratings boon, this time a temporarily unifying one: 9/11. On Tuesday, September 11, 2001, nineteen radical Muslim Arab terrorists from Egypt and Saudi Arabia (a twentieth was prevented from boarding an aircraft by airport security and later arrested), representing the fundamentalist terrorist organization Al-Qaeda and under orders of the organization's leader, Osama bin Laden (1957–2011), hijacked four American passenger planes with intentions of utilizing the aircraft as live missiles against key targets representing American power. At 8:46 a.m. EST, American Airlines Flight 11 crashed into the North Tower of the World Trade Center in New York City, taking out floors ninety-three through ninety-nine. Seventeen minutes later, United Airlines Flight 175 crashed into the South Tower, taking out floors seventy-seven through eighty-five. At 9:37 a.m. EST, American Airlines Flight 77 crashed into the E-Wing of the Pentagon in Washington, DC.

At 9:59 a.m., the South Tower in New York collapsed in ten seconds. At 10:15 a.m., the E-Wing of the Pentagon collapsed, and at 10:28 a.m., the North Tower was the last to fall. By that time, at 10:03 a.m., United Airlines Flight 93 had nosedived into an open field outside of Shanksville, Pennsylvania, killing all aboard. The passengers of Flight 93 head learned through cell phone communications with loved ones on the ground what had happened with the other planes, and they united to overtake their captors and regain control of the plane. Rather than lose control to their hostages, the terrorists purposely crashed the plane. As the sun set on the most horrific day in U.S. history, 2,977 innocent lives had been lost (9/11 Memorial).

American outrage stemming from the event soon launched the War on Terror, which would launch the two longest wars in American history: Afghanistan and Iraq. Enemies in this war were defined by what came to be known as the Bush Doctrine: a policy of preemptive strikes against any nation, organization, or individual who openly threatened the United States, its allies, or interests around the globe. The first target was Afghanistan, under the control of the Taliban regime, which had offered safe haven to Bin Laden and Al-Qaeda in their country. The next target was Iraq, under the leadership of its president, Saddam Hussein (1937–2006). Since the Persian Gulf War (1991), Hussein had insisted that he possessed "weapons of mass destruction" (WMDs) that he intended to use against Israel and Saudi Arabia. Though no concrete evidence of WMDs ever emerged—and none were ever found—the mere fact that Hussein threatened such actions made implementation of the Bush Doctrine relevant. Throughout these events, cable news was there.

By 2001, FOX News had already established itself as the voice of conservatism in the United States. MSNBC soon followed a more radically liberal bend, leading former liberal voice CNN to attempt to find an audience in the political center, ultimately resulting in CNN being the third-rated but legitimately most trusted name in cable news. In hindsight, the partisan nature of cable news can be noted as largely responsible for the short-term nature of the national unity in the wake of 9/11. Since 1982, a popular mainstay on CNN had been the program *Crossfire* (1982–2005; 2013–2016), where a conservative and liberal commentator would debate the issues of the day. By 2004, the program truly represented the vitriol between the two political wings. On October 15, 2004, comedian Jon Stewart, host of Comedy Central's *The Daily Show*, was invited as a guest to promote his show. While there, however, Stewart scolded the show's hosts, liberal pundit Paul Begala (b. 1961) and conservative Tucker Carlson (b. 1969), for adding to the growing political discord in the country. CNN obviously agreed, cancelling the series and firing Carlson three months later.

For the first two decades of FOX News, its most popular program and the highest-rated program on all of cable news was *The O'Reilly Factor* (1996–2017). Hosted by radical conservative commentator Bill O'Reilly (b. 1949), the program was originally called *The O'Reilly Report* and, in its final seasons, simply *The Factor*. O'Reilly became representative of the radicalization of conservatism in America beginning in the late 1990s. His staunch support for Republican president George W. Bush was equaled by his seething hatred of Democratic presidents Clinton and Obama. In 2005, Stephen Colbert (b. 1964), a popular political correspondent on Comedy Central's *The Daily Show with Jon Stewart*, parodied O'Reilly and *The O'Reilly Factor* with his wildly popular satire series, *The Colbert Report* (Comedy Central, 2005–2014). In 2017, O'Reilly was forced from his number-one program due to numerous sexual harassment complaints against him, which became highlighted by the Me Too movement.

The most popular program on MSNBC in the 2000s was *Countdown with Keith Olbermann* (2003–2011). Olbermann (b. 1959) had gained fame as a colorful sports commentator on ESPN. MSNBC utilized his celebrity status from sports to promote a liberal alternative to FOX's *The O'Reilly Factor*. The gamble worked, with *Countdown* quickly becoming MSNBC's top program, second only to O'Reilly in overall news ratings. As intended, Olbermann presented a radically liberal perspective on the day's events, as vitriolic against President Bush as O'Reilly was on Clinton and Obama.

In 2010, Olbermann was suspended by MSNBC management for violating corporate policy against MSNBC employees donating to political campaigns without corporate approval. Though he was reinstated just twelve days later (after considerable fan outcry), Olbermann left MSNBC in January, 2011, for to-date undisclosed reasons. Olbermann briefly took his program to Al Gore's upstart network Current TV, where he also served as news director, but he was dismissed the following year due to his creation of his own, more divisive blog, FOK News Channel ("FOK" standing for "Friends of Keith"). In 2016, Olbermann began twice-weekly episodes of *The Closer with Keith Olbermann*, for GQ's online service. Once Donald Trump (b. 1946) became president, Olbermann continued his GQ broadcasts as *The Resistance* until officially retiring from political commentary in November 2017.

By the time of the political circus that was the 2016 presidential election, Americans were more politically divided than at any point in U.S. history since the American Civil War of 1861–1865. Disagreement between the two political fringes had devolved into outright hatred and—far too often—violence. For the twenty years leading up to 2016, millions of Americans had turned to the three major cable news networks for updates and commentary on the day's events, but, in doing so, they were also feeding their own political frenzy, adding to division, degradation, and hatred on all sides. As the country moves into the 2020 elections, there appears to be no change to this format on the sociopolitical horizon, and although all three networks recognize their part in the continuing and worsening division, none appear to have any solution for alleviating the problem.

SITCOMS

Situation comedies, or sitcoms, remained popular well into the twenty-first century. One of the most popular workplace sitcoms in television history was *Cheers* (NBC, 1982–1993), set in a Boston bar and starring actor Ted Danson (b. 1947) as the bar's owner, Sam Malone. The continuing popularity of the series even in its final season led NBC to seek out a possible spin-off series based on one of the characters. The character they chose was psychiatrist Dr. Frasier Crane. In *Frasier* (NBC, 1993–2004), Kelsey Grammar (b. 1955) moves his character to Seattle, Washington, to be near his aging father and single brother. The series proved nearly as popular as the original, having an eleven-season run just as *Cheers* had.

Perhaps the most popular sitcom of the 1990s—challenged only by *Seinfeld* for the top spot—was *Friends* (NBC, 1994–2004). This series, set around a group of six twenty-to-thirty-something single friends in New York City, starred Jennifer Anniston (b. 1969), Courteney Cox (b. 1964), Lisa Kudrow (b. 1963), Matt LeBlanc (b. 1967), Matthew Perry (b. 1969), and David Schwimmer (b. 1966). The misadventures and hijinks of this tight group of friends won over millions of Americans coming into the 2000s, while simultaneously underscoring the strange mixture of neuroses and pressure to adhere to ever-broadening ideas of political correctness that defined Generation X during the period.

Capitalizing on the obsessive nostalgia of Generation X, FOX took a chance on the sitcom *That '70s Show* (1998–2006). This series was centered on a group of close high school friends in the late 1970s, who hang out in the basement of the show's star, Topher Grace (b. 1978) as Eric Forman. The other main "teenage" stars of the show included Mila Kunis (b. 1983), Ashton Kutcher (b. 1978), Danny Masterson (b. 1976), Laura Prepon (b. 1980), and Wilmer Valderrama (b. 1980). Kunis and Kutcher, who played a romantic couple for the first half of the series, later married in real life in 2015. Much of the show's comedy revolved around young Eric's father, Red Forman (Kurtwood Smith, b. 1943), who frequently referred to the younger characters as "dumbasses" and frequently came up with various methods by which he threatened to put his "foot in your ass." The series remains wildly popular in reruns, as beloved by millennials and iGen audiences as it was with their parents.

Several other family- and friend-based sitcoms that began in the 1990s continued into the new century. In *Everybody Loves Raymond* (CBS, 1996–2005), comedian Ray Romano (b. 1957) starred as Ray Barone, a sportswriter, surrounded by his wife, children, brother, and eccentric parents. Actor Kevin James (b. 1965) saw huge success with his sitcom, *King of Queens* (CBS, 1998–2007). In 1995, the movie studio Paramount Pictures launched its own television network, UPN. One of the new network's biggest early hits was the African American–based series *The Parkers* (1999–2004). This series revolved around the main character, young Kim Parker, played by Countess Vaughn (b. 1978), who discovers that her single mother, Nikki, played by Mo'Nique (b. 1967) has decided to attend the local community college with her daughter.

Possibly the most groundbreaking sitcom of the period was *Will & Grace* (NBC, 1998–2006; 2017–present). This show centered on the close friendship between main characters Will Truman, a gay New York City lawyer played by Eric McCormack (b. 1963), and Grace Adler, a heterosexual interior designer played by Debra Messing (b. 1968). The relationship between the two was closer than most marriages, leading many fans to want them to get together despite Will being gay. Much of the show's hilarity revolved around their friends, side characters Jack McFarland, a flamboyant gay ne'er-do-well played with effervescent glee by Sean Hayes (b. 1970), and Grace's equally flamboyant heterosexual socialite personal assistant Karen Walker, played by Megan Mullally (b. 1958). The show broke ground by "normalizing" the gay community in the eyes of "mainstream" America, breaking down the barriers and stigmatization that had ostracized the LGBTQ+ community for most of the country's history. When the show returned to television in 2017, the focus turned toward how much American society had changed in the decade in between with regard to acceptance of the LGBTQ+ community.

One of the first sitcoms to debut in the 2000s was *Malcolm in the Middle* (FOX, 2000–2006). Meant primarily as another youthful angst series centered on the main character, Malcolm, played by Frankie Muniz (b. 1985), the show's focus quickly turned to Malcolm's quirky parents, played by Jane Kaczmarek (b. 1955) and Bryan Cranston (b. 1956). This was Cranston's first starring role, showing a much more comedic brilliance than his later role as Walter White on the iconic series *Breaking Bad*.

Hot off the massive success of the sitcom *Seinfeld*, series cocreator and head writer Larry David (b. 1947) did a one-hour comedy special for HBO titled *Curb Your Enthusiasm* (1999). In that special, David played a fictionalized version of himself going through day-to-day life constantly frustrated in his efforts to conform to the political correctness of society and, in doing so, pointing out the oftentimes ridiculousness of this facet of society. Massive fan reaction led to the creation of a series along the same lines. The series ran for eight seasons from 2000 to 2011, when David decided he needed a break. The series returned to much applause in 2017 and is scheduled to continue into the fore-seeable future.

The Disney Channel began its long run of successful youth-based sitcoms with *Lizzie McGuire* (2001–2004), starring teen singer and actress Hilary Duff (b. 1987). As with many Disney projects to follow, the series spawned a music and merchandizing bonanza. In 2003, Disney released *The Lizzie McGuire Movie*. The series made a teen sensation of Duff and set the stage for numerous copycat series to come from the cable channel in the years to come.

Family sitcoms continued to dominate the genre during the 2000s. Another popular family sitcom of the period was *My Wife and Kids* (ABC, 2001–2005), starring comedy legend Damon Wayans (b. 1960) as an African American father surrounded by his wife and children. Yet another example of this genre was *Grounded for Life* (FOX, 2001–2003; WB, 2003–2005), starring Donal Logue (b. 1965) as an Irish American father with his wife and children. Superstar Black comedian Bernie Mac (1957–2008) starred in *The Bernie Mac Show* (FOX, 2001–2006). Country music legend Reba McEntire (b. 1955) starred in her own sitcom, *Reba* (WB, 2001–2007), placing a more rural bend on the genre. Although the family-centered sitcoms of the period sought to show different types of families, each series ultimately showed just how similar all families are, regardless of race, ethnicity, religion, or socioeconomic status.

One of the most popular sitcoms of the decade was the workplace series *Scrubs* (NBC, 2001–2010). Following the dramedy (i.e., drama/comedy) approach of the iconic series *M*A*S*H* (CBS, 1972–1983), *Scrubs* focused on the professional and personal lives of the medical personnel at the fictional hospital Sacred Heart. The series starred Zach Braff (b. 1975), Sarah Chalke (b. 1976), and Donald Faison (b. 1974). The hectic work life of a hospital allowed for writers to switch from hilarity to heartbreak in rapid beats. The breakout star of the series, however, was Dr. Perry Cox, played by John C. McGinley (b. 1959), who becomes a multilayered character, breaking away from his initial impression as a cold and insulting instructor and doctor.

One of the more tragic stories in 2000s sitcoms was the series *8 Simple Rules* (ABC, 2002–2005). Originally titled *8 Simple Rules for Dating My Teenage Daughter*, the show originally starred television sitcom veterans John Ritter (1948–2003) and Katey Sagal (b. 1954) as the parents of three children, the oldest of which was a teenage daughter played by Kaley Cuoco (b. 1985). Ritter's untimely death shortly before filming the second season forced a reformatting of the show. Rather than recast Ritter's character, producers decided to write Ritter's death into the show. Hollywood legend James Garner (1928–2014) was cast as Sagal's father, who helped his daughter raise her children. Cuoco would go on to massive success with her next project, *The Big Bang Theory*, and Sagal later appeared on that series, once more playing Cuoco's character's mother.

Diversity appeared again in the family sitcom format before the middle of the decade. Comedian George Lopez starred in *George Lopez* (ABC, 2002–2007) as a fictionalized version of himself, with the show centering on his work and home life. The Disney Channel once more struck sitcom gold with *That's So Raven* (2003–2007). This series starred Raven-Symoné (b. 1985), who had first gained fame as a toddler on the 1980s hit comedy *The Cosby Show*. *Raven* proved to be the most successful show in Disney Channel history to that point, spawning a spin-off ten years later called *Raven's Home*, where the grown-up Raven lives with her best friend, raising their children together. Not since the 1970s had television networks approved so many sitcoms featuring racially and ethnically diverse casts.

One of the most critically acclaimed sitcoms of the decade was *Arrested Development* (FOX, 2003–2006; Netflix, 2013, 2018). The series starred Jason Bateman (b. 1969) as Michael Bluth, a single father trying to raise his son while simultaneously helping his wealthy mother and siblings adjust when the family patriarch, played by Jeffrey Tambor (b. 1944), is sent to prison for financial crimes, locking up the family's vast fortune. Michael's mother, sister, and two brothers burden him with their varying degrees of insanity and dysfunction. Although it was picked up by Netflix in 2013, the series was put on indefinite hiatus in 2018 after sexual harassment reports put an abrupt end to Tambor's career.

CBS enjoyed considerable success with their sitcom *Two and a Half Men* (2003–2015). The series starred Jon Cryer (b. 1965), Angus T. Jones (b. 1993), and, initially, Charlie Sheen (b. 1965). Cryer played a single father, raising his son with the "help" of his hard-partying brother, played by Sheen. Due to continuous bad behavior by Sheen, largely because of his drug addiction, CBS considered halting the series. Instead, they decided to replace Sheen with Ashton Kutcher (b. 1978), who played Cryer's billionaire, womanizing best friend. Despite the cast shake-up, the series had another four successful years after Kutcher joined the cast.

Teenage boys were also at the heart of the hit Nickelodeon series *Drake & Josh* (2003–2007). The series starred Drake Bell and Josh Peck (both born in 1986) as stepbrothers who experience numerous misadventures while working at the local movie theater. The breakout star of the series, however, was Miranda Cosgrove (b. 1993) as their brilliant but evil younger sister. Cosgrove's popularity later led to her own Nickelodeon series, *iCarly* (2007–2012), where she plays an orphan living with her eccentric older brother who launches a popular webcast with her two best friends. These two series proved stiff competition for the Disney Channel with the youth/preteen market. The Disney Channel would soon respond to the challenge with *The Suite Life of Zack & Cody* (2005–2008). This series starred identical twins Cole and Dylan Sprouse (b. 1992) as the sons of a single mother who works as the lounge singer in a prestigious Boston hotel. Part of their mother's contract gives her a permanent room in the hotel, and the series revolves around the misadventures of the boys with a high-rise hotel as their playground.

One of the more controversial sitcoms of the period was *Entourage* (HBO, 2004–2011). The series starred Adrian Grenier (b. 1976) as a Hollywood star and his cadre of childhood friends from New York City. As a pay-cable series free from the confines of network censorship, the series focused a great deal on sex, drugs, alcohol, and harsh language. Despite this—or, perhaps, due to it—the success of the series led to a feature film in 2015. One network series that did attempt to push the boundaries of censorship was *My Name Is Earl* (NBC, 2005–2009). This series starred Jason Lee (b. 1970) as Earl Hickey, a common thief who strikes it rich with a winning lottery ticket, only to lose it when he is hit by an oncoming car while celebrating his win. The experience teaches Earl the meaning of karma, leading to the series' premise of Earl attempting to make amends for his past sins and the comedic results of that quest he takes along with his cadre of moronic friends.

In the summer of 2006, the struggling new networks of the WB and UPN merged to form a single, hopefully stronger, network: the CW. At this time, comedian Chris Rock (b. 1965) had a hit television series with *Everybody Hates Chris* (UPN, 2005–2006; CW, 2006–2009). Rock acts as narrator of this fictionalized version of his upbringing as a teenager in the 1980s. At the end of the fourth season, Chris drops out of high school to become a stand-up comedian (as the real Rock did), leading Rock to decide to end the series, despite its strong ratings and continued success. The show made a star of Terry Crews (b. 1968), who played Chris's hard-as-nails and consistently stressed-out father, based largely on Rock's own father.

NBC experienced massive success with their sitcom *The Office* (2005–2013). A knock-off of a British comedy of the same premise, the main idea of *The Office* was that the entire series was a mockumentary (i.e., mock documentary) of the day-to-day goings-on of a local branch of a fictional paper company. Steve Carell (b. 1962), alum of *The Daily Show with Jon Stewart*, starred as the regional manager of Dunder Mifflin. The breakout star of the series was Rainn Wilson (b. 1966) as salesman Dwight Schrute, whose haplessness is outdone only by his creepy hilarity. The massive popularity of the show's initial run led to a strong push by fans in 2018–2019 to convince the cast to agree to another season.

In the early 1990s, actor Neil Patrick Harris (b. 1973) gained fame for playing child genius doctor Doogie Howser. Long ignored due to his child star status, Harris returned to primetime with one of the most popular characters of the millennium, Barney Stinson, as part of the sitcom *How I Met Your Mother* (CBS, 2005–2014). The premise of the series was that the show's star, Ted Mosby, played by Josh Radnor (b. 1974), is telling his children the story of how he met their mother, and the entire series is a flashback of that story. Harris's Stinson soon became the breakout character, spending the series run by coming up with more and more inventive ways of calling himself "legendary." The series also starred *Buffy the Vampire Slayer* alum Allison Hannigan (b. 1974).

Cable network FX entered the sitcom arena with the popular *It's Always Sunny in Philadelphia* (FX, 2005–2012; FXX, 2013–present). The series centers on a group of friends who call themselves "the Gang" and jointly run an Irish pub in Philadelphia called Paddy's Pub. The main characters are twins Dennis and Deandra Reynolds, played respectively by Glenn Howerton (b. 1976) and Kaitlin Olson (b. 1975). The breakout character of the series is Frank Reynolds, the twins' biological father, played by veteran comedy actor Danny DeVito (b. 1944). Being a cable series, *Philadelphia* possesses more leeway when it comes to vulgar language and sexual situations than would a network program but still not as much as a pay-cable outlet such as HBO.

After her iconic run on *Seinfeld* (NBC, 1989–1998), comedian and *Saturday Night Live* alum Julia Louis-Dreyfus (b. 1961) returned to network sitcoms with *The New Adventures of Old Christine* (CBS, 2006–2010). Louis-Dreyfus played

Christine Campbell, a recent divorcée raising her teenage son. The title's premise comes from the fact that her ex-husband, Richard, has a girlfriend who is also named Christine. The girlfriend, then, is New Christine, while the mother is called Old Christine. Though not as successful as her previous series, *Seinfeld*, or her follow-up series, *Veep* (HBO, 2012–2019), Louis-Dreyfus's impeccable comedic talent carries the show.

By far the most successful sitcom in Disney Channel history was *Hannah Montana* (2006–2011). On this series, young pop and country singer Miley Cyrus (b. 1992) plays Miley Stewart, a "normal" teenage girl who is secretly the popular pop singer Hannah Montana. The series centers on Miley attempting to keep her normal life and professional life separate with the help of her friends, brother, and father and manager, Robby, played by Cyrus's real-life father, country music star Billy Ray Cyrus (b. 1961). The massive commercial success of the series led to four successful soundtrack albums, a Best of Both Worlds music tour, and two feature-film releases: *Hannah Montana and Miley Cyrus: Best of Both Worlds Concert in 3D* (2008) and *Hannah Montana: The Movie* (2009). The show's success also launched Miley Cyrus's own successful music career. During the successful run of *Hannah Montana*, the Disney Channel had continued success with *Wizards of Waverly Place* (2007–2012), starring pop star Selena Gomez (b. 1992) as one of three wizard siblings who compete for total control of the family's magical powers. Like Cyrus, Gomez gained huge success from the show, launching her own singing and acting career.

One of the most popular sitcoms of the period was *30 Rock* (NBC, 2006–2013). This series was the brainchild of *Saturday Night Live* alum Tina Fey (b. 1970), who played Liz Lemon, the head writer of a fictional NBC series called *TGS with Tracy Jordan*, whose star was played by fellow *SNL* veteran Tracy Morgan (b. 1968). The show is perhaps most notable for exposing the considerable comedic talents of actor Alec Baldwin (b. 1958), who played hard-nosed but goofy network executive Jack Donaghy. Through the series' seven seasons, it was nominated for over one hundred Emmy Awards and was a continuous ratings juggernaut for NBC.

By far the most successful sitcom of the twenty-first century has been *The Big Bang Theory* (CBS, 2007–2019). The show centered on four nerdy friends who also happened to be science geniuses: theoretical physicist Dr. Sheldon Cooper, played by Jim Parsons (b. 1973); experimental physicist Dr. Leonard Hofstadter, played by Johnny Galecki (b. 1975); astrophysicist Dr. Rajesh Koothrappali, played by Kunal Nayyar (b. 1981); and engineer Howard Wolowitz, played by Simon Helberg (b. 1980). The primary story line of the series revolved around Leonard's undying love for next door neighbor, waitress and aspiring actress Penny, played by Kaley Cuoco (b. 1985). The series won numerous awards and remained the number one sitcom on television for most of its run, right up through the series finale in 2019.

The sitcom *Community* (NBC, 2009–2014; Yahoo, 2015), while never a ratings juggernaut, garnered a large cult following during its run. The show revolved around seven friends attending the fictional Greendale Community College in Colorado. Joel McHale (b. 1971) played Jeff Winger, a lawyer who has been disbarred for lying about having a bachelor's degree. While attempting to con his way through community college, Winger develops a close-knit and diverse group of friends: *Saturday Night Live* veteran Chevy Chase (b. 1943) as millionaire Pierce Hawthorne, who comes back to college out of loneliness and boredom; Yvette Nicole Brown (b. 1971), as Shirley Bennett, a single mother seeking a degree to help her start her own business; Gillian Jacobs (b. 1982), as Britta Perry, a self-proclaimed liberal anarchist; Danny Pudi (b. 1979), as Abed Nadir, a pop-culture-obsessed eccentric; Alison Brie (b. 1982), as Annie Edison, an innocent studious nerd; and Donald Glover (b. 1983), as Troy Barnes, a former high school football star and classmate of Annie's.

The real breakout characters, however, were college dean Pelton, played by Jim Rash (b. 1971) and Spanish teacher-turned-security guard Señor Chang, played by Ken Jeong (b. 1969). Constant clashes between Chase and the show's creators led to Chase's departure after the third season. Fan backlash after NBC cancelled the series after season four led to Yahoo picking it up for one additional season. The series also launched the feature film careers of brothers Anthony and Joe Russo (b. 1970 and 1971, respectively), who were hired by Marvel Studios after directing several of the more popular and action-packed episodes of *Community*.

The decade closed with the introduction of two iconic sitcoms. *Parks and Recreation* (NBC, 2009–2015) starred *Saturday Night Live* legend Amy Poehler (b. 1971) as Leslie Knope, a local government employee for the fictional town of Pawnee, Indiana. A standard workplace sitcom overall, the breakout character of the series was Knope's boss, Ron Swanson, played with straight-man brilliance by Nick Offerman (b. 1970). Another notable cast member was Chris Pratt (b. 1979), who played Andy Dwyer a slow-witted but good-hearted ne'er-do-well. Pratt's brilliant comedic timing led to one of the most successful Hollywood success stories of the 2010s.

The second sitcom to finish out the decade to go on to iconic status was *Modern Family* (ABC, 2009–2020). The premise follows the lives of three interrelated families, presented to the audience in documentary-style face-to-camera interviews interspersed with the overall narrative. The series starred television icon Ed O'Neill (b. 1946) as successful closet manufacturer and family patriarch Jay Pritchett. Jay is married to his second wife, the much-younger Colombian immigrant Gloria, played by Sofía Vergara (b. 1972), and helps to raise her son from her first marriage. Jay's daughter, Claire, played by Julie Bowen (b. 1970), is married to the dim-witted but good-hearted realtor Phil Dunphy, played by Ty Burrell (b. 1967), and the two have three children. Jay's lawyer son, Mitch, played by Jesse Tyler Ferguson (b. 1975), and his life partner, Cameron, played by Eric Stonestreet (b. 1971), have an adopted Vietnamese daughter. When the U.S. Supreme Court ruled same-sex marriage legal nationally, the series celebrated by dedicating an entire season to the planning of Mitch and Cam's wedding. The series won massive critical and commercial success, becoming ABC's most popular sitcom for the decade to come.

DRAMAS

As with sitcoms, most of the most popular dramas on television coming into the 2000s began in the 1990s. By far, the most successful television drama of all time actually spawned an entire franchise of spin-offs. Coming into the twenty-first century, the longest-running television series of all time had been the western cowboy series *Gunsmoke* (CBS, 1955–1975). In 1990, a series would launch that would match it: *Law & Order* (NBC, 1990–2010). This series was unlike any police or law procedural to date. The premise of the series was that the first half hour focused on police investigation of a crime, while the second half hour focused on the district attorney's office prosecuting the case. Set and filmed in New York City, the constantly revolving cast was filled with top-notch Hollywood talent, but at its height, the main stars were Sam Waterston (b. 1940) as District Attorney Jack McCoy and Jerry Orbach (1935–2004) as NYPD police detective Lennie Brisco.

The continued success of the series led to five spin-off series, three of which were far from successful: *Law & Order: Criminal Intent* (NBC, 2001–2011); *Law & Order: Trial by Jury* (NBC/Court TV, 2005–2006); *Law & Order: Los Angeles* (NBC, 2010–2011); and *Law & Order: True Crime* (NBC, 2017). The first spin-off actually went on to surpass the original—and *Gunsmoke*—to become the longest-running series of all time: *Law & Order: Special Victims Unit* (NBC, 1999–present). This version of the franchise places more focus on the police investigation of the crime of the week, most of which revolves around sex-related crimes. The show's main star since its inception has been Mariska Hargitay (b. 1964) as NYPD detective Olivia Benson. At its peak, the series also starred Christopher Meloni (b. 1961) as Detective Elliot Stabler; Richard Belzer (b. 1944) as Detective John Munch, brought over from another hit NBC series, *Homicide: Life on the Street* (1993–1999); and rap music icon Ice-T (b. 1958), as Detective Fin Tutuola.

Other than police and law dramas, the next most popular genre of dramatic television has always been the medical procedural. The second-longest-running medical drama in television history began in the 1990s and bled into the 2000s: *ER* (NBC, 1994–2009). A standard hospital emergency-room drama set in Chicago, Illinois, the series is most notable for the careers that it launched. The biggest stars to come out of the series were George Clooney (b. 1961), starring on the series from 1994 to 1999; Julianna Margulies (b. 1966), starring on the series from 1994 to 2000; and William H. Macy (b. 1950), starring on the series for its entire run. All three would go on to phenomenal careers in the 2000s and beyond.

Coming into the 2000s, television introduced two of the most empowering female leads in television history: lawyer Ally McBeal and vampire slayer Buffy Summers. *Ally McBeal* (FOX, 1997–2002) was a legal dramedy starring Calista Flockhart (b. 1964) in the titular role as a lawyer at a small Boston, Massachusetts, firm. The show's popularity came largely from the colorful cases in each episode, as well as Flockhart's flawless performance as a neurotic Gen Xer trying to make her way professionally and romantically in a quickly changing American society. The show was equally popular for its quirky characters portrayed by Greg Germann (b. 1958), Portia de Rossi (b. 1973), Lucy Liu (b. 1968), and the endlessly brilliant Peter MacNicol (b. 1954). The series was the first in TV history to portray a coed bathroom in a workplace office. The show was as famous for its musical interludes as for its hilarious dialogue and story lines. Most music, including the title theme, was written and/or performed by Vonda Shepard (b. 1963), who also costarred as a lounge singer in the bar where the coworkers hung out. Another mainstay of the series was frequent use of the 1974 song "You're the First, the Last, My Everything" by Barry White (1944–2003), who even appeared on the show to perform his most iconic hit.

Although never considered a ratings juggernaut, *Buffy the Vampire Slayer* (WB, 1997–2001; UPN, 2001–2003) quickly became a cult classic and remains a solid part of the American zeitgeist more than a decade after its initial television run. The series set in the fictional town of Sunnydale, California, starred Sarah Michelle Gellar (b. 1977) as Buffy Summers, a high schooler of recently divorced parents who has recently discovered that she is the slayer, the latest "Chosen One" in a centuries-long line of young women imbued with enhanced strength and agility in order to protect the world from "vampires, demons, and the forces of darkness," as the series' title credits put it. She is mentored by her high school librarian, who is actually a watcher (a trained guide for the slayer), played by Anthony Stewart Head (b. 1954). Buffy is also backed up by her close-knit group of friends, who come to be known as the Scooby Gang (a reference to the teenage sleuths of the iconic 1970s cartoon *Scooby-Doo*): Willow Rosenberg, played by Alyson Hannigan (b. 1974), and Xander Harris, played by Nicholas Brendon (b. 1971). In an ironic twist, Buffy's greatest romantic love was the vampire with a soul Angel, played by David Boreanaz (b. 1969).

The cult success of *Buffy* all but mandated a spin-off. Angel became the most logical choice. In season two of *Buffy*, it was discovered that to give in to his passion for Buffy, Angel would pay the price of losing his reclaimed soul, which would cause him, then, to revert to his evil vampire persona, Angelus. When Buffy graduates high school at the end of season three, Angel leaves the series, moving to nearby Los Angeles (the City of Angels) to begin his own private detective firm. This launches the series *Angel* (WB, 1999–2004). The show, naturally, starred Boreanaz in the titular role. He was joined by two other *Buffy* alums: Charisma Carpenter (b. 1970), reprising her role as Cordelia Chase, originally Buffy's high school nemesis but later her friend and Xander's girlfriend, and Alexis Denisof (b. 1966) as former watcher Wesley Wyndam-Pryce. Another original cast member was Glenn Quinn (1970–2002), who played the half-human, half-demon Doyle. Due to struggling ratings after the fourth season, producers brought in yet another *Buffy* character, the fan-favorite vampire (also now with a soul) Spike, played by James Marsters (b. 1962). Both *Buffy* and *Angel* would carry on in comic book form after their respective series were cancelled. As of 2019, series creator Joss Whedon (b. 1964) hinted at the possibility of upcoming *Buffy* projects, including a Broadway musical version and a reboot of the original series.

The huge cult success of *Buffy* led to more shows with strong female protagonists. In 1998, the WB launched *Felicity* (WB, 1998–2002), produced by J. J. Abrams and starring Keri Russell (b. 1976) as a New York City college student. The show had a huge following in its first season, but when Russell scandalously cut her hair at the beginning of the second season, ratings fell dramatically (to this day, fans blame the haircut for the series' decline). Along more *Buffy*-esque lines was the cult favorite *Veronica Mars* (UPN, 2004–2006; CW, 2006–2007; Hulu, 2019). Kristin Bell (b. 1980) starred as the title character, a high school (later college) student who moonlights as a private detective. The continued cult following of the original series' run led to a 2014 feature film from Warner Brothers and an additional season that aired on Hulu in 2019.

Pay-cable outlet HBO had considerable success with its drama *Oz* (1997–2003). The title referred to the nickname for the series setting: the fictional prison Oswald State Correctional Facility. The series starred Kirk Acevedo (b. 1971) as inmate Miguel Alvarez, Adewale Akinnuoye-Agbaje (b. 1967) as inmate Simon Adebisi, and Ernie Hudson (b. 1945) as prison warden Leo Glynn. Due to its pay-cable status, the series was able to show a more realistic portrayal of the horrors of prison life than network or basic cable could have allowed. The series is also notable for bringing to light much of the institutional racism that unfortunately still exists within the American criminal justice system.

Another big hit for HBO was *Sex and the City* (1998–2004). Over its six-year run, this series became one of the most influential on television in the areas of representing the modern woman and, tangentially, the world of fashion. The series starred Sarah Jessica Parker (b. 1965), Kim Cattrall (b. 1956), Kristin Davis (b. 1965), and Cynthia Nixon (b. 1966) as four New York City single women whose close-knit friendship saw each through their various crises and love interests. The show emphasized the strength and agency of modern women as well as traditional romantic entanglements. The series was wildly popular among female viewers, and using the four women's various distinct fashions and personalities, fans identified themselves with the character they most resembled. The continued cult success of the series led to two feature films: *Sex and the City* (2008) and *Sex and the City 2* (2010). The one major criticism of the series was that, in reality, most of the four could not afford to live as they did in New York City on the real-world salaries of their respective professions.

HBO struck an even bigger hit with its series *The Sopranos* (1999–2007). This show was a mob-drama centered on the Soprano crime family headed by Tony Soprano, played by James Gandolfini (1961–2013). Several aspects of the series made *The Sopranos* different. First, the series strayed from iconic portrayals of mob families such as *The Godfather* films (1972–1991), where the family's wealth was obvious to all; *The Sopranos* showed a more upper-middle-class crime family. Second, Gandolfini's Tony Soprano spent much of the series talking with his therapist, showing the mental and emotional strain of being deep in a lifestyle that often requires behavior that can be difficult to live with. The controversial finale showed Tony, his wife, son, and daughter in a diner with Tony's enemies moving in for the kill, only to see the camera slowly fade to black.

Another popular legal drama that bridged the 1990s and 2000s was *The Practice* (ABC, 1997–2004). Also set in Boston, *The Practice* focused almost entirely on drama, more so than *Ally McBeal*. Like *Ally McBeal*, this series was centered on a small Boston law firm. The series starred Dylan McDermott

(b. 1961) as Bobby Donnell, the head of the firm, and Camryn Manheim (b. 1961) as attorney Ellenor Frutt. The show garnered considerable commercial and critical success, with two Emmy Award–winning performances by two of its guest stars: James Spader (b. 1960) as unscrupulous attorney Alan Shore and television icon William Shatner (b. 1931) as high-profile and eccentric attorney Denny Crane.

When *The Practice* was cancelled, a spin-off series revolving around Shore and Crane was developed. *Boston Legal* (ABC, 2004–2008) saw Spader's Shore join the big-money law firm Crane, Poole, and Schmidt. While a spin-off of *The Practice*, *Boston Legal* more closely resembled the dramedy structure of *Ally McBeal*. Halfway through its first season, another television legend, Candice Bergen (b. 1946), joined the cast as one of the firm's founding members, Shirley Schmidt. Much of the show's appeal revolved around the close friendship between Shore and Crane and the eccentric Crane's growing concern that his self-diagnosed mad cow disease was actually Alzheimer's, which it ultimately proved to be. The on-air chemistry between Spader and Shatner as well as each actor's brilliant and career-defining performances kept the show alive even as the inclusion of increasingly quirky lawyers began to stretch credulity.

The last 1990s drama to spill over into the new century was also perhaps the most important series of the period: *The West Wing* (NBC, 1999–2006). This series centered on the fictional administration of President Josiah Bartlet, played with iconic gravitas by Martin Sheen (b. 1940). The multi-award-winning cast also included John Spencer (1963–2005) as White House chief of staff Leo McGarry; Bradley Whitford (b. 1959) as Deputy Chief of Staff Josh Lyman, Richard Schiff (b. 1955) as Communications Director Toby Ziegler, Rob Lowe (b. 1964) as Deputy Communications Director Sam Seaborn, Allison Janney (b. 1959) as Press Secretary C. J. Cregg, and Dule Hill (b. 1975) as Charlie Young, the personal aide to the president. It presented an idealized and openly liberal portrayal of what government could and should be. At the height of the controversial recounts for the presidential election of 2000, a commercial for the series promoted Bartlet as "the one president we can all agree on." For the five years after 9/11, *The West Wing* provided American liberals a safe space to see their idealism made manifest in an increasingly conservative country.

The 2000–2001 television season saw the birth of a new legal drama franchise: *CSI*. All of the series focus on different police forensics, or crime scene investigation, units. The original series in the franchise, *CSI: Crime Scene Investigation* (CBS, 2000–2015), was set in Las Vegas and starred William Petersen (b. 1953) and Marg Helgenberger (b. 1958). The second series in the franchise was *CSI: Miami* (CBS, 2002–2012) and starred David Caruso (b. 1956) and Emily Procter (b. 1968). That was followed by *CSI: NY* (CBS, 2004–2013), starring Gary Sinise (b. 1955) and Melina Kanakaredes (b. 1967). The last series in the franchise (to date) was *CSI: Cyber* (CBS, 2015–2016), set in Washington, DC, and centered on an FBI cyberinvestigations unit, starred Patricia Arquette (b. 1968) and James Van Der Beek (b. 1977). The continued popularity of legal series such as *Law & Order*, *CSI*, *NCIS*, and *Criminal Intent* speaks to the enduring respect and admiration that many Americans hold for the American criminal justice system, despite harsher—and unfortunately more realistic—portrayals in the mainstream media.

The upstart network the WB enjoyed some success with another dramedy series: *Gilmore Girls*, which was also caught up in the UPN/WB merger (WB, 2000–2006; CW, 2006–2007). This series starred Lauren Graham (b. 1967) as single mother Lorelai Gilmore and Alexis Bledel (b. 1981) as her only daughter, Rory. The series is set in the fictional small town of Stars Hollow, Connecticut, and focuses on the relationship between mother and daughter against the backdrop of a small town of colorful characters. Like fellow WB series *Buffy*, *Gilmore Girls* was never a high-ratings performer, but it gained a loyal following that continues to call for the series return to this day.

Another popular dramedy of the period was the series *Six Feet Under* (HBO, 2001–2005). The popular HBO show centered on Nate Fisher, played by Peter Krause (b. 1965), and David Fisher, played by Michael C. Hall (b. 1971), as brothers who inherit their father's funeral home, Fisher & Sons. While a traditional family drama to a degree, *Six Feet Under* differed in its constant focus on death—physically, religiously, and philosophically—with the main characters having direct conversations with the corpses they prepare for burial.

The popular *Star Trek* franchise began its fifth decade with the series *Enterprise* (UPN, 2001–2005). Unlike the previous three spin-offs of the 1960s original, *Enterprise* was set a century prior to the original series. The show starred Scott Bakula (b. 1954) as Captain Jonathan Archer, commander of the experimental interstellar starship *Enterprise* (the same name as that of the original series' iconic starship). This *Enterprise* and her crew represented the first in the newly formed Starfleet created by United Earth. The series never received the critical or commercial success of the previous television offerings, and it was cancelled after four seasons. In the series finale, the crew had successfully built alliances with enough other planets to form the United Federation of Planets, the core governing body of the preceding future series.

Two crime dramas in the early 2000s showed the uglier side of law enforcement and the real-world problems that law enforcement officers face every day. *The Wire* (HBO, 2002–2008) was created by real-life crime reporter David Simon (b. 1960), who set his fictional series in Baltimore, Maryland. Though the series centered on law enforcement, each season focused on a different area of crime that the local police had to deal with. Each season had a different main cast, focusing on different local agencies and bureaus each season, with some minor plotlines overarching.

Meanwhile, on basic cable, another police drama was introduced: *The Shield* (FX, 2002–2008). Set in Los Angeles, the show starred Michael Chiklis (b. 1963) as Detective Vic Mackey, the head of a special unit allowed to use whatever means necessary to combat the growing violent crime in the ghetto neighborhoods. Mackey and his unit, as suspected by their commander, are dirty cops, protecting and serving the public while simultaneously filling their own pockets. Unlike more heroic police narratives such as *Law & Order* or *CSI*, *The Wire* and *The Shield*—although, admittedly, in different ways—portrayed American law enforcement in a more realistic and less idealized fashion.

In 1978, in response to the recent *Star Wars* craze, ABC launched the sci-fi series *Battlestar Galactica*, a series about twelve colonies of humanity living in the far reaches of the galaxy, recently decimated by the evil, robotic Cylon race. The series covered the human survivors' quest to find their lost thirteenth colony, Earth. Though highly successful, the series was cancelled after only one and a-half seasons due to its high cost. In 2003, the Sci-Fi Channel debuted a three-hour miniseries relaunching the franchise. The *Battlestar Galactica* miniseries starred Edward James Olmos (b. 1947) as Commander Bill Adama, the commanding officer of humanity's last surviving battlestar, the *Galactica*. Both are tasked with protecting the last remnants of humanity after the devastating Cylon attack leaves their home worlds unlivable. The series also starred Mary McDonnell (b. 1952) as the new president of the Colonies, recent secretary of education Laura Roslin (the original series did not have this political dynamic).

The most controversial aspect of the remake was casting Katee Sackhoff (b. 1980) as series hero, hotshot pilot Starbuck. In the original series, Starbuck was a male character played by Dirk Benedict (b. 1945). The miniseries ended with humanity's decision to seek out Earth. The huge fan response led Sci-Fi to green-light an ongoing series, which ran from 2004 to 2009. Throughout its iconic run, the series examined issues such as the politics of fear, overreaction in the face of uncertainty, and the origins of the human race. The first two of these were issues that most Americans were dealing with in the wake of 9/11. Though the series came to a clear conclusion, fan devotion to the franchise has led to massive support for another reboot in the ten years following the series run.

Another drama series that made the transition after the UPN/WB merger into the CW was *One Tree Hill* (WB, 2003–2006; CW, 2006–2012). This family drama centered on high school athlete brothers, Lucas and Nathan Scott, played respectively by Chad Michael Murray (b. 1981) and James Lafferty (b. 1985). Most of the series focuses on the relationship between these two competitive brothers, both playing on the same high school basketball team, and their rivalry and romances. The fifth season jumped four years into the future, with both brothers now graduated from college and returning to their hometown of One Tree Hill. The seventh season had another time jump, this time of fourteen months. Though serialized in nature, this nighttime soap never reached the over-the-top outlandishness of the 1980s series that spawned the genre.

Police procedural franchises received a new addition in 2003: *NCIS* (CBS, 2003–present). An acronym for Naval Criminal Investigative Service, the series was a spin-off of the popular series *JAG* (NBC, 1995–1996; CBS, 1997–2005), itself an acronym for Judge Advocate General, the legal/justice occupational specialty of the U.S. military branches. *JAG* focused specifically on the Navy JAG Corps and starred David James Elliot (b. 1960) as Lieutenant (later Captain) Harmon Rabb. Combined, *JAG/NCIS* represented, basically, a military *Law & Order*.

NCIS, however, far surpassed the original, becoming the second-longest-running drama series in television history, behind another spin-off series, *Law*

& Order: SVU. NCIS starred Mark Harmon (b. 1951) as Navy senior field agent Leroy Gibbs, head of this Washington, DC–based investigative unit. The enduring popularity of the series led to two spin-offs of its own: *NCIS: Los Angeles* (CBS, 2009–present), starring Chris O'Donnell (b. 1970) and rapper LL Cool J (James Smith, b. 1968), and *NCIS: New Orleans* (CBS, 2014–present), starring Scott Bakula (b. 1954), and C. C. H. Pounder (b. 1952).

A very popular but short-lived program of the decade was the wild-west series *Deadwood* (HBO, 2004–2006). Set in 1876, in the violent Dakota Territory town of Deadwood, the series starred Timothy Olyphant (b. 1968) as real-life former U.S. marshal Seth Bullock (1849–1919) and Ian McShane (b. 1942) as another real-life Deadwood resident, Al Swearengen (1845–1904). The series presented a fictionalized account of life in the violent western town, featuring appearances by other iconic Wild West figures such as Wyatt Earp (1848–1929), Calamity Jane Canary (1852–1903), and Wild Bill Hickock (1837–1876), who famously died in Deadwood, shot in the back during a poker game while holding a hand of two-pair—"aces and eights"—now universally known as the dead man's hand. In the series, Hickock was played by Keith Carradine (b. 1949). Enduring fan devotion to the series eventually led HBO to produce a reunion movie, which aired in 2019.

HBO had success with another historical drama, *Rome* (2005–2007). Set in ancient Rome from 50 to 30 BCE, the series dramatized the events of the First and Second Roman Civil Wars. The two main characters of the series were real-life Roman Gallic War veterans Lucius Vorenus, played by Kevin McKidd (b. 1973), and Titus Pullo, played by Ray Stevenson (b. 1964). As the history-altering events unfold around them, the main focus of the series was the band of brothers–style friendship of the two veterans. Although historians criticized the portrayal of historical events, the portrayal of daily life in ancient Rome was hailed for its preciseness. An interesting aspect of the series, however, was that, while twenty years pass during the series, Vorenus, Pullo, and Vorenus's children remain relatively unaged throughout. Though critically acclaimed and a big hit with fans, HBO cancelled the series after its second season due to its massive budget of over $100 million per season.

One of the most critically and commercially successful series of the decade was the J. J. Abrams creation *Lost* (ABC, 2004–2010). The basic premise of the series centered on the crash of a passenger plane near an uncharted island in the South Pacific; soon, however, the survivors of the crash discover that there is something mysterious about the island and some form of supernatural presence. The large cast consisting, at first, of fourteen main characters featured Matthew Fox (b. 1966), Evangeline Lilly (b. 1979), and Jorge Garcia (b. 1973). Over the course of the series, the survivors experience a strange smoke monster, another group of inhabitants they refer to as the Others, and constant jumps forward and backward through time. The controversial finale suggested that the island was, itself, a limbo state between life and death. The frequent narrative side turns and plot twists kept fans obsessed for the show's six season run.

Another huge hit for ABC debuting in 2004 was *Desperate Housewives* (2004–2012). The series observes the trials and tribulations of a group of friends, upper-middle-class suburban housewives in the fictional town of Fairview. The stars of the series were Marcia Cross (b. 1962), Teri Hatcher (b. 1964), Felicity Huffman (b. 1962), Eva Longoria (b. 1975), and nighttime soap icon Nicollette Sheridan (b. 1963). The narrator of the series is the spirit of a sixth friend, played by Brenda Strong (b. 1960), whose character committed suicide in the series premier. Following many of the tried-and-true tropes of traditional nighttime soaps such as infidelity, divorce, illness, romance, and troubled children, the series was not afraid to poke fun at itself with the hilarity of its own premise, made all-the-more delightful through the top-notch acting, comedic timing, and cast chemistry.

Still another hit veteran of the 2004 season was the medical drama *House, M.D.* (FOX, 2004–2012). Set in a fictional teaching hospital in New Jersey, this series centered on the antisocial diagnostics genius Dr. Gregory House, played with pseudomalevolent charm by British actor Hugh Laurie (b. 1959). House oversees a revolving group of interns, both teaching them proper diagnostics and solving medical mysteries every week. Despite his in-your-face rudeness, excessive egomania, and severe addiction to painkillers, House's students and coworkers are deeply devoted to him, seeing him through his personal eccentricities and physical challenges and constantly in awe of his medical genius. In 2009, Eurodata TV Worldwide, published by *Agence France Presse*, reported that in 2008, *House* was the most watched series in the world, with an average of nearly eighty-two million viewers (Eurodata TV Worldwide 2009).

HBO pay cable rival Showtime also enjoyed success with its series *Weeds* (2005–2012). This series starred Mary-Louise Parker (b. 1964) and Elizabeth Perkins (b. 1960). Parker played Nancy Botwin, a widowed mother of two who begins selling marijuana as a means of supporting her family. Over the course of the series, Botwin becomes increasingly involved in ever-escalating levels of the illegal drug trade. Though similar in many ways to the AMC series *Breaking Bad*, *Weeds* did not become as much a part of the American zeitgeist, due largely to the smaller audiences of pay-cable outlets. Its pay-cable status did, however, allow for much more in the way of violence, sex, and strong language than the basic-cable *Breaking Bad*.

Hot off his success with *Buffy the Vampire Slayer* and *Angel*, actor David Boreanaz (b. 1969) achieved even greater commercial success with his next project: *Bones* (FOX, 2005–2017). In this series, Boreanaz played FBI special agent Seeley Booth, working closely with forensics specialist Dr. Temperance "Bones" Brennan, played by Emily Deschanel (b. 1976). First and foremost a crime investigation procedural drama, over time the series began to focus as much on the budding romantic relationship between the two leads. The series was loosely based on the series of crime novels written by the show's producer, Kathy Reichs (b. 1948). In the *Bones* novels, Brennan is also an author of crime novels based on her cases, and her fictional protagonist is named Kathy Reichs.

Yet another series to survive the UPN/WB merger, and ultimately the most successful series in the CW's history, was *Supernatural* (WB, 2005–2006; CW, 2006–2020). This series starred Jared Padalecki (b. 1982) and Jensen Ackles (b. 1978) as brothers Sam and Dean Winchester, who investigate paranormal activity. Aside from various supernatural creatures from throughout popular culture over the centuries, the series eventually delves more deeply into Christian mythology, making a primary character of fallen angel Lucifer. The series becomes famous for name-dropping numerous related pop-culture franchises such as *Scooby-Doo*, with one episode even animated in the style of the classic cartoon series. The series continues to possess a powerful fan following and has become a pop culture phenomenon going into the 2020s.

Crime and medical procedurals continued to be wildly popular going into and throughout the 2010s. Two such series debuted in 2005: crime procedural *Criminal Minds* (CBS, 2005–present) and medical drama *Grey's Anatomy* (ABC, 2005–present). Both series, due to their longevity, have had revolving casts of characters and actors over their runs. *Criminal Minds* centers on the FBI's Behavioral Analysis Unit, profiling both suspects and victims to solve crimes. The series originally starred Mandy Patinkin (b. 1952), Thomas Gibson (b. 1962), Lola Glaudini (b. 1971), Shemar Moore (b. 1970), and Matthew Gray Gubler (b. 1980). *Grey's Anatomy* centers on the life and loves of Dr. Meredith Grey, played by Ellen Pompeo (b. 1969). Though possessing powerful medical-based weekly story lines, the series focuses more on the personal relationships of the main characters. Aside from Pompeo, the series originally starred Sandra Oh (b. 1971), Katherine Heigl (b. 1978), James Pickens Jr. (b. 1954), and Patrick Dempsey (b. 1966).

In 2005, British network BBC revived one of the most classic series in television history: *Doctor Who* (BBC1, 1963–1989; BBC-Wales/Sci-Fi Channel, 2005; BBC1/BBC-America, 2006–present). This sci-fi series centers on a time and space–traveling alien known only as the Doctor. The Doctor travels with a revolving door of human companions throughout time and space in his mysterious spacecraft, the TARDIS (an acronym for Time and Relative Dimension in Space), which, due to a mechanical malfunction, has taken on the permanent outer shape of a 1960s-sytle British police call box, although the ship is "bigger on the inside." When the iconic and wildly popular series was revived in 2005 after a sixteen-year-long hiatus, it first aired in America on the Sci-Fi Channel (now called SyFy). On its return, the Doctor was portrayed by Christopher Eccleston (b. 1964). Due to the character's ability to regenerate—changing into seemingly another person on one body's death—numerous men have portrayed the Doctor over its fifty-plus year history. In 2017, for the first time, the Doctor regenerated into the form of a woman, played by Jodie Whittaker (b. 1982). Though initially an unpopular idea with some fans, the majority of fans around the world embraced Whittaker's take on the Time Lord, bringing the series its highest ratings since its return.

Another network television hit from the period was the high school family drama *Friday Night Lights* (NBC, 2006–2011). Based on the 2004 film, itself an adaptation of the 1990 novel of the same name, the series starred Kyle Chandler (b. 1965), a high school football coach, and his wife, played by Connie Britton (b. 1967). The original novel and film were based on the real-life story of the 1988 season of an Odessa, Texas, high school football team. Fictionalized and set in the fictional town of Dillon, Texas, on the series, Chandler's character, Eric Taylor, is married to the high school guidance counselor and eventual principal. Set against the backdrop of high school football in Texas, the series was, for the most part, a standard family and workplace drama.

In the back half of the decade, Showtime experienced more success with three back-to-back hits. *Dexter* (2006–2013) starred Michael C. Hall (b. 1971) as Miami forensics specialist Dexter Morgan, who specializes in analyzing blood spatter patterns for the local police department. He also happens to be, in his spare time, a serial killer who specifically murders other murderers who have escaped justice. *The Tudors* (2007–2010) was a historical-based drama centered on the reign of one of England's most iconic monarchs, King Henry VIII (1491–1547; r. 1509–1547). Jonathan Rhys Meyers (b. 1977) played the legendary king famous for his six wives, breaking England away from the Catholic Church, and fathering the empire's most beloved monarch, Queen Elizabeth I (1533–1603; r. 1558–1603). Last, in the dramedy *Californication* (2007–2014), David Duchovny (b. 1960) played Hank Moody, a writer suffering from severe writer's block who experiences numerous misadventures, due largely to his drug and alcohol abuse and excessive womanizing.

Basic cable network FX also had considerable success with dramas in the last half of the 2000s. *Damages* (2007–2012) starred Glenn Close (b. 1947) as legal legend Patty Hewes and her latest protégée, Ellen Parsons, played by Rose Byrne (b. 1979). The series focused on season-long cases and each side's approach to their arguments and strategies. *Sons of Anarchy* (2008–2014) centered on a fictional outlaw biker gang in California. This series starred Charlie Hunnam (b. 1980), Katey Sagal (b. 1954), and Mark Boone Junior (b. 1964). The motorcycle gang, called SAMCRO (for Sons of Anarchy Motorcycle Club, Redwood Original), is involved in gun running, and the series revolves around the interpersonal relationships of the gang members, their families, and their criminal enterprises.

Perhaps the most successful network as the 2000s ended was AMC, with two massive hit series: *Mad Men* (2007–2015) and *Breaking Bad* (2008–2013). *Mad Men* starred Jon Hamm (b. 1971) and Elisabeth Moss (b. 1982). This series was a period drama set against the backdrop of New York advertising firms in the 1960s. It experienced massive commercial and critical success, most notably for its portrayal of the rampant sexism of the 1960s.

Its debut was followed a year later by, perhaps, the most popular series of the decade and an enduring part of the American zeitgeist years after its completion. *Breaking Bad* starred Bryan Cranston (b. 1956), in a career-defining role, as Walter White, a high school chemistry teacher recently diagnosed with near-terminal lung cancer. In order to provide adequate financial security for his family after his death, White utilizes his knowledge of chemistry to begin producing a particularly potent strain of methamphetamine. Like *Weeds* before it, *Breaking Bad* exhibits White's rise in the drug underworld, eventually taking on the identity Heisenberg. White's transformation from a bumbling, docile high school teacher to ruthless drug lord was not only one of the highlights of the series but also an acting tour-de-force that launched Cranston to the top of his art. Continued fan devotion has kept rumors alive of a possible return of the series or reunion movie/miniseries special.

HBO continued its dramatic series success with one of its most successful of all: *True Blood* (2008–2014). This series was based on the popular novel series

The Southern Vampire Mysteries by Charlaine Harris (b. 1951). The series is set in Louisiana and is centered on the character of Sookie Stackhouse, played by Anna Paquin (b. 1982), a small-town waitress who is half-human, half-fairy. The primary story centers on the fact that a new synthetic blood called True Blood has enabled vampires to come out of the shadows and live openly among the living. As the 2000s opened with the vampires of *Buffy,* they ended with the vampires of *True Blood,* a testament to the enduring appeal of vampire fiction well into the twenty-first century.

By the end of the decade, HBO was the number-one pay-cable outlet; this was due in no small part to the considerable commercial and critical success with some of its miniseries events during the decade. *Band of Brothers* (2001) was a historical war drama based on historian Stephen Ambrose's historical account of the same name of Easy Company, of the 2nd Battalion, 506th Paratrooper Infantry Regiment, 101st Airborne Division, in World War II. The miniseries was coproduced by Hollywood legends Steven Spielberg (b. 1946) and Tom Hanks (b. 1956), and it starred an impressive case led by Damian Lewis (b. 1971), Ron Livingston (b. 1967), and Scott Grimes (b. 1971). The miniseries was nominated for twenty Primetime Emmy Awards, winning seven, including Outstanding Miniseries.

Angels in America (HBO, 2003) was based on a Pulitzer Prize–winning play by Tony Kushner (b. 1956). The miniseries was set in 1985, focusing on six New Yorkers and their experiences with angels, all the while acting as a commentary on the sociopolitical climate of America in the Age of Reagan, with heavy emphasis on the AIDS epidemic and the LGBTQ+ community. The star-studded cast included Meryl Streep (b. 1949), Al Pacino (b. 1940), and Emma Thompson (b. 1959). The miniseries was nominated for twenty-one Primetime Emmy Awards (including creative awards), winning eleven, including Outstanding Miniseries.

In 2002, historian David McCullough (b. 1933) won the Pulitzer Prize for his biography of John Adams (1735–1826), the second president of the United States (1797–1801). In 2008, HBO debuted its miniseries based on the book. *John Adams* starred Paul Giamatti (b. 1967) in the titular role. Laura Linney (b. 1964) played Adams's beloved wife, Abigail (1797–1801), and Stephen Dillane (b. 1957) played Adams's close friend, fellow revolutionary, vice president, and temporary political rival, Thomas Jefferson (1743–1826). The miniseries focused on Adams's life from his legal defense of the British soldiers at the heart of the Boston Massacre (1770) through the American Revolution; his time as ambassador to Great Britain, vice president, and president; and his retirement and death, ironically, on the same day as Jefferson, July 4, 1826, the fiftieth anniversary of the Declaration of Independence, which both men signed. The miniseries was nominated for twenty-three Primetime Emmy Awards, winning thirteen, including Outstanding Miniseries.

REALITY PROGRAMMING

With ever-increasing actor pay for the bigger hits on television, the major networks and many cable outlets began investing in reality programming. These usually fall into one of two primary categories: series that give the impression of capturing real-world situations, usually starring "regular" people who are not actors or actresses, often competing in some form of game with the promise of a cash prize; or series that give the appearance of following the day-to-day lives of celebrities or quasi-celebrities. However, by 2000, the year the reality show craze began, the number one show on basic cable throughout most of the 1990s had been a program that already fell tangentially into the realm of reality programming: *WWF Monday Night Raw*.

By the mid-twentieth century, there were several professional wrestling syndicates around the United States. Capitol Wrestling Corporation was cofounded in 1952 by R. J. McMahon (1882–1954). When he died, his interest in the company fell to his son, Vincent J. McMahon (1914–1984). In 1980, Vincent's son Vincent K. McMahon (b. 1945) cofounded Titan Sports with his wife, Linda (b. 1948). In 1982, they purchased Capitol from Vince Sr. and created the World Wrestling Federation. Over the course of the next fifteen years, the McMahons bought up a larger and larger percentage of the overall pro wrestling industry, essentially becoming a monopoly by 2000. The WWF gained a massive following with headlining talent such as Hulk Hogan (b. 1953), "Rowdy" Roddy Piper (1954–2015), and seven-foot, four-inch Andre the Giant (Andre Roussimoff, 1946–1993). In 1985, the company produced the first *WrestleMania*, an annual pay-per-view event that soon became recognized as the Super Bowl of professional wrestling.

In 1993, WWF launched *Monday Night Raw* (USA, 1993–2000; TNN/Spike TV, 2000–2005; USA, 2005–present). Though a strong performer from the beginning, the series became a literal ratings juggernaut during what has come to be known as the Attitude Era, roughly from 1998 to 2002, with wrestling superstars such as "Stone Cold" Steve Austin (b. 1964), Mick "Mankind" Foley (b. 1965), and Dwayne "the Rock" Johnson (b. 1972). By 1999, the Rock was the biggest name in the history of pro wrestling, known throughout the country as "the Most Electrifying Man in Sports Entertainment" and "the People's Champion." His popularity led to the creation of a new WWF program, *Smackdown* (UPN, 1999–2006; CW, 2006–2008; My Network TV, 2008–2010; SyFy, 2010–2015; USA, 2016–present). In 1994, World Wrestling Federation agreed to stop using the acronym "WWF" due to an agreement with the World Wide Fund for Nature, a nonprofit organization that owned the copyright to the acronym. Repeatedly ignoring the agreement, the McMahons were sued, forcing them to change their brand name to World Wrestling Entertainment, or WWE. Throughout the 2000s, *Raw* remained the number one series on basic cable until it was finally dethroned by the AMC sci-fi series *The Walking Dead* (2010–present).

The current reality show craze began in 2000 with two offerings from CBS: *Survivor* (2000–present) and *Big Brother* (2000–present). A knock-off of a Swedish program, by 2000, *Survivor* was already an international phenomenon. The American version copied the format, creating a reality competition program that pitted a group of contestants against each other in a wilderness situation. Contestants form alliances and collectively vote individuals off the program, one at a time, until the last two compete for the grand prize. The first season took place on an island in Malaysia, and the winner was Richard Hatch

(b. 1961), a single gay man, portrayed throughout the season as the villain of the group. In 2013, Hatch was named number thirty-one on a list of TV's Nastiest Villains of all time ("*TV Guide* Picks TV's 60 Nastiest Villains" 2013).

Big Brother is a knock-off of a British program, which, itself, is a knock-off of a Dutch program. Like *Survivor*, this is a competition between a group of contestants, this time all locked in a house together under constant camera surveillance. Throughout the season, contestants are free to speak "privately" to a camera in a booth, making comments and observations that are known only to the home audience. Also like *Survivor*, the group votes to evict members throughout the season until a single winner remains to win the cash prize. It was a continuous ratings powerhouse for the network, and a spin-off was eventually created, *Celebrity Big Brother* (CBS, 2018–present), with the same premise, but with celebrities (actually quasi-, pseudo-, and former celebrities).

Following the success of their first two endeavors, the network struck gold again with *The Amazing Race* (CBS, 2001–present). In this series, ten to twelve pairs of contestants compete against each other in a literal race around the world. Contestants are given a fixed budget with various challenges to lead them to their next destination, which they must reach using various methods of public transit and interacting with local populations. The enduring popularity of the series stems largely from the mixture of traditional reality competition programming with a National Geographic aspect of foreign locales and cultures.

Coming into the twenty-first century, MTV was beginning to lose its place as the go-to outlet for all things teen and twenties pop culture. Their first real foray into reality programming came with *The Osbournes* (2002–2005). This series promoted the idea of following the day-to-day home life of heavy metal legend Ozzy Osbourne (b. 1948); his wife, Sharon (b. 1952); and two of their three children: Kelly (b. 1984) and Jack (b. 1985). Older sibling Aimee (b. 1983) chose not to participate in the spectacle. The opening credit theme was a rendition of Ozzy's hit song "Crazy Train," although it was not performed by Ozzy. The show was an immediate massive success, due largely to the antics of the aging, mumbling rocker and his frequent confusion with modern technology. The series is perhaps most important for making a media darling and reality show superstar of Sharon Osbourne, who, to that point, had been a relatively low-key behind-the-scenes wife and mother for the iconic bat-eating rock star (Ozzy had gained notoriety in the 1980s for biting the head off of a live bat on stage, which was a staged incident utilizing a fake bat with fake blood).

One of the biggest reality-competition programs of the period was *American Idol* (FOX, 2002–2016; ABC, 2018–present). Yet another knock-off of a British import, in *Idol*, contestants compete in rounds of singing competitions, having to sing various genres of music throughout the season to more equitably expose each individual's strengths and weaknesses. They are judged by the viewing audience, with professional input from a panel of three judges. The original panel included singer and record producer Randy Jackson (b. 1956), singer and dancer Paula Abdul (b. 1962), and talent agent and record executive Simon Cowell (b. 1959). Cowell was the "mean" judge, frequently giving the most biting and insulting criticism. The most recent panel included crooner Harry Connick Jr. (b. 1967), country music singer Keith Urban (b. 1967), and singer, dancer, and actress Jennifer Lopez (b. 1969).

Winners with the most successful solo music careers have been 2002 winner Kelly Clarkson (b. 1982) and the 2005 winner, country music legend Carrie Underwood (b. 1983). The massive success of the series led Cowell to produce an international talent competition, the U.S. version of which was *America's Got Talent* (NBC, 2006–present). Like *American Idol*, it is a competition program where contestants show off whatever talent they possess, with input from a panel of celebrity judges and audience feedback deciding the winner. Still another competition-based program is *Top Chef* (Bravo, 2006–present) where would-be chefs compete for a panel of professional judges.

Reality shows are often viewed as guilty pleasures, programs that viewers obsessively watch despite the fact that doing so could bring judgments of low-brow entertainment from those who do not watch. The guiltiest of guilty pleasures are the mirror series *The Bachelor* (ABC, 2002–present) and its spin-off, *The Bachelorette* (ABC, 2003–present). Yet another competition series, the original focused on a single male who must choose from among a group of female contestants all doing whatever it takes to win over their would-be paramour by eliminating their competition. The spin-off was the same premise in reverse, with a single female choosing from a group of male competitors. The winning choice would be presented a rose in the final episode, with the couple presumably going on to live happily ever after . . . although that was rarely the case, as everyone involved actually utilized the series to attempt to gain fame and fortune. The respective series possessed all the beautiful people and biting drama of nighttime soap operas but were presented as reality.

By far, the most socially significant of the reality programs of the 2000s was *Queer Eye for the Straight Guy*, later shortened to just *Queer Eye* (Bravo, 2003–2007). This series was, at its core, a general makeover program, playing into the stereotype that gay men understood fashion, hair, dancing, and fine dining more than straight men. As such, the Fab Five—Ted Allen (b. 1965), Kyan Douglas (b. 1970), Thom Filicia (b. 1969), Carson Kressley (b. 1969), and Jai Rodriguez (b. 1979)—would take on straight men as clients, educating them on areas that would make them more successful with women. Though playing into stereotypes of both gay and straight men, the massive popularity of the show brought gay men into millions of American homes that may have never met, to their knowledge, anyone from the LGBTQ+ community. As such, by playing into, and even celebrating, the stereotypes, *Queer Eye*—along with the sitcom *Will & Grace*—went a long way to breaking down generations-old barriers that had for so long stigmatized the gay community and, in doing so, opened "mainstream" America up to being more accepting of the LGBTQ+ community overall.

A far, far less socially important reality program was *The Simple Life* (FOX, 2003–2005; E!, 2006–2007). This series followed the fish-out-of-water premise, taking real-life best friends and wealthy socialite heiresses Paris Hilton (b. 1981) of Hilton Hotel fame and Nicole Richie (b. 1981), adopted daughter of music icon Lionel Richie, and placing them in "common" low-wage and/or hard-labor jobs. The primary appeal to viewers was to watch "spoiled little rich girls" "suffer" by living the lives of "everyday" Americans. The show gained some unexpected free publicity early on when Hilton's ex-boyfriend uploaded a sex video of the two onto the internet, later releasing it as a home video.

Cashing in on his fame from the popular sitcom *That '70s Show*, actor and well-known prankster Ashton Kutcher (b. 1978) launched his own hidden-camera show, *Punk'd* (MTV, 2003–2007, 2012; BET, 2015). This series featured Kutcher playing elaborate practical jokes on various celebrities, often close personal friends. One of his most popular gags was targeted at Kutcher's close friend, singer and dancer Justin Timberlake (b. 1981), convincing the pop star that he owed massive amounts of back taxes, leading to all of his worldly possessions being confiscated. The scene of Timberlake tearfully talking to his mother on the phone was outshone only by his mixture of anger and glee when discovering that his friend was behind the scam. Another popular gag, focused on pro wrestling champion the Rock (b. 1972), culminated in the giant wrestler-turned-actor chasing Kutcher down a city block.

Several popular reality programs centered on the world of modeling. *America's Next Top Model* (UPN, 2003–2006; CW, 2006–2015; VH1, 2016–2018) was created and hosted by supermodel Tyra Banks (b. 1973) and was, as the title suggests, a reality competition to seek out the next great supermodel. *Project Runway* (Bravo, 2004–2008; Lifetime, 2009–2017; Bravo, 2019–present) was hosted by supermodel Heidi Klum (b. 1973) and iconic fashion critic Tim Gunn (b. 1953) with a very similar format but a focus on seeking out the next great fashion designer. Last, *RuPaul's Drag Race* (Logo, 2009–2016; VH1, 2017–resent) was hosted by iconic drag queen, singer, and actor RuPaul (RuPaul Andre Charles, b. 1960). This series combined the premises of the previous two series, with various drag queens competing in modeling, makeup, and fashion.

One of the more noble reality programs of the 2000s was *Extreme Makeover: Home Edition* (ABC, 2003–2012). This series was hosted by model and carpenter Ty Pennington (b. 1964). The purpose of the program was to conduct surprise remodelings of private homes of lower-income families or families facing health issues or other challenges. The series would also occasionally take on projects such as public schools, community centers, and other public buildings. Though the show has been cancelled for some time, the cable network HGTV announced plans to revive the program on their network in 2020. Another popular makeover show was *Pimp My Ride* (MTV, 2004–2007). This series was hosted by rapper Xzibit (Alvin Nathaniel Joiner, b. 1974), where each episode was dedicated to customizing a previously beat-up or run-down car. The show spawned the copycat series *Trick My Truck* (CMT, 2006–present) which did the same thing for trucks, though with a more rural vibe than the more urban *Pimp*.

Another celebrity-driven reality program was the Donald J. Trump (b. 1946) vehicle *The Apprentice* (NBC, 2004–2017). Series creator Mark Burnett (b. 1960) chose the real estate billionaire as the celebrity host of this American version of his idea. Contestants were first divided into two teams, or "corporations," to compete against each other until one was dominant, with contestants in the winning corporation then competing against each other for a job with the Trump Organization. Trump's trademarked phrase to those selected as the loser was "You're fired."

The popularity of the original led to the spin-off *Celebrity Apprentice* (NBC, 2008–2015), featuring the same format but with contestants of some manner of celebrity or notoriety. Perhaps the most famous—or infamous—contestant of the original show's first season was Omarosa Manigault Newman (b. 1974), who, despite losing the competition, went on to prominent positions both in the Trump Organization and, later, the future president's administration.

Another reality program hosted by a well-known American billionaire was *The Girls Next Door* (E!, 2005–2010). This show centered on the daily life of *Playboy* empire founder Hugh Hefner (1926–2017) and his three live-in Playmate girlfriends: Holly Madison (b. 1979), Bridget Marquardt (b. 1973), and Kendra Wilkinson (b. 1985). When the aged mogul's relationships with the original three ended, they were replaced in 2009 with three new girlfriends: Crystal Harris (b. 1986) and twins Kristina and Karissa Shannon (b. 1989). In 2012, Harris became Hefner's third and final wife, remaining married to the billionaire until his death in 2017. The series was clearly an attempt to lionize the aging publisher's reputation as a lifelong womanizer.

One of the more popular reality competition programs was *Dancing with the Stars* (ABC, 2005–present). Another knock-off of a British original, the series is hosted by Tom Bergeron (b. 1955) and a revolving door of female cohosts, beginning with Lisa Canning (b. 1966) in season one and, most recently, Erin Andrews (b. 1978). Each season pairs one-time celebrities and, occasionally, former political figures with professional dancers whose job it is to turn the celebrity into top-notch dancers. A combination of judges' scores and audience feedback determines which pair will be eliminated each week until a final winner emerges.

Playing off of—and dramatically expanding upon—the perceived venality of the main characters of the drama *Desperate Housewives*, a reality version was launched with *The Real Housewives of Orange County* (Bravo, 2006–present). This guilty pleasure focuses on the often-invented dramas among a group of upper-class housewives. The massive popularity of the original led to eight American and eleven international spin-offs. The cosmetically enhanced, Botoxed stars of each series endlessly compete to project the very worst characteristics often associated with the rich and famous. Their enduring appeal going into the 2020s speaks more than perhaps any other American program to the phenomenon that is Trump's America. American teenagers also received their own dose of banality with the series *Jersey Shore* (MTV, 2009–2012). This series focused on the daily lives of a group of mostly Italian American friends living and partying together over summer break. The show was highly criticized not only for its celebration of a hedonistic lifestyle but also for its stereotyped portrayals of Italian Americans.

By far the most popular and iconic celebrity-based reality program in television history has been *Keeping Up with the Kardashians* (E!, 2007–present). This series centers on the celebrity-for-celebrity's sake members of the Kardashian/Jenner family. Primarily, the show's focus is on model Kim Kardashian-West

(b. 1980), wife of rapper Kanye West (b. 1977). The series also features her sisters, Kourtney (b. 1979) and Khloe (b. 1984); her half-sisters, Kendall Jenner (b. 1995) and Kylie Jenner (b. 1997); and her mother, Kris Jenner (b. 1955). Kris was first married to Kim's father, Robert Kardashian (1944–2003), before marrying Olympic champion Caitlyn Jenner (b. 1949). The series possesses all of the narcissism and rich-and-famous drama of *Real Housewives* but with a slightly more family-focused bend.

As the decade drew to a close, the History Channel entered the reality programming format with the semieducational series *Pawn Stars* (2009–present). The series centers on the day-to-day purchases of the family-owned World Famous Gold and Silver Pawn Shop in Las Vegas, Nevada. The show featured family patriarch and store co-owner Richard "Old Man" Harris (1941–2018); his partner and well-read son, Rick (b. 1965); Rick's son, Corey (b. 1983); and Corey's childhood friend Austin "Chumlee" Russell (b. 1982). The focus of the series is the vast array of interesting and frequently historic objects that patrons bring into the store, haggling with the stars on a sale price once the actual value can be determined—if it can. The series produced two spin-offs: *American Restoration* (History, 2010–2016) and *Counting Cars* (History, 2012–present).

ANIMATION

Prior to the 1990s, animated series had been primarily the purview of Saturday mornings for decades. In 1977, the cable station Nickelodeon became the first cable network directly aimed at children, at first mainly programming popular family-oriented reruns of sitcoms from the past. In 1983, the Walt Disney Corporation launched the Disney Channel to air their own, mostly previously released, programming. Finally, in 1992, Cartoon Network was launched, airing primarily reruns of popular Warner Brothers and Hanna-Barbera cartoons. By that time, the newly launched FOX network had begun the first prime-time animated series since *The Flintstones* decades prior.

One of the first series to air on FOX was *The Tracey Ullman Show* (1987–1990), a sketch comedy program starring the popular British comedian Tracey Ullman (b. 1959). A recurring feature on the series was animated shorts from animator Matt Groening (b. 1954) featuring a dysfunctional family called the Simpsons: father Homer, mother Marge, and their children, Bart, Lisa, and infant Maggie. The popularity of the shorts led FOX executives to green-light a new half-hour series, *The Simpsons* (1989–present). Though the series was initially centered on the rebellious Bart, voiced by Nancy Cartwright (b. 1957), with catchphrases such as "Cowabunga, dude!" and "Eat my shorts!" as well as his frequent prank calls to the local bar, the true breakout character soon became Bart's dim-witted father, Homer, voiced by Dan Castellaneta (b. 1957).

Throughout the 1990s, the show was a cultural phenomenon. Continued high ratings have kept it alive in the decades since, and it is, to date, the longest continuously running fictional series in television history. The show's popularity led to approval for another Groening creation, *Futurama* (FOX, 1999–2003; Comedy Central, 2008–2013), a series centered on the character of Philip

Fry, voiced by Billy West (b. 1952), a pizza delivery guy who inadvertently gets cryogenically frozen, awakening one thousand years in the future. Though not as popular as its predecessor, the series had a devoted cult following, leading the cable network Comedy Central to revive the series in 2008.

A hit series that rivaled *The Simpsons* in both popularity and cultural relevance was *Family Guy* (FOX, 1999–2002, 2005–present). Although it was initially cancelled near the end of its third season, reruns on Cartoon Network inspired FOX to bring the series back for a fourth season in 2005. Though many consider the series highly derivative of *The Simpsons*, *Family Guy* possessed far more controversial material and language than its more family-friendly predecessor. The series centers on the Griffin family: dim-witted father Peter; his wife, Lois; and their children, Chris, Meg, and infant Stewie. Other than content, the one big difference between the series is the character of Brian, the family's intelligent, speaking dog. Peter, Stewie, and Brian are all voiced by the show's creator, Seth McFarlane (b. 1973). Among members of millennials and iGen, the popularity of *Family Guy* has far surpassed *The Simpsons*. Its success led to two other McFarlane animated series: *American Dad* (FOX, 2005–2014; TBS, 2014–present) and the direct spin-off, *The Cleveland Show* (FOX, 2009–2013). Even as new episodes continue, reruns of *Family Guy* air almost daily on TBS and Cartoon Network.

As Generation X began having children of their own (the previously mentioned millennials and iGen), Cartoon Network became a daily part of life for the last generations of the twentieth century. Popular series on the cable network included *Johnny Bravo* (1995–2004), *Dexter's Laboratory* (1996–2006), and *The Powerpuff Girls* (1998–2005). Coming into the twenty-first century, new kids' programs included *Ed, Edd n Eddy* (1999–2009), *The Grim Adventures of Billy and Mandy* (2000–2008), and *Codename: Kids Next Door* (2002–2008). By 2000, however, one thing about Generation X was becoming abundantly clear: they were refusing to grow up. Gen Xers still enjoyed cartoons.

As such, in the early 2000s, Cartoon Network launched Adult Swim, late-night programming of animation aimed at an adult audience. Some of the biggest Adult Swim series in the decade were *Aqua Teen Hunger Force* (2000–2015), *Samurai Jack* (2001–2004; 2017), *The Boondocks* (2005–2014), and *Robot Chicken* (2005–present). *Robot Chicken* was created by *Family Guy* voice actor Seth Green and his friend Matthew Senreich (both born 1974). It is a stop-motion animated series utilizing dolls and action figures, mostly from iconic pop-culture franchises, to create adult-oriented satire. The series has done several specials focused on specific franchises such as DC Comics, *The Walking Dead*, and, most notably *Star Wars*.

Cartoon Network entered the mainstream franchise market with several projects, including the animated series *Justice League* (2001–2004) and *Justice League Unlimited* (Toonami, an offshoot of Cartoon Network, 2004–2006). These were the last two series for the DC Animated Universe from the minds of Bruce Timm (b. 1961), Paul Dini (b. 1957), and, later, Dwayne McDuffie (1962–2011). Their predecessors were *Batman: The Animated Series* (FOX, 1992–1995), *Superman: The Animated Series* (WB, 1996–2000), *The New Batman Adventures* (WB, 1997–1999), *Batman Beyond* (WB, 1999–2001), and *Static Shock* (WB,

2000–2004). *Justice League* and *Justice League Unlimited* centered on DC Comics' superteam, the Justice League. The first series focused primarily on the Big Three: Superman, Batman, and Wonder Woman. The second series broadened its focus on lower-tier characters: Green Lantern, Hawkgirl, and Supergirl (to name but a few).

Cartoon Network also became the primary home for the first two successful *Star Wars* primetime series, both focused on a single event, the Clone Wars, that took place narratively between the films *Star Wars, Episode II: Attack of the Clones* (Lucasfilm, 2002) and *Star Wars, Episode III: Revenge of the Sith* (Lucasfilm, 2005).

In 2003, Cartoon Network tasked *Samurai Jack* animator Genndy Tartakovsky (b. 1970) to create the traditional animated series *Star Wars: Clone Wars* (2003–2005). The first two seasons consisted of twenty episodes of three to five-minute each covering the adventures of Anakin Skywalker, Obi-Wan Kenobi, Yoda, and the other Jedi knights in their fight against the forces of Count Dooku. For the third season, there were only five episodes, with run times of twelve to fifteen minutes, culminating in the opening events of *Revenge of the Sith*.

In 2008, Lucasfilm approached Cartoon Network with a new series, a computer-graphics-animated series covering events taking place between seasons two and three of the original: *Star Wars: The Clone Wars* (Cartoon Network, 2008–2013; Netflix, 2014; Disney+, 2019–present). Continuing the adventures of the galaxy-spanning conflict, this new series focused more on Anakin Skywalker's previously unknown apprentice, Ahsoka Tano. The series was introduced in a 2008 theatrical release, which was, in essence, several episodes strewn together. Though it faced a rocky start with fans, it eventually became a beloved part of the ever-expanding *Star Wars* universe.

Not to be outdone, the other kid-friendly networks began airing their own original animated content. Nickelodeon had considerable success with several series: *Blue's Clues* (1996–2006; 2019–present), *CatDog* (1998–2005), *Dora the Explorer* (2000–2014), *The Fairly OddParents* (2001–2017), *The Adventures of Jimmy Neutron: Boy Genius* (2002–2006), and *All Grown Up* (2003–2008). *All Grown Up* was a spin-off of the wildly popular Nickelodeon series *Rugrats* (1991–2004), featuring the characters from the original series "all grown up." By far the most successful Nickelodeon program—and one of the most successful television series of all time—has been *SpongeBob SquarePants* (1999–present). This series centers on the misadventures of a kindhearted, well-meaning sponge who "lives in a pineapple under the sea" and his array of friends and coworkers. The Disney Channel also had some success with series such as *Kim Possible* (2002–2007) and *Phineas and Ferb* (2007–2015).

By far the most culturally important animated series of the period and perhaps all time did not air on any of the "kids" networks but, rather, on the more adult-oriented Comedy Central. *South Park* (1997–present) was created by Matt Stone (b. 1971) and Trey Parker (b. 1969). The series centers on four grade-school boys in the fictional town of South Park, Colorado: Stan, Kyle, Kenny, and Cartman. Unlike traditional animation, *South Park* was created by making various animated cells with construction paper. The early episodes focused primarily on the foul-mouthed youngsters having various outlandish adventures, Kenny dying horribly in every episode. Over time, however, Stone and Parker began utilizing the series for sociopolitical commentary. Many of the story lines feature the breakout star character Eric Cartman, a malevolent "big-boned" boy of insatiable id. Throughout most of its run, *South Park* has been a direct mirror of current events, with episodes created mere days before airing. Its longevity has allowed it to poke considerable fun at U.S. presidents Clinton, Bush, Obama, and Trump. Its social relevance outmatched only by the burgeoning crop of late-night programming in the 2000s.

Coming into the twenty-first century, *Saturday Night Live* (NBC, 1975–present), or *SNL*, was as popular and socially relevant as ever. It was one of the first programs to return to television in the weeks after the terrorist attacks of 9/11; its location in New York City was paramount to signaling the world that New York would not be frightened. Key components to the show's success in the 2000s was the massive popularity of two of its cast members: Will Ferrell (b. 1967) and Jimmy Fallon (b. 1974). On March 18, 2000, *SNL* played a huge role in launching the film career of professional wrestler the Rock, showcasing his considerable comedic timing and on-screen charisma.

The Late Night Wars on traditional network late night continued with the ratings war between *The Tonight Show with Jay Leno* (NBC, 1992–2009; 2010–2014) and *The Late Show with David Letterman* (CBS, 1993–2015). While Leno (b. 1950) had been the ratings champion through most of the 1990s, Letterman (b. 1947), however, being located in New York City, received a considerable ratings bump in the immediate aftermath of 9/11. Though it was a tight competition, Letterman continued to hold his own throughout the 2000s, leading NBC to pressure Leno into early retirement in 2009 and replace him with Letterman's longtime follow-up personality, Conan O'Brien (b. 1963). The gamble, however, proved disastrous, with many viewers protesting Leno's having been forced out. As a result, NBC brought Leno back, evening out the race between the two programs once more (in essence banishing O'Brien to basic cable).

One of the more controversial figures in late-night television for decades has been Bill Maher (b. 1956). Originally a stand-up comedian like Leno and Letterman before him, Maher found huge success with his late-night program *Politically Incorrect* (Comedy Central, 1993–1996; ABC, 1997–2002). As the title suggests, the program's focus was on pointing a critical finger at the growing political correctness of America at the time and holding a mirror of reality to both the far left and far right. On September 17, 2001, less than a week after 9/11, Maher received massive criticism for agreeing with guest Dinesh D'Souza (b. 1961) that the terrorists on 9/11 were not "cowards," as President Bush had dubbed them, but, rather, it was the United States who had been cowardly for firing missiles at terrorists for years from safe distances. At the time, Maher was considerably upset, as one of his schedule guests for his September 11 program had died in the attacks. Due to considerable outcry, *Politically Incorrect* was cancelled. Though it originally appeared that Maher's career was over, pay-cable outlet HBO decided to give him the unfettered outlet that his brand of comedy required. His new program, *Real Time with Bill Maher* (HBO,

2003–present), has proven a continuous ratings juggernaut for HBO. His clos-ing thoughts at the end of each episode have become some of the most import-ant political commentary on television in the twenty-first century.

In 1997, Comedy Central launched its own late-night program, *The Daily Show* (1997–present). Originally called *The Daily Show with Craig Kilborn* (1997–1998), the series began as a fake news program with celebrity interviews for the last segment, hosted by Craig Kilborn (b. 1962). When Kilborn unexpect-edly left the series to pursue a movie career, Comedy Central was hard-pressed to find a replacement for its most popular program. They ultimately chose talk-show veteran and stand-up comedian Jon Stewart (b. 1962). *The Daily Show with Jon Stewart* (1999–2015) quickly became a very different show. Rather than presenting fake news stories, Stewart and his crew addressed the actual news of the day, squeezing it for comedic fodder (which was never very difficult to do). Additionally, Stewart slowly transitioned the interview segment from celebrities to important political and academic figures. Under Stewart's guid-ance, *The Daily Show* soon became the most trusted source of information on the day's events for the valued eighteen-to-forty-nine-year-old demographic. The series' coverage of the 2004 presidential elections, dubbed In-Decision 2004, launched the show into the stratosphere of must-see political commen-tary as well as the career of *Daily Show* correspondent Stephen Colbert (b. 1964).

In 2005, Colbert launched his own program, immediately following Stewart Mondays through Thursdays, *The Colbert Report* (Comedy Central, 2005–2014). This series was designed as a parody of the FOX News program *The O'Reilly Factor*, with Colbert portraying a fictionalized version of himself carried over from *The Daily Show* as a dim-witted conservative pundit. Like *The Daily Show*, *Colbert* was a massive success, and Stewart and Colbert soon became two of the most important political commentators on television. In 2014, CBS swayed Colbert away from his Comedy Central hit to become Letterman's late-night replacement.

The Late Show with Stephen Colbert (2015–present) became an equally huge ratings juggernaut once the host began to incorporate his brilliant political commentary into the traditional late-night talk-show format. Stewart retired from *The Daily Show* in 2014, mentally and emotionally exhausted and frus-trated with the deteriorating public discourse in America. He was replaced by South African stand-up comedian Trevor Noah (b. 1984). *The Daily Show with Trevor Noah* (2015–present) continues to be a valuable voice of political com-mentary to the present day. Stewart's legacy lives on with Colbert and Noah, as well as other programs launched by *Daily Show* alumni: *Last Week Tonight with John Oliver* (HBO, 2014–present), *Full Frontal with Samantha Bee* (2016–present), *Patriot Act with Hasan Minhaj* (Netflix, 2018–present), *The Break with Michelle Wolf* (Netflix, 2018), *The Nightly Show with Larry Wilmore* (Comedy Central, 2015–2016), *The Opposition with Jordan Klepper* (Comedy Central, 2017–2018), and *Klepper* (Comedy Central, 2019–present).

Television in the 2000s launched what many critics and fans have dubbed a second golden age of television. Going into the 2010s, American network, cable, and streaming television provided more content than ever before in history. Many of the programs discussed above lived throughout the 2010s, with several moving on into the 2020s. As they have always done, the most popular programs of American television have not only reflected American society but also influenced it. The impact that television has had on race and gender relations, LGBTQ+ rights, and American politics cannot be overstated. Even as more and more Americans move from traditional television to online streaming and viewing on phones and tablets, television programming continues to be the most popular form of entertainment in the United States, with no sign of ending any time soon.

FURTHER READING

Assael, Shaun, and Mike Mooneyham. 2004. *Sex, Lies, and Headlocks: The Real Story of Vince McMahon and World Wrestling Entertainment*. Portland, OR: Broadway.

Barker, Cory, Chris Ryan, and Myc Wiatrowski, eds. 2014. *Mapping* Smallville: *Critical Essays on the Series and Its Characters*. Jefferson, NC: McFarland.

Bennett, Jessica. 2019. "This Gen X Mess: The Tech, Music, Style, Books, Trends, Rules, Films and Pills That Made Gen X . . . So So-So." *New York Times*, May 16. https://www.nytimes.com/interactive/2019/05/14/style/generation-xers.html?utm_source=pocket-newtab. Retrieved May 16, 2019.

Bodroghkozy, Aniko. 2018. *A Companion to the History of American Broadcasting*. New York: Wiley-Blackwell.

Brands, H. W. 2011. *American Dreams: The United States since 1945*. New York: Penguin.

Bush, George W. 2001. "Address to the Nation." American Rhetoric, September 11. https://www.americanrhetoric.com/speeches/gwbush911addresstothenation.htm. Retrieved March 31, 2019.

Bush, George W. 2010. *Decision Points*. New York: Crown.

Carter, Bill. 2011. *The War for Late Night: When Leno Went Early and Television Went Crazy*. New York: Plume.

Castleman, Harry, and Walter J. Podrazik. 2016. *Watching TV: Eight Decades of American Television*. 3rd ed. New York: Syracuse University Press.

Chomsky, Noam. 2005. *Imperial Ambitions: Conversations on the Post-9/11 World*. New York: Metropolitan.

Clinton, Hillary Rodham. 2003. *Living History*. New York: Simon & Schuster.

Coontz, Stephanie. 2016. *The Way We Never Were: American Families and the Nostalgia Trap*. New York: Basic.

Crowson, H. Michael, Teresa K. Debacker, and Stephen J. Thoma. 2006. "The Role of Authoritarianism, Perceived Threat, and Need for Closure or Structure in Predicting Post-9/11 Attitudes and Beliefs." *Journal of Social Psychology* 146, no. 6: 733–750.

Cullen, Jim. 2002. *The Art of Democracy: A Concise History of Popular Culture in the United States*. New ed. New York: Monthly Review.

Danesi, Marcel. 2012. *Popular Culture: Introductory Perspectives*. 2nd ed. Lanham, MD: Rowman & Littlefield.

Dittmer, Jason. 2005. "Captain America's Empire: Reflections on Identity, Popular Culture, and Post-9/11 Geopolitics." *Annals of the Association of American Geographers* 95, no. 3: 626–643.

Eurodata TV Worldwide. 2009. "'House' Is World's Most Popular TV Show." *Agence France Presse*, June 12. https://web.archive.org/web/20120401043907/https://

www.google.com/hostednews/afp/article/ALeqM5gGRhjVWTeAVMws
-iEDRJOY3IDH7g. Archived April 1, 2012. Retrieved May 27, 2019.

Evans, Jennifer C. 2002. "Hijacking Civil Liberties: The USA PATRIOT Act of 2001." *Loyola University Chicago Law Journal* 33, no. 4: 933–990.

Fahy, Thomas, ed. 2005. *Considering Aaron Sorkin: Essays on the Politics, Poetics and Sleight of Hand in the Films and Television Series.* Jefferson, NC: McFarland.

Faludi, Susan. 2008. *The Terror Dream: Myth and Misogyny in an Insecure America.* London: Picador.

Farris, Scott. 2012. *Almost President: The Men Who Lost the Race but Changed the Nation.* Guilford, CT: Lyons.

Fink, Moritz. 2019. The Simpsons: *A Cultural History.* Lanham, MD: Rowman & Littlefield.

Goertz, Allie. 2018. *100 Things* The Simpsons *Fans Should Know & Do before They Die.* Chicago: Triumph.

Gournelos, Ted, and Viveca Greene, eds. 2011. *A Decade of Dark Humor: How Comedy, Irony, and Satire Shaped Post-9/11 America.* Jackson: University Press of Mississippi.

Gross, Edward, and Mark A. Altman. 2018. *So Say We All: The Complete, Uncensored, Unauthorized Oral History of* Battlestar Galactica. New York: Tor.

Handley, Rich, and Lou Tambone, eds. 2018. *Somewhere beyond the Heavens: Exploring* Battlestar Galactica. Edwardsville, IL: Sequart Research and Literacy Organization.

Handscombe, Claire. 2016. *Walk with Us: How* The West Wing *Changed Our Lives.* New York: CH Books.

Hart, Kylo-Patrick R., ed. 2016. *Queer TV in the 21st Century: Essays on Broadcasting from Taboo to Acceptance.* Jefferson, NC: McFarland.

Heilemann, John, and Mark Halperin. 2010. *Game Change: Obama and the Clintons, McCain and Palin, and the Race of a Lifetime.* New York: Harper Perennial.

Iannucci, Lisa. 2008. *Ellen DeGeneres: A Biography.* Santa Barbara, CA: Greenwood.

Jennings, John. 2017. *The Wit and Wisdom of Ellen DeGeneres.* Independently published.

Johnson, Dwayne "the Rock," and Joe Layden. 2000. *The Rock Says . . . : The Most Electrifying Man in Sports Entertainment.* New York: Harper Entertainment.

Jones, Brian Jay. 2016. *George Lucas: A Life.* New York: Little, Brown and Company.

Kistler, Alan. 2013. Doctor Who: *Celebrating Fifty Years, a History.* Guilford, CT: Lyons.

Kranz, Gene. 2009. *Failure Is Not an Option: Mission Control from Mercury to Apollo 13 and Beyond.* New York: Simon & Schuster.

Kruse, Kevin M., and Julian E. Zelizer. 2019. *Fault Lines: A History of the United States since 1974.* New York: W. W. Norton.

National Commission on Terrorist Attacks Upon the United States. 2004. *The 9/11 Report.* New York: St. Martin's.

9/11 Memorial. [Posting Date Unknown]. "September 11 Attack Timeline." https://timeline.911memorial.org/#Timeline/2. Retrieved May 8, 2019.

Obama, Barack. 2006. *The Audacity of Hope: Thoughts on Reclaiming the American Dream.* New York: Crown.

Obama, Barack. 2009. "First Inaugural Address." Obama White House, January 20. https://obamawhitehouse.archives.gov/blog/2009/01/21/president-barack-obamas-inaugural-address. Retrieved March 31, 2019.

Oswald, Debra L. 2005. "Understanding Anti-Arab Reactions Post-9/11: The Role of Threats, Social Categories, and Personal Ideologies." *Journal of Applied Social Psychology* 35, no. 9: 1775–1799.

Patterson, James T. 2005. *Restless Giant: The United States from Watergate to* Bush v. Gore. Oxford: Oxford University Press.

Rollins, Peter, and John E. O'Connor. 2003. The West Wing: *The American Presidency as Television Drama*. Syracuse, NY: Syracuse University Press.

Sorkin, Andrew Ross. 2009. *Too Big to Fail: The Inside Story of How Wall Street and Washington Fought to Save the Financial System—And Themselves*. New York: Penguin.

Stewart, Jon, et al. 2004. *America (The Book)*. New York: Warner/Grand Central.

Stratyner, Leslie, and James R. Keller, eds. 2009. *The Deep End of* South Park: *Critical Essays on Television's Shocking Cartoon Series*. Jefferson, NC: McFarland.

Stuller, Jennifer K. 2010. *Ink-Stained Amazons and Cinematic Warriors: Superwomen in Modern Mythology*. London: I. B. Tauris.

Taylor, Chris. 2015. *How* Star Wars *Conquered the Universe: The Past, Present, and Future of a Multibillion Dollar Franchise*. New York: Basic.

Toobin, Jeffrey. 2002. *Too Close to Call: The Thirty-Six-Day Battle to Decide the 2000 Election*. New York: Random House.

TV Guide Editors. 2002. TV Guide: *Fifty Years of Television*. New York: Crown.

"TV Guide Picks TV's 60 Nastiest Villains." 2013. Wordsmithonia, April 22. http://wordsmithonia.blogspot.com/2013/04/tv-guide-picks-tvs-60-nastiest-villains.html. Retrieved August 24, 2018.

Tye, Larry. 2013. *Superman: The High-Flying History of America's Most Enduring Hero*. New York: Random House.

Waldfogel, Joel. 2018. *Digital Renaissance: What Data and Economics Tell Us about the Future of Popular Culture*. Princeton, NJ: Princeton University Press.

Weinstock, Jeffrey Andrew, ed. 2008. *Taking* South Park *Seriously*. Albany: State University of New York Press.

Willis, Susan. 2005. *Portents of the Real: A Primer for Post-9/11 America*. London: Verso.

CHAPTER 2

Sports

In the twenty-first century, American sports across the spectrum would be forced to address the issue of performance-enhancing drugs. Major League Baseball (MLB) would be hardest hit, but it would also eventually destroy the career of professional bicyclist Lance Armstrong. Meanwhile, a professional sport that had long since addressed its own history with steroids—professional wrestling—would enjoy heights of success never seen before (or, arguably, since). Dwayne "the Rock" Johnson would become a household name and an international superstar even outside the professional wrestling ring. Basketball legends Michael Jordan and Dennis Rodman would fade into retirement, while Kobe Bryant would face a scandal far removed from steroid abuse but nonetheless as devastating and then passed away in January, 2020. The world would get its final glimpses of boxing legend Muhammad Ali. The sports world would come to a standstill in the wake of 9/11, but it would emerge more popular and cemented in American popular culture than ever before.

9/11

In the wake of the terror attacks of September 11, 2001, professional sports around the country suspended all games and competitions. Although the country was reeling emotionally and needed the escapism promised by professional sports, Americans en masse were glued to the twenty-four-hour news channels for updates and, subconsciously, breaking news of additional attacks. Professional wrestling was the sole holdout. The World Wrestling Federation/WWF (now known as the World Wrestling Entertainment/WWE) chair, Vincent McMahon, continued performances, believing that to not do so would be to allow the terrorists to win. Six weeks after the attacks, President George W. Bush threw out the first pitch of Major League Baseball's World

Series, pitting the New York Yankees against the Arizona Diamondbacks (the Diamondbacks would go on to win the series, 4–3). By that time, late October 2001, pro sports were back on track, providing their millions of fans the much-needed break from the frightening events of the month before.

LANCE ARMSTRONG

One of the most popular athletes of the early twenty-first century was professional bicycling racer Lance Armstrong (b. 1971). In 1998, after successfully battling testicular cancer at the age of twenty-five, Armstrong returned to pro cycling, winning the Tour de France in 1999. Up to that point, Armstrong had never competed against one of the world's greatest cyclists, German Jan Ullrich (b. 1973). Armstrong went on to win or place in numerous races before announcing his retirement in 2005. He competed in the Tour de France in 2009 and 2010, once more announcing his retirement in 2011 under allegations of steroid abuse, to which he confessed in 2013. For more than fifteen years, however, Armstrong was one of the most famous athletes in the world, and his eventual downfall due to steroids came at a time when all pro sports had begun to crack down on the use of performance-enhancing drugs.

BASKETBALL

After leading Michael Jordan (b. 1963) and the Chicago Bulls to six National Basketball Association (NBA) championships in the 1990s (referred to as the two "three-peats"), head coach Phil Jackson (b. 1945) moved to the Los Angeles Lakers, leading them to dominate the first decade of the new millennium. The Lakers had their own three-peat, becoming NBA champions in 2000, 2001, and 2002. They would finish the decade with two more championship wins in 2009 and 2010. They made it to the playoffs two other years during the decade: 2004 (losing to the Detroit Pistons) and 2008 (losing to the Boston Celtics). The San Antonio Spurs, under head coach Gregg Popovich (b. 1949), were NBA champions in 2005 and 2007. The only other NBA champion of the decade were the Dallas Mavericks in 2006, led by head coach Avery Johnson (b. 1965).

The 2000s saw some of the greatest players in the history of the NBA. In the immediate aftermath of 9/11, basketball legend Michael Jordan (shooting guard) announced his return from his second retirement, joining the Washington Wizards (a team that he co-owned as of 2000). Now thirty-eight-years-old, Jordan suffered an injury soon after his return and retired from pro basketball for good in 2003. One of the greatest names in modern basketball is five-time NBA champion Kobe Bryant (shooting guard; 1978–2020). As part of the Los Angeles Lakers with Jackson, Kobe played a major role in the team's three-peat victories from 2000 to 2002. In 2003, Bryant broke an NBA record for most three-pointers in a game, making twelve such shots against the Seattle Supersonics. Later that year, Bryant was arrested for sexual assault. A woman in Eagle, Colorado, accused the basketball legend of rape. While admitting to an extramarital affair with his accuser, Bryant insisted that their relationship was consensual. The charges were eventually dropped when the accuser refused to testify, but she did win an out-of-court settlement in a civil case, leading Bryant to publicly apologize (while maintaining his innocence) and pay an undisclosed sum.

Dennis Rodman (b. 1961) was another Bulls three-peat alum. In the wake of the second three-peat, Rodman played in the NBA for only two more seasons: one for the LA Lakers and the last for his hometown Dallas Mavericks. After retiring from the NBA in 2000, Rodman played one season with the upstart American Basketball Association (ABA), playing for the Long Beach Jam from 2003 to 2004. He then played for one season for Mexico's Fuerza Regia in 2004. Having dabbled some in professional wrestling in the late 1990s, Rodman came out of retirement one more time in 2008 to compete in the TV show *Hulk Hogan's Celebrity Championship Wrestling*. In 2013, Rodman went to North Korea as a goodwill ambassador to host a basketball exhibition. While there, he met with North Korean leader Kim Jong-un (b. 1983), becoming fast friends with the notorious dictator. Rodman will always, however, hold a place in the American zeitgeist for his amazing performances on the basketball court and the part he played in the Bulls' two three-peat championships in the 1990s.

Another Lakers champion from the period was basketball legend Shaquille O'Neal (center; b. 1972). O'Neal moved to the Lakers from the Orlando Magic in 1996, sticking with the Lakers through their three-peat victories before moving on to the Miami Heat in 2004, the Phoenix Suns in 2008, the Cleveland Cavaliers in 2009, and finally the Boston Celtics for his final season in 2010–2011. He was an NBA all-star from 2000 to 2007 and then again in 2009, and he was named all-star most valuable player (MVP) in 2000, 2004, and 2009. Yet another basketball icon, LeBron James (small forward, power forward; b. 1984), made his NBA debut in 2003, the first-draft pick for the Cleveland Cavaliers (James's hometown team). He played for the Cavaliers throughout the 2000s, leaving the team for the Miami Heat in 2010. He was named an NBA all-star every year from 2005 to 2019 and all-star MVP in 2006, 2008, and 2018. Also in 2008, James was part of the U.S. Olympic basketball team at the Summer Games in Beijing, China.

The 2000s also saw some impressive athletes in the Women's National Basketball Association (WNBA), which was organized in 1996 and had its first season in 1997. Lisa Leslie (center; b. 1972) was an early draft pick for the Los Angeles Sparks, leading the team to the playoffs for each of the WNBAs first five seasons, finally winning the championship in 2001. She was awarded WNBA MVP in 2001, 2004, and 2006. She retired in 2009. Leslie also played for the Women's U.S. Olympic basketball team in 2000, 2004, and 2008. Diana Taurasi (point guard; b. 1982) was the first-draft pick in 2004 for the Phoenix Mercury. At the end of her first season, she was named WNBA rookie of the year. In 2009, she was named WNBA MVP. Taurasi also played for the Women's U.S. Olympic basketball team in 2004, 2008, 2012, and 2016. She currently holds the record for WNBA all-time scoring leader.

Sheryl Swoopes (shooting guard, small forward; b. 1971) was also one of the original WNBA players, beginning her pro career with the Houston Comets. She was named WNBA defensive player of the year for 2000, 2002, and 2003. She played with the Women's U.S. Olympic basketball team in 2000 and 2004.

One of the later additions to the WNBA in the 2000s was Candace Parker (power forward, center; b. 1986). A first-draft pick for the Los Angeles Sparks in 2008, she broke the record for points in a single game by a rookie (thirty-four), which still stood in 2019. She also served on the Women's U.S. Olympic basketball team in 2008 and 2012. In its brief twenty-plus years of activity, the WNBA has introduced some of the greatest female athletes—and athletes overall—of modern times.

BASEBALL

In the few years leading up to the new millennium, numerous MLB players—most notably Mark McGwire (first base; b. 1963) and Sammy Sosa (right field; b. 1968)—gained national attention for their phenomenal batting as they repeatedly broke long-standing records. By 2000, it became clear that there was an epidemic of performance-enhancing drug abuse by some of the league's biggest stars. The scandal hit its peak from 2003 to 2007, scarring the popularity of America's pastime so badly that it is only now beginning to recover. Due to these scandals, future record-breaking performances in professional baseball would remain under scrutiny well into the 2010s. However, several MLB players from the period proved themselves to be considerable athletes even without performance enhancements.

The baseball steroid scandal centered on a San Francisco, California, company known as Bay Area Laboratory Co-operative (BALCO). This company was part of a 2002 government investigation into anabolic steroid use by professional athletes. In 2005, a congressional committee subpoenaed several MLB players who had have tested positive for performance-enhancing drugs. The tests were called for because of the unusually outstanding physical performances of each on the field in the years prior. The players summoned included McGwire, Sosa, José Canseco (outfield/designated hitter; b. 1964), Rafael Palmeiro (first base; b. 1964), Alex Rodriguez (shortstop/third base; b. 1975), and Curt Schilling (pitcher; b. 1966). In defense of his actions, Canseco published the book *Juiced: Wilde Times, Rampant 'Roids, Smash Hits, and How Baseball Got Big* (2005). During the hearings, Canseco admitted to all charges. Palmeiro and Sosa denied them altogether. McGwire chose not to answer to any charges although Canseco had specifically named both Palmeiro and McGwire as fellow users in *Juiced*. Because of his refusal, McGwire was denied admittance to the Baseball Hall of Fame that year. He later admitted in 2010 that he had, in fact, used performance-enhancing drugs for most of his career.

Sammy Sosa had an incredible career with the Chicago Cubs, where he played from 1992 to 2004, in the first half of the 2000s. In 2001, Sosa hit sixty-four home runs, becoming the first MLB player to hit at least sixty runs per season for three seasons, although he did not hit the most runs in any of those seasons. That same year, Sosa recorded personal bests in numerous categories, including runs scored (146) and runs batted in (RBIs, 160), and had a batting average of 0.328. After he spent much of the 2004 season on the disabled list, the Cubs traded Sosa to the Baltimore Orioles, where Sosa played from 2005 to 2006. The Dominican American legend ended his career with the Detroit

Tigers from 2007 to 2009. During his final season, the *New York Times* released a story based on leaked sealed documents, exposing that, despite his strong denials, Sosa had indeed tested positive for performance-enhancing drugs during the 2003 scandal.

Another notable player from the decade was Derek Jeter (shortstop; b. 1974). Playing for the New York Yankees his entire Major League career, he joined the team in national championships five times and was named series MVP in 2000. Jeter gained numerous accolades during the 2000s. He played in the annual all-star game fourteen times in his nineteen-year career. He won the Golden Glove Award five times (2004, 2005, 2006, 2009, and 2010) and the Silver Slugger Award five times (2006, 2007, 2008, 2009, and 2012). Alex Rodriguez ("A-Rod"), despite his own connections with the steroid scandal, also had a considerable decade in the 2000s. He was named the American League home run leader five times: three times with the Texas Rangers (2001, 2002, and 2003) and twice with the Yankees (2005 and 2007). He was twice named the MLB RBI leader: in 2002 with Texas and in 2007 with New York. In 2019, A-Rod announced his engagement to pop-music superstar and actress Jennifer Lopez (b. 1969).

Throughout the decade, several teams became World Series champions, with the New York Yankees and Boston Red Sox making the most appearances in the playoff series. In 2000, the American League (AL) Yankees bested the National League (NL) New York Mets, 4–1. In 2001, the Yankees returned to the series, but they were beaten by the Arizona Diamondbacks (NL), 4–3. In 2002, the Anaheim Angels (AL) defeated the San Francisco Giants (NL), 4–3. In 2003, the Yankees returned again, only to be beaten 4–2 by the Florida Marlins (NL). The 2004 World Series proved historic when the Boston Red Sox (AL) won their first championship since 1918, in a 4–0 win over the St. Louis Cardinals (NL). This victory broke the longtime Curse of the Bambino, caused when the Red Sox (after winning five championships, including the first World Series) sold the Bambino, baseball legend Babe Ruth (1895–1948), to the Yankees.

In 2005, the Chicago White Sox (AL) were victorious over the Houston Astros (NL), 4–0. In 2006, the Cardinals returned to defeat the Detroit Tigers (AL), 4–1. In 2007, the Red Sox chalked up another championship against the Colorado Rockies (NL), 4–0. In 2008, the Philadelphia Phillies (NL) won over the Tampa Bay Rays (AL), 4–1, and in 2009, the Yankees bookended the decade with yet another world championship victory over the Phillies, 4–2. After a decade of scandal, fan support for the MLB had dropped dramatically, and although millions of fans remained dedicated to their respective teams, the days of professional baseball being America's pastime seemed over for good.

FOOTBALL

Unlike the MLB or NBA, no one National Football League (NFL) team dominated the decade, although the New England Patriots had the most impressive record of the decade. In Super Bowl XXXIV (2000), the National Football Conference (NFC) St. Louis Rams defeated the American Football Conference

(AFC) Tennessee Titans, 23–16. In Super Bowl XXXV (2001), the Baltimore Ravens (AFC) defeated the New York Giants (NFC), 34–7. In Super Bowl XXXVI (2002), the Rams returned, only to lose to the New England Patriots (NFC) 20–17. Super Bowl XXXVII (2003) saw the Tampa Bay Buccaneers (NFC) top the Oakland Raiders (AFC) 48–21.

New England returned to win Super Bowls XXXVIII (2004) and XXXIX (2005), defeating the Carolina Panthers (NFC) 32–29, and the Philadelphia Eagles (NFC) 24–21, respectively. Super Bowl XL (2006) saw the Pittsburgh Steelers (AFC) defeat the Seattle Seahawks (NFC) 21–10. In Super Bowl XLI (2007), the Indianapolis Colts (AFC) beat the Chicago Bears (NFC) 29–17. The Patriots returned for Super Bowl XLII (2008), only to lose to the Giants 17–14. In Super Bowl XLIII (2009), the Steelers became champions again, besting the Arizona Cardinals (NFC) 27–23. Rounding out the decade, the winner of the 2009 NFL season was decided in Super Bowl XLIV (2010), seeing the New Orleans Saints (NFC) soundly besting the Colts 31–17.

The NFL was not immune from the BALCO scandal. One of their athletes, Bill Romanowski (linebacker; b. 1966) was named during the congressional investigations. Romanowski was found to have been using both anabolic steroids and synthetic testosterone provided by BALCO, a charge to which he admitted guilt in 2005, two years after leaving the NFL. His steroid use was used as an excuse for a 2003 altercation with his teammate Marcus Williams (tight end; b. 1977) where Romanowski crushed Williams's eye socket with one punch due to a disagreement during practice. The injury ended Williams's football career. After retiring from the NFL, Romanowski became a B-movie actor. Although the BALCO scandal did not affect the NFL to the degree that it did the MLB, the already-daunting size and strength of pro football players make Romanowski an example of the dangers that enhancing such physically powerful players pose on those with whom they work.

Two of the biggest names in the NFL in the 2000s (and 2010s) were the brothers Peyton (quarterback; b. 1976) and Eli (quarterback; b. 1981) Manning. Peyton Manning played for the Indianapolis Colts (AFC) from 1998 to 2011 and the Denver Broncos (AFC) from 2012 to 2015. He led the Colts to victory in Super Bowl XLI (2007) over the Chicago Bears (NFC) and the Broncos to victory in Super Bowl 50 (2016) over the Carolina Panthers (NFC). In the 2000s, Peyton played in every Pro Bowl except in 2001. He was named NFL MVP five times (2003, 2004, 2008, 2009, and 2013) and MVP for Super Bowl XLI. His brother, Eli, also had an impressive decade, playing for the New York Giants (NFC) since 2004. Eli Manning led the Giants to two national championships in Super Bowls XLII (2008) and XLVI (2012), and he was named MVP for both Super Bowl appearances. Eli was also chosen for four Pro Bowls (2008, 2011, 2012, and 2015). The brothers have emerged as two of the most beloved NFL players in history.

A more controversial NFL player is Tom Brady (quarterback; b. 1977), who has led the New England Patriots (AFC) to six Super Bowl victories: XXXVI (2002), XXXVIII (2004), XXXIX (2005), XLIX (2015), LI (2017), and LIII (2019). Brady won Super Bowl MVP for four of those games (2002, 2004, 2015, and 2017). He has played in fourteen Pro Bowls (2001, 2004, 2005, 2007, and every game from 2009 to 2018). He has gained considerable notoriety in recent years due to his part in what has become known as Deflategate. During the NFC playoffs in 2014–2015, Brady was accused of ordering that the balls he used in the game be deflated, which provided a better grip for a more accurate throw, especially during colder weather. Despite his numerous pleas of innocence, a federal appeals court upheld the NFL's punishment (and acknowledgement of guilt) of a four-game suspension, considered by many to be too light a punishment.

In 1999, Vince McMahon (b. 1945) of the World Wrestling Federation/WWF teamed with broadcaster the National Broadcasting Company (NBC) to create a new professional football league: the XFL. Feeling that the NFL had become too safety conscious and denied fans the violence they once loved in the game, McMahon promised audiences a return to "smash mouth" football. The new league consisted of eight teams in two divisions. The Western Division consisted of the Las Vegas Outlaws, the Los Angeles Xtreme, the Memphis Maniax, and the San Francisco Demons. The Eastern Division consisted of the Birmingham Thunderbolts, the Chicago Enforcers, the New York/New Jersey Hitmen, and the Orlando Rage. The names of the teams underscore the increased violence promised by promoters. The XFL had only one season, in 2001. Both television and stadium audiences fell far below expectations, and the WWF and NBC cancelled the league, each recouping less than one-third of their initial investments. However, in 2018, McMahon-owned Alpha Entertainment announced a return of the XFL in 2020. Without NBC involvement, the new XFL will broadcast games on ESPN and the Fox Corporation (the independent company once part of 20th Century Fox).

TENNIS

The twenty-first century began with the waning years of tennis pro Anna Kournikova (b. 1981). After winning several Opens and finally breaking the top ten in pro tennis in 2000, Kournikova experienced a left foot fracture in 2001 that would mark the beginning of the end of her roughly ten-year career. After undergoing surgery in the spring of 2001, she achieved her second career grand slam at the Australian Open, but she had to cancel her next several appearances due to continuing issues from her foot injury. In 2002, she won the Australian Open and made the semifinals at Wimbledon and the quarterfinals at the U.S. Open. She retired from the Women's Tennis Association in 2003, with a career singles record of 209 wins out of 1,291 matches and a career mixed doubles record of 24 wins out of 141 matches. The Russian-born superstar became an American citizen in 2010.

Perhaps the biggest names in professional tennis in the 2000s were the Williams sisters: Venus (b. 1980) and Serena (b. 1981). The two spent the decade dominating the sport in both singles and doubles matches. In Grand Slam women singles matches, Venus won championships at Wimbledon in 2000, 2001, 2005, 2007, and 2008, and at the U.S. Open in 2000 and 2001. Serena won the same titles at the Australian Open (2003, 2005, 2007, 2009, 2010, 2015, and 2017), the French Open (2002, 2013, and 2015), Wimbledon (2002, 2003, 2009, 2010, 2012, 2015, and 2016), and the U.S. Open (1999, 2002, 2008, 2012, 2013, and 2014).

As a team, the sisters dominated Grand Slam women's doubles matches: the Australian Open (2001, 2003, 2009, and 2010), the French Open (1999 and 2010), Wimbledon (2000, 2002, 2008, 2009, 2012, and 2016), and the U.S. Open (1999 and 2009). The two were also Olympic gold medalists throughout the decade. Venus won gold for women's singles in the Sydney Olympic Games in 2000, and Serena won in the same category at the London Games in 2012. As a pair, they won gold in women's doubles in Sydney (2000), Beijing (2008), and London (2012). Both individually and as a team, the Williams sisters emerged from the early 2000s as two of the greatest tennis players—male or female—of all time.

To date, Swiss tennis pro Roger Federer (b. 1981) has a career singles record of 1,237 wins out of 2,701 matches and a doubles record of 131 wins out of 921 matches. In singles competition, he has won the Australian Open (2004, 2006, 2007, 2010, 2017, and 2018), the French Open (2009), Wimbledon (2003, 2004, 2005, 2006, 2007, 2009, 2012, and 2017), and the U.S. Open (2004, 2005, 2006, 2007, and 2008). He won gold for doubles at the Beijing Olympic Games in 2008 and silver for singles at the London Games in 2012. Belgian pro Justine Henin (b. 1982) had a career singles record of 525 wins out of 1,151 matches and a doubles record of 47 wins out of 351 matches. In singles competition, she has won the Australian Open (2004), the French Open (2003, 2005, 2006, and 2007), and the U.S. Open (2003 and 2007). She won gold for singles at the Athens Olympic Games in 2004. The first decade of the millennium was an exciting time for tennis fans around the world.

GOLF

The first decade of the twenty-first century saw the retirement of golfing legend Arnold Palmer (1929–2016). Named *Sports Illustrated* Sportsman of the Year in 1960, Palmer hit the peak of his career in the 1960s but stayed active in the game for decades. In 1974, he was one of the first dozen inductees into the World Golf Hall of Fame. After a career total of sixty-two Professional Golf Association (PGA) Tour wins (the fifth-highest number of all time to date), Palmer officially retired in 2006. In 2004, President George W. Bush awarded him the Presidential Medal of Freedom, one of the highest awards given to civilians, created by President John F. Kennedy in 1963 as an update of the original Medal of Freedom, which was awarded for "an especially meritorious contribution to the security or national interests of the United States, world peace, cultural or other significant public or private endeavors" (President Harry S. Truman, Executive Order 9586, July 6, 1945). In 2009, he was given the Congressional Medal of Freedom.

Few names in PGA sports history stand out more than Tiger Woods (born Eldrick Tont Woods in 1975). He is tied for first place in overall PGA Tour wins alongside Sam Snead (1912–2002). Throughout his career, he has achieved eighty-two PGA Tour wins, forty-one European Tour wins, three Japanese Golf Tour wins, one Asian Tour win, one PGA Australia win, and sixteen other professional and twenty-one amateur wins. He has won the following tournaments: the Masters Tournament (1997, 2001, 2002, 2005, and 2019), the

PGA Championship (1999, 2000, 2006, and 2007), the U.S. Open (2000, 2002, and 2008), and the Open Championship (2000, 2005, and 2006). Already a golf phenomenon at age five, he is, perhaps, the most famous pro golfer of all time. Woods was named PGA Player of the Year in 1997, 1999, 2000, 2001, 2002, 2003, 2005, 2006, 2007, 2009, and 2013. To date, he holds seventeen records in the *Guinness Book of World Records* related to his indomitable golf career. In 2019, Tiger Woods was awarded the Presidential Medal of Freedom by President Donald J. Trump.

In the area of women's professional golf, one of the big names of the 2000s was Swedish-born Annika Sörenstam (b. 1970). A member of the Ladies Professional Golf Association (LPGA), Sörenstam had seventy-two LPGA wins in her career (the third best of all time). In her sixteen-year career (1992–2008), she won the ANA Inspiration (2001, 2002, and 2005), the Women's PGA Championship (2003, 2004, and 2005), the U.S. Women's Open (1995, 1996, and 2006), and the Women's British Open in 2003. She was admitted into the World Golf Hall of Fame in 2003. Another big name in women's golf in the 2000s was Mexican-born Lorena Ochoa (b. 1981). Although she had a very brief professional career (2002–2010), Ochoa had twenty-seven LPGA wins, winning, in particular, the ANA Inspiration in 2008 and the Women's British Open in 2007. She was admitted into the World Golf Hall of Fame in 2017.

OLYMPIC GAMES

The 2000s saw the rise of some historic Olympic performances by Americans. At the 2000 Summer Olympics in Sydney, Australia, the United States won thirty-seven gold medals, twenty-four silver, and thirty-two bronze, coming in first in the overall medal count. At the 2002 Winter Olympics in Salt Lake City, Utah, the United States won ten gold, thirteen silver, and eleven bronze, coming in third behind Norway and Germany, respectively, in the medal count. At the 2004 Summer Olympics in Athens, Greece (the birthplace of the Olympic Games), the United States won thirty-six gold, thirty-nine silver, and twenty-six bronze, once more finishing first in the medal count. At the 2006 Winter Olympics in Turin, Italy, the United States won nine gold, nine silver, and seven bronze medals, finishing an impressive second behind Germany in the overall medal count. Finally, at the 2008 Summer Olympics in Beijing, China, the United States won thirty-six gold, thirty-nine silver, and thirty-seven bronze medals, finishing second to China.

The Olympic Games were not spared the BALCO steroid scandal. Marion Jones (b. 1975) was a former WNBA player for the Tulsa Shock before becoming a track-and-field Olympic gold medalist in the 2000 Summer Olympics in Sydney. After winning three gold medals (100 meter sprint, 200 meter sprint, and 4 x 400 meter relay) and two bronze (4 x 100 meter relay and long jump), she was disqualified and stripped of her medals for steroid use. In 2004, the founder of BALCO admitted in an interview to personally giving Jones illegal performance enhancements. To that point, Jones had never failed a drug test (due to inadequate testing parameters). After confessing in 2007 to perjury for lying to federal authorities about her steroid use, Jones was sentenced to six months in prison, which she served in 2008. The U.S. Olympic Committee voted to strip Jones of her medals, including initially stripping her teammates in the relay events from their medals as well. The teammates, however, won their medals back on appeal.

Though a sport since 1965, snowboarding was not introduced into the Olympic Games until 1998. However, it was the 2002 U.S. Olympic snowboarding team that made the sport an international sensation, winning five medals in that year's games. Ross Powers (b. 1979), who had won the bronze in the 1998 games, won gold for the half-pipe, followed by teammates Danny Kass (b. 1982) winning silver and J. J. Thomas (b. 1981) winning bronze. Kelly Clark (b. 1983) won gold in the women's half-pipe, and Chris Klug (b. 1972) brought home the bronze in the parallel giant slalom. The U.S. team would go on to win seven more medals in the 2006 Turin Games. Together, these athletes brought respect to a sport long derided as a novelty activity.

Perhaps the most famous Olympian of the 2000s was Olympic swimmer Michael Phelps (b. 1985). Phelps holds several considerable records: twenty-three Olympic gold medals, thirteen gold medals in individual events, and sixteen overall medals in individual events. When he won eight gold medals in the 2008 Beijing Olympics, he broke the record previously held by another American Olympic swimmer, Mark Spitz (b. 1950), who won seven in the 1972 Olympics in Munich, Germany (infamous for the kidnapping and murder of the entire Israeli Olympic team by Palestinian terrorists). In 2016, he was chosen to carry the American flag in the Parade of Nations during the Rio de Janeiro Games. He is widely recognized as the greatest swimmer in history.

Another Olympic swimmer with a considerable record was Dara Torres (b. 1967). Long after medaling in the 1984 Los Angeles Games, the 1988 Seoul Games, and the 1992 Barcelona Games, Torres returned to win two gold medals in the 2000 Sydney Games: 4 x 100 meter freestyle and 4 x 100 meter medley. She also won three bronze medals at Sydney: 50 meter freestyle, 100 meter freestyle, and 100 meter butterfly. In 2008, at forty-one years old, Torres gave another outstanding performance: silver medals in 50 meter freestyle, 4 x 100 meter freestyle, and 4 x 100 meter medley. Another female Olympian, Cat Osterman (born Catherine Osterman, b. 1983) won gold at the 2004 Athens Games and silver at the 2008 Beijing Games as part of the Women's Olympic softball team, on which she served as pitcher. In her professional career with the National Pro Fastpitch (NPF), previously known as the Women's Pro Softball League, Osterman held a record of 95 wins out of 241 games, with 1,260 strikeouts and twelve saves. From snow, to water, and to the softball diamond, American Olympians in the 2000s proudly overcame the stigma associated with the BALCO scandal that began the decade, providing examples of the best in human physical achievement over and over again.

SPORTS ENTERTAINMENT

The multimedia empire currently known as World Wrestling Entertainment began in 1952 as Capitol Wrestling Corporation, cofounded by Roderick "Jess" McMahon (1882–1954). When McMahon died two years later, his son, Vincent

(1914–1984), was brought in as partner. In 1980, Vincent Sr.'s son, Vincent Kennedy McMahon (b. 1945), and his wife, Linda, (b. 1948) established the company Titan Sports. Two years later, Titan bought controlling interest in Capitol from McMahon's father, creating the World Wrestling Federation. Professional wrestling by that time was understood by most to be "fake," carefully storied and choreographed for maximum effect and entertainment for the fans. In the late 1980s, McMahon officially began selling his brand as sports entertainment. By the early 1990s, what had once been a dozen or so pro wrestling brands had settled down to two major competitors: the WWF and World Championship Wrestling (WCW). Throughout the 1990s, the two competed for fans and television ratings until the WWF was ultimately successful, sending WCW into bankruptcy. In 2001, the WWF bought many of WCW's key assets, including many of their more popular wrestling superstars.

By that time, the WWF was enjoying the peak of its decades-long success with what came to be known as the Attitude Era (1997–2002). This era made the company's weekly live television series *Monday Night Raw* (and, later, *Rar Is War*) the top-rated program on cable television. This era saw the rise of some of the greatest superstars in professional wrestling history: "Mankind" Mick Foley (b. 1965), "Stone Cold" Steve Austin (b. 1964), "the Undertaker" (Mark Calaway; b. 1965), Paul "Triple H" Levesque (b. 1969), and Dwayne "the Rock" Johnson (b. 1972). During this era, these wrestlers became household names, most notably Johnson. In 2000, the Rock became the only individual in American history to speak at both the Republican and Democratic National Conventions.

The McMahon family became regular stars in the ring, each playing over-the-top fictionalized versions of themselves. Vincent became Mr. McMahon, the corrupt boss of the WWF, and frequent foe of "Stone Cold" Steve Austin. This ongoing story line fed into many fans' fantasies of being able to stick it to their own bosses and gave Stone Cold iconic status among the working class. Linda made occasional appearances, often to thwart the dubious machinations of her husband. The McMahon children, Shane (b. 1970) and Stephanie (b. 1976), also joined the show, often supporting their father's plans but occasionally turning against him to the shock and awe of fans. In 2003, Stephanie married Triple H, working their marriage into the overall story line of the show.

By 2002, WWF was a ratings and pay-per-view powerhouse, scheduling monthly pay-per-view events throughout the year. That same year, as a result of a legal case brought on by the World Wildlife Fund regarding the copyright to the initials "WWF," the McMahon's changed the company's name to World Wrestling Entertainment (WWE). Around that same time, the company took a hit with the retirement of several of its top-tier superstars. Foley was forced to dramatically reduce his time in the ring due to complications from the numerous injuries he received over the years as a hardcore legend, spending much of his career taking metal chairs to the face, being hit with barbed-wire bats, and even exploding small packets of the explosive C4 strapped to his back.

In 2002, Austin left the company and retired after what he viewed as a diminished role in WWE story lines, but he later confessed that an injury that he had sustained in a 1997 bout had begun to plague him (he had been wrestling since then against the advice of his doctors) and that he was informed that any slight injury could be permanently crippling or even, possibly, kill him. He would return to the WWE sporadically in a nonwrestling capacity. By that time, the Rock had already launched a wildly successful Hollywood career that would ultimately make him the top-earning action star in movies. After the departure of so many superstars, the WWE began a slow but steady decline over the next fifteen years. While still a ratings powerhouse, it currently does not possess the fan following that it achieved in the late 1990s and early 2000s. In 2017, Linda McMahon was named U.S. administrator of the Small Business Administration by President Donald J. Trump (a longtime friend of the McMahons and onetime guest on the show as an enemy of Mr. McMahon). She served in the position until the spring of 2019.

ESPORTS

Esports—or electronic sports— is a video game competition that has been in place since 1972, debuting at Stanford University in California. Though it was long called a sport by competitors, China was the first country to officially recognize esports as a sport in 2003. By the 2000s, esports had gone global, due mainly to the increasing worldwide access to the internet, with South Korea becoming a major partner in the competition. A contributing factor to the global expansion of esports was the worldwide implementation of so-called internet cafes, places where internet broadband is available to patrons. Over the first decade of the twenty-first century, esports competitions grew from 10 in 2000 to roughly 260 by decade's end. In 2003, France hosted the first Electronic Sports World Convention (ESWC), featuring competitions for the games Call of Duty, Counter-Strike: Global, and Offensive. In 2005, New York hosted the finals competition for the year-long Cyberathlete Professional League World Tour, with the official game of the competition being Painkiller.

The annual World Series of Video Games (WSVG) launched in 2006, featuring international competitions in the personal computer games *Counter-Strike*, *Quake 4*, and *Warcraft III: The Frozen Throne*. In the *Counter-Strike* team competition, the German team aTTaX won the gold medal, the U.S. team Team 3D won silver, and the British team fnatic won the bronze. In the *Quake 4* singles competition, Swedish player Johan "Toxic" Quick won the gold, and Americans Johnathan "Fatal1ty" Wendel and Jason "Socrates_" Sylka won the silver and bronze, respectively. Finally, in the *Warcraft III* singles competition, Dutch player Manuel "Grubby" Schenkhuizen won the gold, and South Koreans Jung Hee "Sweet" Chun and Dae Hui "FoV" Cho won the silver and bronze, respectively. There were also Xbox competitions in the games *Project Gotham Racing 3*, *Ghost Recon: Advanced Warfighter*, and *Halo* 2. The six-month-long competition was held in numerous locations: Kentucky, United States; Sweden; Texas, United States; China; London, United Kingdom; and New York City, United States. The WSVG was surprisingly cancelled halfway through its 2007 season and was not relaunched until 2014.

CARD GAMES

Beginning in the late 1990s, American youth became obsessed with battle card games. Pokémon, which is short for "Pocket Monsters," was, by far, the most popular. The concept was created in Japan in 1995 by Satoshi Tajiri (b. 1965). The basic concept is that Pokémon are mythical creatures that can be trained to fight each other. The gaming aspect is to collect cards, each of which bears the image of a specific monster with specific power levels and abilities. Competitors, then, battle each other by pitting their Pokémon against those of their opponent, with the winner receiving the losing monster for their own collection. The catchphrase, then, is "Gotta catch 'em all!" Other than buying the packs of cards, the general idea is that Pokémon can be caught by use of a Poké-Ball; if the monster cannot escape the ball, then it has been successfully caught and can now be trained. The popularity of the franchise led to movies, animated television series, video games, and mountains of game-related merchandise. It also spawned similar "knock-off" games, none of which caught the worldwide frenzy of the original.

Another Japanese import—and stiff competition for Pokémon—was Yu-Gi-Oh! Like Pokémon, the core idea is to collect cards, building a deck with as many powerful cards as possible. Combatants then battle to attempt to lessen their opponent's life points, winning their cards (and, presumably, strengthening their own deck). Whereas Pokémon made use of a Poké-Ball, advanced Yu-Gi-Oh! players could purchase a duel disk accessory, a device worn on the arm where cards can be placed into play with portions of the deck readily available. This was inspired by the animated series that accompanied the success of the game.

Both Pokémon and Yu-Gi-Oh!—as well as a plethora of imitators—had legions of fans and players around the world, with competitions available in most communities building toward championships at large conventions. They were, in essence, the next generation of card games to follow the popular role-playing games (RPGs) of the 1990s. By the mid-2000s, the fad had diminished significantly in popularity, but by 2020, there remained loyal fans, leading to an attempted resurgence of Pokémon in 2019 that failed to catch fire on the same level as had the original craze.

VIDEO GAMES

The 2000s was the greatest decade of video gaming to date. Graphics and game design surpassed anything previously imagined. Many of the video games that emerged in the late 1990s and throughout the 2000s spawned franchises that continue well into the 2020s. As games improved, so, too, must gaming consoles. By 2000, Sony, Microsoft, and Nintendo were the dominant gaming systems across the globe, and the competition between the three to dominate the medium would play a major role in the massive advancements in gaming technology throughout the early twenty-first century. Below are just some of the major gaming franchises from the 2000s that remain popular well into the 2020s

Probably the most successful game franchise of all time is Nintendo's *Mario*. He was first introduced as the protagonist in the 1981 arcade game *Donkey Kong*, where he had to jump hurdles of rolling barrels in order to save a princess from the malevolent monkey. Nintendo then took the character to the next level with the introduction of *Super Mario Brothers* in 1985. A growing cast of characters emerged through the 1990s: Luigi, Princess Peach, Bowser, Wario, Toad, and Yoshi, to name a few. The franchise exploded in the 2000s with the following games: *Mario Tennis* (2000), *Mario Kart: Super Circuit* (2001), *Super Mario Sunshine* (2002), *Mario vs. Donkey Kong* (2004), *New Super Mario Bros.* (2006), *Super Mario Galaxy* (2007), *Mario Kart Wii* (2008), and *New Super Mario Bros. Wii* (2009). Mario also crossed over with Nintendo's other heavy-hitter, Sonic the Hedgehog, with *Mario and Sonic at the Olympic Games* (2007). Like *Mario*, the *Sonic* franchise also had numerous incarnations throughout the decade.

Perhaps the most controversial video game of all time has been *Grand Theft Auto*. Designed by Mike Dailly (birth year unknown) and David Jones (b. 1965), it was first released in 1997. The game series is set in various fictional cities. The game allows the player to steal, kill, and physically assault various characters. This emphasis on criminal activity has been seen by some as psychologically scarring and by others to be cathartic release, no different psychologically from watching a gangster movie.

Microsoft had huge success with one of its first Xbox offerings: *Star Wars: Knights of the Old Republic* (2003). The game was developed by BioWare for Lucasfilm. It is a role-playing game that allows players to work their way through the ancient history of the *Star Wars* universe. Players begin as either a scout, soldier, or scoundrel, eventually becoming a Jedi apprentice. The game was popular for exploring a period of *Star Wars* mythology previously only mentioned in passing. Its popularity led to a comic book series and is said to be the subject of an upcoming *Star Wars* film project in the 2020s. *Star Wars* was also the basis for Lego's first franchise video game offerings. In *Lego Star Wars: The Video Game* (2005) available on the Nintendo GameCube, Xbox, and PlayStation 2, players could play their way through Lego versions of the prequel trilogy of the *Star Wars* films (1999–2005). The massive success of that game led to its direct sequels: *Lego Star Wars II: The Original Trilogy* (2006) and *Lego Star Wars: The Complete Saga* (2007). Lego's success with franchise-related video games led to offerings centered on *Indiana Jones*, *Batman/DC* superheroes, *Harry Potter*, *Pirates of the Caribbean*, *Lord of the Rings*, *Jurassic Park*, and Marvel superheroes.

Capcom had considerable success with their *Resident Evil* series, first launched in 1996. Developed by Shinji Mikami (b. 1965) and Tokuro Fujiwara (b. 1961), the game can be played in either third-person or first-person shooter perspective. Originally designed for Sony's PlayStation, the game is a survival horror game requiring players to survive by killing numerous monsters and opponents. The first several incarnations revolved around the T-virus, which turns humans into flesh-eating zombies. The 2000s began with the fourth incarnation of the series: *Resident Evil—Code: Veronica* (2000). Set months after the previous three when the virus had expanded beyond its original locale,

Veronica was the first game in the series to debut on consoles other consoles than just PlayStation. The wildly popular franchise spawned a movie series and has continued developing new games throughout the 2010s.

Xbox dominated the gaming world with its *Halo* franchise. First released in 2001, *Halo* is a first-person strategy game set in futuristic situations. Set in the twenty-sixth century, soldiers of the United Nations Space Command must defend humanity against the encroaching Covenant alliance of aliens using their new breed of supersoldiers. The series quickly became one of the most popular of all time. Activison launched a successful similar franchise in 2003 with *Call of Duty* (*COD*). Another first-person shooter game, rather than set in the far future, *COD* began as a World War II (1939–1945) adventure. Over time, the games proceeded to the Cold War (1947–1992) before moving on to more futuristic venues.

Activision hit gold again with its 2005 offering: *Guitar Hero*. Playable on PlayStation 2, Xbox 360, and Nintendo Wii, this game allowed players to play along with the video game band and included controllers that look like modified Gibson guitars. Harmonix and MTV Games competed in 2007 with the release of *Rock Band*. Also playable on most platforms, *Rock Band* took the original premise a step further, allowing multiple players to play along as either lead guitar, bass guitar, drums, or keyboards, as well as singing with a makeshift microphone. Both were hugely popular, as the controllers gave players the feel of actually being part of a rock band.

Realistic game play was key to the success of *Wii Sports* in 2006. What separated Wii from PlayStation or Xbox was specifically this game. The games allowed players to compete with each other in several sports: baseball, bowling, boxing, golf, and tennis. With controllers resembling the various accoutrements of each sport, the game required players to actually get up and physically move as they would when playing the real sport. The game was not only wildly popular with gamers; it was equally popular with video game critics for its elimination of the couch potato effect of most video games.

In 2004, Blizzard Entertainment released *World of Warcraft* (*WOW*). Unlike the other games mentioned, *WoW* was a PC-based online video game. The game allowed players to interact with others around the nation and the world to form teams to complete quests and build points, powers, and abilities to proceed to greater and greater quests. Players could also simply tour the medieval-style world, taking in the sights and meeting other players. The game became a global phenomenon, eventually coming under the sociological scrutiny of the television series *South Park*, which underscored the couch potato effect of game play.

As the decade drew to a close, two more franchises were launched that would go on to be wildly popular throughout the 2010s. In 2009, Rovio Entertainment launched the gaming phone app *Angry Birds*, which allowed players to launch various-sized birds from a slingshot in an effort to destroy walls and buildings made of green pigs (or just the pig heads?). In 2012, the franchise merged with Lucasfilm to create *Angry Birds Star Wars*, giving a *Star Wars* theme to the same bird-versus-pig game play. The popularity of the original series led to two animated feature films in 2016 and 2019.

The second big offering to debut in 2009 was *Batman: Arkham Asylum*. Based on numerous previous *Batman* adventures, most notably the 1989 graphic novel *Arkham Asylum: A Serious House on Serious Earth* by Grant Morrison (b. 1960) and Dave McKean (b. 1963), the game allows single players to play as Batman, making his way through the rogues' gallery of Arkham on his way to the Joker. Aside from the amazing graphics and exciting game play, the producers of the game hired the amazing voice talents of *Batman: The Animated Series* (FOX Kids, 1992–1995) to reprise their roles. The initial game was one of the most successful of all time, leading to an entire *Arkham* franchise throughout the 2010s as well as a corresponding comic book.

During the first decade of the twenty-first century, steroid use by professional athletes from across the spectrum tainted Americans' trust in individuals once held as heroes. As a result of the incredible stress pro athletes experienced to outperform their predecessors and bring more and more excitement to competitions, many fell to the temptation of performance-enhancing drugs. Despite this drug use by an admittedly small number of athletes overall, many others who did not fall to such temptation went on to break records in their respective sports on the strength of their natural abilities. Teams such as basketball's LA Lakers and football's New England Patriots dominated their respective sports throughout the decade. Baseball's Boston Red Sox broke an eighty-six-year curse to the awe and excitement of baseball fans around the country. The "fake" sport of professional wrestling gained its largest fan base since its inception, and video game competitions were finally recognized globally as a sport. On the home-video game front, graphics and game play reached never-before-imagined heights, and also allowed players to physically interact more with game play. Many of the athletes mentioned above would go on to continued success in the decade to follow, but all have cemented themselves—for good or ill—in the pages of sports history in America.

FURTHER READING

Albergotti, Reed, and Vanessa O'Connell. 2014. *Wheelmen: Lance Armstrong, the Tour de France, and the Greatest Sports Conspiracy Ever*. New York: Penguin/Avery.

Armstrong, Lance, and Sally Jenkins. 2001. *It's Not about the Bike: My Journey Back to Life*. New York: Berkley Trade.

Assael, Shaun, and Mike Mooneyham. 2004. *Sex, Lies, and Headlocks: The Real Story of Vince McMahon and World Wrestling Entertainment*. Portland, OR: Broadway.

Bryant, Kobe. 2018. *The Mamba Mentality: How I Play*. New York: MCD.

Canseco, José. 2005. *Juiced: Wild Times, Rampant 'Roids, Smash Hits, and How Baseball Got Big*. New York: William Morrow.

Canseco, José. 2009. *Vindicated: Big Names, Big Liars, and the Battle to Save Baseball*. New York: Gallery/Simon & Schuster.

Castleman, Harry, and Walter J. Podrazik, 2016. *Watching TV: Eight Decades of American Television*. 3rd ed. New York: Syracuse University Press.

CBS News. 2018. "How Sports Helped America Heal after 9/11." September 8. https://www.cbsnews.com/news/how-sports-helped-america-heal-after-911-new-york-city-exhibit/. Retrieved November 14, 2019.

Dominguez, Eddie, Christian Red, and Teri Thompson. 2018. *Baseball Cop: The Dark Side of America's National Pastime*. New York: Hachette.

Edmondson, Jaqueline. 2005. *Venus and Serena Williams: A Biography*. Santa Barbara, CA: Greenwood.

Elfrink, Tim, and Gus Garcia-Roberts. 2014. *Blood Sport: Alex Rodriguez, Biogenesis, and the Quest to End Baseball's Steroid Era*. New York: Dutton.

Fainaru-Wada, Mark, and Lance Williams. 2006. *Game of Shadows: Barry Bonds, BALCO, and the Steroids Scandal That Rocked Professional Sports*. Los Angeles: Gotham.

Foley, Mick. 2000. *Have a Nice Day: A Tale of Blood and Sweatsocks*. New York: Harper Entertainment.

Gee, James Paul. 2007. *What Video Games Have to Teach Us about Learning and Literacy*. 2nd ed., revised and updated. New York: St. Martin's Griffin.

Geoffreys, Clayton. 2014. *Kobe Bryant: The Inspiring Story of One of Basketball's Greatest Shooting Guards*. Scotts Valley, CA: CreateSpace.

Hodgkinson, Mark. 2019. *Serena: A Graphic Biography of the Greatest Tennis Champion*. London: White Lion.

Johnson, Dwayne "the Rock," and Joe Layden. 2000. *The Rock Says . . . : The Most Electrifying Man in Sports Entertainment*. New York: Harper Entertainment.

Macur, Juliet. 2014. *Cycle of Lies: The Fall of Lance Armstrong*. New York: Harper.

9/11 Memorial and Museum. 2019. "Comeback Season: Sports after 9/11." https://www.911memorial.org/visit/museum/exhibitions/comeback-season-sports-after-911. Retrieved November 14, 2019.

Radomski, Kirk. 2009. *Bases Loaded: The Inside Story of the Steroid Era in Baseball by the Central Figure in the Mitchell Report*. New York: Hudson Street.

Walsh, David. 2015. *Seven Deadly Sins: My Pursuit of Lance Armstrong*. New York: Atria.

CHAPTER 3

Music

The 2000s was a transformative decade for the music industry—not so much in terms of style or genre but in distribution and consumption. As the decade opened, most Americans still purchased compact discs (CDs) to play on home or auto stereo systems. By decade's end, American youth in particular were streaming music on digital platforms such as MP3 players, iPods, and iPhones. In the intervening years, the controversy of sharing music exposed musical artists for the capitalists that they were. In 1999, Shawn Fanning (b. 1980) and Sean Parker (b. 1979) developed the idea for Napster, a file-sharing internet service that allowed members to upload MP3 audio files to freely share with others and share theirs in return.

From the perspective of Napster, this service was no different from friends loaning CDs to each other, allowing one to burn a copy for themselves. From the perspective of the music industry, this allowed millions of people to acquire free copies of songs rather than purchase them, therefore denying money to the artists and companies that owned the copyrights to the songs. In 2000, Napster was sued by the heavy metal band Metallica, rapper Dr. Dre (b. 1965), the record company A&M Records, and the guild organization, the Recording Industry Association of America (RIAA). Napster lost the case and the appeal, and unable to comply with the restrictions placed on them by the court's decision, the company filed for bankruptcy in 2002.

The terror attacks on 9/11 left the country demoralized and frightened, and popular music was there to salve the wounds of a nation in grief. Country music in particular—already established as a very patriotic genre of music—produced songs that both comforted and inspired. Ironically, it would be from the very same genre that the first major backlash against the War on Terror and the policies of President George W. Bush. As a result of this free and understandable expression, the Dixie Chicks would feel the wrath of country music fans around the country and suffer a career setback from which the band, to date, has still not recovered.

Women and minorities would continue their decades-long trajectory of chart dominance in the music industry. A Latin explosion in the early part of the decade made superstars of artists such as Jennifer Lopez (b. 1969), Ricky Martin (b. 1971), and Shakira (b. 1977). Pop star Sheryl Crow (b. 1962) would transition from the pop charts to the country charts. Bubblegum pop stars such as Britney Spears (b. 1981) and Christina Aguilera (b. 1980) would become international superstars, and, by decade's end, the phenomenon that would become Lady Gaga (born Stefani Joanne Angelina Germanotta in 1986) would burst onto the pop music charts, to go on to domination in the decade that followed.

Boy bands such as NSYNC and the Backstreet Boys would peak early on, only to split up and go their separate ways by mid-decade, giving rise to one of the biggest musical stars of the decade: Justin Timberlake (b. 1981). As the decade closed, the world said good-bye to one of its biggest stars: the King of Pop, Michael Jackson (1958–2009). It was a decade of change in so many ways. During the country's darkest hour, music united Americans, and as the world of technology changed, music was center stage during the transition. In the early years of the new millennium, MP3s and iPods helped Americans get through the most devastating event in the country's history: 9/11.

9/11

On September 11, 2001, nineteen terrorists belonging to the international terrorist organization Al-Qaeda hijacked four commercial passenger planes, flying two into the Twin Towers of the World Trade Center in New York City and a third into the Pentagon in Washington, DC. The fourth plane, likely headed for either the White House or Capitol in Washington, experienced a revolt when the passengers, made aware of what was happening by their loved ones on the ground thanks to cell phones, attempted to retake the plane, leading the hijackers to dive-bomb the plane into the ground in a field outside of Shanksville, Pennsylvania. In all, 2,977 people were killed, not including the terrorists, making it the bloodiest attack on the United States in the nation's history. Around the country, millions of people watched events unfold in real time. It would take literally years for the country to overcome the trauma and grief of that day, but, early on, the music industry rose to the challenge, both aiding Americans in dealing with their grief and inspiring them to move forward against our new common foe.

In the immediate aftermath of the attacks, British rock legend and former Beatle Sir Paul McCartney (b. 1942) organized a benefit concert called the Concert for New York City (October 20, 2001). In order of appearance as listed on Wikipedia, the star-studded lineup consisted of David Bowie (1947–2016), Bon Jovi (f. 1983), Jay-Z (b. Shawn Carter, 1969), the Goo Goo Dolls (f. 1986), Billy Joel (b. 1949), Destiny's Child (1990–2006), Eric Clapton (b. 1945) and Buddy Guy (b. 1936), Adam Sandler as Operaman (b. 1966), the Backstreet Boys (f. 1993), Melissa Etheridge (b. 1961), the Who (f. 1964), Mick Jagger and Keith

Richards (both b. 1943), Macy Gray (b. Natalie McIntyre, 1967), James Taylor (b. 1948), John Mellencamp (b. 1951) and Kid Rock (b. Robert Ritchie, 1971), Five for Fighting (b. Vladimir Ondrasik III, 1967), Janet Jackson (b. 1966), Sir Elton John (b. Reginald Dwight, 1947), and McCartney.

Each musical act was introduced by a Hollywood celebrity or political figure. Inspirational short films were produced and presented by filmmakers such as Martin Scorsese (1942), Spike Lee (b. Shelton Lee, 1957), Woody Allen (b. Heywood Allen, 1935), and Kevin Smith (b. 1970). Radio personality Howard Stern and comedian Jerry Seinfeld (both b. 1954) also presented short films. *Saturday Night Live* star Will Ferrell (b. 1967) also appeared in his impersonation of President George W. Bush. The concert was broadcast on cable network VH1 and raised more than $35 million for the families of 9/11 victims.

Americans rallied around music to salve the wounds of grief. Nile Rodgers (b. 1952) re-recorded his 1979 Sister Sledge hit single "We Are Family" (2001). Country artist Lee Greenwood saw a massive resurgence of his 1984 hit "God Bless the USA," which begins with the haunting line "If tomorrow all the things were gone I worked for all my life . . ." and continues with an inspirational chorus.

Country music had long been connected to patriotism and love of nation, and that was never truer than after the events of 9/11, when country artists addressed both America's grief and its anger. One of the earliest songs to address the overwhelming sadness and shock of the country was Alan Jackson's (b. 1958) November 2001 hit "Where Were You (When the World Stopped Turning)." The song presents as what could be any conversation in the wake of the attacks, asking where people were when they heard of what had happened and addressing the idea that many are just simple people living simple lives, calling for unity through "faith, hope and love."

By contrast, the following spring, Toby Keith (b. 1961) released the very angry but equally unifying "Courtesy of the Red, White and Blue (The Angry American)." Expressing all the anger and thirst for vengeance that Americans felt at the time, the final verse of the song ends with "And you'll be sorry you messed with the U.S. of A. / 'Cause we'll put a boot in your ass, / It's the American Way." In 2005, the popular 1990s rock band Green Day (f. 1986, originally) released the song "Wake Me Up When September Ends." Though four years had passed, the song reflects the fact that the events of 9/11 had left deep scars in the American psyche with the refrain "As my memory rests / But never forgets what I lost / Wake me up when September ends."

Controversy eventually arose, however, from the popular country music group the Dixie Chicks (f. 1989). The band consisted of sisters Martie Erwin Maguire (b. 1969) and Emily Erwin Robison (b. 1972) and their lead singer, Natalie Maines (b. 1974). After a chain of hit singles over the previous two years, their last chart-topping hit was "Travelin' Soldier" in 2002, a song about a high school girl who strikes up a pen-pal relationship with a soldier serving in Vietnam. As she reads his latest letter at a football game, the announcer reads a list of recent local deaths in the war, and the soldier's name is among them. The heartrending flashback to a decades-past war struck home for those in 2002 who expected daily to hear their own loved ones' names mentioned among the lost in Afghanistan.

Their wildly successful career took an immediate downturn the following year. While performing in London in 2003, as Maines introduced "Travelin' Soldier," she made the following statement: "Just so you know, we're on the good side with y'all. We do not want this war [the new war in Iraq], this violence, and we're ashamed that the President of the United States [George W. Bush] is from Texas" (Thompson 2019). When news outlets in the United States broke the story, there was immediate backlash against the Dixie Chicks. Their current song, "Landslide" (a cover of a classic Fleetwood Mac song from the 1970s), immediately tanked. It was only eighteen months nearly to the day since 9/11, and the wounds to Americans' souls were still sensitive. When the United States invaded Iraq in 2003, the overwhelming majority of Americans, including both political parties in both houses of Congress, supported the invasion as part of Bush's War on Terror.

Though popular support for the Iraq War would eventually wane and the president's claims that Iraqi President Saddam Hussein possessed weapons of mass destruction proved doubtful, by that time, the Dixie Chicks' career had imploded. One of the few voices of support the Dixie Chicks received, and the only voice from the country music genre, was country legend Merle Haggard (b. 1937) who believed it was un-American to criticize Americans voicing their opinion. Just a few months after Maines's comments, Haggard released "That's the News," a song critical of media coverage of the Iraq War. Haggard, it is important to note, did not receive similar backlash; his status as a music icon—and, perhaps, the fact that he was a man—shielded him from the level of anger experienced by the young women.

Despite massive boycotts by country music fans, repeated cancelled concerts, and even numerous death threats, the Dixie Chicks did return to the pop charts in 2006 with their protest song, "Not Ready to Make Nice." In the song, the women make clear that they are unapologetic about their previous remarks, regardless of the feedback. Maines's original comment was her own, and if she had stepped down or been removed from the group, the Dixie Chicks could have possibly gone on with continued success with another singer. The Erwin sisters, however, stood by their lifelong friend and bandmate, sharing in the backlash.

What is most clear from the Dixie Chicks controversy is the state of the Culture Wars (1992–present) that had been dividing the nation into conservative and liberal since the mid-1990s. While 9/11 briefly brought the two disparate factions together in unity against a common foe, once the dust of Ground Zero settled and the wounds began to heal, the nation was once more divided, and by 2010, the United States would be more divided than at any point in its history, including during the Civil War (1861–1865). Outside of 9/11 and the Culture Wars, however, American music in the 2000s experienced a transition unique in its history. Though past decades had seen music consumption shift from platform to platform (from vinyl to eight-track, to cassette, to compact disc), the internet was producing an entirely new medium for music: online digital streaming. As technology continued to shift throughout the decade, from the CD to the iPhone, the devices in between wound up stuffed in the back of junk drawers, the music within largely lost to the next generation of devices, making the first decade of the twenty-first century "the Deleted Years."

MTV

By the end of the twentieth century, Music Television (MTV) had been the barometer for popular music since the early 1980s. Since 1984, the MTV Video Music Awards were a major event for Generation X. That was followed in 1992 by the MTV Movie Awards. Music, fashion, and everything deemed cool was given credence through MTV. The network experimented with reality programming in 1992 with *The Real World*, placing a diverse group of young people in a house together and recording the inevitable drama.

By 2000, with the rise of the millennials, MTV was losing its cool factor. Expanding the network to include VH1, MTV2, and MTV3 did not help. With the introduction of smartphones in 2007, millennials and Generation Z (or iGen, as they are sometimes called) had all but walked away from the channel, viewing whatever music videos they wanted on their phones. In 2009, MTV introduced two new reality programs aimed at this burgeoning younger demographic: *Jersey Shore* and *Sixteen and Pregnant*. Soon, the network became less and less about the music videos that had brought them national fame, and by 2010, MTV was all but irrelevant to the new generation of America's youth. Whereas the network had launched on August 1, 1981, with the video "Video Killed the Radio Star," by 2010, digital had killed the video star.

THE DELETED YEARS: FROM NAPSTER TO SPOTIFY

Although Napster's bankruptcy ultimately ended the worldwide free sharing of music files, the success of the company was a clarion call to the market that digitally downloaded music was something that the people wanted. In 2003, in the ashes of Napster, Apple opened the Apple Music Store for downloads into the company's new iPods. Since 1997, consumers could purchase MP3 players, devices designed to play digital audio files. In 2001, Apple introduced the iPod. When the Apple Music Store opened, the available music could only be downloaded onto Apple products. The purpose of this, of course, was to put other commercial MP3 players out of business, which it basically did. From 2001 to 2007, Apple continued to improve the quality and interactivity of the iPod before finally introducing the world to the iPhone, one of the first so-called smartphones.

While consumers could access their audio libraries through iTunes, the new iPhones could not download an entire audio library, as the early iPhones did not have the overall memory capacity of the later iPods. Additionally, chargers for iPods and MP3 players became more and more difficult to find, leaving these old devices to collect dust on shelves or become buried in the back of drawers. As a result, since so few people bought CDs (and very few buying vinyl) from 2003 to 2012 roughly, this period has become known as the Deleted

Years (Holmes 2019). Prior to 2003, Americans could show you their music library via their stacks and stacks of CDs, and since 2012, they could show you their entire music library on their phones. The music consumed during the intervening years, however, is stored away in iPods and MP3 players that can no longer be accessed, unless one is lucky enough to find a charger that still works.

Since 2008, consumers have had access to Spotify, an internet music and podcast streaming service. Users can access the app for free, giving them access to roughly fifty million music tracks interspersed with commercials; a commercial-free subscription is also available. As of 2020, Spotify boasted roughly 250 million users, nearly half of whom are subscribers. Though the 2010s would see a nostalgic return to CDs and vinyl, the 2000s forever changed how Americans, especially tech-savvy younger Americans, listened to and collected music. The days of giant boom boxes or smaller Sony Walkmans that forced listeners to carry small cases of portable cassettes are long gone. By 2010, Americans could carry their entire music library wherever they wished, held in the palm of their hand, or clipped to their belt for the admittedly few who kept and used the bulky and garish iPhone belt clips. Say what one will about the music of the Deleted Years, the fact remains that across all genres and subgenres, the decade saw some of the most colorful performers and produced some of the greatest songs in American music history.

ROCK

In every genre of popular music in the 2000s, the music world lost amazing, legendary performers. In the world of rock music, George Harrison (1943–2001), iconic member of the Fab Four, the Beatles, died in Los Angeles in the home of fellow Beatle Paul McCartney, of lung cancer that had spread to his brain. After his death, Harrison's son helped to finish his father's final album, *Brainwashed*, which was released in 2002. By mid-decade, legendary rock band the Ramones had lost three of their founding members: Joey Ramone (Jeffrey Ross Hyman, 1951–2001), Dee Dee Ramone (Douglas Glenn Colvin, 1951–2002), and Johnny Ramone (John William Cummings, 1948–2004). As these rock legends passed, new names were hitting the charts, paving the way for music's future.

The All-American Rejects were founded in 1999 in Oklahoma, headed by lead singer Tyson Ritter (b. 1984). The broke into the alternative rock charts in 2002 with their song "Swing, Swing." They made their way up the overall pop charts, breaking the Top Ten with "Dirty Little Secret" (2005) and "It Ends Tonight" (2006). The band's biggest hit, "Gives You Hell," was released in 2008. To date, the band has not matched their brief mid-2000s success. A more successful artist, also debuting in 1999, was alt-rocker Avril Lavigne (b. 1984). The Canadian singer and songwriter shot to the top of the charts in 2002 with her song "Complicated." That was followed with other hits: "Sk8er Boi" (2002), "Losing Grip" (2003), "Don't Tell Me" and "My Happy Ending" (both in 2004), and "Girlfriend" and "When You're Gone" (both in 2007).

Another popular band making the charts as the new millennium dawned was Blink-182. Originally just called Blink (until 1995), the band was founded in 1992, in Poway, California, by Mark Hoppus (b. 1972), Tom DeLonge (b. 1975), and Scott Raynor (b. 1978). The group's breakthrough hit was "All the Small Things" (2000), at the height of the boy band craze. Future hits included "The Rock Show" (2001) and "I Miss You" (2004). Though the original band split up in 2005, Hoppus relaunched it in 2009 with Matt Skiba (b. 1976) and Travis Barker (b. 1975). DeLonge briefly rejoined the new Blink-182 in 2009, touring with them before leaving the band again in 2015. In 2011, DeLonge dedicated the majority of his time into researching government coverups of the UFO phenomenon.

One of the more colorful groups of the period was the performance art group Blue Man Group, consisting of Chris Wink (b. 1961), Matt Goldman, and Phil Stanton (birth years unknown). Wearing blue face paint and black turtle-necks and slacks, the band has put on artistic performances since its inception in 1987. Their first album, *Audio*, went gold in 1999. It was followed by *The Complex* (2003) and *Live at the Venetian–Las Vegas* (2006). In 2011, the group was bought by Cirque du Soleil in 2017, to be added and expanded upon for their Las Vegas performances.

The British band Coldplay was founded in 1996 by band members Chris Martin (b. 1977), Guy Berryman (b. 1978), Johnny Buckland (b. 1977), and Will Champion (b. 1978), who met while attending University College London. The group had numerous hits in the 2000s: "Yellow" (2000), "In My Place" (2002), "Clocks" (2003), and "Speed of Sound" and "Fix You" (both in 2005). By far, Coldplay's biggest hit to date has been "Viva la Vida" in 2008, expressing a king's lament at having lost his kingdom. The band continued to make the charts throughout the 2010s.

Another popular rock band of the decade was the heavy metal band Disturbed. Founded in Chicago, Illinois, in 1994, the band consisted of Dan Donegan (b. 1968), David Draiman (b. 1973), John Moyer (b. 1973), and Mike Wengren (b. 1971). Their biggest hits from the decade included the following "Down with the Sickness" (2000); "Prayer" and "Remember" (both in 2002); "Liberate" (2004); "Guarded" and "Stricken" (both in 2005); "Just Stop," "Land of Confusion," and "Ten Thousand Fists" (all in 2006); "Inside the Fire" and "Indestructible" (both in 2008); and "The Night" (2009). The band went on hiatus in 2011 but came back strong in 2015 with their haunting rendition of the Simon & Garfunkel classic "The Sound of Silence" in 2015.

Evanescence was a very popular rock band in the 2000s, coming out of Little Rock, Arkansas, in 1995, organized by founding band members Amy Lee (b. 1981), lead singer and pianist, and Ben Moody (b. 1981), on guitar. The rest of the band has had a rotating roster over the years. Evanescence won the Grammy for Best New Artist in 2004. Their biggest hits in the 2000s were the songs "Bring Me to Life" and "My Immortal" (both in 2003) from the album *Fallen*. Their only other chart-topping hit from the decade was "Call Me When You're Sober" (2006), but the band maintains a strong cult following still today.

Fall Out Boy was a pop punk rock band in the 2000s, originating in Chicago, Illinois, in 2001. The band has had rotating members over the years (specifically drummers), but current members include Andy Hurley (b. 1980) on drums, Patrick Stump (b. 1984) on lead vocals and guitar, Joe Trohman (b. 1984) on guitar and backup vocals, and Pete Wentz (b. 1979) on bass. The band's hits from the 2000s include "Sugar, We're Goin' Down" and "Dance, Dance" (both in 2005), "This Ain't a Scene, It's an Arms Race" (2007), and "I Don't Care" (2008).

After the suicide of bandmate Kurt Cobain (1967–1994), Nirvana drummer Dave Grohl (b. 1969) founded the originally one-man group Foo Fighters, eventually joined by Nate Mendel (b. 1968), Pat Smear (b. Georg Ruthenberg, 1959), and William Goldsmith (birth year unknown). By 2000, the band consisted of Grohl, Mendel, and Taylor Hawkins (b. 1972). Their hits in the 2000s included "Learn to Fly" (2000), "All My Life" (2002), "Times Like These" (2003), "Best of You" and "DOA" (both in 2005), "No Way Back/Cold Day in the Sun" (2006), "The Pretender" and "Long Road to Ruin" (both in 2007), and "Wheels" (2009). In 2000, they won a Grammy Award for the video to "Learn to Fly."

One of the more artistic groups of the period was the band Gorillaz. Founded by Damon Albarn and Jamie Hewlett (both born 1968) in 1998, the group is considered a virtual band, meaning a band whose members are animated avatars. The virtual bandmates consist of Russel Hobbes, Murdoc Niccals, Noodle, and Stuart "2-D" Pot. The band's breakthrough hit—and biggest hit to date—was from their debut album, *Gorillaz*, in 2001: "Clint Eastwood." Their 2005 album, *Demon Days*, produced three chart-toppers: "Feel Good Inc." with the group De La Soul (f. 1988), "Dare" with Shaun Ryder (b. 1962), and "Dirty Harry" with Bootie Brown and the San Fernando Valley Youth Chorus. The groundbreaking music video for "Clint Eastwood" won three Billboard Video Music Awards in 2001: the Maximum Vision Award, the Best Modern Rock New Artist Clip, and the Best Rap/Hip-Hop New Artist Clip.

Green Day was one of the biggest rock bands of the 1990s. Founded in 1986 by lead singer Billie Joe Armstrong and bass guitarist Mike Dirnt (both b. 1972), the band was joined by drummer John Kiffmeyer (b. 1969). One of the band's biggest albums was 2004's *American Idiot*, which featured the title song as well as "Boulevard of Broken Dreams," "Holiday," and "Wake Me Up When September Ends" (the last two released as singles in 2005). Yet another hit rock band from the 1990s was Linkin Park. Founded in Agoura Hills, California, in 1996, the band currently consists of Mike Shinoda, Brad Delson, Dave Farrell, Joe Hahn (all born 1977), and Rob Bourdon (b. 1979). Their big hits from the decade included "In the End" (2001), "Somewhere I Belong" and "Faint" (both in 2003), "Breaking the Habit" (2004), "What I've Done" (2007), and "New Divide" (2009).

In 2001, the band previously known as Kara's Flowers changed their name to Maroon 5. The band consisted of lead singer Adam Levine, keyboardist and guitarist Jesse Carmichael, bass guitarist Mickey Madden (all born 1979), lead guitarist James Valentine (b. 1978), drummer Matt Flynn (b. 1970), keyboardist P. J. Morton (b. 1981), and Sam Farrar (b. 1978), who plays multiple instruments. Their debut album, *Songs About Jane* (2002), produced the hits "This Love" and "She Will Be Loved." Another chart-topper was the single "Makes Me Wonder" (2007). The Canadian band Nickleback was formed in 1995. It consists of lead singer Chad Kroeger (b. 1974), keyboardist and guitarist Ryan Peake (b. 1973), drummer Daniel Adair (b. 1975), and Mike Kroeger (birth year unknown). Nickleback's big hits from the 2000s include "How You Remind Me" (2001), "Someday" (2003), "Photograph" (2005), and "Savin' Me" (2006).

Panic at the Disco (originally Panic! at the Disco) was founded in 2004 in Las Vegas, Nevada, by Brendon Urie (b. 1987), Ryan Ross (b. 1986), Spencer Smith (b. 1987), and Brent Wilson (b. 1987). The band had a strong following, with hits on the U.S. alternative charts: "The Only Difference between Martyrdom and Suicide Is Press Coverage" (2005), "I Write Sins Not Tragedies" (2006), and "Nine in the Afternoon" (2008). Perhaps one of the biggest names in rock music in the 2000s was the White Stripes, founded in Detroit, Michigan, in 1997 by the then-married couple Jack and Meg White (b. 1975 and 1974, respectively). Although the couple divorced in 2000, they continued to perform together until 2011. The duo's biggest hits were "Seven Nation Army" and "The Hardest Button to Button" (both in 2003), "Blue Orchid" and "The Denial Twist" (both in 2005), and "Icky Thump" (2007). Although the two were not considered chart-toppers, they were widely respected for their artistry and had a devoted following throughout the 2000s. Some of the biggest chart-toppers of the period came from the genre of pop/dance music.

POP/DANCE

Since the 1980s, the most successful genre of popular music in America appeared on the pop and/or dance charts. One name that exploded onto the pop charts in the 2000s was Amy Winehouse (1983–2011). Born in London, England, Winehouse possessed a powerful voice along the lines of Janis Joplin (1943–1970) decades earlier, who, ironically, died at the young age of twenty-seven, as would Winehouse. Although Winehouse's music has been defined as a mixture of soul, R&B, and jazz, her vocals were reminiscent of female singers from the early days of rock in the 1950s. After a moderately successful debut album, *Frank* (2003), Winehouse exploded onto the American pop charts with back-to-back hits "Rehab" (2006) and "You Know I'm No Good" (2007). On July 23, 2011, Winehouse was found nonresponsive by her bodyguard, who believed she'd been sleeping; ultimately, her death was pronounced the result of accidental overdose of alcohol. Like Joplin forty years earlier, Winehouse's death shocked the world and saddened a generation of fans at the loss of such an amazing talent.

The Black Eyed Peas were a pop, dance, and hip-hop group that saw its peak in the 2000s. The group was first formed in 1988 by rappers will.i.am (b. William Adams in 1975) and apl.de.ap (b. Allan Pineda Lindo in 1974). In 1995, rapper Taboo (b. Jamie Luis Gomez in 1975) joined along with singer Kim Hill (birth year unknown). Hill was replaced around 2000/2001 with new singer Fergie (b. Stacy Ann Ferguson in 1975). It was with Fergie as lead singer that the group would make its greatest chart successes. The Black Eyed Peas burst onto the pop charts in 2003 with the hits "Where Is the Love?" and "Shut Up." They would be followed with other chart-toppers: "Let's Get It Started" (2004); "My Humps" (2005); "Pump It" (2006); and "Boom Boom Pow," "I Gotta

Feeling," "Meet Me Halfway," and "Imma Be" (all in 2009). The band went on hiatus in 2012 as Fergie began her solo career, and it reunited in 2014 with new lead singer Jessica Reynoso (birth year unknown).

Three of the biggest pop stars of the 2000s were former Disney performers Britney Spears (b. 1981), Christina Aguilera (b. 1980), and Justin Timberlake (b. 1981). Both women had been cast as Mouseketeers on Disney's *The All-New Mickey Mouse Club* in 1992, and Justin joined for the 1993–1994 season. Britney burst onto the pop charts in 1998 with ". . . Baby One More Time," followed by back-to-back chart-toppers throughout 1999. In 2000, Britney hit with a long chain of back-to-back hits: "Oops! . . . I Did It Again," "Lucky," and "Stronger" (all in 2000); "Don't Let Me Be the Last to Know," "I'm a Slave 4 U," and "Overprotected" (all in 2001); "I'm Not a Girl, Not Yet a Woman," "I Love Rock 'n Roll," and "Boys" (all in 2002); "Me against the Music" with Madonna (born Madonna Ciccone in 1958) in 2003; "Toxic," "Everytime," and "My Prerogative" (all in 2004); "Piece of Me" (2007); and "Womanizer" (2008). In the 2010s, Britney became less and less visible both on stage and on the charts due to a chain of personal issues.

Christina Aguilera likewise had amazing chart success in the 2000s. Christina had been featured on the soundtrack to the 1998 Disney animated film *Mulan* with the song "Reflections." The following year, her debut album had back-to-back chart-toppers with "Genie in a Bottle" and "What a Girl Wants." Throughout the 2000s, Christina continued to dominate pop charts with more back-to-back hits. In 2001, she released a remake of the song "Lady Marmalade" on the soundtrack for the film *Moulin Rouge!*, singing alongside fellow chart-topping artists Lil' Kim (b. Kimberly Jones in 1974), Mya (b. Mya Harrison in 1979) and Pink (b. Alecia Moore in 1979). Christina had back-to-back hits in 2002 with "Dirrty" and "Beautiful." Her 2006 album, *Back to Basics*, featured the hits "Hurt" and "Candyman." She continued to have chart success as well as serving as a judge on the television singing competition *The Voice* (NBC, 2011–present) from 2011 to 2016.

Justin Timberlake became the lead singer for the boy band NSYNC in 1995, remaining with the band until 2002, when he began a successful solo career. He became embroiled in controversy in 2004 when performing with pop icon Janet Jackson (b. 1966) during the halftime show for Super Bowl XXXVIII. During the performance, Timberlake accidentally exposed Jackson's breast live on national television; according to Timberlake, the intention was to expose a red bra beneath Jackson's outer garment. The two had to issue a public apology or risk being banned from that year's Grammy Awards, where Timberlake was up for numerous awards. His solo hits during the 2000s included "Like I Love You" and "Cry Me a River" (both in 2002), "Rock Your Body" (2003), and "Sexy Back" and "My Love" (both in 2006; the second featuring rapper T.I., born Clifford Harris Jr., in 1980). He also had several hits performing with other artists including "Work It" with Nelly (born Cornell Haynes Jr., in 1974) in 2003 and "4 Minutes" with Madonna and Timbaland (born Timothy Mosley in 1972) in 2008. He also performed in several *Saturday Night Live* satirical music videos with strong sexual themes along with the comedy singing group the Lonely Island, headlined by *SNL* alum Andy Samberg (b. 1978).

The 2000s also saw the beginning of a new musical careers for two young female artists as well as the next chapter in the career of a pop music icon. In 2002, Kelly Clarkson (b. 1982) became the first winner of the television singing competition *American Idol* (FOX, 2002–2016; ABC, 2018–present). She went on to have numerous hits in the 2000s, beginning with the single of her *American Idol* victory song, "A Moment Like This." Her other hits included "Miss Independent" (2003); "Breakaway" and "Since U Been Gone" (both in 2004); "Behind These Hazel Eyes" and "Because of You" (both in 2005); and "My Life Would Suck Without You" (2009). One of the biggest names in pop music well beyond the 2000s was Katy Perry (born Katheryn Hudson in 1984). After her initial 2002 album, she broke into mainstream pop stardom with her second album, *One of the Boys* (2008), producing such Top Ten hits as "I Kissed a Girl" and "Hot n Cold." She would go on to even greater success in the 2010s.

As those two careers began, the undisputed Queen of Pop, Madonna, once more redefined herself for a new generation of fans. After shattering the glass ceiling for American female recording artists in the 1980s, a lackluster movie career, and series of controversies in the 1990s, Madonna returned big in 2000 with her remake of the rock classic "American Pie" (originally released by Don McLean in 1971). That hit was followed by "Music" and "Don't Tell Me" (both in 2000). In 2002, Madonna recorded the song "Die Another Day," the title song for the twentieth *James Bond* film of the same name, in which she also had a cameo. In 2003, she topped charts with the following songs: "American Life," "Hollywood," "Me against the Music" with Britney Spears, "Nothing Fails," and "Love Profusion." Her two biggest hits since 2000 were "Hung Up" (2005) and the previously mentioned "4 Minutes" with Justin Timberlake and Timbaland in 2008. She ended the decade with yet another chart-topper, "Celebration" (2009).

Since the early days of pop music, crooners have been popular. From Frank Sinatra (1915–1998) to Harry Connick Jr. (b. 1967), every generation has had velvety-voiced crooner putting out smooth, easy listening hits. The 2000s answer to this subgenre was Canadian-born Michael Bublé (b. 1975). His first U.S. hit was "Home" in 2005. His other U.S. hits in the decade include "Save the Last Dance for Me" (2006), "Everything" and "Lost" (both in 2007), and "Haven't Met You Yet" and "Hold On" (both in 2009). He was a high-profile artist during the 2010 Winter Olympics in Vancouver, Canada, and took part in the torch relay for the final leg in his homeland of Canada. Some of his music was used for England's coverage of the games, and he was a guest on *The Colbert Report* (Comedy Central, 2005–2014) for its coverage of the Canada games. He remained a popular global star throughout the 2010s.

Miley Cyrus (born Destiny Hope Cyrus in 1992), burst on to the pop culture scene with her smash hit television series, *Hannah Montana* (Disney Channel, 2006–2011). On the series, Cyrus played Miley Stewart, a "normal" teenage girl who lives a secret double life as pop sensation Hannah Montana, under her father and manager Robby Stewart, played by Cyrus's actual father, country music star Billy Ray Cyrus (b. 1961). Hannah hits the charts with "Best of Both Worlds" (2006), the title song of the series. Throughout the series' run, Cyrus released several albums as both Hannah and Miley. As Hannah Montana, she released the songs "The Other Side of Me" (2006), "Make Some Noise" and "Nobody's Perfect" (both in 2007), and "I Wanna Know You" and "He Could Be the One" (both in 2009). As Miley Cyrus, she had hits with "Ready, Set, Don't Go" with her father (2007) and her two biggest hits of the decade, "The Climb" and "Party in the USA" (both in 2009). Miley would experience numerous setbacks and controversies in the 2010s as she attempted to break free from her Disney/Hannah image and be recognized as a serious performer.

One female artist who broke through with a rougher, edgier persona from the beginning was the pop star Pink, or P!nk (born Alecia Beth Moore in 1979). With her short-cropped, upswept pink—sometimes blond—hair, Pink expressed the rebellion of youth and the growing power and agency of women in pop culture. Pink enjoyed a chain of back-to-back hits throughout the decade, including "Most Girls" (2000); "Lady Marmalade" with Christina Aguilera, Lil' Kim, and Mya and "Get the Party Started" (both in 2001); "Don't Let Me Get Me" and "Just Like a Pill" (both in 2002); "Trouble" (2003); "Stupid Girls," "Who Knew," "U + Ur Hand," and "Dear Mr. President" (all in 2006); "So What" and "Sober" (both in 2008); and "Please Don't Leave Me" (2009). Pink continued to top charts and perform to sold-out venues well into the 2010s.

In 2003, a new girl group burst onto the scene. The Pussycat Dolls had begun in the mid-1990s as a dance troupe, switching to pop and R&B in the 2000s. The group's original members included Carmit Bachar (b. 1974), Ashley Roberts (b. 1981), Nicole Scherzinger (b. 1978), Jessica Sutta (b. 1982), Melody Thornton (b. 1984), and Kimberly Wyatt (b. 1982). The original group performed from 2003 to 2010, with such hits as "Don't Cha" with rapper Busta Rhymes (born Trevor Smith Jr., in 1972) and "Stickwitu" (both in 2005); "Beep" with will.i.am and "Buttons" with Snoop Dogg (born Calvin Broadus Jr., in 1971), both in 2006; "When I Grow Up" and "I Hate This Part" (both in 2008); and their 2009 hit, "Jai Ho! (You Are My Destiny)" with A. R. Rahman (b. 1967). The group ultimately disbanded in 2010, due on large part to their management's and the media's overemphasis on Scherzinger as the de facto leader of the ensemble. Since their disbandment, Scherzinger has gone on to a career as a celebrity judge on various singing-competition television series.

One of the biggest pop groups of the 1990s was No Doubt (1986–2004), who rose to international stardom due largely to the voice and stage presence of lead singer Gwen Stefani (b. 1969). The group continued into the 2000s with hits such as "Simple Kind of Life" (2000), "Hey Baby" (2001), "Underneath It All" (2002), and "It's My Life" (2004). By 2004, Stefani had already had chart success outside the group with the 2000 song "South Side" with the artist Moby (born Richard Melville Hall in 1965) and the 2001 hit "Let Me Blow Ya Mind" with rapper Eve (born Eve Jeffers in 1978). Eve was featured in one of Stefani's first solo hits, "Rich Girl" (2004). Stefani then went on to have more chart-topping hits in the 2000s with the songs "Hollaback Girl" (2005) and "The Sweet Escape" featuring the artist Akon (born Aliaune Damala Bouga

Time Puru Nacka Lu Lu Lu Badara Akon Thiam in 1973) and "Wind It Up" (both in 2006). Stefani remains a popular singer into the 2010s. In 2015, Stefani married her second husband, country artist Blake Shelton.

Beginning around 1999 and continuing to thrive into the 2000s and beyond, American pop music experienced an explosion of Latin artists on the charts. Several male artists topped American charts during the period. Spanish-born Enrique Iglesias (b. 1975), son of crooning legend Julio Iglesias (b. 1943), is considered by many to be the King of Latin Pop. After his breakout U.S. hit "Bailamos" (1999), Iglesias went on to top U.S. charts with hits including "Be with You/Solo Me Importas Tu" and "Could I Have This Kiss Forever" with Whitney Houston (1963–2012), both in 2000; "Hero" (2001); "Escape" (2002); "Addicted" (2003); "Do You Know? (The Ping Pong Song)" (2007); and "Can You Hear Me" (2008). Puerto Rican–born Ricky Martin (born Enrique Morales in 1971) had been part of the boy band Menudo from 1983 to 1990. In 1999, he broke into the U.S. English-speaking charts with back-to-back hits "Livin' La Vida Loca" and "Shake Your Bon-Bon." In the 2000s, Martin had hits with "She Bangs" (2000) and "Nobody Wants to Be Lonely" with Christina Aguilera (2001). After a decade of refusing to comment on his sexuality, Martin came out as gay in 2010.

The early 2000s saw hits from the New York/Puerto Rican power couple of Marc Anthony (b. 1968) and Jennifer Lopez (b. 1969). The two were married in 2004 and divorced ten years later. After breaking onto the U.S. English charts with "I Need to Know" in 1999, Anthony followed it with "You Sang to Me" (2000). He also topped U.S. Spanish charts with "Celos" (2001), "Viviendo" (2002), "Ahora Quien" and "Valio la Pena" (both in 2004), and "Que Precio Tiene el Cielo" (2006). Lopez, or J-Lo as she came to be known, also broke out in 1999 with the back-to-back hits "If You Had My Love" and "Waiting for Tonight." Those hits were followed with several throughout the 2000s: "Let's Get Loud" and "Love Don't Cost a Thing" (both in 2000), "I'm Real" (2001), "Jenny from the Block" and "All I Have" with LL Cool J (born James Smith in 1968) in 2002, and "Get Right" (2005). J-Lo continued her movie career throughout the 2000s and beyond and became a judge on *American Idol* in 2010.

Latino rapper Pitbull (born Armando Perez in 1981) burst onto the music scene in the 2000s. Though limited in singles success in the 2000s, "Mr. Worldwide" did have back-to-back chart-topping albums: *M.I.A.M.I.* (2004), *El Mariel* (2006), *The Boatlift* (2007), and *Pitbull Starring in Rebelution* (2009). His Top Ten singles from the decade included "Culo" (2004) and "The Anthem" (2007), both with Lil Jon (born Jonathan Smith in 1973). His biggest hits came in 2009: "I Know You Want Me (Calle Ocho)" and "Hotel Room Service." He remained a considerable success on the dance charts well into the 2010s.

Perhaps the biggest Latina sensation of the 2000s was artist Shakira, born in Colombia in 1977 as Shakira Isabel Mebarak Ripoll to a Lebanese Arab father and Colombian mother. "Shakira" is Arabic for "grateful." Topping American Spanish-speaking charts since 1995's "Estoy Aqui," Shakira broke into the English-speaking U.S. charts with "Whenever, Wherever/Suerte" in 2000. That hit was followed by several throughout the decade: "Underneath Your

Clothes" and "Objection (Tango)" (both in 2001); "La Tortura," with Alejandro Sanz (b. 1968) in 2005; "Hips Don't Lie" with Wyclef Jean (born Nel Ust Wyclef Jean in 1969) in 2006; "Beautiful Liar" with Beyoncé (2007); and "She Wolf" (2009). Shakira continued to top American and international charts well into the 2010s.

As the 2000s came to a close, two future pop superstars made their debut as one of the greatest of all time came to a tragic end. Canadian-born Justin Bieber (b. 1994) was discovered at the age of thirteen due to his popular YouTube videos covering popular songs. As the 2000s ended, Bieber became an overnight superstar with early hits "One Time" and "One Less Lonely Girl" (both in 2009), before his breakthrough hit, "Baby" (2010). Around the same time, New Yorker Lady Gaga launched her debut album, *The Fame* (2008). That album charted three Top Five hits: "Just Dance" and "Poker Face" (both in 2008) and "Paparazzi" (2009). Before the decade ended, Lady Gaga had her breakout number-one hit, "Bad Romance" (2009). Lady Gaga would go on to dominate charts—and eventually the big and small screens—in the 2010s, becoming a major proponent for LGBTQ+ rights and an icon to that community.

On June 25, 2009, the world was shocked to learn of the death of the undisputed King of Pop, Michael Jackson, at the age of fifty. Jackson had become a pop superstar in the 1970s along with his brothers as part of the Motown group the Jackson 5. He finally broke from his childhood shadow and that of his brothers with his 1979 solo album, *Off the Wall*. In 1982, his album *Thriller* became the highest selling album globally of all time (a record it still presently holds). In the 1990s, Jackson's career took a serious setback due to numerous allegations of child molestation. Although his sexuality was always a matter of some public debate, he was married twice, first to Lisa Marie Presley, b. 1968; daughter of the King of Rock-n-Roll, Elvis Presley, and then Debbie Rowe, b. 1958; with whom he had two of his three children, Michael Jr. and daughter Paris. In 2003, Jackson was formally charged on seven counts of child molestation and two counts of providing alcohol to minors. He was found not guilty on all counts in 2005.

After serious financial setbacks leading him to lose his beloved estate, Neverland Ranch, Jackson announced in the spring of 2009 that he would be conducting one final world tour, titled This Is It. Jackson died on June 25 due to cardiac arrest brought on by an overdose of propofol, a powerful sedative, that had been administered to him by his personal physician (along with two other medications) to help him sleep. Despite lingering questions regarding the pop star's sexual preference as well as the accusations of child molestation, what cannot be denied are the contributions that Michael Jackson made to popular music throughout his four-decade career.

HIP-HOP/RAP/R&B/SOUL

Since the 1980s, hip-hop/rap had become a growing force in American popular music; and in the 2000s, it, along with sister genres R&B and soul, dominated popular culture with some of the most amazing performers in the genre's history. Originally hitting the mainstream with the Sugarhill Gang's

"Rapper's Delight" (1979), the genre rocketed to the top of pop charts with Run-DMC's cover of Aerosmith's "Walk This Way" (1986; original version, 1975). In the 1990s, hip-hop/rap took a more political turn with artist such as Dr. Dre (born Andre Young in 1965), Ice-T (born Tracy Marrow in 1958), Ice Cube (born O'Shea Jackson in 1969), and—perhaps the most influential rapper of all time—Tupac Shakur (born Lesane Crooks, 1971–1996). In the decades since its inception, hip-hop/rap has transcended its inner-city origins to become a dominant force in American popular music in the twenty-first century, and the artists who produce it have become household names.

Rapper 50 Cent (born Curtis Jackson III in 1975) had a background that has become synonymous, to the point of stereotypical, of mainstream rappers: a Black kid from a New York inner-city borough (Queens) who got in trouble with the law (selling drugs) and broke into rap music, speaking to the inner-city experience of the minority male in America. He dominated music charts in 2003 with back-to-back hits: "In da Club," "21 Questions" with Nate Dog (born Nathaniel Hale, 1969–2011), and "P.I.M.P." with Snoop Dogg, Lloyd Banks (born Christopher Lloyd in 1982), and Young Buck (born David Brown in 1981). He hit again in 2007 with "Ayo Technology" with Justin Timberlake. 50 Cent's career almost ended before it had really begun when he was shot nine times outside his grandmother's home in 2000, just as his debut album was set to release. His career then took another hit when, as he was recovering from the gunshot wounds, his label, Columbia Records, dropped him and blacklisted him in the entire industry due to his 1999 song "Ghetto Qu'ran." The rapper was tenacious, however, and overcame the blacklisting to go on to become one of the most popular rappers of the 2000s.

The early 2000s saw the rise of two iconic female performers. Alicia Keyes (b. 1981) was a child protégée who began writing songs as a preteen. She had numerous hits in the decade, including "Fallin'" (2001); "You Don't Know My Name" (2003); "If I Ain't Got You," "Diary" with Tony! Toni! Tone! (f. 1988), and "My Boo" with Usher (born Usher Raymond IV in 1978), all in 2004; and "No One" (2007). One of her most iconic songs of the period was "Empire State of Mind" (2009), which she recorded with Jay-Z. Though the song was not directly related to 9/11, its expression of the strength, resilience, and diversity of New York City very much defined how the city was perceived internationally since the terrorist attacks of 2001. Ashanti (born Ashanti Douglas in 1980) burst on to the music scene in 2002, featured in two of that year's biggest songs: "What's Luv?" with Fat Joe (born Joseph Cartagena in 1970) and "Always on Time" with Ja Rule (born Jeffrey Atkins in 1976). She also had her own number-one hit that year with "Foolish." Since her early successes, she has also found fame through songwriting, record producing, and acting.

Without question, however, the biggest female artist of the 2000s was Beyoncé (born Beyoncé Knowles in 1981). The Houston, Texas, native entered the decade as the lead singer of the wildly popular girl group Destiny's Child, along with Kelly Rowland (b. 1981) and Michelle Williams (b. 1979). The trio stormed into the decade like an unstoppable force with back-to-back hits: "Say My Name," "Jumpin', Jumpin'," and "Independent Women, Part I" (all in 2000); "Survivor" and "Bootylicious" (both in 2001); and "Lose My Breath" (2004).

Beyoncé's outgoing charm and presence soon led her to strike out on a solo career. She hit charts right away in 2003 with "Crazy in Love" with future husband, Jay-Z. Her other hits from the decade include "Naughty Girl" (2004), "Irreplaceable" (2006), "Beautiful Liar" with Shakira (2007), and, perhaps her biggest hit to date, "Single Ladies (Put a Ring on It)" (2008). She ended the decade in 2009 with two more hits: "Halo" and "Sweet Dreams." In 2008, Beyoncé and Jay-Z were married, creating the most powerful supercouple in the music industry.

Jay-Z is one of the most legendary figures in hip-hop/rap history. Beginning his music career in 1995, he has become one of the most powerful record producers in the music industry. His personal hits from the 2000s include "I Just Wanna Love U (Give It 2 Me)" (2000); "03 Bonnie & Clyde" with Beyoncé (2002); "Excuse Me Miss" and "Change Clothes" both with Pharrell (born Pharrell Williams in 1973) in 2003; "Show Me What You Got" (2006); "Swagga Like Us" with T.I., Lil Wayne, and Kanye West (2008); and "Run This Town" with Kanye West and Rihanna and "Empire State of Mind" with Alicia Keyes (both in 2009). With wife Beyoncé, Jay-Z has gone on to dominate the music industry well into the 2010s.

One of the more controversial rappers to come on to the scene in the 2000s was Chris Brown (b. 1989). His hits from the decade include "Run It!" with Juelz Santana (born LaRon James in 1982) in 2005, "Say Goodbye" (2006), "Kiss Kiss" with T-Pain (born Faheem Najm in 1985) and "With You" (both in 2007), and "No Air" with Jordin Sparks (b. 1989) and "Forever" (both in 2008). In 2009, Brown met controversy and a considerable career setback when he was charged with felony assault for a domestic dispute with current girlfriend and fellow music star Rihanna (born Robin Rihanna Fenty in 1988). Brown took a guilty plea with five years of probation, community service, and required counseling. Although his career would rebound in the 2010s, because his victim was such a high-profile and popular celebrity herself, Brown's public image remains justifiably tainted.

Throughout the history of rap music, white performers have gained little recognition or spotlight. The most famous exception to this is the artist known as Eminem (born Marshall Mathers III in 1972). Not only did Eminem stand out as a white artist in a predominantly Black genre, but he was also from the Midwest (St. Joseph, Michigan) rather than the inner cities of the coasts. He burst onto the music scene in 2000 with back-to-back hits "The Real Slim Shady" and "Stan" featuring Dido (born Dido Florian Cloud de Bounevialle O'Malley Armstrong in 1971). He had additional back-to-back hits in 2002 with "Without Me," "Cleanin' Out My Closet," and "Lose Yourself," the last coming from the soundtrack to his feature film debut, 8 Mile. His other hits from the decade include "Just Lose It" (2004), "Mockingbird" and "When I'm Gone" (both in 2005), and "Crack a Bottle" with Dr. Dre and 50 Cent and "We Made You" (both in 2009).

Perhaps the most over-the-top and complex artists in music in the twenty-first century, Kanye West (b. 1977) has become pop culture royalty in his own right. After some lackluster chart performance early in the decade, Kanye broke through with his smash hit single "Gold Digger" (2005). The main lyrics were interspersed with samples from the classic Ray Charles (1930–2004) hit "I Got a Woman" (1954) sung by famous comedy actor and singer Jamie Foxx (born Eric Bishop in 1967) who had just played the iconic blues/R&B singer in the film *Ray* (2004). Kanye would go on to have other hits throughout the decade: "Stronger" and "Good Life" featuring T-Pain (both in 2007); "Love Lockdown" and "Heartless" (both in 2008); and "Forever" with Drake (born Aubrey Drake Graham in 1986), Lil Wayne, and Eminem in 2009. His 2014 marriage to reality-show superstar Kim Kardashian (b. 1980) secured his status as pop culture icon.

A very popular artist from the decade that many other artists were eager to work with was Lil Wayne (born Dwayne Carter Jr. in 1982). Working with big names from Destiny's Child and Shakira to T-Pain and Chris Brown, one would be hard-pressed to find a hip-hop/rap chart in the 2000s without Lil Wayne's name appearing somewhere. His own hits from the decade include "Go DJ" (2004); "Stuntin' Like My Daddy" with Birdman, b. 1969 (2006); "Lollipop" with Static Major (born Stephen Garrett, 1974–2008), "A Milli," "Got Money" with T-Pain, and "Mrs. Officer" with Bobby Valentino (born Bobby Wilson in 1980) and Kidd Kidd (born Curtis Stewart in 1986), all in 2008. Throughout the 2010s, Lil Wayne would struggle with epilepsy and would have several high-profile seizures throughout the decade.

Prior to becoming a successful actor, rapper Ludacris (born Christopher Bridges in 1977) was one of the more successful rap artists of the 2000s. He is a cousin of legendary comedian Richard Pryor (1940–2005). Since 2001, he has appeared in thirty-five feature films, television series, and documentaries. His music hits from the period include "Stand Up" with Shawnna (born Rashawnna Guy in 1978) and "Splash Waterfalls" (both in 2003), "Get Back" (2004), "Pimpin' All over the World" with Bobby V (born Bobby Wilson in 1980) and "Number One Spot" (both in 2005), "Money Maker" with Pharrell (2006), "Runaway Love" with Mary J. Blige (2007), "One More Drink" with T-Pain (2008), and "How Low" (2009). He also provided guest vocals on several big hits from the decade: "Yeah!" with Usher (2004) and "Glamorous" with Fergie (2007).

One of the most iconic female artists of any genre of recent decades has been Mary J. Blige (b. 1971). Like Ludacris, Blige is a musical artist and actor. She has worked with some of the biggest names in hip-hop/R&B, including Jay-Z and Sean "Puff Daddy" Combs. Her hits from the period include "Family Affair" (2001), "Be without You" (2005), "Enough Cryin" and "Take Me as I Am" (both in 2006), "Just Fine" (2007), and "I Am" (2009). In the 2010s, she would become more focused on acting—particularly in music-related projects. She was a judge on *American Idol* in 2010 and 2012 and starred as the Wicked Witch of the West in the live televised broadcast of *The Wiz* in 2015. Another popular Black female artist from the 1990s who continued her career into the 2000s was Missy Elliott (b. 1971). Her biggest hits from the decade were "Get Ur Freak On" (2001), "Work It" (2002), and "Lose Control" with Ciara (born Ciara Harris in 1985) and Fatman Scoop (born Isaac Freeman III in 1971) in 2005. She was also featured in Ciara's "1, 2 Step" (2004) and alongside Lil' Kim in Keyshia Cole's (b. 1981) "Let It Go" (2007).

Nas (born Nasir bin Olu Dara Jones in 1973) began his rap career in the 1990s. For the first half of the 2000s, Nas partook in a highly publicized feud with Jay-Z, which appears to have begun with Jay-Z releasing songs that dissed Nas, presenting the younger rapper as a fraud (for reasons that are unclear). Nas responded in kind, and the two continued their public exchange of insults until around 2005, just prior to Nas signing on with Def Jam Records, run by Russell Simmons (b. 1957), who was even more powerful and influential in the business than Jay-Z. Nas's hits from the early 2000s include "Got Ur Self A . . ." (2001), "One Mic" (2002), and "Made You Look" and "I Can" (both in 2003). Nas has not hit the Top Thirty on any U.S. chart since 2003.

Missouri native Nelly (born Cornell Haynes in 1974) began his career in 1993 before signing on with Universal Records before the dawn of the new century. His hits included "Country Grammar (Hot Shit)" (2000), "Ride wit Me" with City Spud (born Lavell Webb in 1975) in 2001, "Hot in Herre" and "Dilemma" with Kelly Rowland (both in 2002), "Shake Ya Tailfeather" with P. Diddy (born Sean Combs in 1969) and Murphy Lee (born Torhi Harper) in 2003, and "My Place" with Jaheim (born Jaheim Hoagland in 1978) and "Over and Over" with Tim McGraw (b. 1967), both in 2004. He was also a featured guest on hit singles from stars such as NSYNC, P. Diddy, and Janet Jackson.

The hip-hop duo Outkast consisted of artists Andre 3000 (born Andre Benjamin in 1975) and Big Boi (born Antwan Patton in 1975). They were pioneers of the subgenre of southern rap (also known as Dirty South): a version of hip-hop/rap that emerged from the southern United States in places such as Atlanta, Georgia; New Orleans, Louisiana; and Miami, Florida. The two performed together from 1992 to 2006 and reunited in 2014. Their biggest hits from the 2000s were "Ms. Jackson" (2000), "Hey Ya!" and "The Way You Move" with Sleepy Brown (born Patrick Brown in 1970), both in 2003, and "Roses" (2004). "Hey Ya!" went on to be the duo's biggest hit ever, topping numerous charts in the United States and around the world.

One of the most powerful individuals in rap music in the 2000s was Sean Combs (b. 1969). Also known by his various professional names—Puff Daddy, P. Diddy, Puffy, and Diddy—Combs came into the decade as a popular rapper and left it a powerhouse in the industry, one of its most prolific producers and talent scouts, through his record label, Bad Boy Entertainment (f. 1993). He spent the first half of the decade going by P. Diddy before changing mid-decade to Diddy. In 2002, he released the back-to-back singles "I Need a Girl (Parts One and Two)." The first featured Usher and Loon (born Chauncy Hawkins in 1975). The follow-up saw the return of Loon along with Ginuwine (born Elgin Lumpkin in 1970) and Mario Winans (birthdate unknown). In 2003, Diddy released the hit "Shake Ya Tailfeather" with Nelly and Murphy Lee (born Torhi Harper).

In 2005, Def Jam Records signed a young up-and-coming singer from Barbados, Rihanna (born Robyn Rihanna Fenty in 1988). She was an immediate success, with a chain of chart-topping hits throughout the rest of the decade. Her hit singles included "Pon de Replay" (2005); "SOS," "Unfaithful," and "Break It Off" with Sean Paul (born Sean Paul Francis Henriques in 1973), all in 2006;

her two biggest hits of the decade, "Umbrella" with Jay-Z and "Don't Stop the Music" (both in 2007; "Take a Bow" and "Disturbia" (both in 2008); and "Russian Roulette" (2009). Her second-biggest hit was as a backup for Eminem on his 2010 song "Love the Way You Lie." As mentioned earlier, Rihanna was abused in 2009 by then-boyfriend Chris Brown.

Two artists in the 2000s became popular for their collaborations with other established artists but also made names for themselves in the area of record production and songwriting. One was T-Pain (born Faheem Rasheed Najm in 1985). Working with nearly every hip-hop/rap artist of the period, his most notable collaborations in the 2000s were on the songs "Kiss Kiss" with Chris Brown and "Low" with Flo Rida (born Tramar Lacel Dillard in 1979), both in 2007. He also collaborated with Jamie Foxx on his 2009 song "Blame It." In 2019, T-Pain won the first season of the television singing-competition program *The Masked Singer* (FOX, 2019–present), performing behind the costumed persona of "the Monster" and showing the world that—outside of rapping, producing, and writing—he possesses an amazing singing voice. Another artist famous for his collaborations is Timbaland. His hits in the 2000s included "Give It to Me" with Nelly Furtado (b. 1978) and Justin Timberlake, "The Way I Are" with Keri Hilson (b. 1982), and "Apologize (Remix)" with OneRepublic, all in 2007. He also collaborated with Timberlake and Madonna on their 2008 hit, "4 Minutes."

One of the most successful musical artists of the last quarter-century has been Usher. Beginning his career in 1994, Usher was already topping charts before the twenty-first century began. His chain of hip-hop hits in the 2000s included "U Remind Me" and "U Got It Bad" (both in 2001); "U Don't Have to Call" (2002); "Yeah!" with Lil Jon and Ludacris, "Burn," "Confessions, Part II," and "My Boo" with Alicia Keyes, all in 2004; "Love in This Club" with Young Jeezy (born Jay Wayne Jenkins in 1977) and "Love in This Club, Part II" with Beyoncé and Lil Wayne, both in 2008.

While the 2000s saw some amazing hip-hop/rap artists emerge and thrive, however, the decade also bade farewell to many great artists, some passing long before their time. Young hip-hop artist Aaliyah (born Aaliyah Haughton in 1979) died unexpectedly in a plane crash in the Bahamas on August 25, 2001. She was twenty-two years old. In 2002, Lisa "Left Eye" Lopes (b. 1971) of the hit 1990s R&B group TLC died in a car crash. She was thirty years old. That same year, rap pioneer Jam Master Jay (born Jason William Mizell in 1965) of the rap group Run-DMC was shot and killed. He was thirty-seven years old. On July 4, 2003, R&B legend Barry White (born Barry Carter in 1944) died from a stroke at the age of fifty-eight.

Another R&B legend—one of the most iconic performers of all time—Ray Charles (born Ray Charles Robinson in 1930) died on June 10, 2004, of liver failure at age seventy-three. Just a couple months later, on August 6, funk superstar Rick James (born James Johnson Jr. in 1948), passed away of heart failure at the age of fifty-six. On Christmas Day 2006, the Godfather of Soul, James Brown (b. 1933), died at the age of seventy-three from heart failure brought on by severe pneumonia. Funk/soul artist Isaac Hayes (b. 1942), most known for his iconic theme song for the 1971 film *Shaft* as well as the voice for the character Chef on the hit animated series *South Park* (Comedy Central, 1997–present), died of a stroke on August 10, 2008, just shy of his sixty-sixth birthday.

COUNTRY

Country music in the 2000s became more mainstream, crossing more and more on to pop charts, due in no small part to the events of 9/11 and the genre's already substantial connection to patriotism and Americana. Country artists from the decade ran the gambit from traditional country/western music of Toby Keith and Alan Jackson to more of a country/pop subgenre with up-and-coming artists such as Carrie Underwood and Taylor Swift. The decade would see one-time rapper Kid Rock blend his genre in with traditional country music, becoming more recognized for the latter than the former by decade's end. Also, like all other genres discussed above, country music would say good-bye to longtime legends before the decade was done.

Alan Jackson remains one of the more popular classic country artists in the twenty-first century. The Georgia native has won nearly every award that country music offers. His hits from the 2000s include "It Must Be Love" and "www.memory" (both in 2000); "When Somebody Loves You," "Where I Come From," and his 9/11 tribute, "Where Were You (When the World Stopped Turning)" (all in 2001); "Drive (for Daddy Gene)," "Work in Progress," and "That'd Be Alright" (all in 2002); "It's Five O'Clock Somewhere" with Jimmy Buffett (b. 1946) and "Remember When" (both in 2003); "Small Town Southern Man" (2007); and "Good Time" and "Country Boy" (both in 2008).

Another country artist along the classical vein is Alison Krauss (b. 1971). She began performing professionally at age fourteen. Krauss began playing with her backup band, Union Station, in 1989. Her hits in the early twenty-first century included "The Lucky One" (2001), "Restless" (2004), and a cover of John Waite's 1980s love song "Missing You," which she recorded with Waite (b. 1952) in 2007. Her biggest hits from the decade were "Whiskey Lullaby" with Brad Paisley (b. 1972) in 2004 and "Gone, Gone, Gone (Done Moved On)" with former Led Zeppelin front man Robert Plant (b. 1948) in 2007. Her cover of the song "Down to the River to Pray" (2000) is widely considered one of the most beautiful renditions of that song.

The modern country duo Big & Rich debuted in 1998. The team consists of Big Kenny (born William Kenneth Alphin in 1963) and John Rich (b. 1974). In the 2000s alone, they picked up more than thirty awards for their music. Their biggest hits from the decade include "Save a Horse (Ride a Cowboy)" and "Holy Water" (both in 2004), "8th of November" (2006), and their biggest hit of the decade, "Lost in This Moment" (2007). In 2006, along with Gretchen Wilson (b. 1973) and Van Zant (a duo consisting of Donnie and Johnny Van Zant, born 1952 and 1960, respectively, brothers to Lynyrd Skynyrd front man Ronnie Van Zant, 1948–1977), they were featured on the song "That's How They Do It in Dixie" by country legend Hank Williams Jr. (b. 1949). In 2007, the duo released a cover of the 1980 AC/DC hit "You Shook Me All Night Long."

One country artist to debut in the decade was Blake Shelton (b. 1976). His hits from his first decade included "Austin" (2001), "The Baby" (2002), "Some Beach" (2004), "Nobody but Me" (2005), "Home" and "She Wouldn't Be Gone" (both in 2008), and "I'll Just Hold On" and "Hillbilly Bone" with Trace Adkins (b. 1962), both in 2009. Since 2011, Shelton has been a coach on the long-running television talent program *The Voice* (NBC, 2011–present). From 2011 to 2015, Shelton was married to fellow country artist Miranda Lambert, and since his divorce, he married fellow *Voice* coach, Gwen Stefani in 2015.

Brad Paisley (b. 1972) carries on the tradition of a more classic style of country/western music in the 2000s. Throughout the decade, Paisley had a long, unbroken chain of Top Five hits, most of them reaching number one on the country charts. These songs include "We Danced" (2000); "Two People Fell in Love" and "Wrapped Around" (both in 2001); "I'm Gonna Miss Her (The Fishin' Song)" (2002); "Celebrity" and "Little Moments" (both in 2003); "Whiskey Lullaby" with Alison Krauss and "Mud on the Tires" (both in 2004); "Alcohol" and "When I Get Where I'm Going" with Dolly Parton (born 1946), both in 2005; "The World" and "She's Everything" (both in 2006); "Ticks," "Online," and "Letter to Me" (all in 2007); "I'm Still a Guy," "Star a Band" with Keith Urban (b. 1967), and "Waitin' on a Woman" (all in 2008); and "Then," "Welcome to the Future," and "American Saturday Night" (all in 2009). He continued to dominate the Top Ten country charts well into the 2010s.

Carrie Underwood (b. 1983) was voted the fourth American Idol on the television singing competition of the same name in 2005. From that point on, Underwood went on to massive success in country music. She had an impressive list of number-one hits in the last half of the 2000s, including "Inside Your Heaven" and "Jesus, Take the Wheel" (both in 2005); "Before He Cheats" (2006); "Wasted" and "So Small" (both in 2007); "All-American Girl," "Last Name," and "Just a Dream" (all in 2008); and "Cowboy Casanova" and "Temporary Home" (both in 2009). Also in 2009, Underwood recorded a cover of Randy Travis's "I Told You So" with the legendary Travis (b. 1959).

New Zealand–born Keith Urban (b. 1967) made his U.S. debut in 1999. He, too, had a long chain of Top Five hits throughout the decade: "Your Everything" and "But for the Grace of God" (both in 2000); "Where the Blacktop Ends" (2001); "Somebody Like You" (2002); "Raining on Sunday" and "Who Wouldn't Wanna Be Me" (both in 2003); "You'll Think of Me," "Days Go By," and "You're My Better Half" (all in 2004); "Making Memories of Us," "Better Life," and "Tonight I Wanna Cry" (all in 2005); "Stupid Boy" (2006); "I Told You So" (not to be confused with the Randy Travis classic) and "Everybody" (both in 2007); "You Look Good in My Shirt" and "Sweet Thing" (both in 2008); and "Kiss a Girl," "Only You Can Love Me This Way," and "Till Summer Comes Around" (all in 2009). In 2006, Urban married Hollywood actress Nicole Kidman (b. 1967), and in the 2010s, he has served as a coach and judge on *The Voice* and *American Idol*.

Another country artist along the more classic vein is Kenny Chesney (b. 1968). Popular since the mid-1990s, Chesney's long list of number-one hits in the 2000s include "Don't Happen Twice" (2001); "The Good Stuff" (2002);

"No Shoes, No Shirt, No Problem" and "There Goes My Life" (both in 2003); "When the Sun Goes Down" with Uncle Kracker (born Matthew Shafer in 1974), in 2004; "Anything but Mine" (2005); "Living in Fast Forward" and "Summertime" (both in 2006); "Beer in Mexico," "Never Wanted Nothing More," and "Don't Blink" (all in 2007); "Better as a Memory," "Everybody Wants to Go to Heaven" with the Wailers, the former backup band for reggae legend Bob Marley (1945–1981), and "Down the Road" with Mac McAnally (born Lyman McAnally Jr. in 1957), all in 2008; and "Out Last Night" (2009).

Popular rapper Kid Rock made the transition to country music in the 2000s, due largely to his close friendship with country legend Hank Williams Jr. His biggest hits in this genre were "Picture" with Sheryl Crow (b. 1962) in 2002 and his rap/rock/country hybrid hit "All Summer Long" in 2008. "All Summer Long" was a massive hit across all genres due to its sampling of the two rock classics "Sweet Home Alabama" by Lynyrd Skynyrd (f. 1964) from 1974 and "Werewolves of London" by Warren Zevon (1947–2003) from 1978. In the 2010s, Kid Rock has experienced considerable ostracism in the hip-hop and rock communities due to his radically conservative political views.

Miranda Lambert was born in Texas in 1983. In 2003, she was the second runner-up on the country-television singing-competition program *Nashville Star* (USA, 2003–2007; NBC, 2008). She had several Top Forty country hits in the 2000s, including "Me and Charlie Talking" (2004); "Bring Me Down" and "Kerosene" (both in 2005); "New Strings" (2006); "Famous in a Small Town" (2007); "Gunpowder & Lead" and "More Like Her" (both in 2008); and "Dead Flowers" and her biggest hit of the decade, "White Liar" (both in 2009). Her career became even more successful in the 2010s.

One of the biggest music stars of the 2000s across all genres of music burst on to the scene in 2006. Taylor Swift (b. 1989) was only seventeen when she was launched to overnight superstardom. Her Top Forty hits from the 2000s include "Tim McGraw" (2006); "Teardrops on My Guitar" and "Our Song" (both in 2007); "Picture to Burn," "Should've Said No," "Change," "Love Story," and "White Horse" (all in 2008); and "You Belong with Me" and "Fifteen" (both in 2009). In 2009, as Swift was accepting the award for Best Female Video for her song "You Belong with Me" at the MTV Video Music Awards, an awkward moment arose when controversial hip-hop artist Kanye West interrupted her speech to insist that Beyoncé should have won for "Single Ladies."

By far the biggest power couple in country music throughout the 2000s was Tim McGraw (b. 1967) and his wife, Faith Hill (born Audrey Faith Perry in 1967). The two have had a chain of chart-topping hits both together and as solo artists. McGraw's number-one hits from the 2000s include "My Next Thirty Years" (2000); "Grown Men Don't Cry," "Angry All the Time," and "The Cowboy in Me" (all in 2001); "Unbroken" (2002); "Real Good Man" and "Watch the Wind Blow By" (both in 2003); "Live Like You Were Dying" and "Back When" (both in 2004); "Last Dollar (Fly Away)" (2007); and "Southern Voice" (2009). Hill's number-one hits from the decade were "The Way You Love Me" (2000) and "Mississippi Girl" (2005). The two had Top Ten hits with "Let's Make Love" (2000) and "I Need You" (2007). McGraw continued to top charts throughout the 2010s.

Toby Keith (born Toby Keith Covel in 1961) sprang onto the country music scene in the 1990s. He was one of the first artists of any genre to release a song in response to the 9/11 terrorist attacks in 2001. His number-one hits from the 2000s included "You Shouldn't Kiss Me Like This" (2000); "I'm Just Talkin' about Tonight" and "I Wanna Talk about Me" (both in 2001); "My List," "Courtesy of the Red, White and Blue (The Angry American)," and "Who's Your Daddy?" (all in 2002); "Beer for My Horses" with country music legend Willie Nelson (b. 1933), "I Love This Bar," and "American Soldier" (all in 2003); "Whiskey Girl" (2004); "As Good as I Once Was" (2005); "Love Me If You Can" (2007); "She Never Cried in Front of Me" and "God Love Her" (both in 2008); and "American Ride" (2009).

Another artist to hit the mainstream around the same time as Keith was Trace Adkins (b. 1962). Very similar in tone and style to Keith's brand of more classic country music, Adkins also had a very successful decade in the 2000s. He hit the Top Ten with the following songs: "I'm Tryin'" (2001); "Chrome" (2002); "Then They Do" and "Hot Mama" (both in 2003); "Songs about Me" (2004); "Honky Tonk Badonkadonk" (2005); and the number-one hit "Ladies Love Country Boys" (2006) and, lastly, "You're Gonna Miss This" (2008).

Like the other genres of popular music mentioned above, country music lost some of its most legendary performers in the 2000s. Waylon Jennings (1937–2002) was one of the pioneers of the outlaw movement in country music in the 1970s. Two of his biggest hits were the number-one songs "I'm a Ramblin' Man" (1974) and "Luckenbach, Texas (Back to the Basics of Love)" (1977). He was perhaps most widely known for being the narrator and singer of the theme song for the wildly popular television series *The Dukes of Hazzard* (CBS, 1979–1985). He passed away on February 13, 2002, of complications from diabetes. His legacy lives on, not only through his impressive catalog of hits but also through his son, Waylon "Shooter" Jennings (b. 1979), who has gained a considerable following for his blend of country and rock since his father's passing.

The following year, the world lost two true American legends. Johnny Cash (1932–2003) and his wife June Carter Cash (1929–2003) are country music icons. Their storied romance was the basis for the 2005 film *Walk the Line*, starring Joaquin Phoenix (b. 1974) and Reese Witherspoon (b. 1976). Their list of hits could fill volumes. June died on May 15, 2003, from complications from heart surgery. Johnny followed shortly after, on September 12, most presume from a broken heart. In his last few months of life, Cash recorded three songs that have come to be some of his most popular: "Hurt" (a cover of the Nine Inch Nails hit from 1994) in 2003; "God's Gonna Cut You Down" (2006); and "Ain't No Grave" (2010). The losses of Jennings, Carter, and Cash were devastating to generations of country music fans around the world.

As the above-mentioned artists—just a small sampling of the decade—prove, the 2000s was an amazing decade for American popular music, across all genres. New faces arrived on the scene just as longtime legends took their final bows. Despite the given moniker of the Deleted Years, the artists and songs listed here will long outlive the period that spawned them. During a decade of healing from the worst disaster in American history, music artists from across the spectrum came together to provide comfort, inspiration, and hope to a country desperately in need of all three. Their contributions to American society during its darkest hour will never be forgotten.

FURTHER READING

Bailey, Julius, ed. 2015. *The Cultural Impact of Kanye West*. London: Palgrave Macmillan.

Breihan, Tom. 2011. "VH1 100 Greatest Songs of the '00s." Stereogum, September 29. https://www.stereogum.com/826992/vh1-100-greatest-songs-of-the-00s/fran chises/list/. Retrieved November 23, 2019.

Chambers, Veronica. 2019. *Queen Bey: A Celebration of the Power and Creativity of Beyoncé Knowles-Carter*. New York: St. Martin's.

Chang, Jeff. 2005. *Can't Stop Won't Stop: A History of the Hip-Hop Generation*. London: Picador.

Charnas, Dan. 2011. *The Big Payback: The History of the Business of Hip-Hop*. New York: Berkley.

Chomsky, Noam. 2005. *Imperial Ambitions: Conversations on the Post-9/11 World*. New York: Metropolitan.

Crowson, H. Michael, Teresa K. Debacker, and Stephen J. Thoma. 2006. "The Role of Authoritarianism, Perceived Threat, and Need for Closure or Structure in Predicting Post-9/11 Attitudes and Beliefs." *Journal of Social Psychology* 146, no. 6: 733–750.

Dennis, Steve. 2010. *Britney: Inside the Dream*. New York: Harper.

Dominguez, Pier. 2003. *Christina Aguilera: A Star Is Made*. Dubai: Amber.

Faludi, Susan. 2008. *The Terror Dream: Myth and Misogyny in an Insecure America*. London: Picador.

Fast, Susan, and Kip Pegley, eds. 2012. *Music, Politics, and Violence*. Middletown, CT: Wesleyan University Press.

Ferrence, Matthew J. 2014. *All-American Redneck: Variations on an Icon, from James Fenimore Cooper to the Dixie Chicks*. Knoxville: University of Tennessee Press.

Goodman, Lizzy. 2018. *Meet Me in the Bathroom: Rebirth and Rock and Roll in New York City 2001–2011*. New York: Dey Street Books.

Hal Leonard Corp. 2010. *#1 Country Hits of the 2000s*. Milwaukee, WI: Hal Leonard.

Holmes, Dave. 2019. "A Decade of Music Is Lost on Your iPod. These Are the Deleted Years. Now Let Us Praise Them: From 2003 to 2012 Music Was Disposable and Nothing Survived." *Esquire*, September 4. https://www.esquire.com/entertainment /music/a28904211/2003-to-2012-forgotten-music-era/. Retrieved November 23, 2019.

Isaacson, Walter. 2011. *Steve Jobs*. New York: Simon & Schuster.

Kruse, Kevin M., and Julian E. Zelizer. 2019. *Fault Lines: A History of the United States since 1974*. New York: W. W. Norton.

Malone, Bill C., and Tracey Laird. 2018. *Country Music USA: 50th Anniversary Edition*. Austin: University of Texas Press.

Meacham, Jon, and Tim McGraw. 2019. *Songs of America: Patriotism, Protest, and the Music That Made a Nation*. New York: Random House.

Menn, Joseph. 2003. *All the Rave: The Rise and Fall of Shawn Fanning's Napster*. New York: Crown.

9/11 Memorial. [Posting Date Unknown]. "September 11 Attack Timeline." https:// timeline.911memorial.org/#Timeline/2. Retrieved May 8, 2019.

Oswald, Debra L. 2005. "Understanding Anti-Arab Reactions Post-9/11: The Role of Threats, Social Categories, and Personal Ideologies." *Journal of Applied Social Psychology* 35, no. 9: 1775–1799.

Reed, Ryan. 2018. "Metallica's Kirk Hammett: 'We're Still Right' about Suing Napster." *Rolling Stone*, May 14. https://www.rollingstone.com/music/music-news/metallicas-kirk-hammett-were-still-right-about-suing-napster-630185/. Retrieved November 23, 2019.

Ritter, Jonathan. 2007. *Music in the Post 9/11 World*. London: Routledge.

Rolling Stone. 2011. "100 Best Songs of the 2000s." June 17. https://www.rollingstone.com/music/music-lists/100-best-songs-of-the-2000s-153056/damian-marley-welcome-to-jamrock-159253/. Retrieved November 23, 2019.

Smith, Michael. 2017. *Streaming, Sharing, Stealing: Big Data and the Future of Entertainment*. Cambridge, MA: MIT.

Spears, Britney. 2000. *Britney Spears' Heart to Heart*. New York: Three Rivers.

Starr, Larry, and Christopher Waterman. 2017. *American Popular Music: From Minstrelsy to MP3*. New York: Oxford University Press.

Street, John. 2011. *Music and Politics*. Cambridge: Polity.

Sullivan, Randall. 2012. *Untouchable: The Strange Life and Tragic Death of Michael Jackson*. New York: Grove.

Taraborrelli, J. Randy. 2010. *Michael Jackson: The Magic, the Madness, the Whole Story, 1958–2009*. New York: Grand Central.

Terry, Josh. 2019. "Sixteen Years Later, Country Radio Is Still Mad at the Dixie Chicks." *Vice*, September 10. https://www.vice.com/en_us/article/evjvqe/sixteen-years-later-country-radio-is-still-mad-at-the-dixie-chicks-taylor-swift-soon-youll-get-better. Retrieved November 23, 2019.

Thompson, Gayle. 2019. "16 Years Ago: Natalie Maines Makes Controversial Comments about President George W. Bush." Boot, March 10. https://theboot.com/natalie-maines-dixie-chicks-controversy/. Retrieved November 28, 2019.

Tinsley, Omise'eke Natasha. 2018. *Beyoncé in Formation: Remixing Black Feminism*. Austin: University of Texas Press.

Waldfogel, Joel. 2018. *Digital Renaissance: What Data and Economics Tell Us about the Future of Popular Culture*. Princeton, NJ: Princeton University Press.

Weinstein, Deena. 2015. *Rock'n America: A Social and Cultural History*. Toronto, ON: University of Toronto Press.

Willis, Susan. 2005. *Portents of the Real: A Primer for Post-9/11 America*. London: Verso.

Witt, Stephen. 2016. *How Music Got Free: A Story of Obsession and Invention*. New York: Penguin.

CHAPTER 4

Movies

The 2000s produced some amazing feature films and launched some of the most successful film franchises in Hollywood history. Tom Hanks and Meryl Streep continued their storied careers as two of the most brilliant and prolific actors in the history of the English-speaking world. George Lucas completed his *Star Wars* saga—or so audiences were led to believe at the time—and he, Steven Spielberg, and Harrison Ford brought Indiana Jones back to the big screen. *Saturday Night Live*'s Will Ferrell made the transition from television to feature films to become one of the biggest names in comedy in the twenty-first century. The *Star Trek* franchise saw its biggest big-screen failure, only to be rebooted before the decade's end. Disney made Johnny Depp (b. 1963) an international box-office superstar. DC Comics and Warner Brothers hit and missed with their superhero films, while the massive success of the *X-Men* films for 20th Century Fox and *Spider-Man* at Sony Pictures led Marvel Entertainment to launch its own movie studio and usher in the most successful film franchise in history throughout the 2010s.

DRAMA

American audiences continued to enjoy serious drama in the 2000s, even in the wake of the 9/11 attacks. Many such films were based, sometimes loosely, on historical events, while others were transcribed from popular fiction or nonfiction books. One historical based film was the drama/comedy, or dramedy, film *Almost Famous* (2000). Produced by Columbia Pictures and Dream-Works, the film was directed by Cameron Crowe (b. 1957) and starred Patrick Fugit (b. 1982) as *Rolling Stone* magazine reporter William Miller recalling how, at the age of fifteen, he did his first story for the iconic magazine in the 1970s. Michael Angarano (b. 1987) played the younger Miller. Crowe won the Academy Award for Best Original Screenplay.

A darker film from the same year was *American Psycho* (2000), based on the 1991 novel of the same name by Bret Easton Ellis (b. 1964). The film was produced by Columbia Pictures, directed by Mary Harron (b. 1953), and starred Christian Bale (b. 1974), Willem Dafoe (b. 1955), and Jared Leto (b. 1971). Set in the late 1980s, Bale plays Patrick Bateman, a wealthy New York banker who, through the course of the story, commits several brutal murders, mostly of fellow bankers and businessmen. Only at the end do audiences discover that Bateman has either gotten away with his crimes utterly hallucinated each violent act; either way, he is a psychopath, and he is out there. Many were disturbed by the graphic violence of the film (and the fact that the antagonist failed to see justice), particularly since the film was released only a year after the deadly school shooting at Columbine High School in Columbine, Colorado, where twelve students and a teacher were killed by the two gunmen before the assassins killed themselves.

Having already cemented himself as one of the greatest actors of all time with films such as *Forrest Gump* (1994), *Apollo 13* (1995), and *Saving Private Ryan* (1998), acting legend Tom Hanks (b. 1956) had his first big hit of the new decade with *Cast Away* (2000). In this film, produced by ImageMovers and Playtone and directed by Robert Zemeckis, Hanks plays Chuck Noland, a problem solver for FedEx who also happens to be persnickety about time. When the FedEx plane his is traveling on crashes, killing all but him, he finds himself on a deserted island, with nothing but coconuts, rainwater, and the contents of the surviving FedEx packages to keep him alive. For three-fourths of the film, Hanks is alone, with nothing but a soccer ball he names Wilson to interact with. Hanks was nominated for an Academy Award for Best Actor for this film, the first of many successes throughout the decade.

Will Smith (b. 1968) secured his status as a dramatic actor by portraying heavyweight boxing legend Muhammad Ali (born Cassius Clay Jr., 1942–2016) in the biopic *Ali* (2001). Directed by Michael Mann (b. 1943), the film portrays the life of the sports icon from the years 1964–1974. This period, the most storied of his legendary career, covers Ali's conversion to the religion of Islam, the controversy surrounding his refusal to be drafted to serve in Vietnam, the loss of his title, and his return to the top. Smith was nominated for an Academy Award for Best Actor, along with castmate Jon Voight (b. 1938), though neither achieved the win. From this point on, however, Smith would be known for his dramatic work as equally as for his comedic and action endeavors.

One of the most successful historical epics of modern times was director Ridley Scott's film *Gladiator* (2000), starring Russell Crowe (b. 1964) as the fictional Spanish Roman general Maximus Decimus Meridius and Joaquin Phoenix (b. 1974) as the evil Emperor Commodus (161–192 CE). Meridius's refusal to follow Commodus leads to the Roman officer losing his family, his home, and his freedom, becoming an enslaved gladiator to the new emperor. The film's use of CGI technology for the gladiator bouts against lions and tigers was considered groundbreaking at the time, and Meridius's cry of "Are you not entertained?" became part of the American lexicon. Though possessing several historical inconsistencies, it was a huge box-office success, winning five Academy Awards including Best Picture and Best Actor for Crowe.

Crowe returned the following year with another success: the biographical picture *A Beautiful Mind* (2001). Based on the 1998 book of the same name by journalist Sylvia Nasar (b. 1947), the film tells the story of John Nash (1928–2015), winner of the Nobel Prize in Economics in 1994. Due to his natural gift for deciphering code in his head, he begins working for military intelligence, where he becomes embroiled in Cold War espionage. He is later diagnosed with paranoid schizophrenia, and the film focuses a good deal on his deteriorating mental state and his relationship with his wife, played by Jennifer Connelly (b. 1970). The film won four Academy Awards, including Best Picture, Best Supporting Actress for Connelly, and Best Director for Hollywood legend Ron Howard (b. 1954).

Yet another historically based film that year was *Black Hawk Down* (2001). Based on the 1999 book by Mark Bowden (b. 1951), journalist for the *Atlantic*, the film was produced by Columbia Pictures and directed by Ridley Scott. The movie tells the story of the chaotic events of U.S. special forces and UN peacekeepers assigned to the African nation of Somalia in 1993, specifically about the shooting down of U.S. Army Black Hawk helicopters, with the call signs Super Six One and Super Six Four during a rescue attempt for a fallen comrade. The soldiers bravely fight off Somali militia loyal to warlord Mohamed Farrah Aidid (1934–1996), while air and ground units back them up. The film starred Josh Hartnett (b. 1978) and Ewan McGregor (b. 1971), and it won two Academy Awards, one for sound and the other for editing.

Monster's Ball (2001) was directed by Swiss German filmmaker Marc Forster (b. 1969) and starred Billy Bob Thornton (b. 1955), Heath Ledger (1979–2008), and Halle Berry (b. 1966). Thornton stars as a career corrections officer, working with his son, played by Ledger. Continued disputes between father and son lead the son to die by suicide and the father to retire. Berry, meanwhile, plays the widow of a recently executed prisoner under Thornton's and Ledger's care. Berry's character, Leticia, inadvertently meets Thornton's Hank, and the two strike up a relationship, unaware of their connection. The crux of the film focuses on troubled families. It is most notable for Berry's Academy Award win for Best Leading Actress, the first African American woman to win the award.

Rapper Eminem (born Marshall Mathers III in 1972) made his big screen debut in the film *8 Mile* (2002). Directed by Curtis Hanson (1945–2016), the film tells the story of a white rapper (Eminem) trying to make his way in the African American–dominated field of hip hop. Kim Basinger (b. 1953) played the rapper's troubled mother, and Brittany Murphy (1977–2009) as his girlfriend. The film won the Academy Award for Best Song ("Lose Yourself"), making Eminem the first rap/hip-hop artist to win the award.

Tom Hanks returned the following year with anther biopic, *Catch Me If You Can* (2002), directed by Steven Spielberg (b. 1946) and produced by his Amblin Entertainment. The film starred Leonardo DiCaprio (b. 1974) as professional con man Frank Abagnale Jr. (b. 1948) and Hanks as fictional FBI agent Carl Hanratty, based on real FBI agent Joseph Shea (1919–2005). Their game of cat and mouse eventually leads to Abagnale's capture and sentence of working for the FBI. The film received two Academy Award nominations: Best Score and Best Supporting Actor for Christopher Walken (b. 1943), who played Abagnale's father. Although it did not receive Academy recognition, the film did gain DiCaprio considerable attention for his growing acting skills.

That reputation would be enhanced further with *Gangs of New York* (2002), directed by Martin Scorsese (b. 1942) and based on the 1927 historical book of the same name by Herbert Asbury (1889–1963). Set during the New York City Draft Riots of 1863 protesting conscription in the American Civil War, the story is set primarily around the already-existent tension between poor Protestants and Catholics in the city. Leo DiCaprio played Irish-Catholic leader "Priest" Amsterdam Vallon, and Daniel Day-Lewis (b. 1957) played William "Bill the Butcher" Cutting, leader of the Protestant nativists. Though the film was nominated for ten Academy Awards, it won none, and DiCaprio was once more denied a nomination.

Another historical film—this time a biopic—was *Frida* (2002). Directed by Julie Taymor (b. 1952), the film was based on the book *Frida: A Biography of Frida Kahlo,* by art historian Hayden Herrera (b. 1940). Starring and coproduced by Salma Hayek (b. 1966), the film tells the life story of the iconic Mexican artist and communist revolutionary Frida Kahlo (1907–1954). The film also starred Alfred Molina (b. 1953) as Frida's equally iconic artist husband, Diego Rivera (1886–1957). The film was nominated for six Academy Awards, including a Best Actress nomination for Hayek, winning only two—for makeup and original score.

By 2000, Meryl Streep (b. 1949) was already considered one of the greatest actresses to ever grace the silver screen, and her performance in *The Hours* (2002) only enhanced her reputation. Directed by Stephen Daldry (b. 1960) and based on the Pulitzer Prize–winning 1998 novel by Michael Cunningham (b. 1952), the film tells the stories of three women, from three generations, connected through the Virginia Woolf (1882–1941) novel *Mrs. Dalloway* (1925). Streep plays a woman in the early twenty-first century dealing with a friend suffering from AIDS. Julianne Moore (b. 1960) plays an unhappy pregnant housewife and mother in the 1950s, and Nicole Kidman (b. 1967) plays the tragic author, Woolf. It was nominated for nine Academy Awards, including Best Picture and Best Supporting Actress for Moore, winning only Best Actress for Kidman.

The Sum of All Fears (2002) was the fourth film based off of the *Jack Ryan* spy novels from author Tom Clancy (1947–2013). The novel of *The Sum of All Fears* was released in 1991. Directed by Phil Alden Robinson (b. 1950), the film was set to reboot the *Jack Ryan* franchise, casting the much younger Ben Affleck (b. 1972) in the role previously made famous by Alec Baldwin (b. 1958) and Harrison Ford (b. 1942). The story pits Ryan against a plot by an Austrian neofascist to manipulate a nuclear war between the United States and Russia. In the original novel, the antagonists were Arab terrorists, but as anti-Arab sentiments were on the rise in the immediate aftermath of the September 11, 2001, terrorist attacks, the villain in the film was changed mid-production to be a white European. Though considered a box-office success, hardline Clancy fans and the author himself did not care for the reboot aspect associated to a story that, in the novels, occurred after the events of the previous three films.

Since the 2002 film and the author's death in 2013, the *Jack Ryan* franchise has had difficulty finding an audience outside of the author's original novels.

The year 2003 would produce two of the more thought-provoking dramas of the decade. Tim Burton (b. 1958) directed *Big Fish*, based on the 1998 novel by Daniel Wallace (b. 1959). The film and novel tell the story of a dying man played by Albert Finney (b. 1936) and his estranged son, played by Billy Crudup (b. 1968), attempting to mend their relationship in the brief time they have left. Finney's character regales his son with fantastical tales of his adventures as a young man, tales that push the boundaries of credulity. The son does not believe these tall tales until, during his father's funeral, he sees some of the characters from his father's stories, realizing that there was a kernel of truth to his father's "big fish" stories, allowing the son to understand the father to a deeper degree than perhaps anything else could have accomplished. The film was nominated for only one Academy Award, Best Original Score. It did not win.

Another of the more out-of-the-box dramatic offerings from 2003 was *Lost in Translation*, a romantic dramedy written and directed by Sofia Coppola (b. 1971). It starred comedy icon Bill Murray (b. 1950) and Scarlett Johansson (b. 1984) in one of her first adult roles. Murray plays a Hollywood actor suffering a midlife crisis and dissolving marriage, and Johansson plays a young college student in her own difficult marriage. The two form a bond as they deal with their respective crises. The film was nominated for four Academy Awards, including Best Picture, Best Actor for Murray, and Best Director for Coppola, and it won Best Original Screenplay for Coppola.

The following year produced a wide array of dramas. *The Alamo* (2004), directed by John Lee Hancock (b. 1956), was the most recent film incarnation of the famous last stand of Texas revolutionaries in 1836, whose sacrifice inspired the revolutionary movement leading to Texas's independence later that year. It starred Patrick Wilson (b. 1973) as William Travis (1809–1836), Jason Patric (b. 1966) as Jim Bowie (1796–1836), and Billy Bob Thornton (b. 1955) as frontier legend Davy Crockett (1786–1836). Although the film was a massive failure at the box office, the set of the Alamo, the largest movie set ever built in North America, is the most accurate representation of the original Alamo (only a small fraction of which survives today) ever set to film.

The Aviator (2004) was yet another biopic, this time of aviation pioneer and eccentric millionaire Howard Hughes (1905–1976), and once more teamed director Scorsese with Leo DiCaprio. The film was based on the 1993 Hughes biography, *Howard Hughes: The Secret Life* (1993), and covers the famous aviator's life during the twenty-year period from 1927 to 1947. Cate Blanchett (b. 1969) also stars as Hollywood icon Katharine Hepburn (1907–2003), Hughes's then girlfriend. The film gained eleven Academy Award nominations, including, finally, a Best Actor nod to DiCaprio, and it won five: Art Direction, Cinematography, Costumes, Editing, and Best Actress for Blanchett.

Yet another historical drama was released by director Mel Gibson (b. 1956): *The Passion of the Christ* (2004). The story retells the final twelve hours of the life of Jesus of Nazareth (c. 4 BCE–30 CE). The film starred Jim Caviezel (b. 1968) as Jesus. Gibson made the controversial choice to script the film in the original Aramaic, Latin, and Hebrew languages with English subtitles. It is the most graphically violent representation of the death of Jesus ever committed to film, and it gained notoriety and accusations of anti-Semitism for its emphasis on the role played by Jewish authorities in pushing for the crucifixion of the renegade preacher. Though nominated for three Academy Awards,--Cinematography, Makeup, and Original Score—it won none.

Actor Jamie Foxx (born Eric Bishop in 1967) showcased both his dramatic acting and singing chops in the film *Ray* (2004), a biopic of R&B music icon Ray Charles (born Ray Charles Robinson, 1930–2004). Directed by Taylor Hackford (b. 1944), the film covers a thirty-year period in the long life and career of the music legend. The film was nominated for six Academy Awards, including Best Picture and Best Director for Hackford, and won two, Best Sound Mixing and Best Actor for Foxx. Foxx became only the second actor in Hollywood history to win Best Actor on all five major awards shows: the Academy Awards, BAFTAs (the British Academy Awards), Critics' Choice, Golden Globes, and Screen Actors' Guild.

One of the biggest films of the decade was *Brokeback Mountain* (2005), a dramatic romance featuring two men in a homosexual relationship. It was directed by Ang Lee (b. 1954) and based on a 1997 short story by Annie Proulx (b. 1935). The film starred Heath Ledger and Jake Gyllenhaal (b. 1980) as two hired ranch hands who spend a summer herding sheep in 1963 an develop a deeply romantic relationship. At the end of summer, both men go their separate ways, marry women, and have children. Though Jack, played by Gyllenhaal, wants a more permanent relationship, Ennis, played by Ledger, is haunted by childhood memories of a gay man beaten to death. The two never find happiness—either together or apart. Jack dies young (presumably beaten to death for his sexuality), and Ennis mourns him for the rest of his life. The film was groundbreaking for being a major Hollywood production featuring a romance between two men. The film was nominated for eight Academy Awards, only winning Best Director, Best Adapted Screenplay, and Best Score.

By 2005, the wounds of 9/11 had still not healed, but Americans' thirst for justice and vengeance was beginning to wane. That year, director Steven Spielberg released his film *Munich*, starring Eric Bana (b. 1968) as Israeli Mossad agent Avner Kaufman (based on real-life Agent Juval Aviv, b. 1947), who leads a secret team of Israeli assassins to hunt down and assassinate members of the Palestinian terrorist group Black September, who were responsible for the terror attacks at the 1972 Olympic Games in Munich, Germany, and the deaths of the Israeli Olympic team. The film explores the fine line between justice and vengeance, as well as the emotional toll on those who seek them. The film was nominated for six Academy Awards, winning none.

Mel Gibson returned to the director's chair for the film *Apocalypto* (2005). Set in the early 1500s, the film focuses on a group of Maya natives in the Yucatan Peninsula just prior to the Mayan civilization's demise and the arrival of the Spaniards, under threat from the growing Aztec empire of the region. The film starred Native Mexican actors Rudy Youngblood (b. 1982), Raoul Trujillo (b. 1955), and Dalia Hernández (b. 1985). Like *The Passion of the Christ*, Gibson chose to go with the original ancient languages of the peoples of the region, or as close a proximation as possible, as the languages have been unspoken for centuries. The film was nominated for three logistical Academy Awards, winning none.

One of the biggest books of the 2000s was the novel *The Da Vinci Code* (2003) by Dan Brown (b. 1964). In 2006, director Ron Howard brought the book to the big screen, starring Tom Hanks as Harvard professor Robert Langdon, a "symbologist" (someone who studies the meanings behind symbols, particularly in the area of religions). Both the film and the book came under attack by Christian institutions around the world for its suggestion that Jesus had a child by Mary Magdalene and that a secret order has existed since the Middle Ages to protect this secret and keep track of the members of this familial line. Howard and Hanks would team up for the sequel, *Angels and Demons* (2009), although, in the novels, the events of *Angels and Demons* come before those of *The Da Vinci Code*. *Angels and Demons* brings Langdon in the middle of the centuries-long feud between the Catholic Church and a group known as the Illuminati, attempting to prevent the latter from bringing on an apocalyptic attack on the Church. Both films were moderate successes but failed to achieve the success of their literary sources.

By 2006, it had been five years since the 9/11 attacks, and Hollywood commemorated the anniversary with three major feature films. *World Trade Center* was directed by Oliver Stone (b. 1946) and starred Nicolas Cage (b. 1964), focusing on first responders to the attacks on the Twin Towers of the World Trade Center in New York City on that day. Another film focused on the events on board United Airlines Flight 93, which was stopped from its planned attack on Washington, DC, when passengers, who had been made aware of the events in New York and the Pentagon, attempted to take back control of the plane, forcing the terrorists to crash the plane in an Pennsylvania field, killing all aboard. *United 93* was directed by Paul Greengrass (b. 1955) and starred Christian Clemenson (b. 1958).

Two of the most critically acclaimed dramas of the decade were released in 2007. *No Country for Old Men*, based on the 2005 novel by Cormac McCarthy (b. 1933), was directed by Joel and Ethan Cohen (b. 1954 and 1957, respectively) and starred Tommy Lee Jones (b. 1946) as a Texas sheriff on the hunt of an escaped convict, played by Javier Bardem (b. 1969), who has been hired to hunt down a man who has confiscated a briefcase full of drug money, played by Josh Brolin (b. 1968). The film was nominated for eight Academy Awards, winning four: Best Picture, Best Director, Best Adapted Screenplay, and Best Supporting Actor for Bardem. The second—and equally violent—of these two films was *There Will Be Blood*, based on the novel *Oil!* (1926) by Upton Sinclair (1878–1968). Directed by Paul Thomas Anderson (b. 1970), the film is set in 1898 New Mexico. Starring Daniel Day-Lewis as a mining and oil tycoon, the film explores the corruptions, lies, and betrayals that come with the quest for power and money. It was nominated for eight Academy Awards, winning two: Cinematography and Best Actor for Day-Lewis.

Advancements in special effects were greatly responsible for the success of the film *The Curious Case of Benjamin Button* (2008), partially based on the 1922 short story by F. Scott Fitzgerald (1896–1940). Directed by David Fincher

(b. 1962), the film stars Brad Pitt (b. 1963) as the title character as an "adult" with an odd condition that causes him to age backward. The story of the odd man is told from the present by an elderly woman (played by Cate Blanchett) who tells her daughter the story of a clock built in 1918, set to tell time backward, so that the boys lost in World War I could come home. Shortly after, a child is born with the appearance and physical ailments of an elderly man. Abandoned by his father (after the mother dies in childbirth), the elderly child meets a young girl, and throughout the remainder of the twentieth century, the two repeatedly meet, Benjamin younger on each meeting and Daisy (the girl) growing older. Benjamin dies an infant in the elderly Daisy's arms. Daisy dies in New Orleans as Hurricane Katrina comes ashore. Although nominated for thirteen Academy Awards, it won only three: Makeup, Art Direction, and Visual Effects.

The Hurt Locker (2008) was directed by Kathryn Bigelow (b. 1951) and starred Jeremy Renner (b. 1971) and Anthony Mackie (b. 1978) as U.S. Army explosives ordinance disposal specialists serving in the Iraq War. Over the course of their dangerous missions, Mackie's character decides that he can no longer deal with the job and returns to civilian life, while Renner' character attempts to do the same but realizes that he thrives on the danger and the mission. The film was nominated for nine Academy Awards, winning six: Original Screenplay, Sound Mixing, Sound Editing, Film Editing, Best Picture, and Best Director, making Bigelow the first woman to win that award.

As the decade drew to a close, Hollywood released three of the most beloved films of the decade. *The Blind Side* (2009), based on the 2006 book by Michael Lewis (b. 1960), was directed by John Lee Hancock Jr. (b. 1956). It tells the true story of NFL offensive lineman Michael Oher (b. 1986), who, as a young African American teenager in Tennessee, had a troubled life, tossed around the foster care system due to a drug-addicted single mother. Because of his size, he is considered a prime candidate for high school football and is admitted to a private school. He is eventually taken in by the wealthy white Tuohy family, primarily under the care of family matriarch, the very outspoken and daunting Leigh Anne Tuohy, played by Sandra Bullock (b. 1965). The Tuohys help Michael, played by Quinton Aaron (b. 1984), excel in football and do better academically, and he becomes a member of the family. The heartwarming film became a phenomenon in box offices around the country. The film won Bullock an Academy Award for Best Lead Actress.

Precious (2009), based on the 1996 novel *Push* by the author Sapphire (born Ramona Lofton in 1950), was directed by Lee Daniels (b. 1959) and starred Gabourey Sidibe (b. 1983). Set in the late 1980s, Claireece "Precious" Jones is a teenage Black girl living on welfare with her abusive mother in Harlem, New York. Precious has two children, drops out of high school, and discovers that she has contracted HIV from her sexually abusive father, who dies of AIDS. Through all of her trials and torments, she does find occasional kindness, particularly from a nurse's assistant at the hospital played by rock star Lenny Kravitz (b. 1964). The film received six Academy Award nominations, winning for Best Adapted Screenplay and Best Supporting Actress for Mo'Nique (born Monique Hicks in 1967), who played Precious's abusive mother, Mary. It also gained considerable notoriety for Sidibe's performance.

Slumdog Millionaire (2009) was a British film loosely based on the 2005 novel *Q&A* by Vikas Swarup (b. 1963) and directed by Danny Boyle (b. 1956). The film begins with teenager Jamal Malik (played by Dev Patel, b. 1990), on the cusp of winning India's version of the television program *Who Wants to be a Millionaire?*, answering every single question correctly, which leads to accusations of cheating. Malik then tells his life story to police, including his own love story revolving around the young woman Latika, played by Frieda Pinto (b. 1984). The police believe his amazing tale, and Malik is released to win the show and then the girl. It was nominated for ten Academy Awards, winning eight, including Best Picture, Best Director, Best Adapted Screenplay, Best Score, Best Song, Cinematography, Editing, and Mixing.

One of the most prolific dramatic actors of the period was Denzel Washington (b. 1954). Already one of Hollywood's most successful leading actors by 2000, Denzel had a string of successful films during the decade, including *Remember the Titans* (2000), *Training Day* (2001), *John Q* (2002), *Antwone Fisher* (2002), *Out of Time* (2003), *Man on Fire* (2004), *The Manchurian Candidate* (2004), *Inside Man* (2006), *Déjà Vu* (2006), *American Gangster* (2007), *The Great Debaters* (2007), and *The Taking of Pelham 123* (2009). In 2002, he won the Academy Award for Best Actor for *Training Day*, becoming only the second African American man to win that award. As memorable as the dramatic films of the 2000s were, however, the comedies of the decade were just as memorable.

COMEDY

The 2000s produced some of the most hilarious comedies of all time. This was due in large part to bold filmmakers who pushed the boundaries on what had previously been considered acceptable for American audiences. That is not to say that only sophomoric or prurient comedy is funny, but it did break down barriers that had been put in place since the 1970s. During that decade, many filmmakers, Mel Brooks and Monty Python to name but a few, pushed comedy to the edges of offense. "Offense," however, is an important aspect to comedy, as comedy and science fiction are the best methods of social commentary in American popular culture; offense forces thought and conversations on topics often considered taboo in polite society. The 2000s returned comedy on the big screen to these high levels—or low levels, depending on one's perspective—last seen three decades earlier.

A new comedy franchise was introduced as the 1990s came to a close. *American Pie* (1999), directed by Paul and Chris Weitz (b. 1965 and 1969, respectively), starred Jason Biggs (b. 1978), Chris Klein (b. 1979), Thomas Ian Nicholas (b. 1980), and Eddie Kaye Thomas (b. 1980) as four high school seniors who make a pact to lose their virginity by graduation (with prom night as the desired goal). After a chain of comedic misadventures and comedies of errors, all four achieve their goal, although Klein's character remains gentlemanly silent on the matter, but over the course of events, each learn lessons on respect and seeing women as more than sexual objects. The breakout characters, however, were Stifler, played by Sean William Scott (b. 1976), whose over-the-top immaturity plays perfectly into the stereotype of high school jerk, and

Michelle, played by Alyson Hannigan (b. 1974) of *Buffy the Vampire Slayer* fame, a seemingly innocent and nerdy band girl who turns out to be very sexually active, going against stereotypes.

The entire cast reunited in 2001 for *American Pie 2*, this time directed by James B. Rogers (birth year unknown), continuing the misadventures of the group after a year at college. The focus this time was the burgeoning romance between Biggs's Jim and his first-time partner, Michelle. The third chapter in the saga, *American Wedding* (2003), directed by Jesse Dylan (b. 1966), centers on Jim and Michelle's wedding, and the final film, *American Reunion* (2012), reunites the original cast thirteen years after high school and explores how their lives have changed during adulthood. Each film was rich in sophomoric and prurient humor while simultaneously having heart and holding a mirror to the uncomfortableness, awkwardness, and hijinks many face during the transition from teenager to adulthood.

Another film to make fodder of awkward situations, including those of a sexual nature, was the film *Meet the Parents* (2000), directed by Jay Roach (b. 1957). Ben Stiller (b. 1965) plays Gaylord "Greg" Focker, a nurse who plans to propose to his girlfriend, Pam, played by Teri Polo (b. 1969) while the two spend the weekend at her parents' home for her sister's wedding. Honoring tradition, Greg hopes to gain the permission of Pam's father, Jack, played by Robert De Niro (b. 1943), a protective, tough-as-nails former CIA interrogator, who even his own family believes is a retired florist. The film is loaded with comedies of error, making everyone who has ever met a significant other's parents feel every awkward moment deeply, painfully, and hilariously. The film's success led to two sequels. In the first, *Meet the Fockers* (2004), again directed by Roach, the ultraconservative Byrnes meet Greg's radically liberal parents, played to comedic perfection by Dustin Hoffman (b. 1937) and Barbara Streisand (b. 1942). A third film, *Little Fockers* (2010), this time directed by Paul Weitz, closes the tale with an ailing Jack considering naming Greg the official head of the family once Jack dies, dubbing Greg "the Godfocker," a not-so-subtle nod to De Niro's iconic role as Don Vito Corleone in *The Godfather, Part II* (1974).

One of the biggest low-budget comedies of the 1990s was the film *Friday* (1995), starring and cowritten by rapper Ice Cube (born O'Shea Jackson in 1969) and costarring Chris Tucker (b. 1971) and directed by F. Gary Gray (b. 1969). Cube and Tucker play two stoner friends taking it easy on a presumably ordinary Friday. A series of comedic misadventures and brilliant writing by Cube and DJ Pooh (born Mark Jordan in 1969) simultaneously poke fun at, dispel, and embrace the stereotypes often associated with poor Black communities in America. The original film is also the source for the 2010s meme "Bye Felisha." The commercial and continuing cult success of the film led to two sequels in the 2000s: *Next Friday* (2000), directed by Steve Carr (birth year unknown), and *Friday After Next* (2002), directed by Marcus Raboy (b. 1965).

Two of the most successful comedy directors of the 2000s were the Coen brothers, Joel and Ethan (b. 1954 and 1957, respectively). They began the decade with their hit *O Brother, Where Art Thou?* (2000), starring George Clooney (b. 1961), John Turturro (b. 1957), and Tim Blake Nelson (b. 1964). The film follows the misadventures of three escaped convicts in Depression-era Mississippi in search of buried treasure. They soon meet up with Tommy, played by Chris Thomas King (b. 1962), a Black guitar player who claims to have achieved his talent through a deal with the devil. They go to a local radio station and record a song with Tommy that, after they part ways with him, becomes a successful record, unbeknown to the trio. Throughout their misadventures, the film provides a window into the 1930s Jim Crow South. Though set in early twentieth-century America, the script was a modern adaptation of the Greek classic *The Odyssey* (c. early 700s BCE) by the poet Homer. The film won two Academy Awards: Best Adapted Screenplay and Best Cinematography.

Film parodies became wildly popular in the 2000s. The most successful, however, was the *Scary Movie* series, beginning with the 2000 original directed by Keenan Ivory Wayans (b. 1958) and cowritten by his brothers Shawn (b. 1971) and Marlon (b. 1972). Marlon also costarred in the film. The main character was Cindy Campbell, played by Anna Faris (b. 1976). The film—and its sequels, *Scary Movie 2* (2001), *Scary Movie 3* (2003), *Scary Movie 4* (2006), and *Scary Movie 5* (2013)—satirized popular slasher films, most notably the *Scream* series (1996–2011). Other films that became fodder for ridicule were the films of M. Night Shyamalan (b. 1970) and Steven Spielberg's 2005 remake of *War of the Worlds*. The Wayan brothers parted ways with the series after the second film. The third and fourth parts were directed by David Zucker (b. 1947), who also cowrote part five, which was directed by Malcolm D. Lee (b. 1970).

Comedian and television sitcom star Martin Lawrence (b. 1965) starred in the film *Big Momma's House* (2000), directed by Raja Gosnell (b. 1958). Lawrence plays undercover FBI agent Malcolm Turner, assigned to impersonate elderly Georgia grandmother Hattie Mae "Big Momma" Pierce in order to capture a runaway convict through his ex-girlfriend, Big Momma's granddaughter. Hijinks ensue in the standard man-dressed-as-a-woman trope, with a southern African American twist. The film was wildly popular, spawning two sequels to date: *Big Momma's House 2* (2006) and *Big Mommas: Like Father, Like Son* (2011).

Christmas 2000 saw the release of Ron Howard's live-action remake of the children's classic *How the Grinch Stole Christmas*, the 1957 book by Dr. Seuss (born Theodor Seuss Geisel, 1904–1991). The film perfectly cast comedy icon Jim Carrey (b. 1962) as "the mean one" best described as "stink, stank, stunk." Carrey's blend of physical comedy and comedic timing brought the holiday favorite to an entirely new level. The film has achieved required-annual-viewing status alongside such other holiday classics as *It's a Wonderful Life* (1946), *A Christmas Story* (1983), *Home Alone* (1990), *The Muppet Christmas Carol* (1992), *The Santa Clause* (1994), and the dozen-or-so film renditions of Charles Dickens's *A Christmas Carol*, first published in 1843. Carrey went on to continued success throughout the decade with a chain of other hit films: *Me, Myself & Irene* (2000), *Bruce Almighty* (2002), *Lemony Snicket's A Series of Unfortunate Events* (2004), *Fun with Dick and Jane* (2005), and *Yes Man* (2008).

George Clooney returned in 2001 with what may become his most iconic film: *Ocean's Eleven*, directed by Steven Soderbergh (b. 1963), a remake of the 1960 film by Frank Sinatra (1915–1998) and the rest of the Rat Pack. Clooney stars alongside a star-studded cast: Brad Pitt, Matt Damon (b. 1970), Don

Cheadle (b. 1964), Bernie Mac (1957–2008), Casey Affleck (b. 1975), Carl Reiner (1922–2020), Elliot Gould (b. 1938), Julia Roberts (b. 1967), and Andy Garcia (b. 1956). Danny Ocean (Clooney) is a recently paroled thief who quickly teams up with longtime associate Rusty (Pitt) with a scheme to rob three Las Vegas casinos simultaneously, all owned by dangerous tough-guy Terry Benedict (Garcia). As the two assemble their diverse team of professional con artists and thieves, Danny's true motive is revealed: steal his ex-wife (Roberts) away from Benedict. Both goals, of course, succeed, and the success of the film led to two less successful direct sequels: *Ocean's Twelve* (2004) and *Ocean's Thirteen* (2007). A more successful sequel or spin-off, *Ocean's Eight* (2018), starred Sandra Bullock leading a team of female con artists on a jewel heist.

Ben Stiller also returned in 2001 as star, director, and cowriter of *Zoolander*. The film centers on the narcissistic and utterly idiotic male model Derek Zoolander who is being unseated as America's top male model by newcomer, and only slightly-less idiotic, Hansel, played by Owen Wilson (b. 1968). The two become embroiled in an international plot to assassinate the Malaysian prime minister. The film came under some scrutiny when Bret Easton Ellis, author of *American Psycho*, claimed that the entire film was based upon his 1998 novel, *Glamorama*. An out-of-court settlement forbids either side from confirming or denying the accusations.

One of the biggest surprise hits of the decade was the independent film *My Big Fat Greek Wedding* (2002), a romantic comedy, or rom-com, written by Nia Vardalos (b. 1962), who also stars in the film, and directed by Joel Zwick (b. 1942). Vardalos plays Toula Portokalos, who—in the face of her family's traditionalist beliefs—foregoes her Greek culture. In order to gain her parents' acceptance when she agrees to marry a man who is not Greek, she concedes to a traditional Greek wedding, with all the traditions that come with it. The heartwarming rom-com impressed audiences nationwide. The film's success led to a short-lived television series, *My Big Fat Greek Life* (CBS, 2013), and a sequel, *My Big Fat Greek Wedding 2* (2016).

By 2000, young actress Lindsay Lohan (b. 1986) was a well-established movie star in Disney films. In 2003, she starred in a second remake of the film *Freaky Friday*, directed by Mark Waters (b. 1964) and costarring Jamie Lee Curtis (b. 1958). The original 1976 film starring Jodie Foster (b. 1962) was based on the 1972 novel by Mary Rodgers (1931–2014). Lohan plays a rebellious teenage daughter of a widowed mother on the cusp of remarriage. As mother and daughter argue at a Chinese restaurant, the restaurant owner's mother presents the two with fortune cookies possessing magical qualities. The next morning mother and daughter wake up having swapped bodies and spend the day literally in each other's shoes, seeing each other in a new light by the end of the day. Though the third incarnation of basically the same film, *Freaky Friday* was highly successful with both adult and teen audiences.

Comedy actor Jack Black (b. 1969) had a huge hit in 2003 with *School of Rock*, directed by Richard Linklater (b. 1959). Black plays a down-on-his-luck guitarist for a struggling rock band facing eviction from his friend's apartment for failure to make rent. He takes a temporary job as a substitute teacher at a preparatory grade school (a job meant for his friend). Dewey (Black) uses his love of music, particularly classic rock, to break down the barriers between him and his high-society students. The students likewise begin to love music, and with Dewey's help, they organize the band School of Rock and sneak away from school to audition for a competition. The film also features Nickelodeon television star Miranda Cosgrove (b. 1993) in one of her earliest roles.

Tom Hanks made a return to comedy—the genre that made him famous in the 1980s—with the film *The Ladykillers* (2004), directed by the Coen brothers. This film was a remake of a 1955 British film of the same name. In it, Hanks plays Professor Goldthwaite Higginson Dorr, a professor of literature renting a room from the elderly and ultrareligious Mrs. Munson, played by Irma P. Hall (b. 1935). Dorr, however, is actually a con man, needing access to Mrs. Munson's home to drill into a neighboring casino. He passes his team off as an amateur band of musicians. Although the heist is successful, Mrs. Munson discovers their plot and demands that they make good and return the money and go to church. When attempts to convince her otherwise fails, the group decides they must kill her. Continual mishaps result in most of the team dying instead. Left with the money, Mrs. Munson attempts to report it to the police, but they do not believe her, and she donates the money to a Christian university. Though not a commercial success, it was critically acclaimed and underscored once more Hanks's comedic talents.

Lindsay Lohan teamed up again with director Mark Waters in 2004 with perhaps her most famous film, *Mean Girls*. The screenplay was written by *Saturday Night Live* head writer Tina Fey (b. 1970) and produced by *SNL* creator Lorne Michaels (b. 1944). It was based on the psychological study *Queen Bees and Wannabes* (2002) by Rosalind Wiseman, a self-help book written to help teenage girls deal with the phenomenon of social cliques and bullying. Lohan plays a high schooler named Cady who, to this point, had always been homeschooled by her academic parents. Now thrust into the clique system of public high school, Cady is ill-equipped both mentally and emotionally to deal with the level of bullying experienced by so many public and even private school students. The film sees her social development, as she eventually overcomes the mean girls in school, led by Regina, played by Rachel McAdams (b. 1978). The film became an instant classic, leading to the term "mean girls" becoming part of the American vernacular still to this day.

The year 2004 also saw the release of two films that have become cult classics. *Napoleon Dynamite*, was directed and cowritten by Jared Hess (b. 1979), based on his college short film *Peluca* (2002). The film starred Jon Heder (b. 1977) as the title character, an odd, nerdy, and socially awkward high schooler. The film follows the misadventures of Dynamite and his friends Deb, played by Tina Majorino (b. 1985), and Mexican immigrant Pedro, played by Efren Ramirez (b. 1973). Like *Mean Girls*, the film underscores the plight of the unpopular and the significance of social cliques and bullying in public schools, once more allowing the underdog to overcome adversity and be the hero.

The same year, director Edgar Wright (b. 1974) cowrote the horror/comedy cult classic *Shaun of the Dead* along with the film's star, Simon Pegg (b. 1970). Taking advantage of the recent resurgence in popularity of zombie apocalypse fiction, the film—not so much a satire as a comedic twist on the genre—

focuses on Shaun (Pegg), a salesman at a London electronics store, and his unemployed ne'er-do-well friend Ed, played by longtime Pegg collaborator Nick Frost (b. 1972), as they fight their way through a zombie outbreak in the United Kingdom. Following the similar trajectories of the iconic *Dead* films of George A. Romero (1940–2017), the film follows a group of everyday people, with many casualties along the way. Unlike the horror films, however, *Shaun of the Dead* does provide an ending, as the zombies are eventually brought under control to serve various purposes once civilization is back on track. As a bit of brilliant social commentary, however, the film opens with the everyday citizenry drudging through their daily lives like living zombies, causing the hero to take a considerable bit of time before he notices that the dead are walking and attacking people. The film launched Pegg, already well known to British audiences, into an international star.

The classic television series *The Dukes of Hazzard* (CBS, 1979–1985) received a big-screen adaptation in 2005. Taking a somewhat more adult and realistic take on the original subject matter, the Duke Boys, Bo and Luke, played by Sean William Scott and Johnny Knoxville (b. 1971) respectively, use their wits to thwart the corrupt machinations of Hazzard County, Georgia, businessman "Boss" Jefferson Davis Hogg, played by Burt Reynolds (1936–2018) as he plans to confiscate local farms to open them for fracking. They avoid Hogg and his cadre of corrupt police led by Sheriff Roscoe P. Coltrane, played by M.C. Gainey (b. 1948). As in the series, the true star of the film is the boys' souped-up orange 1969 Dodge Charger, called General Lee after the legendary Confederate general of the American Civil War. As 2004 was a far more politically correct era than the early 1980s, the film takes time to address the controversial Confederate flag that has always emblazoned the roof of the car, though never really apologizing for or explaining celebrating the name of the Confederate general. The film was a box-office disaster.

Also in 2005, the Black-man-as-elderly-woman trope returned to massive success with the launch of the *Madea* franchise by iconic movie and television magnate Tyler Perry (b. 1969). Perry first appeared as Madea—a hilariously angry, violent, and vindictive older Black woman—in the 1999 stage play *I Can Do Bad All by Myself*. The first big-screen adaptation was in the film *Diary of a Mad Black Woman*, an adaptation of Perry's stage play sequel to the original *Madea* play. The massive success of the film has led to a legion of sequels: *Madea's Family Reunion* (2006), *Madea Goes to Jail* (2009), *Madea's Big Happy Family* (2011), *Madea's Witness Protection* (2012), *A Madea Christmas* (2013), *Boo! A Madea Halloween* (2016), *Boo 2! A Madea Halloween* (2017), and *A Madea Family Funeral* (2019).

Television comedy actor Steve Carell (b. 1962) broke into big screen leading man success with *The 40-Year-Old Virgin* (2005), the directorial debut of now comedy icon Judd Apatow (b. 1967), cowritten by Carell and Apatow. As the title suggests, the film centers on a forty-year-old man (Carell) facing his first sexual encounter. The massive success of this film, along with the following year's *Little Miss Sunshine* (2006), codirected by Jonathan Dayton (b. 1957) and Valerie Faris (b. 1958), secured Carell's standing as one of Hollywood's most respected comedic and dramatic actors. The latter film was nominated for four Academy Awards, winning two: Best Original Screenplay and Best Supporting Actor for Alan Arkin (b. 1934).

Controversial comedian Sacha Baron Cohen (b. 1971) had international success with his film *Borat: Cultural Learnings of America for Make Benefit Glorious Nation of Kazakhstan* (2006), cowritten, coproduced, and starring Cohen and directed by Larry Charles (b. 1956). In the film, Cohen plays Kazakhstani reporter Borat Sagdiyev who has been granted sanction by his government to go to the United States to make a documentary and raise awareness of Kazakhstan. Borat interviews several American politicians and ordinary citizens, none of whom are informed that they are taking part in a comedic film but are led to believe that it is, in fact, a documentary. Some of those interviewed were angered by the ruse but unable to do anything about it, having signed releases to not sue anyone involved in the "documentary." One person who was in on the joke was 1990s *Playboy* icon Pamela Anderson (b. 1967), who plays herself as the object of Borat's obsession. As the film was based on a character previously created for Cohen's television series *Da Ali G Show* (BBC4, 1999–2004; HBO, 2003–2004), it was nominated for an Academy Award for Best Adapted Screenplay but failed to win.

Actress Meryl Streep, best known for her iconic dramatic work, took a turn at comedy in the film *The Devil Wears Prada* (2006), directed by David Frankel (b. 1959) and based on the 2003 novel by Lauren Weisberger (b. 1977). The film starred Anne Hathaway (b. 1982) as Andy, a recently graduated journalist who attains a job as a personal assistant to fashion icon Miranda Priestly (Streep), the editor of a respected fashion magazine. The film pokes fun at the mean girl atmosphere of high society fashion, with Streep manifesting the pinnacle of that world with devilish glee. Once more proving that she can play any role, Streep received a Best Actress nomination at the Academy Awards, losing to Hellen Mirren (b. 1945).

By far, the most frightening comedy of the decade was the cult classic *Idiocracy* (2006), directed by Mike Judge (b. 1962) and starring Luke Wilson (b. 1971), who plays an army librarian chosen to be frozen as an experiment. When the project is forgotten, he finds himself woken up in the year 2505, where American society has been severely dumbed down, as intellectuals in the twenty-first century stopped having children while the less intelligent continued to breed excessively. Now, five hundred years in the future, Americans are monumentally stupid, and they are on the brink of starvation, primarily due to using an energy drink on crops rather than water. Unable to return to the past, Wilson's character, Joe, eventually becomes president of the United States and marries his fellow time traveler Rita, played by Maya Rudolph (b. 1972), to produce the world's most intelligent children. As a considerable faction of American society since 2006 has grown to distrust and ignore simple, basic facts—and intellectualism has become increasingly vilified—the future presented in *Idiocracy* becomes frighteningly more possible than ever.

The year 2007 produced two of the most beloved teen comedies of the decade. *Juno* was directed by Jason Reitman (b. 1977) and starred Ellen Page (b. 1987) in the title role. The film follows the life of teenage Juno who has become pregnant by her friend (and ardent admirer), Paulie, played by Michael

Cera (b. 1988). The same year saw the release of *Superbad*, directed by Greg Mottola (b. 1964) and starring Cera, Jonah Hill (b. 1983), and Emma Stone (b. 1988). The film follows the two male leads along their misadventures over one night as high school seniors and lifelong friends soon facing separation as they go separate ways after graduation. Together, the two films give a broad overview of the various issues and thoughts of high schoolers in the 2000s.

Ben Stiller returned to direct, star, and cowrite the 2008 film *Tropic Thunder*. In this action satire, Stiller plays action star Tugg Speedman filming his new project, *Tropic Thunder*, based on the memoir of a war hero. His cast are dropped into the jungle to interact with what they've been assured are actors firing blanks in order to add a degree of realism to the guerilla fighting scenes. They are inadvertently thrown into the mix with real-world guerillas who call themselves Flaming Dragon. The guerillas soon discover Tugg's identity and that he is the star of their favorite film, where the actor played a person with a mental disability. Despite its success, the film garnered some criticism for constant use of the word "retard" in reference to Tugg's previous character. Added to that was Robert Downey Jr.'s (b. 1965) character, Kirk Lazarus, an white Australian method actor who plays a Black character (in blackface) in the fictional *Tropic Thunder*, playing into racial stereotypes and, being a method actor, staying in character even when off camera. The film also featured real-life action star Tom Cruise, whom Stiller gained considerable fame imitating throughout his career, in a brief cameo as a bald, overweight studio executive.

Christmas 2008 saw another holiday classic released in theaters. *Four Christmases*, directed by Seth Gordon (b. 1976), starred Reese Witherspoon (b. 1976) and Vince Vaughn (b. 1970) as lovers Kate and Brad, who for the last three years have gone out of their way—literally—to avoid their respective families on Christmas. When their planned trip to Fiji is postponed and they are shown on television as examples of the many trapped by fog at the airport, the two have no choice but to make appearances at their parents' homes for Christmas. As both sets of parents are divorced, the result is four Christmases. Their hilarious encounters expose the respective traumas of the two leads, allowing each to know the other even better. Since its theatrical debut, it has become a holiday constant on cable television.

The most commercially successful comedy of the decade, and perhaps all time, was the film *The Hangover* (2009). Directed by Todd Phillips (b. 1970), the film starred Bradley Cooper (b. 1975), Ed Helms (b. 1974), and Zach Galifianakis (b. 1969) as three friends who take their soon-to-be-married best friend, Doug, played by Justin Bartha (b. 1978), to Las Vegas for a bachelor party. When Alan (Galifianakis) unknowingly spikes the drinks of all four with rohypnol, believing it to simply be ecstasy, the three friends wake up the following morning unaware of what has transpired over the previous night, and Doug is missing. The three embark on a hilarious string of misadventures as they attempt to find their friend and piece together what they did the night before. All ends well, and the massive success of the film led to two sequels: *The Hangover Part II* (2011) and *The Hangover Part III* (2013). The film also launched comedian Ken Jeong, who played sexually ambiguous international crime lord Leslie Chow, to superstardom.

As the decade drew to a close, the zombie genre was even more popular, and another cult classic was born with the film *Zombieland* (2009). Directed by Ruben Fleischer (b. 1974), the film starred Jesse Eisenberg (b. 1983), Emma Stone, Woody Harrelson (b. 1961), and Abigail Breslin (b. 1996). With the old world a thing of the past, people are allowed to reinvent themselves, right down to their identities. Each member of the group identifies themselves by their hometowns: Columbus (Eisenberg), Tallahassee (Harrelson), Wichita (Stone), and Little Rock (Breslin). The four reluctantly become a group as romance builds between Columbus and Wichita. The film became an immediate cult classic, finally resulting in a sequel, *Zombieland: Double Tap* (2019).

One of the biggest names in comedy in the 2000s was *Saturday Night Live* alum Adam Sandler (b. 1966). With several box-office hits throughout the 1990s, Sandler entered the 2000s with another huge hit in *Little Nicky* (2000). That was followed by several succeeding hits: *Mr. Deeds* and the animated feature *Eight Crazy Nights* (both in 2002), *Anger Management* (2003), *50 First Dates* and *Spanglish* (both in 2004), *The Longest Yard* (2005), *Click* (2006), *I Now Pronounce You Chuck & Larry* (2007), *You Don't Mess with the Zohan* (2008), *Funny People* (2009), and *Grown Ups* (2010). Though he continued to make movies throughout the 2010s and beyond, Sandler has yet to recapture the popularity of his 1990s and 2000s projects.

Perhaps the most prolific comedic actor of the 2000s was Will Ferrell (b. 1967). Like Sandler, coming into the 2000s, Ferrell had already reached superstar status as a cast member of *Saturday Night Live*, from 1995 to 2002. After several noteworthy cameos in films in the late 1990s, Ferrell launched a massively successful lead career in the 2000s. His films included *Zoolander* (2001); *Old School* and *Elf* (both in 2003), *Anchorman: The Legend of Ron Burgundy* (2004); *The Producers*, *Bewitched*, and *Kicking & Screaming* (all in 2005); *Stranger Than Fiction*, *Talladega Nights: The Ballad of Ricky Bobby*, and *Curious George* (all in 2006); *Blades of Glory* (2007); *Semi-Pro* and *Step Brothers* (both in 2008); and *Land of the Lost* (2009). Of those films, *Anchorman*, *Elf*, and *Talladega Nights* were three of the most successful comedies of the decade. In 2008, Ferrell was given the James Joyce Award by the University College Dublin's Literary and Historical Society, recognizing his excellence in his field. His massive success would continue throughout the 2010s.

ACTION

In the 1990s, Hollywood produced an action film that would launch one of the most successful franchises of the twenty-first century. In 1996, Tom Cruise (b. 1962) starred in *Mission: Impossible*, directed by Brian De Palma (b. 1940) and based on the popular television series that aired on CBS from 1966 to 1973. Unlike the series, however, the film franchise centers on Ethan Hunt, an agent for the Impossible Missions Force (IMF), a fictional American intelligence agency. On the series and in the films, every mission begins by informing the lead agent of the mission, "Your mission, should you choose to accept it . . ." Each briefing ends with, "If any member of your IMF team should be captured or killed, the secretary will disavow any knowledge of your activities . . . . This message will self-destruct in five seconds." The massive popularity of the film led to numerous sequels: *Mission: Impossible 2* (2000), *Mission: Impossible III* (2006), *Mission: Impossible—Ghost Protocol* (2011), *Mission: Impossible—Rogue Nation* (2015), and *Mission: Impossible—Fallout* (2018).

The decade opened with yet another television-to-screen adaptation with the big-screen version of *Charlie's Angels,* directed by McG (born Joseph McGinty Nichol in 1968) and based on the popular television series that aired on ABC from 1976 to 1981. The premise of both is that Charles Townsend hires teams of three beautiful, brilliant, and cunning female detectives to handle various cases. The original television series was connected to the women's liberation movement of the 1970s, underscoring that women could do anything men could do. The initial film version starred Drew Barrymore (b. 1975), Cameron Diaz (b. 1972), and Lucy Liu (b. 1968). The film was massively popular, spawning a sequel, *Charlies Angels: Full Throttle* (2003), and a less successful reboot in 2019.

Another twenty-first-century update of a 1970s classic was the film *Shaft* (2000), directed by John Singleton (1968–2019) and based on the iconic blaxploitation 1971 action film that starred Richard Roundtree (b. 1942) as the titular private detective, John Shaft. The 2000 film was neither a remake nor a reboot but, rather, a continuation of the original, with Roundtree's retired John Shaft replaced by his nephew of the same name played by Samuel L. Jackson (b. 1948). A sequel, also called *Shaft* (2019), was directed by Tim Story (b. 1970); it updates the story to reveal that the original John Shaft was actually the father of Jackson's Shaft, a fact only revealed to the son in the years since the previous film, and reunites John Shaft II with his own estranged son, John Shaft III, played by Jessie Usher (b. 1992). As Roundtree's and Jackson's Shafts represented the ultimate in African American machismo, the most recent film examined twenty-first century ideas of manhood and Blackness.

Yet another throwback to 1970s nostalgia in 2000 was the Chinese martial arts film *Crouching Tiger, Hidden Dragon,* directed by Ang Lee and starring Chow Yun-fat (b. 1955) and Hong Kong action icon Michelle Yeoh (b. 1962). The film is set in China in the 1700s. Its mixture of amazing martial arts and groundbreaking special effects made it an international sensation. It was nominated for ten Academy Awards, winning four: Best Foreign Language Film, Best Art Direction, Best Original Score, and Best Cinematography. It also secured Yeoh as an American movie star. In the late 2010s, Yeoh used her fame to move into the science fiction and comedy genres.

The Transporter (2002) was a French film based on an internet series, *The Hire,* and directed by Hong Kong director Corey Yuen (b. 1951). The film made an American action star of Jason Statham (b. 1967), who played Frank Martin, a transporter who will deliver any package anywhere for the right price (the "packages" are objects—or people—of an important and possibly illegal nature). The film's popularity led to Statham returning for two sequels: *Transporter 2* (2005) and *Transporter 3* (2008). A far less successful reboot was attempted in 2015 without Statham.

Matt Damon (b. 1970) made the move to action star with the film *The Bourne Identity* (2002), directed by Doug Liman (b. 1965). Damon plays Jason Bourne, a highly skilled CIA assassin suffering from amnesia and hunted by other CIA assassins to eliminate what he knows. As he uncovers his identity and out-smarts or kills those hunting him, Bourne makes his way back to CIA head-quarters to confront his superiors. The film was a huge commercial success, leading to a new franchise of films: *The Bourne Supremacy* (2004), *The Bourne Ultimatum* (2007), *The Bourne Legacy* (2012), and *Jason Bourne* (2016).

Director Robert Rodriguez (b. 1968) completed his popular Mexico Trilogy with the film *Once Upon a Time in Mexico* (2003). The first two chapters—the independent film *El Mariachi* (1993) and the big budget film *Desperado* (1995)—had established the character of El Mariachi, a nameless gunslinger who car-ries a guitar and goes from town to town in Mexico taking out drug cartels. In the final installment, El Mariachi, played by Antonio Banderas (b. 1960), is mourning the loss of his wife, played by Salma Hayek, and young daughter, when he is approached by an American CIA agent, played by Johnny Depp, to assassinate the Mexican general who murdered El Mariachi's family. The film is a sweeping and violent epic filled with Rodriguez's trademark action brilliance.

Rodriguez's close friend and frequent collaborator, Quentin Tarantino (b. 1963), released his own blood-soaked revenge epic masterpiece the same year with *Kill Bill, Vol. 1* (2003), inspired by the popular samurai and martial arts films of the 1970s. Uma Thurman (b. 1970) plays the nameless Bride bent on revenge against her former employer and ex-lover, Bill, played by David Carradine (1936–2009), and his team of assassins who attempted to murder her at her wedding and presumably murdered her unborn child. Working her way halfway through her list of targets, the first film ends with the audience's discovery that her daughter is still alive. In *Kill Bill, Vol. 2* (2004), the Bride com-pletes her quest and is reunited with her daughter. If *Pulp Fiction* (1994) is con-sidered Tarantino's greatest film, *Kill Bill, Vols. 1 and 2* surely rank a close second.

Brad Pitt and Angelina Jolie (b. 1975) teamed up for the action romantic comedy *Mr. & Mrs. Smith* (2005), directed by Doug Liman. In the film, Pitt and Jolie play John and Jane Smith, a couple facing the dissolution of their mar-riage and attempting counseling. Each believe the other to live a boring, aver-age life; meanwhile, they secretly work for different intelligence agencies as top-notch field agents. When their missions collide, each is left with the job of killing the other, exposing their respective years of lies. Ultimately, getting to the bottom of their cases reunites them and reignites their love for each other.

Action legend Sylvester Stallone (b. 1946) reignited his two most iconic action franchises in the 2000s. *Rocky Balboa* (2006), which Stallone also wrote and directed, is the sixth film in the *Rocky* series. In the film, a retired and widowed Balboa decides to enter the ring again against a much-younger heavyweight champion. The bout ends in a draw, giving the official win to the reigning champ, but Rocky proves once more what a champion he is. Rocky's story would continue in the spin-off *Creed* franchise in 2015, where Rocky becomes the seasoned trainer for Adonis Creed, played by Michael B. Jordan (b. 1987), the son of his late sparring partner and friend, Apollo Creed, played by Carl Weathers (b. 1948). Stallone also directed and cowrote *Rambo* (2008), reintroducing audiences to the skilled Vietnam vet, who now lives in Thailand. When he is hired by missionaries to ferry them upriver, Rambo is once more called into action when his charges come under threat. This film led to another sequel, *Rambo: Last Blood* (2019).

Northern Irish actor Liam Neeson (b. 1952) made the transition to action star in the film *Taken* (2008), directed by Pierre Morel (b. 1964). Neeson plays Brian Mills, a retired CIA operative whose daughter is kidnapped by sex traffickers during her trip to Europe. Possessing "a very particular set of skills," Neeson tracks the perpetrators across the globe and successfully rescues his daughter. The film was a massive success, leading to two sequels: *Taken 2* (2012) and *Taken 3* (2014).

Tarantino produced one more epic film in the 2000s: *Inglourious Basterds* (2009). Starring Brad Pitt, Christoph Waltz (b. 1956), and Michael Fassbender (b. 1977), the story is a reimagining of the events of World War II. Pitt plays U.S. Army lieutenant Aldo "the Apache" Raine, who leads a team of predominantly Jewish soldiers as an assassin squad proud to be in the "Nazi killin' business." In a side story, Shoshanna LaPadite, played by Melanie Laurent (b. 1983), seeks revenge against the Nazis for the murder of her family. Pitt's squad eventually team with Shoshanna to use her movie theater to assassinate the entire Nazi high command, including Hitler. The film is ultimately a revenge fantasy epic. The film was nominated for eight Academy Awards, winning only one: Best Supporting Actor for Waltz.

The *James Bond* film franchise continued into the twenty-first century. Based on the spy novels of Ian Fleming (1908–1964), the film franchise began with *Dr. No* (1962). In 2002, Pierce Brosnan (b. 1953), the fifth actor to play Bond in the official franchise, made his swan song as the most famous superspy in film history with the film *Die Another Day*, directed by Lee Tamahori (b. 1950). The next Bond, Daniel Craig (b. 1968), rebooted the entire franchise with his first film in the series, *Casino Royale* (2006), directed by Martin Campbell (b. 1943). Craig continued his run through the rest of the decade and the 2010s with three more films: *Quantum of Solace* (2008), *Skyfall* (2012), and *Spectre* (2015). Craig is scheduled to complete his run as James Bond in the 2020 film *No Time to Die*.

The most prolific action star of the 2000s also made his debut in the same decade: Dwayne "the Rock" Johnson (b. 1972). Having already become an international superstar as "the Most Electrifying Man in Sports Entertainment" as a professional wrestler, the Rock made his film debut as the Scorpion King in the film *The Mummy Returns* (2001). His other films in the 2000s were *The Scorpion King* (2002), *The Rundown* (2003), *Walking Tall* (2004), *Be Cool* and *Doom* (both in 2005), *The Game Plan* (2007), *Get Smart* (2008), and *Race to Witch Mountain* (2009). He went on to appear in twenty-six more films in the 2010s.

ANIMATED

The most successful animated franchise of the 2000s was the *Shrek* tetralogy. The series was a satire of traditional fairy tales centered on a green ogre named Shrek, voiced by Mike Myers (b. 1963); his friend Donkey, voiced by Eddie

Murphy (b. 1961); and Shrek's love interest, the Princess Fiona, voiced by Cameron Diaz. The original film, *Shrek* (2001), was massively successful and spawned three direct sequels: *Shrek 2* (2004), *Shrek the Third* (2007). and *Shrek Forever After* (2010). The series also produced a spin-off film, *Puss in Boots* (2011), featuring the iconic fairy tale swords cat, voiced by Antonio Banderas.

Other popular animated films in the decade included *Chicken Run* (2000), *Lilo & Stitch* (2002), *The Polar Express* (2004), *Team America: World Police* (2004), *Madagascar* (2005), *Happy Feet* (2006), *Horton Hears a Who* (2008), *Kung Fu Panda* (2008), and *Cloudy with a Chance of Meatballs* (2009). Director Tim Burton (b. 1958) returned to the world of stop-motion animation in the 2000s. In the tradition of his holiday classic, *The Nightmare Before Christmas* (1993), Burton returned with another creepy classic, *Corpse Bride* (2005). Another stop-motion hit of the decade was *Coraline* (2009), based on the 2002 children's book by Neil Gaiman (b. 1960).

Throughout the decade, another hit franchise was the *Ice Age* films, beginning with the 2002 original. The series centered on a group of mammals experiencing the end of the Paleolithic ice age approximately three million years ago. The films featured the voice talents of Ray Romano (b. 1957), John Leguizamo (b. 1964), Dennis Leary (b. 1957), and Chris Wedge (b. 1957). In addition to short films and television specials, the original film also spawned four sequels: *Ice Age: The Meltdown* (2006), *Ice Age: Dawn of the Dinosaurs* (2009), *Ice Age: Continental Drift* (2012), and *Ice Age: Collision Course* (2016).

The biggest success story of the decade came from Pixar Studios. After their masterful debut with their first CGI-animated film, *Toy Story* (1995), Pixar became *the* name in animated entertainment by the beginning of the twenty-first century. Their chain of successes in the 2000s included the following films: *Monsters, Inc.* (2001), *Finding Nemo* (2003), *The Incredibles* (2004), *Cars* (2006), *Ratatouille* (2007), *WALL-E* (2008), and *Up* (2009). *Up* is most remembered for the most heartrending, emotional, and tear-inducing opening in film history. Of their films from the decade, all but two won the Academy Award for Best Animated Feature. The two exceptions—*Monsters, Inc.* and *Cars*—were both nominated for the award. In 2006, Disney purchased Pixar, beginning the corporation's quest to buy out American popular culture that would dominate the 2010s with Disney's purchases of Marvel Entertainment, Lucasfilm, and 20th Century Fox.

MUSICALS

For the first four decades of Hollywood history, musicals were a vital genre in moviemaking. That trend all but dropped off in the 1970s, and few musicals were produced for the rest of the twentieth century. The genre made a big comeback in the first decade of the twenty-first century. *Moulin Rouge!* (2001) was directed by Baz Luhrmann (b. 1962) as the third chapter of his Red Curtain Trilogy, which consisted of the earlier musicals *Strictly Ballroom* (1992) and *Romeo + Juliet* (1996). The film starring Nicole Kidman and Ewan McGregor was nominated for eight Academy Awards and won two: Costume Design and Art Design.

In 2002, Rob Marshall (b. 1960) directed *Chicago*, the feature film version of the 1975 Broadway musical (cowritten by Bob Fosse, 1927–1987, and Fred Ebb, 1928–2004, with music by John Kander and lyrics by Ebb), which, itself, was based on a 1926 stage play by Maurine Dallas Watkins (1896–1969), all of the same name. Set in 1920s Chicago, the film starred Renée Zellweger (b. 1969) as a wannabe jazz singer who is convicted for murder. The film also starred Richard Gere (b. 1949) and Catherine Zeta-Jones (b. 1969). The film was nominated for thirteen Academy Awards, winning six: Best Picture, Best Supporting Actress for Zeta-Jones, Art Direction, Costume Design, Editing, and Sound.

Another Broadway-to-screen adaptation from the decade was *Phantom of the Opera* (2004). Directed by Joel Schumacher (1939–2020), the film was based on the 1986 Broadway musical by Andrew Lloyd Webber (b. 1948), which, itself, was based on the 1925 horror film of the same name directed by Rupert Julian (1879–1943), which was based on the French 1910 novel *Le Fantôme de l'Opéra* by Gaston Leroux (1868–1927). The film starred Emmy Rossum (b. 1986) and Gerard Butler (b. 1969). The film was nominated for three Academy Awards but failed to win one.

Walk the Line (2005) was a biographical musical telling the love story of country music icons Johnny Cash (1932–2003) and June Carter Cash (1929–2003). The two icons were played by Joaquin Phoenix and Reese Witherspoon, respectively. Directed by James Mangold (b. 1963), the film was based on two autobiographies of Cash: *Man in Black: His Own Story in His Own Words* (1975) and *Cash: The Autobiography* (1997). The film was nominated for five Academy Awards, winning one: Best Actress for Witherspoon.

The year 2007 was a big one for hit musicals. Director Tim Burton took a turn to musicals with his rendition of *Sweeney Todd: The Demon Barber of Fleet Street*. The film is based on the 1979 Broadway play by Stephen Sondheim (b. 1930), which was based on the fictional villain of a nineteenth-century British novella serial, *The String of Pearls* (1846–1847, author unknown). The film starred Johnny Depp as the serial-killing barber and Helena Bonham Carter (b. 1966) as his assistant, Mrs. Lovett. The film was nominated for three Academy Awards, including a Best Lead Actor nod for Depp, winning only one: Best Art Direction.

That same year, Beatles fans were treated to *Across the Universe*. Directed by Julie Taymor, the film tells the story of various youths (mostly Americans) at the height of the Vietnam War. Interspersed throughout the narrative are more than thirty Beatles songs. The film starred Evan Rachel Wood (b. 1987) and Jim Sturgess (b. 1978). It was nominated for one Academy Award, Costume Design, but failed to win. Disney entered the foray of live-action musicals with the 2007 film *Enchanted*, directed by Kevin Lima (b. 1962) and starring Amy Adams (b. 1974). Last, 2007 also saw a remake of *Hairspray*, based on the 2002 Broadway play (cowritten by Mark O'Donnell, 1954–2012, and Thomas Meehan, 1929–2017; music and lyrics by Marc Shaiman, b. 1959, and Scott Wittman, b. 1954) that, itself, was based on the 1988 musical film by John Waters (b. 1946). The update was directed by Adam Shankman (b. 1964) and starred Nikki Blonsky (b. 1988), Amanda Bynes (b. 1986), and John Travolta (b. 1954) in the gender-bending role of Edna Turnblad.

The decade ended with the release of the film *Mamma Mia!* (2009), based on the 1999 British stage play by Catherine Johnson (b. 1957), Benny Andersson (b. 1946), and Björn Ulvaeus (b. 1945). The theatrical version was directed by Phyllida Lloyd (b. 1957) and starred Meryl Streep, Pierce Brosnan, Colin Firth (b. 1960), Stellan Skarsgård (b. 1951), and Amanda Seyfried (b. 1985). The story revolves around a young bride (Seyfried) who has secretly invited three of her mother's former lovers to her wedding in hopes of discovering which of them is her father. Both the film and original play feature the music of the 1970s disco band ABBA, of which both Andersson and Ulvaeus were members. The massive success of the film led to a sequel, *Mamma Mia! Here We Go Again* (2018), which would include a cameo and musical number by pop icon Cher (born Cherilyn Sarkisian in 1946).

HORROR

In the twenty-first century, horror films remain as popular as in their 1930s heyday. As the decade opened, Hollywood released *Final Destination* (2000), directed by James Wong (b. 1959). The film centers on a group of teenagers, one of whom has a premonition of an impending plane crash, leading the group to avoid the flight; however, the group is chased by death in order to restore the balance of what should have happened. The film was wildly popular, spawning several sequels: *Final Destination 2* (2003), *Final Destination 3* (2006), *The Final Destination* (2009), and *Final Destination 5* (2011).

The zombie genre was given a modern twist in the film *28 Days Later* (2002). This British horror film was directed by Danny Boyle (b. 1956) and starred Cillian Murphy (b. 1976). Cillian plays Jim, a bicycle courier in London who wakes up from a coma twenty-eight days after the outbreak of a virus that turns people into mindless, rage-filled monsters. His experiences show how quickly civilization has collapsed as he and a growing number of acquaintances make their way to safety. The popularity of the film led to a sequel, *28 Weeks Later* (2007).

Rocker Rob Zombie (born Robert Cummings in 1965) made his Hollywood debut by writing and directing the horror classic *House of 1,000 Corpses* (2003). Set in the late 1970s, the film's plot is reminiscent in many ways to the horror classic *The Texas Chainsaw Massacre* (1970). Zombie, however, adds considerably more violence, gore, and blood in his tale of insanity and the supernatural. This secured Rob Zombie's directing credentials, which would lead him to remake the classic *Halloween* (1978). *The Texas Chainsaw Massacre* receive a remake in 2003, directed by Marcus Nispel (b. 1963) and starring Jessica Biel (b. 1982). Another horror remake occurred the following year with *Dawn of the Dead* (2004), directed by Zack Snyder (b. 1966), updating the 1978 classic by zombie progenitor George A. Romero. The success of these remakes would lead to remakes of other horror and slasher classics by decade's end.

Japan had a considerable impact on American horror films in the 2000s. *The Ring* (2002), directed by Gore Verbinski (b. 1964) and starring Naomi Watts (b. 1968), was based on a Japanese film and novel of the same name. The premise of the film was that there existed a videotape that, once viewed, caused the viewer to die within seven days. The film's horrific groundbreaking effects made it a national phenomenon. It inspired three sequels: *The Ring Two* (2005); a short-film, *Rings* (2005); and another theatrical film, *Rings* (2017). Another Japanese inspiration came from *The Grudge* (2004), directed by Takashi Shimizu (b. 1972) and starring *Buffy the Vampire Slayer* alum Sarah Michelle Gellar (b. 1977). It is an American adaptation of Shimizu's Japanese horror film *Ju-On: The Grudge* (2002). The film's frightening special effects made it an instant classic, inspiring two sequels before the end of the decade: *The Grudge 2* (2006) and *The Grudge 3* (2009). A reboot of the original was released in 2020, directed by Nicolas Pesce (b. 1990).

Horror met reality with the film *The Exorcism of Emily Rose* (2005). Directed by Scott Derrickson (b. 1966) and starring Laura Linney (b. 1964) and Tom Wilkinson (b. 1948), the film is loosely based on the story of Anneliese Michel, a young German woman who died from epileptic psychosis, earlier considered to be demonic possession. The story follows the agnostic lawyer Erin (Linney) who defends a Catholic priest (Wilkinson) accused of complicit negligence in the death of Emily Rose, the character based on Michel, played by Jennifer Carpenter (b. 1979). Possessing both the horror of an exorcism film and the drama of a courtroom, the film was met with mixed critical and commercial success.

In 2007, one of the most innovative and successful horror franchises of the twenty-first century was launched with the release of *Paranormal Activity*, directed by Oren Peli (b. 1970). The movie is filmed with a series of edited clips from video cameras set throughout a house in an attempt to capture proof of paranormal activity. The horror of the film comes largely from the anticipation of activity appearing on the film, very similar in many ways to the 1999 mega-hit movie *The Blair Witch Project*. The film was a massive success, leading to multiple sequels utilizing the same premise and telling an overarching story of a family's history with a demon. The succeeding films were *Paranormal Activity 2* (2010), *Paranormal Activity 3* (2011), *Paranormal Activity 4* (2012), *Paranormal Activity: The Marked Ones* (2014), and *Paranormal Activity: The Ghost Dimension* (2015). The found footage concept was given a new twist with the film *Cloverfield* (2008), directed by Matt Reeves (b. 1966), focusing on video footage of an invasion of New York City by a massive monster.

The film *30 Days of Night* (2007) was based on a horror comic-book miniseries, created by Steve Niles (b. 1965) and Ben Templesmith (b. 1984) and published by IDW. Directed by David Slade (b. 1969), the film starred Josh Hartnett (b. 1978) as a sheriff in a small Alaskan town that experiences an annual thirty-days of nighttime. This makes the town a particular draw for vampires, which is where the horror begins. The series continued in direct-to-home-video movies.

As the decade drew to a close, audiences were given a special Halloween treat with aptly named film *Trick 'r Treat* (2009). Directed by Michael Dougherty (b. 1974), the film is an anthology, telling multiple scary and funny tales of events that take place on Halloween night in a small Ohio town. The film starred Rochelle Aytes (b. 1976), Dylan Baker (b. 1959), Brian Cox (b. 1946), and Anna Paquin (b. 1982). The element that connects the stories is the character of

Sam, played by Quinn Lord (b. 1999), a seemingly paranormal child dressed in a makeshift pumpkin-headed costume. Since its release, the film has become cult favorite.

By 2000, the aging Generation X was beginning to feel nostalgic for the 1980s. As such, the 2000s saw several throwbacks to the horror and slasher films of that decade. The *Friday the 13th* franchise returned with its most recent installment, *Jason X* (2001). Directed by James Isaac (1960–2012), it brings America's favorite immortal serial killer into the future, where he becomes a cyborg immortal serial killer. The tagline for the film stated, "Evil gets an upgrade." The two greatest slasher franchises of the 1980s merged with the long-hoped-for mash-up *Freddy vs. Jason* (2003), directed by Ronny Yu (b. 1950). This film finally gave fans the ultimate showdown between *A Nightmare on Elm Street*'s Freddy Kreuger and *Friday the 13th*'s Jason Voorhees, with the outcome predictably uncertain. Rob Zombie returned with his remakes of the Halloween classics *Halloween* (2007) and *Halloween 2* (2008). The success of Zombie's remakes and continued demand for more Jason Voorhees led to one last remake for the decade: *Friday the 13th* (2009). Directed by Marcus Nispel of *The Texas Chainsaw Massacre* remake fame, the attempted reboot failed to gain an audience.

SCIENCE FICTION/FANTASY

The most successful sci-fi/fantasy franchise of all time returned just as the twentieth century came to a close. After years of fan demand, writer and director George Lucas (b. 1944) attempted to meet the insanely high fan expectations with the first of his prequel trilogy: *Star Wars: Episode I—The Phantom Menace* (1999). This trilogy would seek to explore how the villainous Darth Vader from the original trilogy fell from heroic Jedi knight to evil Sith Lord. The first film was followed by its two concluding chapters: *Star Wars: Episode II—Attack of the Clones* (2002) and *Star Wars: Episode III—Revenge of the Sith* (2005). Overly reliant on green-screen special effects, the entire trilogy was derided by fans for years, with *Episode I* frequently tagged as the worst *Star Wars* film. Fan reaction led Lucas to declare that *Episode III* would be the last *Star Wars* film ever. He did, however, have one more theatrical release during the decade: *Star Wars: The Clone Wars* (2008). Directed by Dave Filoni (b. 1974), this CGI-animated film was designed as a launch for the new television series of the same name (Cartoon Network, 2008–2012; Netflix, 2014; Disney+, 2020). In 2012, Lucas sold his company, Lucasfilm, along with all rights to *Star Wars*, to the Walt Disney Corporation, which would lead to five more live-action feature films in the 2010s.

In 2001, longtime Lucas friend and colleague Steven Spielberg returned to the realm of science fiction with his film *A.I.: Artificial Intelligence*. Set in the twenty-second century, the film centers on David, played by Haley Joel Osment (b. 1988), a "mecha" (or android) specifically programmed with the ability to feel and, therefore, love. He is given to a couple whose son has been placed in suspended animation due to an incurable disease. Eventually abandoned by his human parents when their son is revived and feeling jealous of the robot, David embarks on a series of adventures to turn into a real boy (á la Pinocchio). Trapped underwater for two thousand years, David is revived into a world where humans have long since died away and where evolved mechas are the only "life" on Earth. The film concludes with David being given one day with a mechanized version of his human mother and experiencing one happy day of real love. The film was nominated for two Academy Awards but won none.

One of the most popular sci-fi franchises in Hollywood history was the *Planet of the Apes* films (1968–1973). In 2001, 20th Century Fox attempted to reboot the franchise with a new *Planet of the Apes*, directed by Tim Burton and starring Mark Wahlberg (b. 1971) and Helena Bonham Carter. Similar to the original film, Wahlberg plays an American astronaut in the twenty-first century who is inadvertently thrust three thousand years into the future to a distant planet dominated by intelligent apes. On a twist from the original, which exposed the "alien" planet to actually be a future Earth, the astronaut returns to Earth and his own time only to discover that it is now populated and run by apes and that his nemesis from the future alien world is now memorialized in what had originally been the Lincoln Memorial in Washington, DC. The confusing and unexplained ending led to the film being a box-office flop. The studio would have more success in the 2010s with a new prequel trilogy to the original films.

Director Robert Rodriguez made the foray into children's films with *Spy Kids* (2001). The film begins with retired spies Gregorio and Ingrid Cortez, played, respectively, by Antonio Banderas and Carla Gugino (b. 1971), settling down and beginning a family. Unaware of their parents' past, their children, played by Alexa Vega and Daryl Sabara (b. 1988 and 1992, respectively), are thrust into action to rescue their parents when a foe from their past comes back seeking revenge. The massive success of the film led to three sequels: *Spy Kids 2: The Island of Lost Dreams* (2002), *Spy Kids 3-D: Game Over* (2003), and *Spy Kids: All the Time in the World* (2011).

Two of the most popular films of the 1990s were *Jurassic Park* (1993) and *The Lost World: Jurassic Park* (1997), both based on novels by Michael Crichton (1942–2008). A third, original, film was released in 2001: *Jurassic Park III*. Directed by Joe Johnston (b. 1950), it starred Sam Neill (b. 1947) reprising his role from the original film. In this first film not based on a novel, Neill's Dr. Alan Grant is hired by two distraught parents to retrieve their son lost on the island of Isla Sorna (Jurassic Park's Site B, last seen in *The Lost World*), unaware that Grant has never been to that island. Terror ensues as the group consisting of the parents, Grant, his grad student, and a small team of mercenaries find the boy and attempt to escape the island before being devoured by the local dinosaur population. Though the film was largely successful, the franchise would not continue until fourteen years later with the release of *Jurassic World* (2015).

Director Peter Jackson (b. 1961) brought the beloved literary classic trilogy *The Lord of the Rings* by the iconic J. R. R. Tolkien (1892–1973) to the big screen in the 2000s. The first chapter, *The Fellowship of the Ring*, was released in 2001, followed annually by *The Two Towers* (2002) and *The Return of the King* (2003). A huge critical and commercial success, all three films won Academy Awards. *The Fellowship of the Ring* was nominated for thirteen Academy Awards, winning four in logistical categories. *The Two Towers* was nominated for six Oscars, winning two: Sound Editing and Visual Effects. The final installment, *The Return of the King* was the biggest winner of all, nominated for eleven Academy Awards and winning all eleven, including Best Picture, Best Director, and Best Adapted Screenplay.

Without question, however, the most successful film franchise of the decade was the *Harry Potter* series, based on the best-selling children's books of all time by author J. K. Rowling (b. 1965). The massive success of the books was matched by the films produced by Warner Brothers. The series tells the story of the boy wizard, Harry Potter, played by Daniel Radcliffe (b. 1989), and his friends fighting the evil forces of Lord Voldemort, played primarily by Ray Fiennes (b. 1962). The series consisted of the following films: *Harry Potter and the Sorcerer's Stone* (2001), *Harry Potter and the Chamber of Secrets* (2002), *Harry Potter and the Prisoner of Azkaban* (2004), *Harry Potter and the Goblet of Fire* (2005), *Harry Potter and the Order of the Phoenix* (2007), *Harry Potter and the Half-Blood Prince* (2009), *Harry Potter and the Deathly Hallows, Part 1* (2010), and *Harry Potter and the Deathly Hallows, Part 2* (2011). The global success of the film led Warner Brothers to all but beg Rowling to produce more original work, which she finally began to do by agreeing to write five straight-to-screen prequel films beginning with *Fantastic Beasts and Where to Find Them* (2016), which promise to show the rise of legendary wizard Albus Dumbledore, played by Richard Harris (1930–2002) in the first two *Harry Potter* films, Michael Gambon (b. 1940) in the final six, and Jude Law (b. 1972) in the prequel films.

Spielberg returned to science fiction with the film *Minority Report* (2002), based on the short story by Philip K. Dick (1928–1982). Set in the mid-twenty-first century, the film stars Tom Cruise as a PreCrime agent tasked with arresting individuals for crimes that they will one day commit. The tables turn when Agent Anderton (Cruise) is predicted to commit a murder the following day. As he avoids the authorities, he discovers that among the mutant Precogs (the humans who predict the future), there is one that often disputes the claims of the others, producing a "minority report" and picturing an alternate time line. In order to keep the public's faith in the program, the existence of the minority report has been kept secret. Anderton then embarks on a quest to expose the minority report and, hopefully, exonerate himself. Spielberg and Cruise would reunite before the decade's end for one more sci-fi venture.

The highly successful *Star Trek* franchise hit a massive stumbling block with the release of *Star Trek: Nemesis* (2002). Directed by Stuart Baird (b. 1947) and starring the cast of the massively successful television series *Star Trek: The Next Generation* (Syndication, 1987–1994), this was the fourth and final film with that cast. The story revolved around the evil plans of a Romulan clone, played by Tom Hardy (b. 1977), of Federation Starfleet captain Jean-Luc Picard, played by Sir Patrick Stewart (b. 1940). The film was a critical and commercial disaster, suggesting the end to the aging franchise. Director J. J. Abrams (b. 1966) would be tasked with resuscitating the property, which he did with considerable acclaim with *Star Trek* (2009), which attempted to reboot the entire franchise by essentially erasing all that had come before. Despite the film's success, thanks to the conundrum regarding the rights to the franchise divided as they are between CBS TV and Paramount Pictures, the overall future of *Star Trek* remained unclear throughout the 2010s.

In 2003, 20th Century Fox became the first Hollywood studio to make an adaptation of an Alan Moore (b. 1953) comic book, *The League of Extraordinary Gentlemen, Vol. 1* (1999–2000). Directed by Stephen Norrington (b. 1964), the film, like the comic, collects some of the most iconic characters from nineteenth-century British literature, bringing them together to save the world as part of a top-secret government organization. The film starred Sir Sean Connery (1930–2020) as adventurer Allan Quartermain, Peta Wilson (b. 1970) as Mina Harker from *Dracula*, Stuart Townsend (b. 1972) as Dorian Gray, and Jason Flemyng (b. 1966) as Dr. Jekyll and Mr. Hyde. Though a special effects extravaganza, the film was a commercial and critical disaster.

Disney had massive success with their launch of the *Pirates of the Caribbean* franchise, starring Johnny Depp in perhaps his most iconic role, pirate Captain Jack Sparrow. The series originally consisted of the following films: *The Curse of the Black Pearl* (2003), *Dead Man's Chest* (2006), and *At World's End* (2007). All three were huge commercial and critical successes and made an international superstar of Depp. Demand for more films led to two more in the 2010s: *On Stranger Tides* (2011) and *Dead Men Tell No Tales* (2017). The lackluster response to the last two films, as well as personal controversies surrounding Depp, led Disney to announce that the original series would be discontinued, with a reboot of the entire series in the 2020s, presumably without Depp.

Will Smith made his return to sci-fi and fantasy in the 2000s with two successful films. Directed by Alex Proyas (b. 1963), *I, Robot* (2004) was loosely based on the 1950 novel of the same name by sci-fi icon Isaac Asimov (1920–1992). Smith plays a Chicago detective in the not-too-distant future where robots have become servants to humans. Distrustful of robots in general, the detective uncovers a plot that will lead to a robot uprising. Another Smith sci-fi offering from the decade was *Hancock* (2008), directed by Peter Berg (b. 1964). Smith plays John Hancock, a reluctant alcoholic superhero who cares little about the collateral damage of his superhero antics. A public relations specialist played by Jason Bateman (b. 1969) makes it his mission to clean up Hancock's public image, making him the superhero that the people need.

The year 2005 saw an explosion of remakes of old films and adaptations from literature. Directed by Tim Burton and starring Johnny Depp, *Charlie and the Chocolate Factory* was a remake of the 1971 classic *Willy Wonka and the Chocolate Factory*, though much more loyal to the source material written in 1964 by Roald Dahl (1916–1990). The 1933 classic film *King Kong* received a big-budget, CGI-heavy remake directed by Peter Jackson. *The Chronicles of Narnia* (1950–1956) by C. S. Lewis (1898–1963) were transformed into major motion pictures: *The Lion, the Witch, and the Wardrobe* (2005), *Prince Caspian* (2008), and *The Voyage of the Dawn Treader* (2010). In 2005, Spielberg made his last foray into sci-fi in the decade with a remake of the 1953 classic *War of the Worlds* (based on the 1897 novel), starring Tom Cruise. Finally, director Robert Rodriguez created an artistic masterpiece interpretation of the comic book series *Sin City*, by comic-book legend Frank Miller (b. 1957). The film had a star-studded cast led by Mickey Rourke (b. 1952) and became a cult classic. Its success led to a less-successful prequel, *Sin City: A Dame to Kill For* (2014).

Possibly the most original and fantastical sci-fi and fantasy offering from the decade was *Pan's Labyrinth* (2006), written and directed by Guillermo del Toro (b. 1964). It was set during World War II–era Spain. The film works as a parable, fairy tale, and morality tale connected thematically to his earlier film *The Devil's Backbone* (2001). One of the most successful foreign language films in U.S. history, it was nominated for six Academy Awards, winning three: Best Art Direction, Cinematography, and Makeup.

One of the most profitable film franchises of the twenty-first century launched in 2007. *Transformers*, directed by Michael Bay (b. 1965), brought the wildly popular "robots in disguise" toy line to the big screen in their first live-action/CGI film. Bay would return for the series' four sequels: *Transformers: Revenge of the Fallen* (2009), *Transformers: Dark of the Moon* (2011), *Transformers: Age of Extinction* (2014), and *Transformers: The Last Knight* (2017). Voice actor Peter Cullen (b. 1941), best known for voicing Autobot leader Optimus Prime in the original animated television series (Syndication, 1984–1987), returned to the role to voice the CGI big-screen version of the character. A spin-off film, *Bumblebee*, was released in 2018, directed by Travis Knight (b. 1973).

In 2008, Lucas and Spielberg reunited for the fourth installment of their *Indiana Jones* franchise: *Indiana Jones and the Kingdom of the Crystal Skull*. Set in the 1950s, aging professor and archaeologist Dr. Indiana Jones, once more played by Harrison Ford (b. 1942), this time spars with Soviet agents in a quest to discover mysterious alien artifacts. The film also introduces Jones's son, Mutt Williams, played by Shia LaBeouf, b. 1986. Although it was a commercial success and fans were happy to see Indiana Jones in action once more, the film was panned by critics and audiences, largely due to the alien story line and LaBeouf's performance. A fifth film, starring Ford one last time, is scheduled for release in the early 2020s.

Hot off the success of *Transformers*, another popular 1980s toy line was brought to the big screen with *G. I. Joe: The Rise of Cobra* (2009), directed by Stephen Sommers, who opened the decade with *The Mummy Returns*. The film starred Channing Tatum (b. 1980) as team leader Duke and Dennis Quaid (b. 1954) as corps commander General Hawk, leaders of G. I. Joe, America's elite anti-terrorist organization. Their adversary, the international terrorist organization Cobra, attempts to infiltrate and take over the U.S. government. Their success leads to the attempted elimination of the Joes in the sequel, *G. I. Joe: Retaliation* (2013), directed by Jon Chu (b. 1979) and starring Bruce Willis (b. 1955) and the Rock. The series failed to reach the commercial success of the *Transformers* franchise.

After his massive success with *Iron Man* (2008), Robert Downy Jr. revived a century-old franchise with the release of *Sherlock Holmes* (2009). Directed by Guy Ritchie (b. 1968), the film also starred Jude Law as Dr. John Watson. The film was a commercial and critical success, bringing a steampunk, fantasy element to the nineteenth-century hero. A sequel, also directed by Ritchie, was released in 2011: *Sherlock Holmes: A Game of Shadows*. A third film, once more including Downy and Law, is set for release in 2021, to be directed by Dexter Fletcher (b. 1966).

In 1999, director James Cameron (b. 1954) directed the highest-grossing film of all time: *Titanic*. Ten years later, as the 2000s drew to a close, he would beat his own record with a film that he both wrote and directed: the CGI/3D epic *Avatar* (2009). By the twenty-second century, humans have completely depleted Earth of all its natural resources. In need of a new planet to exploit, they discover Pandora, a planet rich with the aptly named mineral unobtanium. Utilizing advanced genetically connected technology called avatars, the humans can interact with the native populations without detection. One of their operatives, Jake, played by Sam Worthington (b. 1976), in his avatar guise, falls in love with a native, Neytiri, played by Zoe Saldana (b. 1978). The film became an international phenomenon, due primarily to its groundbreaking special effects. It was nominated for nine Academy Awards, winning three: Art Direction, Cinematography, and Visual Effects. Four sequels are planned to be released throughout the 2020s.

THE COMIC BOOK WARS

Since the early 1960s, comic book publishers DC Comics and Marvel Comics have dominated the industry, as each other's primary competitors. In the late 1970s, DC Comics brought their products to the big screen with *Superman: The Movie* (1978). DC would dominate the superhero genre in cinema for the next twenty years. That would begin to change with the box-office disaster of *Batman & Robin* (1997), followed soon after with Marvel Comics' first success, *Blade* (1998). Beginning in 2000, Marvel Comics would begin two decades of dominating the big screen in American popular culture as former powerhouse DC desperately attempted to remain relevant.

There are two main reasons for DC's supremacy at the box office prior to 2000. The first is special effects. The only big-screen offerings from DC from 1978 to 1997 were *Superman* and *Batman*. While Batman possesses no superpowers requiring special effects, Superman's powers were easily reproducible with the effects of the time. The complex superpowers of the Marvel heroes were much more complicated and difficult to replicate realistically prior to 1999. The second reason was simple economics. By the late 1970s, DC Comics was owned by the movie studio Warner Brothers. Marvel had no such big brother. In fact, due to the collapse of the comic book market in the mid-1990s, Marvel was forced to declare bankruptcy in 1996. This led to them selling the movie and television rights to some of their more lucrative properties to major movie studios. Sony Pictures purchased the rights to *Spider-Man*, and 20th Century Fox purchased the rights to the *Fantastic Four* and Marvel's *most* profitable property, the *X-Men*.

The first major superhero blockbuster of the 2000s was the 20th Century Fox film *X-Men* (2000). Directed by Bryan Singer (b. 1965) and starring Sir Patrick Stewart, Sir Ian McKellan (b. 1939), and Australian actor Hugh Jackman (b. 1968), *X-Men* brought Marvel's "band of merry mutants" to the big screen and to the attention of a broader swath of American audiences than ever before. The X-Men represent a minority class of humanity blessed/cursed with mutant genes that give many miraculous powers and others simply physical oddities. As they had done in comics for forty years, the X-Men spoke to anyone who has ever felt "other" in society. This—along with the film's amazing special effects—was a huge draw to millions of Americans. The film was followed by two direct sequels: the equally successful *X2: X-Men United* (2003, also directed by Singer) and the disastrous *X-Men: The Last Stand* (2006), which was directed by Brett Ratner (b. 1969).

As in the comics, the breakout character of the films was the mutant anti-hero Wolverine, played by Jackman. Wolverine received a solo trilogy beginning with *X-Men Origins: Wolverine* (2009), directed by Gavin Hood (b. 1963). The film was a commercial and critical flop, but the character's popularity allowed for two more stand-alone films in the 2010s: *The Wolverine* (2013), directed by James Mangold (b. 1963), and the biggest commercial and critical success of all the 20th Century Fox *X-Men* films, *Logan* (2017), also directed by Mangold. The studio would reboot the *X-Men* series in the 2010s, merging the new films with the originals by creating an alternate time line. Disney bought out 20th Century Fox, and the *X-Men* franchise with it, in 2019, just prior to the release of the studio's final *X-Men* offering: the commercial and critical bomb, *Dark Phoenix*, directed by Simon Kinberg (b. 1973).

Sony Pictures had equally strong initial success with the first *Spider-Man* trilogy. *Spider-Man* (2002) was directed by Sam Raimi (b. 1959) and starred Tobey Maguire (b. 1975) as Peter Parker/Spider-Man and Willem Dafoe (b. 1955) as Norman Osborn/Green Goblin. Debuting nearly eight months after the events of 9/11, the film was a massive success, as it did what comic book superheroes had always done on the printed page: provided comfort and hope in frightening times. The sequel, *Spider-Man 2* (2004), was also directed by Raimi, this time pitting Maguire's Spider-Man against Doctor Octopus, played by Alfred Molina. The third film of the original trilogy was far less successful, both critically and commercially. *Spider-Man 3* (2007) would be Raimi's and Maguire's last installment of the franchise. Sony would reboot the series in the early 2010s to limited success before combining their efforts with Marvel Studios in the late 2010s to produce truly lucrative films for the property.

Another Marvel property bought by Fox was *Daredevil*. In 2003, Mark Steven Johnson (b. 1964) directed *Daredevil*, starring Ben Affleck (b. 1972) as the blind vigilante. The film was moderately successful, leading to a spin-off project, *Elektra* (2005), directed by Rob Bowman (b. 1960) and starring Jennifer Garner (b. 1972) as the ninja assassin. The failure of the latter film killed the franchise. Another Marvel-based flop was Universal Pictures' offering *Hulk* (2003), directed by Ang Lee and starring Eric Bana as the beleaguered scientist Dr. Bruce Banner/the Hulk. Universal would have a more successful stab at the character by working directly with the newly established Marvel Studios in 2008 with *The Incredible Hulk*, directed by Louis Leterrier (b. 1973) and starring Edward Norton (b. 1969). A key selling point for the latter *Hulk* film was a cameo during the postcredits by Robert Downey Jr.'s Tony Stark, who had just debuted months earlier in *Iron Man*.

One of Marvel's earliest attempts at a feature film was the 1989 box-office disaster *The Punisher*, starring Dolph Lundgren (b. 1957) as the military-vet-turned-vigilante. Lionsgate Films would have moderately more success with their turn on the character in 2004, directed by Jonathan Hensleigh (b. 1959) and starring Thomas Jane (b. 1969). A third attempt would be released in 2008. *Punisher: War Zone* was directed by Lexi Alexander (b. 1974) and starred Ray Stevenson (b. 1964). After three failed attempts, the character was shelved until Marvel Television was finally able to launch a critically acclaimed Netflix series (2017–2019), starring Jon Bernthal (b. 1976).

Another 20th Century Fox purchase, the *Fantastic Four*, would have some limited success in the mid-2000s. *Fantastic Four* (2005) was directed by Tim Story (b. 1970). It starred Ioan Gruffudd (b. 1973) as Dr. Reed "Mister Fantastic" Richards, Jessica Alba (b. 1981) as Susan "Invisible Woman" Storm, Michael Chiklis (b. 1963) as Ben "the Thing" Grimm, and Chris Evans (b. 1981) as Johnny "Human Torch" Storm. The first film was successful enough to greenlight a sequel, *Fantastic Four: Rise of the Silver Surfer* (2007). The second film reunited the entire team from the original and introduced professional mime Doug Jones (b. 1960) as the body of the Silver Surfer, with Laurence Fishburne (b. 1961) providing the character's voice. The second film was a disaster. Evans would go on to achieve legendary status with his portrayal of Captain America throughout the 2010s.

Another Sony purchase, *Ghost Rider*, would experience only slightly less success than the *Fantastic Four*. *Ghost Rider* (2007) was directed by Mark Steven Johnson (b. 1964) and starred lifelong comic-book enthusiast Nicolas Cage (b. 1964) as Johnny Blaze/Ghost Rider. Like *Fantastic Four*, the film was just successful enough to garner a sequel. Cage returned in *Ghost Rider: Spirit of Vengeance* (2011), this time directed by Mark Neveldine (b. 1973) and Brian Taylor (birth year unknown). The massive box-office failure of the second film led to the discontinuation of the franchise.

With much of the criticism of the Marvel superhero films to date focusing on a lack of consistency with the source material, the company launched its own big-budget studio, Marvel Studios, and began to focus on films of the properties still held by the mother company. Their first offering was a grand slam hit. *Iron Man* (2008) launched what has come to be known as the Marvel Cinematic Universe (MCU). Directed by Jon Favreau (b. 1966), the film rejuvenated the troubled career of Robert Downey Jr. His masterful performance as Tony Stark/Iron Man (many have said a role he was born to play) not only helped to take a previously B-list comic-book superhero and make it a household name but also was a key factor in selling the MCU to audiences around the world. Over the next eleven years, the MCU would become the most profitable film franchise in Hollywood history.

Though with fewer offerings in the 2000s than its longtime rival, DC's record of hits and misses closely mirrored that of Marvel's throughout the decade. By far, DC's most successful franchise was the Dark Knight trilogy. After the disaster of *Batman & Robin* (1997), many thought the Caped Crusader's big-screen career was all but over. That changed with *Batman Begins* (2005), directed by Christopher Nolan (b. 1970) and starring Christian Bale (b. 1974) as

Bruce Wayne/Batman. The first film of the trilogy was a reboot, setting up Batman's origin. It was the series' second offering, *The Dark Knight* (2008), that would take the franchise to its greatest heights. With Nolan and Bale both returning, *Dark Knight*'s massive global success was due largely to the Oscar-winning performance of Heath Ledger (1979–2008) as the Joker, still considered by many to be the greatest rendition of the character ever committed to film. Ledger's death by drug overdose just prior to the film's release gave the film considerable media coverage. The last film of the trilogy saw Nolan and Bale return one last time in *The Dark Knight Rises* (2012). Though a huge commercial success due to the buzz from the previous film, it was panned by critics and fans alike.

Two more Alan Moore projects were translated for the big screen by Warner Brothers/DC: *V for Vendetta* (2005) and *Watchmen* (2009). *V for Vendetta* was based on the 1988 graphic novel from Vertigo/DC that, itself, was originally published by Moore in England in the early 1980s. The film was directed by James McTeigue (birth year unknown) and starred Hugo Weaving (b. 1960) and Natalie Portman (b. 1981). Weaving played V, an anonymous vigilante standing up to the neofascist, radical conservative British government from a not-too-distant future. *Watchmen* was based on Moore's iconic and groundbreaking 1986–1987 graphic novel miniseries. Directed by Zack Snyder, the film starred Jackie Earle Haley (b. 1961), Billy Crudup, Patrick Wilson, and Malin Åkerman (b. 1978) as former vigilantes in a fictional mid-1980s that no longer needs (or wants) superheroes and stands on the verge of global nuclear war. As with the film version of *The League of Extraordinary Gentlemen* and all film and television versions of his works, Moore refused to allow his name to be connected with the projects and refused any financial compensation from them. Both *V for Vendetta* and *Watchmen* were considered box-office failures.

After the success of *Batman Begins*, DC decided to take another chance on *Superman*, not seen in theaters since the disastrous *Superman IV: The Quest for Peace* in 1987. The result was *Superman Returns* (2006), directed by Bryan Singer and starring Brandon Routh (b. 1979) as the Man of Steel. Pretending that the films *Superman III* (1983) and *Superman IV* never happened, *Superman Returns* acts as a direct sequel to the last successful *Superman* film, *Superman II* (1980). The gamble did not work, and the film was considered a massive failure. Superman would not return to theaters until *Man of Steel* (2013). Routh's performance, however, would be honored with his return to the tights in December 2019 to January 2020 as part of the "Crisis on Infinite Earths" crossover story line from DC's several popular television series airing on the CW network at the time.

The only other DC offering in theaters in the 2000s was the film *300* (2007). Directed by Zack Snyder and based on the 1998 graphic novel by Frank Miller, *300* was a fictional and highly stylized retelling of the historic Battle of Thermopylae (479 BCE). The film starred Gerard Butler (b. 1969) as the legendary King Leonidas, who led his small band of three hundred Greek Spartans against the countless legions of the Persian Empire and their king Xerxes, played by Rodrigo Santoro (b. 1975). The film became a cultural phenomenon and is second only to *The Dark Knight* in DC's successes from the decade. It spawned a less-successful sequel, *300: Rise of an Empire*, in 2014.

The films of the 2000s provided a broader array of entertainment than perhaps any period in Hollywood history, potentially opening the door for a new golden age. Meryl Streep and Tom Hanks secured their places as two of the greatest actors in the history of the English-speaking world. The Rock made the transition from the wrestling ring to international big-screen superstar. Special effects reached heights heretofore unthought of. Superheroes once more saved the day in the immediate wake of America's darkest days and opened the door for some of the biggest box-office successes of the decade to follow. Old franchises were given new life, and new franchises were brought to life. The 2000s were a preview of what was possible and what was to come in the decades that followed.

FURTHER READING

Ashby, LeRoy. 2006. *With Amusement for All: A History of American Popular Culture since 1830.* Lexington: University Press of Kentucky.

Bond, Jeff, and Joe Fordham. 2014. Planet of the Apes: *The Evolution of the Legend.* London: Titan.

Carlson, Erin. 2019. *Queen Meryl: The Iconic Roles, Heroic Deeds, and Legendary Life of Meryl Streep.* New York: Hachette.

Chomsky, Noam. 2005. *Imperial Ambitions: Conversations on the Post-9/11 World.* New York: Metropolitan.

Conrad, Dean. 2018. *Space Sirens, Scientists and Princesses: The Portrayal of Women in Science Fiction Cinema.* Jefferson, NC: McFarland.

Coontz, Stephanie. 2016. *The Way We Never Were: American Families and the Nostalgia Trap.* New York: Basic.

Cullen, Jim. 2002. *The Art of Democracy: A Concise History of Popular Culture in the United States.* New ed. New York: Monthly Review.

Danesi, Marcel. 2012. *Popular Culture: Introductory Perspectives.* 2nd ed. Lanham, MD: Rowman & Littlefield.

Dittmer, Jason. 2005. "Captain America's Empire: Reflections on Identity, Popular Culture, and Post-9/11 Geopolitics." *Annals of the Association of American Geographers* 95, no. 3: 626–643.

Edwards, Gavin. 2018. *The World According to Tom Hanks: The Life, the Obsessions, the Good Deeds of America's Most Decent Guy.* New York: Grand Central.

Fahy, Thomas, ed. 2005. *Considering Aaron Sorkin: Essays on the Politics, Poetics and Sleight of Hand in the Films and Television Series.* Jefferson, NC: McFarland.

Faludi, Susan. 2008. *The Terror Dream: Myth and Misogyny in an Insecure America.* London: Picador.

Gardner, David. 2006. *The Tom Hanks Enigma: The Biography of the World's Most Intriguing Movie Star.* London: John Blake.

Haskell, Molly. 2017. *Steven Spielberg: A Life in Films.* New Haven, CT: Yale University Press.

Howe, Sean. 2012. *Marvel Comics: The Untold Story.* New York: Harper Perennial.

Iger, Robert. 2019. *The Ride of a Lifetime: Lessons Learned from 15 Years as CEO of the Walt Disney Company.* New York: Random House.

Jones, Brian Jay. 2016. *George Lucas: A Life.* New York: Little, Brown and Company.

Kaminski, Michael. 2008. *The Secret History of* Star Wars. Kingston, ON: Legacy Books.

McIlwaine, Catherine. 2018. *Tolkien: Maker of Middle-Earth.* Oxford: University of Oxford.

9/11 Memorial. [Posting Date Unknown]. "September 11 Attack Timeline." https://timeline.911memorial.org/#Timeline/2. Retrieved May 8, 2019.

Oswald, Debra L. 2005. "Understanding Anti-Arab Reactions Post-9/11: The Role of Threats, Social Categories, and Personal Ideologies." *Journal of Applied Social Psychology* 35, no. 9: 1775–1799.

Price, David A. 2009. *The Pixar Touch: The Making of a Company.* New York: Vintage.

Salkowitz, Rob. 2012. *Comic-Con and the Business of Pop Culture: What the World's Wildest Trade Show Can Tell Us about the Future of Entertainment.* New York: McGraw-Hill.

Schroeder, Wallace. 2019. *The New York Times Book of Movies: The Essential 1,000 Films to See.* New York: Universe.

Stuller, Jennifer K. 2010. *Ink-Stained Amazons and Cinematic Warriors: Superwomen in Modern Mythology.* London: I. B. Tauris.

Taylor, Chris. 2015. *How* Star Wars *Conquered the Universe: The Past, Present, and Future of a Multibillion Dollar Franchise.* New York: Basic.

Tucker, Reed. 2017. *Slugfest: Inside the Epic 50-Year Battle between Marvel and DC.* New York: Da Capo.

Tye, Larry. 2013. *Superman: The High-Flying History of America's Most Enduring Hero.* New York: Random House.

Willis, Susan. 2005. *Portents of the Real: A Primer for Post-9/11 America.* London: Verso.

CHAPTER 5

Literature

As the twenty-first century dawned, the printed word continued to be as popular as ever. While the first decade of the new millennium would see the rise of e-books, the vast majority of American readers continued to prefer holding a book in their hands, flipping back if needed for review, and smelling the pages. All of that continues to add to the reading experience more than electronic devices ever could. Key to publishing's continued to success was the online juggernaut Amazon. Founded in 1994 by Jeff Bezos (b. 1964), Amazon has been one of the major success stories of the Internet, surviving the dot-com bubble of the late 1990s.

Americans' obsession with books caught the attention of Hollywood. While books had been a source for major motion pictures throughout the film industry's history, the major movie studios began to rely more heavily on published material than ever before throughout the first two decades of the new century. From classics like J. R. R. Tolkien's *Lord of the Rings*, to comic book superheroes, to the worldwide phenomenon of *Harry Potter*, literature was responsible for some of the most profitable films of the 2000s. They all began with excited readers and their voracious appetite for printed adventures and stories both real and imagined. Like all other areas of popular culture in the 2000s, the events of 9/11 proved such a traumatic event that the medium of literature was forced to respond.

9/11

Just six weeks prior to the terror attacks, iconic African American poet Maya Angelou (1928–2014) republished her 1978 poem "Still I Rise" in a small booklet illustrated with art by famed Mexican artist Diego Rivera (1886–1957). The release proved timely, as its words would be needed by a traumatized nation.

The major comic book publishers, headquartered in New York City, felt a particular call to respond, utilizing their significant talents to do what they could for the families of the victims. Smaller publishers Dark Horse, Image, and Chaos! released *9/11: Artists Respond, Volume One*. Contributors included such comic book legends as Will Eisner (1917–2005), Frank Miller (b. 1957), Alan Moore (b. 1953), Dave Gibbons (b. 1970), Jeph Loeb (b. 1958), Trina Robbins (b. 1938), and dozens more.

DC Comics responded with *9/11: The World's Finest Comic Book Writers & Artists Tell Stories to Remember, Volume Two*. With cover art by Alex Ross (b. 1970), others involved included such icons as Neil Gaiman (b. 1960), Stan Lee (1922–2018), Dwayne McDuffie (1962–2011), Dave Gibbons, Denny O'Neil (b. 1939), Neal Adams (b. 1941), and Marv Wolfman (b. 1946). Both volumes donated their proceeds to the following charities: the September 11th Fund, the World Trade Center Relief Fund, the Twin Towers Fund, and the Survivors' Fund. Marvel Comics published two books whose proceeds went to the Twin Towers Fund: *Heroes* and *A Moment of Silence*, the latter with an introduction by New York mayor Rudy Giuliani (b. 1944). Marvel also commemorated the event with a special issue of *The Amazing Spider-Man* featuring several Marvel superheroes responding to the collapse of the towers (J. Michael Straczynski and John Romita Jr., *The Amazing Spider-Man*, Vol. 2, #36, December 2001).

In the world of nonfiction, the book that all of America awaited was *The 9/11 Commission Report* (9/11 Commission 2004). The culmination of more than two years of investigation, the report provided detailed descriptions of how the attacks were planned and executed and by whom. The report concluded that the international terror organization Al-Qaeda and its leader, Osama bin Laden (1957–2011), were entirely responsible and that, though mistakes were made, neither President Bill Clinton (in office 1993–2001) nor President George W. Bush (in office 2001–2009) could have foreseen or prevented the attacks. After leaving office, President Bush (b. 1946) released his book, *Decision Points* (2010), in which he explains his reasoning behind the decisions he made on that day, along with his decisions regarding the war in Iraq, Hurricane Katrina, and the economic collapse of 2008. The trauma left in the wake of the terror attacks would require years of healing and escapism through many forms. Literature was there to help salve the wounds.

Just weeks after the initial terrorist attacks, on October 26, 2001, Congress passed the Uniting and Strengthening America by Providing Appropriate Tools Required to Intercept and Obstruct Terrorism Act (the USA PATRIOT Act). This act, originally widely accepted by the American people, granted sweeping powers to U.S. intelligence agencies to access phone transcripts, text messages, and emails in order to more quickly find and eliminate potential terror threats. In the ashes of 9/11, the American people welcomed this action, but by 2006, as fears had abated, the issue of liberty versus security no longer appeared black-and-white to a growing number of Americans. The divisiveness of the issue was fictionalized by Marvel Comics in perhaps the most important comic book narrative of the decade, *Civil War* (2006–2007).

Written by Mark Millar (b. 1969) and drawn by artist Steve McNiven (b. 1967), the story revolves around a catastrophe in the wake of a superhero battle with a supervillain that caused hundreds of civilian casualties, mostly children. Outrage and fear led the American people and Congress to support a Superhero Registration Act, requiring all superpowered vigilantes to register their identities with the U.S. government and undergo required training to act as law enforcement officers. Some heroes—most notably, Tony Stark/Iron Man, Hank Pym/Yellow Jacket, and Reed Richards of the Fantastic Four—fully supported the idea. Others, led by Captain America, strongly opposed the idea, fearing that any list of identities—no matter how well protected—could make heroes vulnerable, endangering the lives of their loved ones.

Captain America argued that superheroes provided a service, free of charge, out of a sense of duty. Iron Man argued that registration would provide economic stability and benefits to heroes (many of whom, like Spider-Man, struggled financially), as well as calm the angry public. The result was a civil war, pitting heroes against each other. The war came about due to the passing of the Registration Act and the death of Captain America, itself a separate commentary on how the World War II hero was no longer relevant in modern-day Bush America. The comic sparked a national conversation about liberty versus security and what society was losing out of fear. While this work spoke directly to the issues of the day, however, most of the fiction of the 2000s was geared much more toward escapism, allowing American readers to free themselves from the stresses of the new millennium, even if only for a little while—many to such a successful degree that they would be translated into equally successful feature films.

FICTION

Coming into the 2000s, the entire world was already enraptured by perhaps the most successful book series in the history of the printed word. In 1997, British author J. K. Rowling (born Joanne Rowling in 1965) introduced the world to the boy wizard Harry Potter in her first book, *Harry Potter and the Philosopher's Stone* (sold in the United States as *Harry Potter and the Sorcerer's Stone*). The first book begins the tale of eleven-year-old orphan Harry Potter learning that he is, in fact, a wizard and has been invited to attend Hogwarts School of Witchcraft and Wizardry. Soon, Harry, along with friends Ron Weasley and Hermione Granger, discover that he is under threat from his parents' murderer, Lord Voldemort. Each succeeding book recounts another year at Hogwarts and Voldemort's growing threat. After two more globally best-selling books, *Harry Potter and the Chamber of Secrets* (1998) and *Harry Potter and the Prisoner of Azkaban* (1999), Rowling released the fourth (and to date largest) book of the series in 2000: *Harry Potter and the Goblet of Fire*.

While audiences waited three years for the fifth book, Warner Brothers launched the film versions that would ultimately yield nearly $8 billion worldwide, with another $10 billion in DVD and merchandise sales (Rapp and Thakker 2017). In 2003, the darkest book of the series, *Harry Potter and the Order of the Phoenix*, was finally released. The final two books of the series were *Harry Potter and the Half-Blood Prince* (2005) and *Harry Potter and the Deathly Hallows* (2007). By 2017, the books had sold roughly four hundred million copies worldwide in sixty-eight different languages. The enduring success of the franchise led Rowling to write a highly successful stage play, *Harry Potter and the Cursed Child*, in 2016 and to pen a new five-film prequel series beginning with *Fantastic Beasts and Where to Find Them* (also in 2016).

In the immediate wake of 9/11, American audiences were desperate for fantastical escapism. The success of Peter Jackson's *Lord of the Rings* film trilogy (2001–2003) led to a resurgence of the classic books on which the films were based. From 1937 to 1949, iconic British author J. R. R. Tolkien (1892–1973) wrote his epic *The Lord of the Rings*, published in three parts over a fifteen-month period from 1954 to 1955: *The Fellowship of the Ring*; *The Two Towers*; and *The Return of the King*. The trilogy was a sequel to Tolkien's earlier work, *The Hobbit, or There and Back Again* (1937). All four books had been massively popular among baby boomers, maintaining a strong audience among Generation X before being introduced to millennials through the feature films. Along with the *Harry Potter* series, these books were largely responsible for a massive jump in book sales in the early 2000s.

In 2000, author Michael Chabon (b. 1963) published *The Amazing Adventures of Kavalier & Clay*, which would win the Pulitzer Prize for fiction in 2001. The book follows the lives of teenager Josef Kavalier, a Czechoslovakian refugee in the 1930s, and his teenage cousin Sammy Klayman. Both boys are of Jewish descent and are in New York at the birth of the comic book industry, where they become celebrities by the end of World War II. The boys are a fictionalization of the lives of many iconic comic-book superhero creators. The superheroes mentioned in the novel were incorporated into a Dark Horse comic from 2004 to 2006, and Brian K. Vaughn (b. 1976), a contributor to the comic book, also published a sequel to the novel called *The Escapist* (2004).

Dan Brown (b. 1964) launched his *Robert Langdon* series in 2000 with the novel *Angels and Demons*. Langdon is a symbologist, specializing in the historic secret organization the Illuminati. He is called into investigate a threat against the Catholic Church apparently by members of a modern-day Illuminati. Though successful, the book would be outshone by its sequel, *The Da Vinci Code* (2003). This Langdon adventure was based largely on the nonfiction book *The Holy Blood and the Holy Grail* (1982), which suggests that the Holy Grail of legend is, in fact, a bloodline descended directly from Jesus and Mary Magdalene. The fictional adventure places Langdon between a group that seeks to keep this millennia-old bloodline a secret and a radical Catholic faction that wishes to eliminate all evidence of it. The novel became a global phenomenon and reopened the controversial research of the original work. *Da Vinci's* massive success was followed by *The Lost Symbol* (2009), in which Langdon investigates the Founding Fathers' connection to the Free Masons and the secret organization's role in organizing Washington, DC. Brown's Langdon would return in *Inferno* (2013) and *Origin* (2017).

In 2001, readers were introduced to two more works of fiction that would go on to be best sellers. Yann Martel (b. 1963) published *Life of Pi*, which tells the story of Pi, a boy from India, trapped on a lifeboat with a living Bengal tiger. The book examines philosophy and perceptions of reality. In 2012, it was adapted into a feature film. Another 2001 fictional offering was *The Secret Life of Bees* by Sue Monk Kidd (b. 1948). Set in the 1960s, the book is a coming-of-age, on-the-road adventure centered on a teenage girl named Lily. Mourning the loss of her mother, Lily escapes her abusive father by helping their maid, Rosaleen, escape authorities, and the two embark on an adventure. Like *Pi*, *Bees* was adapted into a feature film in 2008 starring Dakota Fanning (b. 1994) and Jennifer Hudson (b. 1981).

A hugely successful novel series launched in 2001 with *Dead until Dark*, by Charlaine Harris (b. 1951), launching what came to be known as *The Southern Vampire Mysteries*. The series consists of thirteen novels and eighteen short stories/novellas. Set in the early 2000s, vampires have gone public after a synthetic blood substitute called True Blood allows them to live without killing humans. The stories are told from the perspective of the main protagonist, Sookie Stackhouse, a telepathic human from Louisiana. The huge success of the books led to an equally successful HBO series, *True Blood* (2008–2014), starring Anna Paquin (b. 1982) as Stackhouse.

In 2002, famed sci-fi and fantasy author Neil Gaiman published the popular children's book *Coraline*. Coraline Jones is a little girl who moves into an old house that has been transformed into multiple apartments. Meeting her strange neighbors, she is warned to not open a door in her apartment that links to a neighboring—presumably empty—apartment. Giving in to curiosity, Coraline does so, entering a magical world that she enjoys more than her own. Over time, however, Coraline discovers that Other Mother, who rules this other realm, is not what she appears, and she works to free herself and the other children who have been trapped there. In 2009, it was adapted into a stop-motion animated film by Tim Burton (b. 1958).

In 2003, first-time author Audrey Niffenegger (b. 1963) published *The Time Traveler's Wife*. Beginning in the early 1990s, Henry DeTamble is a man with a rare medical condition that causes him to randomly travel through time, with no control of when or for how long he disappears. The book examines how his wife, Clare, handles the difficulties inherent with the disorder and shows how love conquers all travails. The novel was made into a feature film in 2009 from Director Robert Schwentke (b. 1968). According to many fans of the television series *Doctor Who* (BBC, 1963–1989; 2005–present), this book influenced writer Stephen Moffat's to create the time-traveling character River Song and her romance with the time-traveling Doctor.

Another popular fiction series of the 2000s was *The Inheritance Cycle*, by Christopher Paolini (b. 1983). The first book of the series was *Eragon* (self-published in 2001; published professionally in 2003). The series follows the adventures of elves and humans who are dragon riders. The other books of the series were *Eldest* (2005), *Brisingr* (2008), and *Inheritance* (2011). *Eragon* was adapted into a feature film in 2006.

Author Elizabeth Kostova (b. 1964) hit big with her debut novel, *The Historian* (2005). The story is told through the perspective of an unnamed woman in the 1970s recalling the adventures of her father, Paul, a history professor, and his wife-to-be, Helen, on a quest in the 1950s to connect the fictional novel *Dracula* (1897) to the real-world Wallachian dictator Vlad Tepes (c. 1430–1477), also known as Vlad the Impaler and Vlad Dracul. Paul seeks to locate Tepes's tomb, and the narrator tells the tale of her parents' investigations. On discovering the empty tomb, they are informed that Dracula is alive. The heroes unite and battle to destroy the vampire, ultimately believing they are successful. The story ends in the early twenty-first century, and the author is led to believe that Dracula may still be alive. Kostova would go on to publish two more books, *The Swan Thieves* (2010) and *The Shadow Land* (2018).

One of the best-selling novels of the decade was *The Girl with the Dragon Tattoo* (2005), by Swedish author Stieg Larsson (1954–2004), published after his death. The story is a murder investigation centered on a troubled teen, Lisbeth Salander, the girl of the title. The story is the first of a trilogy, also written by Larsson and published after his death, called *Millennium*. The other two books in the series are *The Girl Who Played with Fire* (2006) and *The Girl Who Kicked the Hornets' Nest* (2007). A Swedish version of the first novel was adapted into a feature film in 2009 by Director Niels Arden Oplev (b. 1961). The book's international success led to a Hollywood production in 2011 by Director David Fincher (b. 1962).

Possibly the second most popular book series of the 2000s, behind only *Harry Potter*, was the *Twilight* series by Stephanie Meyer (b. 1973). The series consisted of four books: *Twilight* (2005), *New Moon* (2006), *Eclipse* (2007), and *Breaking Dawn* (2008). The fantasy series revolved around a love triangle between Bella Swann (a human teenager), Edward Cullen (a vampire), and Jacob Black (a Native American werewolf). Behind the conflict between the vampire and werewolf for the human girl's love, a centuries-long war exists between vampires and werewolves. The massive success of the novels led to an equally successful film series, released from 2008 to 2012. Another offshoot of the novels was an entirely separate, and equally popular, series of books, *Fifty Shades*. Originally written as *Twilight* fan fiction, author E. L. James (b. 1963) transformed her original idea into a modern tale of sexual exploration, largely told through texting. Those books included *Fifty Shades of Grey* (2011) and *Fifty Shades Darker* and *Fifty Shades Freed* (both in 2012). The novels, like the fantasy romance on which they were based, became a national phenomenon.

Just as the last of the *Twilight* novels hit bookstores, a new and equally popular series was just debuting. In 2008, author Suzanne Collins (b. 1962) published *The Hunger Games*. The book takes place in the dystopian future nation of Panem, which would appear to be the modern-day United States, Canada, or both. The nation is divided into fourteen districts. The Capitol is populated by the government and the wealthy, and it enjoys all the comforts life has to offer. The other thirteen districts live in abject poverty. (District 13 has been destroyed by the first book's opening due to a rebellion against the government.) The districts survive largely on self-reliance, but, once annually, a teenage boy and girl are selected by lottery from each of the thirteen districts to come to the Capitol and compete in the Hunger Games: a televised competition to the death, the winner of which wins food and supplies for their district. The games also offer a reminder of who is in charge.

In the first book, readers meet Katniss Everdeen, a skilled hunter from District 12, the poorest of the remaining districts. Katniss volunteers for the

Hunger Games in order to replace her younger sister, who has been chosen by lottery. When Katniss and the only other surviving participant choose joint suicide rather than victory, a groundswell of support and strength emerges from the districts, forcing the authorities to step in and save both. Katniss becomes a national celebrity and a symbol of hope, something those in charge cannot abide. The adventures continue in the next two books: *Catching Fire* (2009) and *Mockingjay* (2010). The massive success of the trilogy led to equally successful Hollywood adaptations. A prequel novel, *The Ballad of Songbirds and Snakes*, was released in 2020.

As the decade drew to a close, Kathryn Stockett (b. 1969) published *The Help*. Set in Mississippi in the 1960s, the novel tells the story of African American domestic workers in the waning years of the Jim Crow South. Skeeter Phelan is a young white woman recently graduated from college. On her return home, Skeeter is surprised by the sudden disappearance of her family's maid, Constantine, who essentially raised Skeeter. During her investigation into what happened to Constantine, Skeeter discovers how horribly Black domestic workers are treated and sets out to write a book about their experiences, exposing the deeply embedded racism in the South. Like most of the books mentioned so far, *The Help*, too, was adapted into a major feature film in 2011 by Director Tate Taylor (b. 1969).

In the late 1970s and early 1980s, the *Star Wars* films were an international sensation, becoming some of the highest-grossing films of all time and spawning a multi-billion-dollar toy and merchandise industry. After the last film, *Return of the Jedi* (1983), *Star Wars* fans were ravenous for more adventures with their beloved characters. In 1991, Lucasfilm authorized a novel, *Heir to the Empire*, by Timothy Zahn (b. 1951), continuing the *Star Wars* story in print as officially authorized canon. The massive success of the book led to the creation of the Expanded Universe (EU). For the next twenty years, dozens of *Star Wars* novels maintained a huge following, even after new *Star Wars* films and an animated television series opened new avenues of adventures with new characters.

The success of the EU continued well into the 2000s. *Dark Lord: The Rise of Darth Vader* (2005) by James Luceno (b. 1947) acted as a sequel to the recently released film *Star Wars: Episode III—Revenge of the Sith*. The nine-book series *Legacy of the Force* (2006–2008) by authors Aaron Allston (b. 1960), Troy Denning (b. 1958), and Karen Traviss (birth year unknown) continued the stories of the heroes from the original film trilogy, set forty years after the first film. With the primary protagonists—Luke Skywalker, Han Solo, and Leia Organa-Solo—in their sixties, the crux of the story revolves around Han and Leia's twin children. Both force-sensitive Jedi, their son, Jacen, falls to the dark side, and only his twin sister, Jaina, can stop him. In 2006, author Drew Karpyshyn (b. 1971) published *Darth Bane: Path of Destruction*, examining the origin of the modern Sith Lords in the *Star Wars* saga. It was followed by two more novels: *Darth Bane: Rule of Two* (2007) and *Darth Bane: Destiny of Evil* (2009).

In 2007, Michael Reaves (b. 1950) and Steve Perry (b. 1947) published *Death Star*. This novel recovers the events of the original *Star Wars* film (1977) from the perspectives of other, previously unknown characters working on the doomed battle station and showing that not everyone working for the bad guys were bad people. *Star Wars* literature experimented with the horror genre with *Death Troopers* (2009), by Joe Schreiber (b. 1969). This book unfolds a tale of a zombielike outbreak on an imperial star destroyer. The decade ended with the launch of another nine-book series: *Fate of the Jedi* (2009–2012), by Allston, Denning, and Christie Golden (b. 1963).

Although the *Star Wars* EU novels continued to be best sellers, when Disney bought Lucasfilm in 2012, they announced that, as part of their overall plan for the future of *Star Wars*, they were erasing the canon status of all previously published novels and comic books. This outraged fans across the globe who had dedicated themselves to these stories, clinging to them as the official word on their heroes' postfilm adventures. Though a new EU would be relaunched, it is too soon to tell if the franchise has maintained its original fan base.

One of the most popular suspense writers of modern times has been Mary Higgins Clark (1927–2020). Her mystery novels from the 2000s included *Before I Say Goodbye* (2000), *On the Street Where You Live* (2001), *The Second Time Around* (2003), *Nighttime Is My Time* (2004), *I Heard That Song Before* (2007), *Where Are You Now* (2008), and *Just Take My Heart* (2009). Some of her works had Christmas themes: *Deck the Halls* (2000), *Santa Cruise: A Holiday Mystery at Sea* (2002), *The Christmas Thief* (2004), and *Dashing through the Snow* (2008). She continued to be a best-selling author throughout the 2010s.

By 2000, Anne Rice (b. 1941) was a mainstay on U.S. fiction sales charts with her *Vampire Chronicles*, beginning with *Interview with the Vampire* (1976). The *Chronicles* continued in the early 2000s with the following works: *Merrick* (2000), *Blood and Gold* (2001), *Blackwood Farm* (2002), and *Blood Canticle* (2003). Rice reconnected with the Catholic Church in 1998, and after her husband, Stan, died in 2002, Anne Rice put aside all things occult and committed herself more to her Catholic faith. She then embarked on a trilogy of novels covering the life of Jesus Christ called *Christ the Lord: Out of Egypt* (2005), *The Road to Cana* (2008), and a third, so far unpublished, novel, *Kingdom of Heaven*. In 2014, Rice returned to her beloved *Chronicles*—some say having once more moved away from the Catholic Church due to its continued stance against the LGBTQ+ community—with the release of *Prince Lestat*. Her *Vampire Chronicles* continue into the 2020s, with a television series announced to appear on the Hulu streaming service.

Horror legend Stephen King (b. 1947) continued his prolific best-selling career in the first decade of the twenty-first century. In those ten years, he published the following works: *On Writing: A Memoir of the Craft* and *Riding the Bullet* (both in 2000); *Dreamcatcher, Black House,* and *The Death of Jack Hamilton* (all in 2001); *Everything's Eventual* and *From a Buick 8* (both in 2002); *The Things They Left Behind, Harvey's Dream,* and *Wolves of the Calla: The Dark Tower V* (all in 2003); *Song of Susannah: The Dark Tower VI* and *The Dark Tower* (both in 2004); *The Colorado Kid* (2005); *Lisey's Story, Cell,* and *Willa* (all in 2006); *Blaze* and *The Gingerbread Girl* (both in 2007); *Wastelands: Stories of the Apocalypse, Duma Key,* and *A Very Tight Place* (all in 2008); and *Stephen King Goes to the Movies* and *A Good Marriage* (both in 2009). Continuing to publish throughout the 2010s, since 2016, King has been equally prolific on Twitter with frequent condemnations of the actions of policies of President Donald Trump.

NONFICTION

Though fiction continued to prove wildly popular, especially in the wake of 9/11, Americans continued to consume some of the best nonfiction works of all time, many winning the Pulitzer Prize. In the realm of nonfiction, history continued to fascinate Americans of all ages, and the 2000s added considerably to the history of the United States. From a continued examination of America's racial history to a reconnecting with the Founding Fathers to the Cold War and beyond, readers in the 2000s gained fascinating insights into American history, expanding their understanding of who we have been as a nation and how we came to be who we are in the twenty-first century.

The decade opened with a Pulitzer Prize–winning biography, the second volume of a massive biography of W. E. B. Du Bois (1868–1963), the first African American to receive a PhD from Harvard University and one of the most important icons in American civil rights history. *W. E. B. Du Bois: The Fight for Equality and the American Century, 1919–1963* (2000) by David Levering Lewis (b. 1936) covers Du Bois's decades of service with the NAACP, his communist ideology during the Second Red Scare, and his death in Ghana on August 27, 1963, at the age of ninety-five. The first volume of the biography, *W. E. B. Du Bois: Biography of a Race, 1868–1919* (1994), also won the Pulitzer Prize. To date, Lewis's work is still considered the authoritative source on the subject.

As Americans built a bridge to the twenty-first century, they began looking back, finding renewed interest in the Founding Fathers and the country's origins. *Founding Brothers* (2000) by Joseph Ellis (b. 1943) won the Pulitzer Prize for history in 2001. Rather than a biographical examination of any specific Founding Father, Ellis focuses on specific events in the early decades of the republic: the duel that cost Alexander Hamilton (c. 1756–1804) his life, the famous dinner where the location for Washington, DC, was negotiated, the farewell address of President George Washington (1732–1799), and the strained relationship between onetime friends John Adams (1735–1826) and Thomas Jefferson (1743–1826). In 2002, the History Channel premiered a documentary based on the book.

David McCullough (b. 1933), one of the most popular historians in the United States, published his own tome to the Founders with *John Adams* (2001). Rather than a full-life biography, *John Adams* begins with Adams's life as a lawyer in and around Boston, Massachusetts, and particularly with his defense of the nine British soldiers arrested for the Boston Massacre of 1770. The book then follows Adams through his involvement with the American Revolution; his time as the U.S. ambassador to Great Britain; his terms as the new country's first vice president and second president; and his postpolitical life at his home of Braintree. The book won the Pulitzer for biography in 2002 and was adapted into an award-winning miniseries on HBO in 2008. Above all, however, it returned Adams to the American consciousness, as he had been pushed to the back of American memory for nearly two centuries.

Another Pulitzer Prize–winning offering from 2001, this time for general nonfiction, was *Carry Me Home: Birmingham, Alabama, the Climactic Battle of the Civil Rights Revolution* by Diane McWhorter (b. 1952). A native of Birmingham and only around ten-years-old at the time of the historic 1963 protests, McWhorter brings to the narrative a sense of identity often missing in history. She recounts the brutal tactics of Birmingham commissioner of public safety Eugene "Bull" Connor (1897–1973), including his attacks against the Children's Marchers and the movement as directed by Dr. Martin Luther King (1929–1968). The events in Birmingham would not only gain national and international sympathy for Blacks in the South but would also push President John F. Kennedy (1917–1963) to push what would become the Civil Rights Act of 1964.

An even darker moment in American history appeared in *The Devil in the White City: Murder, Magic, and Madness at the Fair That Changed America* (2003) by Erik Larson (b. 1954). This book covers both the amazing and horrific events surrounding the 1893 World's Fair in Chicago, Illinois. This particular world's fair is notable for numerous firsts: the first time the Pledge of Allegiance was recited publicly, the first nighttime events illuminated with electrical light, the first appearance of Cracker Jacks, the first public presentation of Aunt Jemima pancake mix, the first appearance of zippers, and the first use of the Ferris wheel, to name but a few. The fair was also notable, however, for murders perpetrated by Dr. H. H. Holmes (1861–1896), considered to be America's first serial killer and also a likely suspect for the true identity of the legendary London murderer, Jack the Ripper.

Steve Coll (b. 1958) published yet another Pulitzer Prize winner (for general nonfiction) with *Ghost Wars: The Secret History of the CIA, Afghanistan, and Bin Laden, from the Soviet Invasion to September 10, 2001* (2004). At the height of America's post-9/11 trauma, Coll's book examines how Osama bin Laden (1957–2011) came to be the international threat that brought a superpower to its knees. After the Soviet Union invaded Afghanistan in 1979, the CIA began training freedom fighters, many recruited from Saudi Arabia and Pakistan, to fight against the Soviet aggressors. Bin Laden was one such recruit. An expanded edition as published in 2005, with added material from the *9/11 Report*.

The Founding Fathers led to another Pulitzer Prize winner for history with *Washington's Crossing* (2004) by David Hackett Fischer (b. 1935). This was a major turning point in the American Revolution. As 1776 came to a close, General Washington faced the very real possibility that much of his army would not reenlist when their commitments expired in January, 1777. The crossing immortalized in the 1851 painting by Emanuel Leutze (1816–1868) led to the sneak attack Battle of Trenton, where Washington successfully subdued a detachment of British-hired Hessian mercenaries. The victory inspired his men to reenlist, leading to eventual American victory.

Doris Kearns Goodwin (b. 1943), considered by many to be America's premier presidential historian, published her sixth book, *Team of Rivals: The Political Genius of Abraham Lincoln*, in 2005. This book is a multipronged biography examining not only Lincoln's rise to the presidency but also minibiographies of the men who opposed him for the nomination. Lincoln would go on to convince these men to support him as members of his cabinet, where each transformed from hating the back-country, self-educated lawyer to revering him as perhaps the greatest president in American history. Steven Spielberg (b. 1946) utilized the last portion of the book—the political maneuvering behind passing the Thirteenth Amendment to the Constitution, abolishing slavery in the United States—as the basis for his film *Lincoln* (2012).

Three amazing histories were published in 2006–2007. Civil rights were once more at the center with *The Race Beat: The Press, the Civil Rights Struggle, and the Awakening of a Nation* (2006) by Gene Roberts (b. 1932) and Hank Klibanoff (b. 1949). The book examines how journalists, for both television and print media, covered the civil rights movement. Both authors were, themselves, journalists. The book won the Pulitzer for history in 2007. Robert Dallek (b. 1934) is another highly respected presidential historian, most famous for his works on President John Kennedy and his multivolume work on President Lyndon Johnson (1908–1973). In 2007, he published *Nixon and Kissinger: Partners in Power.* The book examines the relationship between President Richard Nixon (1913–1994) and his national security advisor, Dr. Henry Kissinger (b. 1923). It was nominated for the Pulitzer in history but lost to *The Race Beat.* David Halberstam (1934–2007) was a journalist who gained notoriety covering both the Vietnam War and the civil rights movement. He gained considerable notice as an historian for his book *The Fifties* (1993), a general history of the decade, its major figures and events. His last completed work was *The Coldest Winter: America and the Korean War,* published after his death in an automobile accident in 2007. *The Coldest Winter* is, perhaps, the most detailed and thorough account of the Korean War (1950–1953) ever published.

In 2008, the United States elected its first African American president, Barack Obama (b. 1961). That year, two more incredible works of African American history were published. Douglas Blackman (b. 1964) published *Slavery by Another Name: The Re-Enslavement of Black Americans from the Civil War to World War II.* This book examined the Jim Crow South, with its de facto slave labor of sharecropping, its segregationist policies, racist Jim Crow Laws, and enforcement of all the above through lynching. In 2009, it won the Pulitzer for general nonfiction. *The Hemingses of Monticello* by Annette Gordon-Reed (b. 1958) examines the family history of the slave woman Sally Hemmings (c. 1773–1835), who gave birth to at least one child by President Thomas Jefferson. Many believe all five of her children were fathered by Jefferson, but, to date, only her youngest son, Eston (1808–1856), has been genetically tied to the Founding Father. Gordon-Reed won the Pulitzer for history for this work in 2009.

Two more Pulitzer Prize winners were published as the decade closed. *The First Tycoon: The Epic Life of Cornelius Vanderbilt* (2009) by T. J. Stiles (b. 1964) won the Pulitzer for biography for this narrative of the first robber baron in the United States, known during his life as the Commodore and founder of the Vanderbilt dynasty. *The Dead Hand: The Untold Story of the Cold War Arms Race and Its Dangerous Legacy* (2009) by David E. Hoffman (b. 1953) won the Pulitzer for general nonfiction for this account of the long-classified details of the American-Soviet arms race. It is clear that the histories and biographies produced in the 2000s were not only widely read but also widely respected.

Other nonfiction works from the decade focused more on current events and sociopsychological issues facing Americans in post-9/11 America. Some books presented various bits of wisdom, others analysis of current events, and still others apparent political manifestos for potential presidential runs, which has become standard in the twenty-first century. During the election year of 2000, celebrity businessman Donald Trump (b. 1946), with the assistance of Dave Shiflett (birth year unknown), published *The America We Deserve*. This book was meant to gauge interest in and gain support for a possible third-party run for the presidency that year. In it, Trump puts forth some of his conservative viewpoints, such as stronger immigration laws and a flat income tax. He also made vague predictions of impending terrorist attacks on U.S. soil. The book gained little notice among conservatives and was written off as ridiculous by liberals. Trump would, however, ride very similar talking points to presidential victory with the Republican Party in 2016.

As the twentieth century came to a close, a book was released celebrating perhaps the most famous band of the century: *The Beatles Anthology* (2000). A companion piece to their multivolume documentary DVD release, as well as their CD recording anthology, both released in the mid- to late 1990s, the book collects interviews and photographs of the Fab Four: John Lennon (1940–1980), Paul McCartney (b. 1942), George Harrison (1943–2001), and Ringo Starr (born Richard Starkey in 1940). The three-piece collection was a must for Beatles fans. The CD included two "new" recordings from the band, incorporating unreleased music and lyrics from the late Lennon mixed with vocals and music from the remaining three Beatles.

Less than a month after 9/11, lawyer, legal analyst, and political pundit Jeffrey Toobin (b. 1960) published *Too Close to Call: The Thirty-Six-Day Battle to Decide the 2000 Election* (2001). What was expected to be a close but relatively uninteresting presidential election quickly became one of the most divisive events in modern American history. Confusion over who won the vital state of Florida, whose electoral votes would decide the victor, led the team behind Texas governor George W. Bush, led by former secretary of state James Baker (b. 1930), and the team supporting Vice President Al Gore (b. 1948), led by campaign staffer Ron Klain (b. 1961), to turn Florida into a near-literal battleground. More than a month after election day, repeated recounts failed to cement a victor. Ultimately, the U.S. Supreme Court, in *Bush v. Gore* (2000), ordered the recounts halted, giving the state's electoral votes and the presidency to Bush.

On the same day as Toobin's book, authors Judith Miller (b. 1948), William Broad (b. 1951), and Stephen Engelberg (birth year unknown) released their book, *Germs: Biological Weapons and America's Secret War* (2001). Utilizing declassified American and Soviet documents, as well as countless interviews with scientists and government officials, the three authors provide a vivid analytical account of American and Soviet/Russian biological weapons research since the 1980s and discuss America's ability in 2000 to counter bioweapons attacks. Though viewed by some to be overly critical and pessimistic, the authors' research was presented shortly after the book's release on the television science program *Nova* (PBS, 1974–present).

On a much lighter note, Bradford W. Wright (b. 1968) published *Comic Book Nation: The Transformation of Youth Culture in America* (2001). The book provides perhaps the most comprehensive study to date on the history of superhero comic books, an industry in steep decline at the time of the book's writing but about to experience a massive resurgence by the time of publication. A second edition was printed in 2003 with a new epilogue examining superhero comics' reactions to 9/11. The book became the basis for the 2003 History Channel documentary *Comic Book Superheroes Unmasked*. Considering the massive impact of comic book superheroes in the decades that followed 9/11, the book, in hindsight, proves quite prescient.

Investigative reporter Bob Woodward (b. 1943), famous for being one of the first reporters to deeply investigate the Watergate break-in in 1972, along with his partner, Carl Bernstein (b. 1944), that ultimately brought down President Richard Nixon, utilized his decades of Washington insider connections to publish his book *Bush at War* (2002). With access to significant notes from National Security Council meetings in the immediate wake of 9/11, Woodward recounts the decisions made by the Bush administration leading up to the invasion of Afghanistan less than a month after the terrorist attacks. Woodward's reputation also gained him access to personal interviews with key members of the Bush administration: Vice President Dick Cheney (b. 1941), Secretary of State Colin Powell (b. 1937), National Security Advisor Condoleezza Rice (b. 1954), and President Bush himself.

In November, 2000, outgoing first lady Hillary Rodham Clinton (b. 1947) was elected senator from New York, taking office shortly before her husband stepped down from the presidency. In 2003, Clinton published her second book, *Living History*. Many bought the book in hopes that it would provide juicy information regarding President Clinton's extramarital affairs, particularly his affair with intern Monica Lewinsky (b. 1973), which ultimately led to his impeachment in 1998. Those who hoped for such details would be disappointed. Others believed that the book may perhaps have been a prelude to an announcement that the senator would run for president in 2004. Ultimately, however, Rodham Clinton's quest for the Oval Office would wait another four years, only to be defeated for the Democratic nomination by Illinois senator Barack Obama. She would ultimately gain the Democratic nomination in 2016, winning the national popular vote by nearly three million votes but losing the electoral college to Donald Trump.

The War on Terror declared after the 9/11 attacks ultimately led to the American invasion of Iraq in 2003. In 2004, embedded journalist Evan Wright (b. 1966) published *Generation Kill: Devil Dogs, Iceman, Captain America, and the New Face of American War*. The book recounts Wright's time with the 1st Recon Battalion, USMC, and their encounters in Iraq. Though trained as reconnaissance soldiers, the mission in Iraq used—or, as some military specialists would say, misused—the battalion more as military police in the wake of the U.S. invasion. The book has become a must-read for commissioned and noncommissioned officers in the military for its insights into the realities of modern warfare. Originally released as a three-part article in *Rolling Stone* magazine in 2003, the book was adapted into an HBO miniseries in 2008.

In 2005, economics professor Dr. Steven Levitt (b. 1967) and journalist Stephen J. Dubner (b. 1963) published *Freakonomics: A Rogue Economist Explores the Hidden Side of Everything*. The best-selling book examines the role of incentives in overall economics. Of the many fascinating topics discussed, the book takes on controversial material such as the role of the legalization of abortion in crime reduction since the 1970s. Although the book has met considerable criticism, most notably about the research used to back up arguments, Levitt and Dubner's overall conclusions still prove fascinating food for thought. In the end, the book succeeded in what academic research does best: opening the door for debate.

American football, the new American pastime by 2000, was the topic of the book *The Blind Side: Evolution of a Game* (2006) by Michael Lewis (b. 1960). The first part of the book examines how field strategy has changed in recent decades. With most quarterbacks throwing right-handed, a literal blind side is created on the quarterback's left, opening him up for easier tackling. This has led many football teams to focus on more powerful left tackles. The second half of the book focuses on the life of pro footballer Michael Oher (b. 1986). A poor Black youth from Tennessee, Oher was taken in by a wealthy white family who adopted him and helped him get through high school and on to successful college and pro football careers. The latter half of the book was later adapted into the feature film *The Blind Side* (2009) by Director John Lee Hancock (b. 1956).

Two books published in 2006 gained considerable notoriety. Elizabeth Gilbert (b. 1969) published her own journey of self-discovery in the book *Eat, Pray, Love: One Woman's Search for Everything Across Italy, India and Indonesia* (2006). This book was a memoir of the author's overseas travels in the wake of her divorce. The title explains how she used her travels: eating in Italy, learning to meditate in India, and combining the two in Indonesia. The book was a best seller and was later adapted into a feature film in 2010 directed by Ryan Murphy (b. 1965) and starring Julia Roberts (b. 1967) as the troubled author. Oxford biologist Dr. Richard Dawkins (b. 1941) published the controversial book *The God Delusion* in 2006. The essential premise, clearly stated in the title, is that there exists no concrete evidence whatsoever of a supernatural God and that anyone who believes in such a deity is suffering from a delusion. Like *Freakonomics* before it, the book was met with considerable criticism, but it opened the door of debate on the subject.

By 2004, *The Daily Show* (Comedy Central, 1996–present) had become perhaps the most influential political program on television. The brilliant satire and political commentary of comedian and host Jon Stewart (b. 1962) and his staff of commentators made this previously comedic send-up of network news the go-to source for actual news among Americans under forty-five. In 2006, Stewart and company published their satirical work, *America (The Book)*, a satirical textbook explaining how American government and democracy works. In 2005, popular *Daily Show* commentator Stephen Colbert (b. 1964) spun off his satirical conservative pundit character into his own series, *The Colbert Report* (Comedy Central, 2005–2014), itself a send-up of conservative pundit programming like *The O'Reilly Factor* (FOX News, 1996–2017). In 2007,

Colbert (or, rather, his on-screen character) published *I Am America (And So Can You!)*, a faux autobiography of the radical conservative character. These two comedians became some of the most important political influencers of the 2000s.

In 2004, a little-known state senator from Illinois, Barack Obama, running for the U.S. Senate seat from Illinois that year was chosen as he keynote speaker at the Democratic National Convention, which gave the presidential nomination that year to Senator John Kerry (b. 1943). His powerful speech immediately launched him to celebrity status within the Democratic Party, and after he won his Senate race in 2004, whispers began of a future presidential run. In 2006, Obama published *The Audacity of Hope: Thoughts on Reclaiming the American Dream*. The book, spelling out most of what would become his 2008 presidential campaign platform, was Obama's second book; his first was the memoir *Dreams from My Father: A Story of Race and Inheritance* (1995). Once he was running for the presidency in 2008, Obama's campaign released *Change We Can Believe In: Barack Obama's Plan to Renew America's Promise*. The book would become a manifesto for Obama's historic rise to the presidency of the United States.

By 2008, the ongoing wars in Afghanistan and Iraq had devolved into quagmires, and popular support for both were waning fast. War correspondent Dexter Filkins (b. 1961) published his experiences covering both wars in the book *The Forever War* (2008). That same year, in the midst of a presidential election, the stock market collapsed under the weight of overleveraged Wall Street banks, threatening another Great Depression. *New York Times* financial correspondent Andrew Ross Sorkin (b. 1977) deeply researched the events leading to what would ultimately become known as the Great Recession, publishing his research in the book *Too Big to Fail: The Inside Story of How Wall Street and Washington Fought to Save the Financial System—and Themselves* (2009). The book provided considerable insight into the behind-the-scenes maneuverings to keep the American and global economies afloat, with particular attention paid to the three government officials most closely tied to the unfolding crisis: U.S. secretary of the treasury Hank Paulson (b. 1946), Chair of the U.S. Federal Reserve Ben Bernanke (b. 1953), and President of the New York Federal Reserve Bank Tim Geithner (b. 1961). The book was adapted into a 2011 HBO film.

The presidential election of 2000 and the terrorist attacks of 9/11 threw the United States into a state of chaos, one that would continue to define the decade that followed. The overwhelming grief and fear felt by the vast majority of Americans in the wake of the attacks called for a degree of escapism not needed since the social and economic chaos of the 1960s and 1970s. American literature was there to answer that call. From fantastical novels and comic books that transported American readers to realms other than what was presented on cable news, to rich histories that reminded Americans of all strata how far the county had come and how much Americans could accomplish together, to biographies, memoirs, and analyses that expressed the greatness of American thought and spirit, the printed word provided a salve to wounds that were once thought to be unhealable.

FURTHER READING

Abad-Santos, Alex. 2016. "Marvel's Civil War and Its Politics, Explained." *Vox*, May 3. https://www.vox.com/2016/5/3/11531348/marvel-civil-war-explained. Retrieved January 2, 2020.

Angelou, Maya. 1978. "Still I Rise." Poets.org. https://poets.org/poem/still-i-rise?gclid=EAIaIQobChMI9cnh2fHn5gIVrP_jBx1BYAPHEAAYASAAEgKFMPD_BwE. Retrieved January 3, 2020.

Beahm, George. 2015. *The Stephen King Companion: Four Decades of Fear from the Master of Horror*. New York: St. Martin's Griffin.

Bennett, Jessica. 2019. "This Gen X Mess: The Tech, Music, Style, Books, Trends, Rules, Films and Pills That Made Gen X . . . So So-So." *New York Times*, May 16. https://www.nytimes.com/interactive/2019/05/14/style/generation-xers.html?utm_source=pocket-newtab. Retrieved May 16, 2019.

Bowen, Michelle. 2018. *J. K. Rowling: From Welfare to Billionaire, a Biography*. Scotts Valley, CA: CreateSpace.

Cancel, Nola. 2014. *Anne Rice the Interviews: A Compilation of Interviews with the Iconic Author on Everything from the Writing Process to Her Extraordinary Life*. Scotts Valley, CA: CreateSpace.

Colbert, Stephen. 2009. *I Am America (and So Can You!)*. New York: Grand Central.

Crowson, H. Michael, Teresa K. Debacker, and Stephen J. Thoma. 2006. "The Role of Authoritarianism, Perceived Threat, and Need for Closure or Structure in Predicting Post-9/11 Attitudes and Beliefs." *Journal of Social Psychology* 146, no. 6: 733–750.

Danesi, Marcel. 2012. *Popular Culture: Introductory Perspectives*. 2nd ed. Lanham, MD: Rowman & Littlefield.

Dittmer, Jason. 2005. "Captain America's Empire: Reflections on Identity, Popular Culture, and Post-9/11 Geopolitics." *Annals of the Association of American Geographers* 95, no. 3: 626–643.

Evans, Jennifer C. 2002. "Hijacking Civil Liberties: The USA PATRIOT Act of 2001." *Loyola University Chicago Law Journal* 33, no. 4: 933–990.

Faludi, Susan. 2008. *The Terror Dream: Myth and Misogyny in an Insecure America*. London: Picador.

Howe, Sean. 2012. *Marvel Comics: The Untold Story*. New York: Harper Perennial.

Irwin, William, and Gregory Bassham, eds. 2010. *The Ultimate* Harry Potter *and Philosophy: Hogwarts for Muggles*. Hoboken, NJ: Wiley.

McIlwaine, Catherine. 2018. *Tolkien: Maker of Middle-Earth*. Oxford: University of Oxford.

Mulholland, Neil. 2007. *The Psychology of Harry Potter: An Unauthorized Examination of the Boy Who Lived*. Dallas, TX: Smart Pop.

National Commission on Terrorist Attacks Upon the United States. 2004. *The 9/11 Report*. New York: St. Martin's.

9/11 Commission. 2004. "The 9/11 Commission Report." National Commission on Terrorist Attacks Upon the United States. https://www.9-11commission.gov/report/. Retrieved January 3, 2020.

Obama, Barack. 2006. *The Audacity of Hope: Thoughts on Reclaiming the American Dream*. New York: Crown.

Pate, Nancy. 2003. "Lord of the Rings Films Work Magic on Tolkien Book Sales." *South Florida Sun-Sentinel*, August 20. https://www.sun-sentinel.com/news/fl-xpm-2003-08-20-0308190249-story.html. Retrieved January 4, 2020.

Rapp, Nicholas, and Krishna Thakker. 2017. "Harry Potter at 20: Billions in Box Office Revenue, Millions of Books Sold." *Fortune*, June 26. https://fortune.com /2017/06/26/harry-potter-twentieth-anniversary/. Retrieved January 4, 2020.

Rice, Anne. 2010. *Called out of Darkness: A Spiritual Confession*. New York: Anchor.

Richmond, Kia Jane. 2018. *Mental Illness in Young Adult Literature: Exploring Real Struggles through Fictional Characters*. Santa Barbara, CA: Libraries Unlimited.

Sorkin, Andrew Ross. 2009. *Too Big to Fail: The Inside Story of How Wall Street and Washington Fought to Save the Financial System—And Themselves*. New York: Penguin.

Stewart, Jon, et al. 2004. *America (The Book)*. New York: Warner/Grand Central.

Stone, Brad. 2013. *The Everything Store: Jeff Bezos and the Age of Amazon*. Boston: Little, Brown and Company.

Topping, Seymore, and Sig Gissler. [Posting Date Unknown]. "History of the Pulitzer Prizes." Pulitzer Prizes. https://www.pulitzer.org/page/history-pulitzer-prizes. Retrieved January 2, 2020.

Tucker, Reed. 2017. *Slugfest: Inside the Epic 50-Year Battle between Marvel and DC*. New York: Da Capo.

Veloso, Francisco, and John Bateman. 2013. "The Multimodal Construction of Acceptability: Marvel's *Civil War* Comic Books and the PATRIOT Act." *Critical Discourse Studies* 10, no. 4: 427–443.

Waldfogel, Joel. 2018. *Digital Renaissance: What Data and Economics Tell Us about the Future of Popular Culture*. Princeton, NJ: Princeton University Press.

Whitehead, John W., and Steven H. Aden. 2002. "Forfeiting 'Enduring Freedom' for 'Homeland Security': A Constitutional Analysis of the USA Patriot Act and the Justice Department's Anti-Terrorism Initiatives." *American University Law Review* 51, no. 6: 1081–1133.

Willis, Susan. 2005. *Portents of the Real: A Primer for Post-9/11 America*. London: Verso.

Wright, Bradford W. 2003. *Comic Book Nation: The Transformation of Youth Culture in America*. Baltimore, MD: Johns Hopkins University Press.

CHAPTER 6

Technology

By the end of the twentieth century, the United States was a very different place than it had been just ten years prior. Much of the intervening change can be connected directly to the internet. Conceived in the 1960s and expanded to some limited commercial use in the 1980s, the internet—or "interconnected network" of computers—truly went mainstream in the mid-1990s. Due to the popular response to chat rooms, search engines, and a rapidly growing number of commercial websites, Americans quickly adapted to this new Digital Age. Most of the technological advances of the 2000s would be tied one way or other to accessing and utilizing the internet. Likewise, computer-based technology would create massive strides in home video games, motion picture special effects, and space exploration. Coming into the twenty-first century, Americans were expecting a brighter future, and to a considerable degree, they attained it.

9/11

The technology of the day provides an interesting window into the terror attacks of September 11, 2001. Today, with most Americans possessing 4G smartphones, a breakdown of communication seems alien. In 2001, most of America was still running on the technology of the previous decade. With the suddenness of the attacks in New York City, 911 and first-responder radio frequencies were quickly overwhelmed. Many people trapped above the impact zones of the Twin Towers were unable to call for help, although, to be fair, by the time such calls were pouring in, first responders were already well aware that an emergency situation was underway. Even with the ultra high frequency (UHF) handheld radios used by police and firefighters, responders discovered difficulties once they reached the higher floors.

Even aboard *Air Force One,* President George W. Bush (b. 1946) experienced massive frustration, on top of the pressure from the events of the day, as the presidential plane's communications abilities proved inadequate for maintaining contact with the White House Situation Room and the Pentagon. Added to that, the plane had no access to satellite television. As such, the televisions on board could only pick up standard antennae transmissions from local news outlets on the ground, outlets whose ranges the plane would fly over quickly, requiring staffers to surf the channels to find another local outlet. Reporters were denied cell phone use so as to not accidentally give away the president's location to other potential terrorists. Due to these inadequacies, the commander in chief was essentially blind and deaf during the greatest crisis in the nation's history.

By 2001, more Americans owned cell phones than at any point prior. Cell phones and pagers played a key role in loved ones tracking each other during the chaos of the day. Unfortunately, however, the cellular tower technology of the day also experienced overwhelming traffic, causing thousands of calls to be dropped or not go through at all. On board the hijacked planes, cell phones and credit-card phones allowed passengers to make final calls to loved ones on the ground. Cell phones became particularly important when it came to the fate of United 93, flying over Pennsylvania on its way to Washington, DC. By the time the plane was over Pennsylvania, the other three planes had already hit their targets in New York and DC, and the news was already reporting that the planes had been hijacked by terrorists who then used the planes as human-bearing projectiles. As such, the passengers of Flight 93 were informed of what had happened and what the terrorists were probably planning. This led the passengers to make the fateful decision to attempt to retake the plane.

Utilizing nothing more than the available kitchen implements, the passengers appear to have gotten to the cockpit door. Unfortunately, as they made their way to the cockpit, the terrorists, fearful that the passengers might be successful, chose instead to nosedive the plane into a field in Pennsylvania, killing the four passengers and all forty passengers and crew. Thanks to cell phones, the passengers' foreknowledge allowed them to take actions that saved countless lives in Washington, thwarting the plans of one of the four teams of terrorists. Unbeknown to most Americans, the federal government collected transcripts of all phone calls and text messages from that day, some of which never reached their intended destinations. The technology of the day has allowed the voices of the lost to be preserved for all posterity, providing an invaluable window into the horror and confusion felt during America's darkest day.

THE INTERNET

Google

Possibly the biggest success story in internet history would be the search engine Google. Founded in 1998 by Sergey Brin and Larry Page (both born 1973), Google quickly surpassed Yahoo! as the world's primary search engine.

Throughout the 2000s, it has added numerous other attributes to its overall brand: Google Earth (2001); Gmail (2004); Google Maps (2005); Google Docs, Google Calendar, and Google Translate (all in 2006); and Google Street View (2007). In 2006, Google purchased YouTube—launched in 2005 by Steve Chen (b. 1978), Chad Hurley (b. 1977), and Jawed Karim (b. 1979)—an online video-sharing website that has become one of the most popular sites on the Web. In 2008, Google became the primary marketer of the Android mobile operating system, which became the operating system of Samsung Galaxy smartphones, first launched in 2009.

Amazon

As the twentieth century drew to a close, American society was already undergoing one of the most dramatic changes in its history: becoming an online society. The internet went fully mainstream in 1996. One of the earliest successful websites was Amazon.com, founded in 1994 by Jeff Bezos (b. 1964) as Cadabra, Inc., changing the name to Amazon the following year. Originally an online bookseller, throughout the 2000s, Amazon began broadening its offerings to include essentially anything anyone could want or need. In 2005, Amazon launched Amazon Prime. For an annual fee, Prime members could receive free shipping on most items. In 2007, Amazon began selling the Kindle, an e-reader device. During the 2000s, e-books became increasingly popular, with many Americans preferring reading on electronic devices rather than traditional books. In 2011, Prime expanded to include online streaming services.

The success of Amazon, and all online shopping, proved problematic for traditional brick-and-mortar stores. Successful chains such as Barnes & Noble, Books-A-Million, Sears, J. C. Penney, Target, K-Mart, Toys "R" Us, and even superstore Walmart felt the pressure from the convenience provided by home shopping. Some—Barnes & Noble, Books-A-Million, Target, and Walmart— would eventually transition to offer online options for their shoppers. In the 2010s, Sears, J. C. Penney, K-Mart, and Toys"R" Us were barely viable, some going out of business altogether.

Despite Amazon's success, however, the company has experienced continued criticism for the poor treatment of their workers. Though there were calls for boycotts of Amazon to support the workers' cause, so many Americans had become addicted to the convenience of the company. By 2020, Bezos's estimated net worth was $110 billion (Kiersz and Rogers 2019). Despite its controversies and ever-increasing competition online, Amazon continues to reign supreme as *the* online retailer well into the 2020s.

Napster

In 1999, Shawn Fanning (b. 1980) and Sean Parker (b. 1979) developed Napster, an online file-sharing website that allowed users to share music files for free. It was originally only available through Microsoft Windows, until a separate company, Black Hole Media, developed a version that would make the service available on Apple Macintosh as well. The site became wildly popular almost overnight, especially among college-age young people. The ethical question quickly arose as to whether Napster was a violation of copyright laws. From the perspective of Napster, the website was no different from the previous generation's common practice of recording mixed tapes from the radio and sharing them with friends.

From the perspective of record producers and musical artists—most notably the hard-rock band Metallica (f. 1981)—this was clear copyright infringement. Several lawsuits throughout 2000 and the Ninth U.S. Circuit Federal Court of Appeals order to shut down led Napster to settle the suits and shut down its free services in 2001. In 2008, the bankrupt Napster was purchased by electronics retail outlet Best Buy, and in 2011, Best Buy allowed Napster to merge with the record company Rhapsody in exchange for a minority stake in the record company. By that time, however, the service would be unable to compete with the popular iTunes and Spotify, which launched in 2006.

TELECOMMUNICATION DEVICES

Cell Phones

The idea of portable phones had been around throughout the twentieth century, with the first digital cellular networks going online in the mid-1990s. Japanese company Sony was the first to market 2G technology in 1991. It was followed by 3G in 2001 and 4G in 2009. By 2000, the majority of cell phones on the market were flip phones that only provided phone and texting options. By the end of the decade, the smartphone became the standard for American consumers and would literally change American society forever.

Bluetooth

The concept of wireless short-range radio technology, known commonly today as Bluetooth, was first developed in the late 1980s by Swedish engineer Nils Rydbeck for Ericsson Mobile for wireless headsets. Modern Bluetooth was designed for consumer markets in 1998 through a cooperation of five major companies: Ericsson, IBM, Intel, Nokia, and Toshiba. They became common offerings in the U.S. market in 2001, and by the end of the decade, Bluetooth would be the primary offering in wireless headset technology.

Apple

Perhaps the biggest tech success story of the 2000s was Apple, Inc. Apple began as the Apple Computer Company in 1976, founded by Steve Jobs (1955–2011), Ronald Wayne (b. 1934), and Steve Wozniak (b. 1950). The company originally focused on personal computers and hardware. In the 1990s, Apple experienced near collapse due to two main reasons: firing founder and chief innovator Jobs and losing the PC (personal computer) wars to companies like

Dell and Gateway, due largely to their deals with Microsoft, provider of the most popular PC software. The company enjoyed a massive resurgence in 1997 with the return of Jobs and a deal with Microsoft to provide software for their Macintosh personal computers.

In the early 2000s, the music industry saw a massive change when consumers began to prefer downloading music content into digital MP3 players, a digital format for audio files first launched in the mid-1990s. Apple responded immediately with the introduction of the iPod in October 2001. Consumers could now carry literally thousands of their favorite songs in one small device. After the Napster controversy led to the online purchase of music, Apple introduced iTunes in January 2001. The caveat, however, was that iTunes material could only be downloaded into the iPod. Consumers could now carry literally thousands of their favorite songs in one small device. As cell phones evolved into smartphones, Jobs introduced his next innovation, one that would help Apple dominate both the cell phone and music markets: the iPhone, launched on June 29, 2007. The first iPhone featured a cell phone, email, visual voicemail, Safari internet access, Google Maps, YouTube, and, of course, an iPod. Apple would go on to dominate the market throughout the 2010s with the iPad and ever-evolving versions of the iPhone.

BlackBerry

A key inspiration for the iPhone was the popularization throughout the 2000s of the BlackBerry smartphone, originally introduced in 1999 by the Canadian company BlackBerry Limited. BlackBerry allowed users to send emails or instant messages (i.e., texting). In 2002, BlackBerry launched the 5810, running on a 2G network. The 6710, also launched in 2002, also had an integrated phone. The 6210 (2003) was the first BlackBerry to have a full color screen. The 7290 (2003) incorporated the new Bluetooth technology. These early models were designed primarily for business use. The 7100 series (2003) was the first to be marketed to general consumers. The BlackBerry Curve arrived in 2007, incorporating a camera for the first time. Though the arrival of the iPhone proved stiff competition, BlackBerry was able to maintain considerable market share due to the fact that it was 2008 presidential candidate Barack Obama's smartphone of preference (O'Boyle 2019). By 2010, however, BlackBerry began to see a steep decline as the iPhone became Americans' smartphone of preference.

Motorola Razr

Motorola released its first Razr flip phone in July 2004, with the V3. While not a smartphone per se, the V3 did include a camera and an ISB port. It was soon followed by the V3i after Motorola reached a deal with Apple allowing the company to incorporate iTunes access to their devices. An updated model, the Razr2 or V8, was released in 2007 providing a screen on the outer, closed shell. However, with BlackBerry and the iPhone, flip phones quickly went out of fashion. In 2020, expected nostalgia for the old days led Motorola to announce the release of a new Razr, available only through the cell carrier Verizon.

Skype

In 2003, Skype Technologies introduced the first widely used video-chatting program. While users could make use of text messaging, sending audio files and image files, Skype has become most popular for its video conferencing abilities. Skype is readily available on home computers, smartphones, watches, tablets, and the Xbox One video gaming system. The system, in essence, combines the technologies of teleconferencing and webcams, both of which have been available since the early 1990s.

The ever-increasing use of online retailing and smartphones, however, led to one massive unintended consequence: easier methods of identification theft. Websites and internet-accessing devices were forced to constantly stay one step ahead of increasingly cunning computer hackers. As Americans began to upload more and more private information—birthdates, Social Security numbers, credit card numbers, and the like—hackers could access more and more information with which to appropriate people's identities, download their texts for blackmail, or often both. The market would respond with more and more companies that promised to protect private information and monitor the internet for potential identity theft. From 2000 to 2009, millions of Americans would be affected by identity theft and other forms of cybercrime.

AUTOMOTIVE ADVANCEMENTS

Back-Up Cameras

Another tech innovation that would become commonplace by 2020 is the back-up camera installed in private automobiles. A rear-mounted camera connected to a dashboard monitor had been experimented with since the mid-1950s. Japanese automaker Nissan was the first company to make the back-up camera standard in some vehicles in the United States in 2001. By 2009, the cameras became standard in most high-end private vehicles, and by 2020, full-color monitors with computer-generated guiding lines and audible alarms were standard in most vehicles produced in the United States.

GPS

The Global Positioning System (GPS) was developed by the U.S. military in 1978. The concept is to use radio navigation coordinated by positioned satellites to provide directional guidance for military transportation and weaponry. By the time of the Persian Gulf War (1991), GPS was utilized for many military vehicles. By 2009, all military vehicles and launchable weaponry had GPS, and all military drivers, pilots, and long-range weapons operators were trained in its use. In the 2000s, civilian use of GPS became more widespread.

Everything from land survey and mining operations, to air traffic control, to cellular phones commonly used GPS by 2009. The decade also saw implementation of GPS for civilian vehicles, becoming standard in most commercial automobiles by 2020.

Sirius/XM Satellite Radio

Aside from GPS, satellites also became valuable for commercial radio broadcasting. In 2002, Sirius satellite radio launched in four states, providing pay radio, which was commercial-free (in theory), not unlike premium television cable networks. By 2006, the company was beginning to show a profit, and Sirius was offered as a free thirty-day trial in most commercial vehicles sold in the United States. In 2008, Sirius merged with rival XM, and in 2011, the two separate companies officially became Sirius/XM. By 2020, Sirius/XM offered such stations as Sixties on 6, Seventies on 7, and Eighties on 8 (featuring popular music from each decade); radio broadcasts of cable news outlets CNN, FOX News, and MSNBC; sports broadcaster ESPN; and the company's flagship channel, the Howard Stern Channel, featuring programming based on legendary shock jock Howard Stern (b. 1954).

HOME ENTERTAINMENT

Plasma TV

The original convex picture tube television sets, standard since the inception of the medium, were on their way out by 2000, with flat screens becoming the preference for most consumers. Originally, flat-screen televisions were primarily plasma screen, featuring ionized gas that responded to electric fields and produced a high-quality picture more capable of taking full advantage of the high-definition picture promised by DVD technology. Plasma screens, however, proved problematic; they caught fire easily, and once the plasma went bad, the entire set had to be replaced. By 2007, plasma screens were essentially replaced by cheap liquid-crystal display (LCD) or the much more expensive organic light-emitting diode (OLED) sets. Today, most flat screen televisions and computer monitors are LCD.

Blu-Ray versus HD-DVD

By 2000, home video options were changing rapidly. Original home video champ, VHS/VCR was quickly going the way of the dinosaur, replaced by DVD (digital video discs). As higher quality monitors became economically available for consumers, DVD technology had to push further to maximize picture quality. By 2007, there were two primary contenders for the next-gen DVD: Blu-Ray and HD-DVD. Both were developed in 2006: HD-DVD by Toshiba and Blu-Ray by Sony. HD-DVD merely expanded the existing DVD technology to provide higher-resolution picture quality. Blu-Ray allowed for high-definition video to be recorded in higher capacity and quantity, gaining its name from the blue laser used to read the disc. It is primarily used for home video and video games. Competition remained stiff, and consumers would ultimately decide which would reign as the next generation of home video and gaming entertainment. In 2008, Toshiba announced that it was discontinuing its HD-DVD format, handing the market to Sony's Blu-Ray.

DVR

As VCRs went the way of the dinosaur, digital video recorders (DVRs) hit the market in 1999. Not only could DVRs record television programming the same as its video-tape-based predecessor, but connected to one's cable or satellite box, DVRs allowed the viewer to pause or even rewind live broadcasting. Its storage capacity, likewise, could hold more and higher-quality content than old-school VHS cassette tapes. Originally, DVRs were sold as separate machines, connected to the television or cable or satellite box via cable. One of the most popular original DVR boxes was TiVo, launched in 1999. In 2002, the release of HDMI cables improved picture quality from DVRs, cable, and satellite boxes. By the end of the decade, DVRs were standard in all cable and satellite television boxes, all but eliminating the market for separate devices.

Netflix

Home video rentals of movies and video games represented a major market since the mid-1980s. Throughout the 1990s, Blockbuster was *the* name in home entertainment rentals. In 1997, a new competitor emerged: Netflix. Founded by Reed Hastings (b. 1960) and Marc Randolph (b. 1958), Netflix offered the option of renting movies or video games online and receiving the respective discs in the mail, with no due dates or fees. Renters could keep the disc as long as they wished, although they were unable to request another until the previous was returned. Though not a big money maker, Blockbuster saw the company's potential and offered to buy it out in 2001, but Netflix declined. The company truly began to take off in 2002 when DVD player sales began to skyrocket. In 2007, the company began offering online streaming services. By 2010, Blockbuster was on its way to bankruptcy; its last stores closed in 2014, except for one outlet in Alaska, which stayed open until 2019. As the Streaming Wars began near the end of the 2010s, Netflix had the distinct advantage.

Video Gaming Systems

Home video-gaming consoles had hit the market big in the late 1970s with the Atari 2600. In the 1980s, Nintendo would make a considerable dent in market share, and in the 1990s, Sega became equally competitive. By 2000, gamers were insisting on ever-increasing picture and gaming quality, and the war to dominate the home video-gaming market was on. Sony introduced the first PlayStation in 1994, with PlayStation 2 hitting the market in 2000, followed by PlayStation 3 in 2006. Microsoft entered the fray with Xbox in 2001, followed by the Xbox 360 in 2005. Nintendo, with its corner of the market somewhat secure with its globally popular *Mario Brothers* franchise, introduced the Wii in 2006. The Wii offered what no other gaming console had to date: physically interactive games that allowed players to engage in full-body interplay (with "outdoor" games such as tennis and baseball). While Nintendo would continue to hold a decent amount of market share, by 2009, the true contest was between PlayStation and Xbox, each developing their next-gen offerings in the 2000s: PlayStation 4 and Xbox One both released within days of each other in 2013.

SPACE

Columbia Disaster

The National Aeronautics and Space Administration (NASA) space shuttle *Columbia* (Orbital Vehicle-102) had been the first manned space shuttle, originally launched on April 12, 1981. By the end of the twentieth century, space shuttle missions had become so commonplace that few Americans took time to notice them. To that point, the only disaster had been the explosion of the shuttle *Challenger* (OV-099) on January 28, 1986, resulting in the deaths of all on board, including the first teacher in space, Christa McAuliffe (1948–1986). By 2003, Americans never imagined that such a disaster could happen again. Then, on February 1, 2003, the *Columbia* exploded on reentry. Unknown to the crew, a piece of the underbelly heat shield's foam insulation near the orbiter's external tank broke away; the excessive heat from reentry ignited the tank and destroyed the shuttle.

Those lost were U.S. Air Force colonel Rick Husband (1957–2003), the mission commander; U.S. Navy commander William McCool (1961–2003), the pilot; U.S. Air Force commander Michael Anderson (1959–2003), the payload commander; Israeli Air Force colonel Ilan Ramon (1954–2003); NASA engineer Kalpana Chawla (1961–2003); U.S. Navy captain David Brown (1956–2003); and U.S. Navy captain Laurel Blair Salton Clark (1961–2003). As in the wake of the *Challenger* incident, all shuttle missions were suspended for three years pending full investigation and adjustments to safety protocols. The return, however, was short-lived as NASA completely shut down the space shuttle program in 2011. This left America in a weakened position, forcing the country to rely on Russia or other space-faring nations to provide transport for continued NASA research, repairs to damaged satellites (commercial, governmental, and military), and trips to the International Space Station.

Mars Rover

Prior to 2000, NASA had made three attempts to place roving robots on the surface of Mars; the first failed, and the following two lost communications months after landing. Success was finally attained in 2004. Mars exploration rover A (MER-A), named *Spirit*, landed on Mars on January 4, 2004, and continued to send images from the surface for nearly six years before becoming trapped in sand. MER-B, named *Opportunity*, landed three weeks after *Spirit*.

Opportunity continued to send transmissions for an unexpected fourteen years before a global dust storm prevented the rover from being able to recharge its solar batteries. The most recent Mars mission, the Mars Science Laboratory, named *Curiosity*, landed on the Red Planet in 2011 and was still transmitting as of 2020.

SpaceX

In 2002, world-renowned engineer Elon Musk (b. 1971) opened Space Exploration Technologies Corporation (SpaceX) for the purpose of exploring civilian approaches to space travel with the ultimate goal of establishing human settlements on Mars. In 2008, the SpaceX rocket *Falcon 1* became the first liquid-propelled rocket funded by a private corporation to reach orbit. In 2010, SpaceX began its Dragon program, similar to NASA's space shuttles, to provide working orbiters, and by the end of the 2010s, the company was well into the planning stages of manning the Dragon with a human crew. In 2016, the company announced plans for the Interplanetary Transport System—called *Starship*—moving the company closer to its original plans for interplanetary travel and potential settlement of Mars.

MOVIES

Computer-Generated Imagery (CGI)

Since its inception, the movie industry had experimented with what we today call special effects. For the bulk of that history, these special effects required camera and lighting trickery. For example, in the 1941 film *The Wolf Man*, the transformation of Larry Talbot from man to wolf and back required one of two slights-of-hand: either filming a close-up of actor Lon Chaney Jr. (1906–1973) with a quick cut, placing some "fur" on his face, and another quick cut, then more and cut, until he was fully transformed or having the actor walk behind a pillar (and cut) then emerging with some fur, walking behind another pillar (and cut), and so on until there was full transformation. In the mid-1940s throughout the early 1970s, model spaceships hung from strings were filmed in front of a screen of stars. In the 1973 film *The Exorcist*, in order to create the illusion that actress Linda Blair (b. 1959) was possessed by a demon, she was filmed in full makeup slowly turning her head, and then the film cut while the actress put her bed clothes on backward and then resumed filming as she turned her head again, making it seem that her head had turned a full 360 degrees.

In 1975, innovative filmmaker George Lucas (b. 1944) created the special effects shop Industrial Light and Magic (ILM). After the jaw-dropping practical and blue-screen special effects of his *Star Wars* trilogy (1977–1983), ILM became the go-to shop for state-of-the-art special effects. In 1993, ILM produced the amazing dinosaur effects for the film *Jurassic Park*. While some of the dinosaur shots were traditional practical puppets and robots, many of the shots were computer-generated imagery. Lucas utilized this new technology to update his iconic sci-fi/fantasy trilogy, rereleasing the films in 1997 as *The Star Wars: Special Edition*. That experiment led Lucas to begin work on a prequel trilogy to the franchise, beginning with *Star Wars: Episode 1—The Phantom Menace* (1999).

All three of the prequel films were primarily CGI, with the actors forced to work on sets that were 90 percent green screen. *The Phantom Menace* also included film's first fully interactive CGI character: the much-maligned Jar Jar Binks. Many of the most popular films of the 2000s made full use of this new technology: from the *Harry Potter* and *Lord of the Rings* films to 2009's *Avatar*. The technology works by filming live actors in front of a green screen (originally blue screens in the 1980s) and then utilizing computer technology to insert fantastical backgrounds and characters. When one looks closely at 1999's *Phantom Menace* and 2009's *Avatar*, one can see how dramatically the technology advanced throughout the decade. One company that was particularly adept at this technology was Pixar.

Pixar

Originating in 1974 as the Computer Graphics Lab, the new team of computer animators went to work for ILM as a separate computer division in 1979. In 1983, Lucasfilm was in need of money and decided to sell off its computer division. In 1986, Steve Jobs, recently fired from Apple, purchased the division for $5 million, setting up the company as Pixar, named for the Pixar Image Computer that was the centerpiece of their technology. In 1995, Pixar released *Toy Story*, the first fully CGI-animated feature film. After Pixar had back-to-back box-office successes, the Walt Disney Corporation purchased the company in 2006 for $7.4 billion, becoming the first of what would be several major pop-culture studio purchases by the animation and theme-park giant over the next decade. Throughout the 2010s, it would be difficult to find a major box-office blockbuster that did not make considerable use of CGI technology or to find a Pixar film that did not dominate the box office.

Three-Dimensional Movies

Since the 1950s, American audiences have, from time to time, become obsessed with the concept of three-dimensional movies (3D). When most people think of 3D movies, they often think back to the genre's heyday, the 1950s. These classic 3D films required audiences to wear cheap plastic eyeglasses with one blue lens and one red lens in order to view the three-dimensional aspects. Though there were many, particularly sci-fi and horror, 3D films in the 1950s, possibly the one most remembered was *Creature from the Black Lagoon* (1954). By 1960, the popularity of 3D had waned, and the technology all but disappeared for two decades before returning to brief popularity in the early 1980s with films such as *Jaws 3D* and *Friday the 13th, Part III—In 3D*, both released in 1983 and both equally panned by critics and audiences alike.

In the early 2000s, 3D movies made a huge comeback. Technology had progressed to a degree that audiences no longer had to wear the blue- and red-lensed paper glasses, but, instead, audiences could enjoy the films in full color through clear-lensed 3D glasses. Early 3D hits from the 2000s included *Spy Kids 3D: Game Over* (2003) and *The Adventures of Shark Boy and Lava Girl in 3D* (2005). In 2008, Disney Channel sensation Hannah Montana/Miley Cyrus (b. 1992) released the theatrical 3D concert film *Hannah Montana and Miley Cyrus: Best of Both Worlds*. By far the biggest 3D sensation of all was *Avatar* (2009) by writer and director James Cameron (b. 1954). The continued popularity of the gimmick led studios for the next decade to release most films in both 3D and traditional 2D formats. with the 3D tickets being more expensive. By 2015, however, the popularity of 3D movies once more severely waned, and studios all but abandoned the format once more.

MEDICAL

Human Genome Project

From 1990 to 2003, twenty universities and research facilities from around the world contributed to the Human Genome Project mapping human DNA and all of the genes that form the human genome from both a functional and biological perspective. The original idea sprang from the University of California, Santa Cruz in 1985, but the project would not gain considerable interest until the Federal Office of Health and Environmental Research fully funded the Santa Fe Workshop in 1986. Advances in genomics and computer technology throughout the 1990s allowed the project to advance somewhat rapidly, and a "complete" mapping of DNA was released to the world in 2004, with 92 percent of samples achieving at least 99.9 percent accuracy.

At the close of the decade, the Genome Reference Consortium, consisting of all of the research and researchers from contributing nations, provided a more accurate mapping, although they admitted that more than three hundred gaps remained in the overall research. By 2019, those gaps had been reduced to just over eighty. The research has been responsible for huge advancements in all areas of bioscience and has been key in advances in research into cancers, viruses, mutations, and brain-related syndromes. As the science continues to advance, more and more human ailments will be within reach of treating or curing outright. The mapping of the human genome will likely go down in history as being responsible ultimately not only for prolonging human life but for improving quality of life as well.

Prosthetics

Throughout the 2000s, advancements in prosthetics have added considerably to the quality of life for those who have lost limbs or been born without them. All through the decade, advancements were made in brain and computer interface technology. In 2004, technology allowed a man with no arms to work a computer cursor with his mind. High-intensity lightweight running blades allowed people with no legs to run. In 2012, South African sprinter Oscar Pistorius (b. 1986) became the first legless Olympian to compete in track-and-field events. Indeed, most of the prosthetics advancements of the 2010s came about due to diligent research throughout the decade prior.

The 2000s was a transformative decade, taking the technologies developed in the 1990s to create the world of the 2010s and beyond. This has proved a double-edged sword in some ways. One the one hand, smartphones have made daily life in America easier than at any point in human history. On the other hand, as Americans have become so dependent on their smart devices that if something were to happen to the internet or satellites linking these devices, many Americans would have a difficult time reverting to the old ways, even many of those who can remember them. Additionally, such a computer-linked society has opened the door for identity theft to a degree never before experienced in American history. Data protection has become its own, constantly evolving, 24-7 industry.

Just as space exploration technology reached zeniths never imagined a generation before, the government began dramatically reducing funding for NASA, leaving the premier space agency to look to private sector support. This has opened the door for private engineers to profit considerably from developing space exploration technology. Allowing such massive power in the hands of a wealthy few, rather than the equalizing capabilities of government funding, creates the possibility of an all-new power dynamic, further enhancing class differences in America.

Advances in movie special effects have allowed Hollywood studios to create worlds never before dreamed of for the entertainment of audiences around the world. On the one hand, this opens the door for all new areas of storytelling that would not have been as believable during the days of old school practical effects, such as the Marvel Cinematic Universe of the 2010s. On the other hand, with directors and editors possessing the ability to alter onscreen performances, the day will soon come when studios no longer need actors to act but, rather, to provide release of their images and allow the computer graphics teams to create their own performances. Add to that the fact that, by 2020, computer graphics teams have gone from trying to make video games look more like movies to making movies look more like video games.

The considerable medical advancements of the 2000s have already had a profound effect on human life in the 2010s and beyond. From mapping human DNA to advancements in prosthetics, longevity and quality of life by 2020 are already increasing at a faster rate than any decade prior. The upside of this is obvious, already benefiting millions around the world and potentially billions in the generations to come. The potential downside is that it will require "old" and "disabled" to be redefined. As humans live longer, either retirement ages will have to be raised or more money will be required to support the ever-increasing numbers of retirees. When the original retirement age was set at sixty-five in the 1930s, few Americans lived past seventy; as more live to one hundred and beyond, new ideas about age and retirement will have to be developed.

Overall, the United States in 2010 was a significantly different world than that of just ten years earlier, a more significant change than in any previous ten-year period. More and more, tedious and mundane tasks are being passed on to smart devices, leaving more leisure time for Americans than ever before. The world of the twenty-first century is a much smaller, more connected world than that of the twentieth century. Instant gratification has never been more instantaneous, and the future promises to make life even easier than now. Individuals are more empowered than ever before, making the old adage "With great power, there must also come . . . great responsibility" (Stan Lee, *Amazing Fantasy #15*, 1962) all the more important.

FURTHER READING

Bennett, Jessica. 2019. "This Gen X Mess: The Tech, Music, Style, Books, Trends, Rules, Films and Pills That Made Gen X . . . So So-So." *New York Times*, May 16. https://www.nytimes.com/interactive/2019/05/14/style/generation-xers.html?utm_source=pocket-newtab. Retrieved May 16, 2019.

Carr, Nicholas. 2011. *The Shallows: What the Internet Is Doing to Our Brains*. New York: W. W. Norton.

Chossudovsky, Michel. 2004. "What Happened on the Planes on September 11, 2001? The 9/11 Cell Phone Calls. The 9/11 Commission 'Script' Was Fabricated." GlobalResearch, August 10. https://www.globalresearch.ca/more-holes-in-the-official-story-the-911-cell-phone-calls/5652872. Retrieved January 10, 2020.

Eriksson, Maria, Rasmus Fleischer, Anna Johansson, Pelle Snickars, and Patrick Vonderau. 2019. *Spotify Teardown: Inside the Black Box of Streaming Music*. Cambridge, MA: MIT.

Essinger, James. 2014. *Ada's Algorithm: How Lord Byron's Daughter Ada Lovelace Launched the Digital Age*. New York: Melville House.

Graff, Garrett M. 2019. "Pagers, Pay Phones, and Dialup: How We Communicated on 9/11." *Wired*, September 11. https://www.wired.com/story/pagers-pay-phones-and-dialup-how-we-communicated-on-911/. Retrieved January 10, 2020.

Holmes, Dave. 2019. "A Decade of Music Is Lost on Your iPod. These Are the Deleted Years. Now Let Us Praise Them: From 2003 to 2012 Music Was Disposable and Nothing Survived." *Esquire*, September 4. https://www.esquire.com/entertainment/music/a28904211/2003-to-2012-forgotten-music-era/. Retrieved November 23, 2019.

Isaacson, Walter. 2011. *Steve Jobs*. New York: Simon & Schuster.

Jones, Brian Jay. 2016. *George Lucas: A Life*. New York: Little, Brown and Company.

Kaminski, Michael. 2008. *The Secret History of* Star Wars. Kingston, ON: Legacy Books.

Kiersz, Andy, and Taylor Nicole Rogers. 2019. "Jeff Bezos Might Lose His Spot as the World's Richest Person as Amazon Shares Tank. Here's How He Makes and Spends His Billions." *Business Insider*, October 25. https://www.businessinsider.com/jeff-bezos-net-worth-life-spending-2018-8. Retrieved January 8, 2020.

Klemens, Guy. 2010. *The Cellphone: The History and Technology of the Gadget That Changed the World*. Jefferson, NC: McFarland.

Kranz, Gene. 2009. *Failure Is Not an Option: Mission Control from Mercury to Apollo 13 and Beyond*. New York: Simon & Schuster.

Kwon, Amos. 2012. "Life & Limb: The Evolution of Prosthetics." Gear Patrol, August 1. https://gearpatrol.com/2012/08/01/life-limb-the-evolution-of-prosthetics/. Retrieved January 11, 2020.

Lakdawalla, Emily. 2018. *The Design and Engineering of Curiosity: How the Mars Rover Performs Its Job*. New York: Springer.

Leinbach, Michael, and Jonathan H. Ward. 2018. *Bringing Columbia Home: The Untold Story of a Lost Space Shuttle and Her Crew*. New York: Arcade.

Levy, Janey. 2019. *The Human Genome Project: History Just before You Were Born*. New York: Gareth Stevens.

Linzmayer, Owen W. 2004. *Apple Confidential 2.0: The Definitive History of the World's Most Colorful Company*. San Francisco, CA: No Starch.

Manning, Rob, and William L. Simon. 2017. *Mars Rover Curiosity: An Inside Account from Curiosity's Chief Engineer*. Washington, DC: Smithsonian.

Menn, Joseph. 2003. *All the Rave: The Rise and Fall of Shawn Fanning's Napster*. New York: Crown.

9/11 Commission. 2004. "The 9/11 Commission Report." National Commission on Terrorist Attacks Upon the United States. https://www.9-11commission.gov/report/. Retrieved January 3, 2020.

9/11 Memorial. [Posting Date Unknown]. "September 11 Attack Timeline." https://timeline.911memorial.org/#Timeline/2. Retrieved May 8, 2019.

O'Boyle, Britta. 2019. "The History of BlackBerry: The Best BlackBerry Phones That Changed the World." Pocket-Lint, January 16. https://www.pocket-lint.com/phones/news/137319-farewell-blackberry-os-here-are-the-23-best-blackberry-phones-that-changed-the-world. Retrieved January 8, 2020.

Pearlman, Robert Z. 2011. "NASA's Space Shuttle Program Officially Ends after Final Celebration." Space.com, September 1. https://www.space.com/12804-nasa-space-shuttle-program-officially-ends.html. Retrieved January 10, 2020.

Price, David A. 2009. *The Pixar Touch: The Making of a Company*. New York: Vintage.

Ramsay, Randolph. 2008. "Blu-Ray vs. HD DVD: Which Video Format Is for You?" C-Net, August 14. https://www.cnet.com/news/blu-ray-vs-hd-dvd-which-video-format-is-for-you/. Retrieved January 9, 2020.

Randolph, Marc. 2019. *That Will Never Work: The Birth of Netflix and the Amazing Life of an Idea*. Boston: Little, Brown and Company.

Redding, Anna Crowley. 2018. *Google It: A History of Google*. New York: Feiwel & Friends.

Reed, Ryan. 2018. "Metallica's Kirk Hammett: 'We're Still Right' about Suing Napster." *Rolling Stone*, May 14. https://www.rollingstone.com/music/music-news/metallicas-kirk-hammett-were-still-right-about-suing-napster-630185/. Retrieved November 23, 2019.

Ridley, Matt. 2006. *Genome: The Autobiography of a Species in 23 Chapters*. New York: Harper Perennial.

Simons, Iain, and James Newman. 2019. *A History of Videogames: In 14 Consoles, 5 Computers, 2 Arcade Cabinets . . . and an Ocarina of Time*. London: Carlton.

Sivolella, Davide. 2017. *The Space Shuttle Program: Technologies and Accomplishments*. Cham, Switzerland: Springer Praxis.

Smith, Michael. 2017. *Streaming, Sharing, Stealing: Big Data and the Future of Entertainment*. Cambridge, MA: MIT.

Spitzmiller, Ted. 2017. *The History of Human Space Flight*. Gainesville: University Press of Florida.

Starr, Larry, and Christopher Waterman. 2017. *American Popular Music: From Minstrelsy to MP3*. New York: Oxford University Press.

Stone, Brad. 2013. *The Everything Store: Jeff Bezos and the Age of Amazon*. Boston: Little, Brown and Company.

Tsonga, Taj. 2019. "Remembering the Greatest Con in Silicon Valley History." *Wired*, January. https://www.wired.com/wiredinsider/2019/01/remembering-greatest-con-silicon-valley-history/. Retrieved May 16, 2019.

Vance, Ashlee. 2015. *Elon Musk: Tesla, SpaceX, and the Quest for a Fantastic Future.* New York: Ecco.

Waldfogel, Joel. 2018. *Digital Renaissance: What Data and Economics Tell Us about the Future of Popular Culture.* Princeton, NJ: Princeton University Press.

Wheeler, Tom. 2019. *From Gutenberg to Google: The History of Our Future.* Washington, DC: Brookings Institution.

Willis, Susan. 2005. *Portents of the Real: A Primer for Post-9/11 America.* London: Verso.

Witt, Stephen. 2016. *How Music Got Free: A Story of Obsession and Invention.* New York: Penguin.

CHAPTER 7

Media

As in most other areas of popular culture, the 2000s was a transformative decade for media across the board. As the political divide in America grew wider, so, too, did differences in cable news coverage. American audiences began to not only choose who reported the news to them, but also what "facts" they chose to believe. News was no longer an arena for informing the public. By decade's end, it would become more and more an entertainment medium, with Americans choosing their news outlet based on which one backed up their preconceived ideas of the facts. As cable news became less and less trust-worthy factual outlets, American audiences—particularly young, college-age Americans—began looking to another source: politically themed comedian pundits.

By 2010, Jon Stewart, Stephen Colbert, and Bill Maher had emerged as the go-to sources for what was really going on in America. Network and cable entertainment channels shifted to reality TV over scripted dramas and come-dies, primarily due to their much-cheaper budgets and the decreasing adver-tising dollars connected to continually falling viewership. Though television maintained a certain dominance in American pop culture overall, the internet began to widen, offering Americans and people around the world access to information on an unprecedented level. By the end of the 2010s, television as it had always been known was quickly going the way of radio.

Print media also saw a massive decline throughout the 2000s. Americans no longer needed to wait for tomorrow's newspaper to tell them yesterday's news. Even widely circulated magazines such as *Time* and *Newsweek* found it diffi-cult to compete with the instantaneous information and opinion outlets that the internet increasingly offered. The sole exception to the rule appeared to be the medium of superhero comic books. On the verge of collapse as an industry in 2000, by 2009 the market had rebounded, due in no small part to

Americans' need for the escapism of heroic narratives in the wake of 9/11. As the internet evolved and gained popularity and accessibility throughout the 2000s, it led by decade's end to the advent of social media, a simple concept that would change the world (both for better and worse) in the decade that followed.

CABLE NEWS

As the last decade of the twentieth century began, the Cable News Network (CNN) was "the most trusted name in news." Created by cable-TV entrepreneur Ted Turner (b. 1938), CNN debuted on June 1, 1980. Originally intended to bring 24-7 news coverage of events around the world, ratings soon dictated that most Americans cared little for news outside their borders, and the news outlet began focusing only on American news, with a different CNN International for outlets in other nations. This led to limiting news reporting in favor of argumentative punditry (essentially, ten minutes of news and fifty minutes of arguing about the news every hour). Though the networked billed itself as a balanced account of the daily events, audiences soon began to complain that CNN had become too leftist in its presentation of the news. By mid-decade, many began to refer to the station as either the Clinton News Network or the Communist News Network. While there was some semblance of truth to the criticisms, the decision by CNN to be more left leaning derived largely from the fact that those of politically liberal leanings were more likely to watch the news for hours at a time.

In 1996, two more cable news outlets joined the fray. On July 15, 1996, NBCUniversal debuted MSNBC (a partnership between Microsoft and NBC News), answering the call for liberal-leaning news coverage. In an attempt the make the field "fair and balanced," the Fox Corporation's Rupert Murdoch (b. 1931) and conservative media specialist Roger Ailes (1940–2017) launched FOX News, a source for a conservative alternative to what was seen as a liberal biased media. FOX's tagline of "fair and balanced" was misunderstood from day one. It was not the intent of FOX to present "fair and balanced" coverage of the news but, rather, to provide fairness and balance to the news media by presenting the news from a strictly conservative perspective in order to "balance" the coverage of CNN and MSNBC. MSNBC's hold on the far left and FOX's hold on the far right, CNN was ultimately pushed back toward the political center, where the American audience was consistently shrinking.

In the wake of the Cold War (1947–1992), and the perceived threat of Al-Qaeda still years away, Americans in the 1990s, for the first time since before World War II, had no external enemy to fear. Unfortunately, for the last half of the twentieth century, Americans had become accustomed to seeking out, fearing, and defeating enemies. As such, Americans began to look inward for perceived threats, and the Culture Wars began. With Democrats in apparent control of the political left and center, the Republican Party began to seek out votes in the far-right fringes of American society.

Conservatives and liberals began to see each other as the enemy, and the cable news media was quick to pick sides and add fuel to the growing fire. The first major battleground in this emerging civil war was the presidential election of 2000. Republicans chose as their candidate the very conservative governor of Texas, George W. Bush (b. 1946), son of former and politically moderate president George H. W. Bush (1924–2018). Democrats chose Vice President Al Gore (b. 1948), the two-term number two to the still very popular president Bill Clinton (b. 1946).

The contest was heated, with Republicans painting the Democrats as socialist and the Democrats promising a continuation of the policies that had led to the greatest economic expansion in American history throughout the 1990s. By that time, however, left and right were already so polarized that the results of the election on November 7, 2000, proved too close to call. At 7:48 p.m. (all times EDT), the Associated Press (AP) and CNN reported that Gore had won the state of Florida and its twenty-five electoral votes (Florida would ultimately be the deciding factor in who won the overall election). At 2:18 a.m. (November 8), the network and cable news outlets change their call for Florida, awarding it instead to Bush. At 2:30 a.m., the vice president called Governor Bush to concede defeat only to withdraw that concession an hour later (History on the Net). The Gore campaign demanded recounts in some Florida districts, and the thirty-six-day fight for Florida began.

Soon both campaigns had teams on the ground overseeing the recounts. Additionally, Americans from across the country descended on the Sunshine State, making it a battlefield, each side convinced that the other was trying to steal the election. While it was the responsibility of news outlets to reassure both sides, explain the details of the process, and return trust in the system, all too often, pundits devolved into the same accusations and name-calling possessing the mob mentality on the ground. Finally, the Bush campaign took the matter directly to the U.S. Supreme Court, and in *Bush v. Gore* (2000), the Court ordered the end to all recounts, relying on the most recent results and giving Florida's electoral votes and the presidency to Bush. The paper-thin popular vote count and the controversial manner in which Bush won the highest office in the land strongly suggested that the Bush administration would attempt to stay relatively low-key politically and that Bush would likely follow his father's fate as a one-term president. That would change on the following September 11.

After the election was called, most Americans who had been obsessively watching cable news for the duration of the recounts returned to their previous viewing habits, and cable news ratings returned to their preelection numbers. That changed on September 11, 2001. By 9:00 a.m. (all times EDT), all cable and network television news outlets turned from scheduled programming to cover the unfolding events at the World Trade Center in New York City. At 8:46 a.m., an airplane of unknown size and origin struck the North Tower of the World Trade Center. As reporters scrambled to determine the origin of the plane and the cause of the crash, a second passenger jet (this time caught on film as the networks were covering the tower live) struck the South Tower at 9:03 a.m. Reporters from all outlets were in Washington, DC, on the ground at the Pentagon when the third plane hit that building at 9:37 a.m. By 10:00 a.m. it was clear: America was at war.

The new War on Terror boosted cable news ratings beyond their postelection highs, with Americans in a constant state of fear as to when and where the next attack would happen. Initially, all three cable news outlets maintained a strong pro-American stance, as Americans put aside their political differences in light of the common threat. Over time, however—particularly after the American invasion of Iraq in 2003 due to White House assurances that Iraqi president Saddam Hussein (1937–2006) possessed weapons of mass destruction—Americans began to divide on the issue of the wars, and cable news reflected those differences. While CNN and MSNBC insisted that it was patriotic to question those in power, FOX News argued that any criticism of the president during wartime was just this side of treason. By midway through Bush's second term, Americans and cable news were more divided than ever; and "facts" gave way to "what feels like facts."

Prior to the 2000 election, news outlets utilized a combination of red and blue coloring to monitor election maps, with no uniformly assigned color representing any particular party. After the election, that changed. Network and cable television news outlets universally began to use the color red to identify Republicans and blue to identify Democrats. Just like that, the United States were now a mere amalgamation of red states and blue states (ironically similar to the 1990s national gang war between the Crips and Bloods, who identified their enemies by the colors they wore, blue for Crips and red for Bloods). By 2008, the United States was more divided than at any point in its history since the Civil War (1861–1865).

As the cable news outlets began to cement specific political demographics, they needed on-air personalities who could act as mouthpieces for the rhetoric of the left or right. On the left, MSNBC contracted sports commentator Keith Olbermann (b. 1959). His program, *Countdown with Keith Olbermann* (2003–2011), was MSNBC's most popular program. Every weeknight, Olbermann would count down the top stories of the day, topped by his declaration of three newsmakers (almost always conservative) from which he chose "the worst person in the world." In 2008, the network added *The Rachel Maddow Show* (2008–present). Maddow (b. 1973) took a more meticulous, well-documented approach to pointing out the dubious actions of right-wing politicians, while simultaneously praising the heroics of the left wing.

FOX News countered with louder, more boisterous personalities such as Bill O'Reilly (b. 1949) and his show, *The O'Reilly Factor* (1993–2017), which promised a "no spin zone." FOX also contracted Glenn Beck, a popular conservative radio commentator, from 2009 to 2011. FOX did attempt a "balanced" program with *Hannity & Colmes* (1996–2009), hosted by conservative radio host Sean Hannity (b. 1961) and liberal radio host Alan Colmes (1950–2017). By 2009, the liberal perspective was removed, and the series was renamed *Hannity* (2009–present). With the back-to-back powerhouses of O'Reilly and Hannity, FOX News soon dominated primetime cable news ratings in post-9/11 America.

When President Barack Obama (b. 1961) took office in January 2009, cable news perspectives suddenly shifted. Overnight, CNN and MSNBC were less critical of the administration, while FOX News (despite the fact that the country was still at war) began to be far more critical. Celebrity businessman Donald Trump (b. 1946), among numerous others, frequently appeared on FOX suggesting that Obama was not born in the United States. The opposing coverage further divided an already-split American society, pitting conservatives against liberals in a blood feud rivaling the legendary Hatfields and McCoys.

On October 15, 2004, in the midst of yet another presidential election, the late-night comedian and host of *The Daily Show* (Comedy Central, 1996–present), Jon Stewart (b. 1962), appeared on the program *Crossfire* (CNN, 1982–2005; 2013–2014), where one conservative pundit and one liberal pundit would debate the day's news. Stewart used his appearance to voice his serious concerns about the failures of cable news discourse, stating, "It's hurting America. Here is what I wanted to tell you guys: Stop! You have a responsibility to the public discourse, and you fail miserably" ("Jon Stewart on Crossfire," You-Tube, https://www.youtube.com/watch?v=aFQFB5YpDZE). Conservative host Tucker Carlson (b. 1969) attempted to defend the network's actions by stating that Stewart was no different in his coverage. Stewart pointed out that he was a comedian on a comedy show, not a journalist. With audiences strongly supporting Stewart's take, CNN canceled *Crossfire* three months later. Despite this one act of resistance to the devolution of cable news and this one company's response, the discourse continued to get worse throughout the decade and throughout the decade that followed.

TELEVISION

With the internet still in its infancy by 2001, television entered the twenty-first century still the predominant entertainment medium in the United States. Television, as stated above, was where the overwhelming majority of Americans followed the events of 9/11, with cable news the country's go-to source for information in the days, weeks, and months that followed the terror attacks. Television entertainment, however, also responded to the attacks as the primary source for salving the wounds of a traumatized nation. Television production came to an abrupt halt for days after the attacks, but it got back on its feet to meet the needs of the nation faster than almost any other industry. The first to directly address the mass trauma being experienced was the fictional television series *The West Wing* (NBC, 1999–2006).

The West Wing was a workplace drama set in the White House of the fictional U.S. president Josiah "Jed" Bartlet, played by Martin Sheen (b. 1940) and his staff. The series was one of the most popular on NBC, with weekly audiences in the tens of millions. The writing on the show, led by series creator Aaron Sorkin (b. 1961) was extremely sophisticated for a primetime drama (which gave NBC some pause in green-lighting it), but American audiences responded to the idealist view of what politics and government could be. In September 2001, *The West Wing* was about the begin its third season with a premier that would address the cliff-hanger from the previous spring. In the wake of 9/11, however, Sorkin strongly believed that since the series was about a sitting U.S. president, the show needed to address the national catastrophe that had just happened. His response was the last-minute episode "Isaac and Ishmael" (October 3, 2001).

Written, filmed, and put to air in just three weeks, all commercial proceeds from "Isaac and Ishmael" were donated to 9/11 charities, as were the pay that the cast and crew received for the episode. In this stand-alone episode, a student group is touring the White House, led by Deputy Chief of Staff Josh Lyman, played by Bradley Whitford (b. 1959), when the White House is placed on lockdown. National Security has located a possible terrorist working inside the White House. The episode allows all of the show's primary characters to reflect on fundamentalist Muslim terrorism, overall tensions with the Middle East, and the uncertainty of the future (Sorkin, *The West Wing*, Special Episode 1, October 3, 2001). As it aired in the immediate aftermath of the attacks when a vast majority of Americans were angry, wanting vengeance (some against the entire Muslim world) with a violence equal to the attacks, Sorkin could have played into this anger to great acclaim. Instead, he produced an episode that warned, "Wait. Calm down. Think." In the overall history of post-9/11 America, *The West Wing* proved remarkably prescient.

While many late-night television programs were produced in and around Los Angeles, California, two very popular nightly shows were filmed in New York City: *The Late Show with David Letterman* (CBS, 1993–2015) and *The Daily Show* (Comedy Central, 1996–present). David Letterman (b. 1947) returned to work on September 17, 2001. He did not attempt to be funny or in any way make light of recent events. Rather, he opened his show somberly, with reverence to those whose lives were lost and thankfulness to first responders for their heroism. His primary guest was CBS news anchor Dan Rather (b. 1931) to help put recent events into perspective. Rather experienced an emotional breakdown during the interview, with Letterman taking his hand in support.

Jon Stewart reopened *The Daily Show* on September 20, 2001. Like Letterman, he opened with an expression of the grief that he, himself, was experiencing, even noting during the opening monologue that his view from his apartment had been the Twin Towers of the World Trade Center but that, now, his view was the Statue of Liberty. Both Letterman and Stewart acknowledged that they could not be funny yet and were unsure when they could be—or *if* they could be—again.

The New York institution *Saturday Night Live* (NBC, 1975–present) took a bit longer to return, finally airing a new live episode on September 27, 2001. The cold open featured New York City mayor Rudy Giuliani (b. 1944) and representatives of the New York City Police and Fire Departments. After a heartwarming brief speech declaring that New York City was "open for business," Giuliani was joined by *SNL* creator and producer Lorne Michaels (b. 1944), who asked the mayor, "Can we be funny?" Giuliani sardonically responded, "Why start now?" This brief, subtle exchange showed Americans that it was okay to laugh again. The cast, led by *SNL* icon Will Ferrell (b. 1967), gave Americans their first real laughs since the tragic events. Singer Paul Simon (b. 1941) sang a heartrending rendition of his song "The Boxer" during the cold open. In response to Mayor Giuliani's urge for New York to reopen for business, Hollywood legend Robert De Niro (b. 1943) organized the Tribeca Film Festival in New York City in 2002.

Since World War II, Americans have frequently met periods of fear and uncertainty with a turn to fictional hero narratives. The idea of a hero sweeping in to save the day has proved comforting throughout modern U.S. history. Two new television series were set to debut in the fall of 2001 that would meet that very need, and both would go on to considerable commercial success throughout the decade. The WB, a fledgling network, premiered *Smallville* (WB, 2001–2006; CW, 2006–2011), the most recent update of the sixty-three-year-old *Superman* franchise.

In this unique take on the character, however, actor Tom Welling (b. 1977) played a teenage Clark Kent, just learning of his alien origins and dealing with his ever-evolving superpowers. With a promise of "no tights, no flights" from show creators Alfred Gough and Miles Millar (both b. 1967), this post-9/11 Superman would have no costume, no cape, and no ability to fly (yet) and would never be referred to as Superman or even the Man of Steel. The series was, instead, modeled along the lines of the WB's previous hit teen series, *Buffy, the Vampire Slayer* (WB, 1997–2001; UPN, 2001–2003), with the superpowered lead battling a monster of the week alongside an entourage of nonpowered teenage friends.

Actor Kiefer Sutherland (b. 1966) debuted his spy thriller *24* (FOX, 2001–2010; 2014) on November 6, 2001. Sutherland played Agent Jack Bauer of the Counter Terrorist Unit (CTU), tasked each season with stopping a potential terrorist threat within twenty-four hours. Over time, the series would be criticized for its excessive violence and clear violation of due process for accused terrorists. To an America still in fear, however, Bauer proved a cathartic release for their pent-up tensions. By 2010, American fears had subsided and Americans were questioning the liberties they had sacrificed in the wake of their immediate trauma, and *24* was cancelled. It made a brief appearance in a miniseason in 2014, with conservative audiences still very taken with the idea of a Jack Bauer protecting Americans from future threats.

One of the career casualties of the American sensitivities after 9/11 was comedian Bill Maher (b. 1956), host of the late-night series *Politically Incorrect* (Comedy Central, 1993–1997; ABC, 1997–2002). Known for speaking his mind, Maher created *Politically Incorrect* to address how, in the 1990s, political correctness in America had evolved, or devolved, depending on one's perspective, from "Don't be offensive" to "No matter what you say, you will offend someone, so don't say anything at all." As a result, most of the major social issues facing America could not be fully discussed out of fear of someone being offended, thus solving nothing. The series was very popular throughout the 1990s. One of the guests scheduled to appear on the September 11, 2001, episode, Barbara Olsen (1955–2001), was on board American Flight 77, which hit the Pentagon that day. The following week on September 17, 2001, another panelist, controversial filmmaker Dinesh D'Souza (b. 1961), stated on air that the terrorists were "warriors." Maher supported the comment by furthering that America was cowardly by attacking the enemy with long-range missiles and that the terrorists, though horrible, were not cowards. Dramatically declining ratings and advertising dollars led to the series' cancellation the following summer.

Many in the media, however, saw the irony and ridiculousness of cancelling a program called *Politically Incorrect* because its host had said something politically incorrect. One such critic was pay-cable outlet HBO, who immediately offered Maher his own show on their network, *Real Time with Bill Maher* (HBO, 2003–present). Since its debut, Maher has become a powerful voice in political punditry. What makes Maher unique in the twenty-first century—and a key factor of his popularity among his audience—is that, rather than coming out strongly liberal or conservative, Maher speaks "common sense," with a left-of-center approach to commentary. Throughout the 2000s and 2010s, Maher continued to occasionally offend those on the right and left, but the support he receives from his audience and HBO remains strong.

By far the biggest name in comedic political punditry to emerge from the 2000s was the aforementioned Jon Stewart. When *The Daily Show* debuted in 1996 with Craig Kilborn (b. 1962) as host, the series was a straightforward parody of nightly news broadcasts. At the end of 1998, Kilborn left the show, and producers replaced him with popular comedian Jon Stewart. Despite four failed talk shows of his own throughout the late 1980s and early 1990s and a lackluster movie career, Stewart achieved new heights for both himself and the show with his new take on the concept. Stewart would report and make jokes about the actual news of the day, and his new correspondents, including Stephen Colbert (b. 1964), Steve Carrell (b. 1962), Samantha Bee (b. 1969), and John Oliver (b. 1977), would record in-depth feature stories utilizing comedy and sarcasm to underscore either the seriousness or ridiculousness of the story. Most important, perhaps, Stewart faded out the celebrity interviews in each episode's last segments with interviews of politicians, scientists, journalists, and other professionals.

This new, smarter approach led to their coverage of the 2000 elections as Indecision 2000, followed four years later by Indecision 2004. By 2004, Stewart and company had cemented themselves as legitimate political pundits, and more and more young people began turning to Comedy Central for factual coverage of the news. Improv comedian Colbert created a caricature of himself in his role as correspondent, passing himself as a buffoonish hardline conservative and quickly becoming the most popular correspondent on the show. His and the show's popularity soon led to a spin-off series, *The Colbert Report* (Comedy Central, 2004–2014), a parody of FOX News' *The O'Reilly Factor*. The back-to-back pundit shows soon became a ratings powerhouse, and by decade's end, Stewart and Colbert were two of the most respected political pundits in television history.

Colbert and Stewart would leave their posts in 2014 and 2015, respectively. Colbert went on to host *The Late Show* on CBS in the wake of David Letterman's retirement. Stewart, frustrated and disheartened by the widening divide in American discourse (which, he, himself, possibly felt some responsibility for), stepped aside for his handpicked successor, South African comedian Trevor Noah (b. 1984). During the controversial and divisive presidential election of 2016, Colbert soon turned *The Late Show* into a broader form of his previous politically centered *Colbert Report*. Noah followed Stewart's model, providing a fresh, young, and international perspective on the news of the day. After a successful stint filling in for Stewart during the summer of 2013, British-born comedian and *Daily Show* correspondent John Oliver was given his own series, *Last Week Tonight with John Oliver* (HBO, 2014–present). Popular longtime *Daily Show* correspondent, Canadian-born Samantha Bee, was given her own program, *Full Frontal with Samantha Bee* (TBS, 2016–present). By 2020, Jon Stewart's impact on political punditry in America had transformed into a legacy.

Throughout the 1970s, a contributing factor to the successes of the women's liberation movement was the strong support given by network television. Series such as *The Mary Tyler Moore Show* (CBS, 1970–1977), *Maude* (CBS, 1972–1978), *Wonder Woman* (ABC, 1975–1977; CBS, 1977–1979), and *Charlie's Angels* (ABC, 1976–1981) normalized strong, empowered, and professional women to American audiences to a massive degree of success. In the late 1990s and early 2000s, television responded to social change once again with their increasing support for the LGBTQ+ community. *Will & Grace* (NBC, 1998–2006; 2017–2020) was a sitcom centered on the very deep friendship between a gay man, Will Truman, played by Eric McCormack (b. 1963), and his straight former fiancée, Grace Adler, played by Debra Messing (b. 1968). The series brilliantly made fun of gay stereotypes, while at the same time presenting why those stereotypes exist. The writers, directors, and actors strove to show those opposed to the LGBTQ+ community the flaws in their thinking without insulting or talking down to their way of thinking.

In 2003, the cable network Bravo launched the reality series *Queer Eye for the Straight Guy* (2003–2007). The series starred five gay men—Ted Allen (b. 1965), Kyan Douglas (b. 1970), Thom Filicia (b. 1969), Carson Kressley (b. 1969), and Jai Rodriguez (b. 1979)—who provided grooming, fashion, and style advice to straight men. The show was wildly popular and gave rise to the "metrosexual" movement: straight men who cared about stereotypically "gay" topics such as grooming, fashion, and style. The stars became known as the Queer Eye Guys and the Fab Five, a play on the equally culturally significant Fab Four of the 1960s, the Beatles. An updated series, *Queer Eye*, was launched in 2018 with new guys. While by the time these two series ended their initial runs the majority of states had voted to ban same-sex marriage, in less than a decade the tide dramatically turned, and, in 2015, same sex marriage was protected nationally by the U.S. Supreme Court in *Obergefell vs. Hodges*.

Perhaps the greatest influence on "normalizing" the LGBTQ+ community to a wider range of straight Americans was stand-up comedian Ellen DeGeneres (b. 1958). A hugely successful stand-up comic in the late 1980s and early 1990s, Ellen received her own sitcom in the mid-1990s, *Ellen* (ABC, 1994–1998). The series was built along the same premise of the iconic 1990s sitcom *Seinfeld* (NBC, 1989–1998), where Ellen played a slightly fictionalized version of herself. In the spring of 1997, at the height of her sitcom's success, Ellen came out as lesbian to Oprah Winfrey (b. 1954) on her daytime talk show. Later that evening, *Ellen* aired an episode where the fictional Ellen also came out to her therapist, also played by Winfrey. Conservative backlash was immediate, and ratings and advertising dollar drops led ABC to cancel the show the following season.

Ellen's career collapsed overnight. However, in the wake of 9/11, awards shows were finding it difficult to recruit comedians to host their awards events. The Emmy Awards turned to Ellen, who rose to the challenge. Her performance, walking the fine line between respect for the national trauma and comedic brilliance, was hailed from that night. Ellen received numerous standing ovations throughout the evening, becoming America's sweetheart overnight. One of her grand slam jokes from the evening was an opener: "What would bug the Taliban more than seeing a gay woman in a suit surrounded by Jews?" (Ford 2013; "2001 Emmy Awards, Ellen DeGeneres Highlights," YouTube, https://www.youtube.com/watch?v=ZY06m4tro2E). As a result of Ellen's massive appeal after the Emmys, she was given her own *Oprah*-esque daytime talk show, *The Ellen DeGeneres Show* (Syndication, 2003–present), which has become the top-rated show on daytime television throughout the 2000s and 2010s. By 2020, Ellen had truly become a beloved American icon.

Television took a massive hit in the early 2000s in a way no one saw coming. For the last two decades of the twentieth century, cable network Music Television (MTV) reigned as the go-to channel for all things music, fashion, and overall popular culture. MTV defined Generation X and was a consistent ratings powerhouse on cable. That took a dramatic nosedive almost overnight in the 2000s. Launched on August 1, 1981, as a twenty-four-hour music-video channel, MTV originally showed only rock videos. In 1983, the channel broadened to include artists such as Michael Jackson (1958–2009), Lionel Richie (b. 1949), Prince (1958–2016), and Madonna (b. 1958). MTV helped launch rap/hip-hop as a nationally popular genre of music.

In the 1990s, it broadened its programming to include shows such as the hugely popular but equally sophomoric animated series *Beavis and Butt-Head* (MTV, 1993–1997; 2011). Beginning in 1984, the *MTV Video Music Awards* became one of the most popular annual events on television. By 2000, however, millennials began to view MTV and sister channel VH1 as passé. Even though the franchise would expand with MTV2 and MTV3 (the latter primarily speaking to aging Gen Xers), the cultural impact of MTV would remain an artifact of the twentieth century. With the expansion of the internet throughout the 2000s, video services such as MTV would be replaced by YouTube. It would be that same internet that would account for the downfall of another major twentieth century medium: print media.

PRINT MEDIA

With the advent of the internet, print media's days were numbered. At the height of the Monica Lewinsky scandal in 1997–1998, more and more Americans began turning to the website the Drudge Report for up-to-the-minute events. Throughout the first decade of the twenty-first century and the rapid evolution and expansion of the internet, the problem only got worse. According to the *Atlantic*, "Between 2000 and 2015, print newspaper advertising revenue fell from about $60 billion to about $20 billion, wiping out the gains of the previous 50 years" (Thompson 2016). This decline was logical and inevitable. With 24-7 cable news coverage, cable news' own eventual postings to the internet, and news sites like Drudge, Americans no longer needed to wait for tomorrow's morning paper to receive in-depth coverage of the previous day's news.

As much as newspapers felt the crunch, weekly and monthly periodicals felt it even more. Magazines such as *Time* and *Newsweek*, which provided more detailed analysis of recent news events and news-making individuals, were hit even harder. Americans in the 2000s became more and more addicted to instant notification. Online stories could be updated as more information came in; plus with the advent of smartphones, news was available at the touch of a button. Most big-name news outlets began to shift with the times, providing website or app versions of their publications. What appears to have kept print media afloat at all is older Americans, more comfortable with sifting through the morning paper than reading a digital report on their phones. However, as the Greatest Generation and the baby boomers retire and die, print media may be a matter of history in another generation.

Print books remained popular throughout the 2000s and beyond. Despite the advent of e-books and reading devices such as Amazon's Kindle, Americans continued to overwhelmingly prefer holding a book in their hands and shifting through the pages, as their ancestors had done for centuries. As such, book sales continued to do well even as periodical sales declined. One periodical that struggled throughout the 2000s only to collapse entirely as the next decade dawned was *Wizard: The Magazine of Comics, Entertainment and Pop Culture*. Launched in 1991, at the height of what would come to be known as the collectors' bubble in the comic book media, *Wizard* was the go-to source for all things comics and comics related. Each month's issue also provided a price guide, allowing comics collectors to maintain up-to-the-minute estimates on the value of their comic book collections. In the early 2000s, the magazine cut its issue size and content by half to save costs, and in 2011, the magazine shut down entirely, unable to compete with the same content being provided by dozens of legitimate websites and apps.

Even before periodicals began feeling the crunch from the internet, one medium—comic books—was already on the verge of collapse as the twentieth century came to a close. When the collectors' bubble burst (around 1995), publishers struggled to stay afloat. Dark Horse Comics maintained an audience primarily through their offerings of original *Star Wars* comics, and industry giant DC Comics was able to maintain stability primarily due to the fact that it was a subsidiary of a much larger company, Warner Brothers, who marketed DC's superhero catalog through their film and television divisions. Marvel Comics, however, barely survived the 1990s. At the end of 1996, Marvel filed for bankruptcy under Chapter 11, and in 1997, the company was saved when it was bought out by Toy Biz. The toy company's chief executive officer, Avi Arad (b. 1948), believed that although Marvel possessed no real physical assets, their intellectual properties (i.e., their superhero characters) represented millions of dollars of value. He would ultimately be proven very prophetic, as, by 2020, the Marvel superheroes proved to be worth billions. Still, however, comic book sales continued a steep decline in the last half of the 1990s.

That changed after the terror attacks of 9/11. As stated earlier, since the advent of superheroes in the late 1930s, Americans had consistently turned to hero narratives for escapism during uncertain times, and 9/11 provided the most uncertain times in American history. A new generation of writers and artists began taking these old heroes and moving them in new and fresh directions. The rise in interest in comic book superheroes led Hollywood to reinvest in the genre, which was in a steep decline in box office revenue by the end of the 1990s. Films such as *Iron Man* and *The Dark Knight* (both in 2008) became some of the highest-grossing films in history, and the comic book medium escaped extinction for the third time in its history. Throughout the 2010s, the continued success of superhero films and merchandise—as well as comics publishers' offerings of old and new comics on digital platforms—kept the print division of their industry alive.

One thing that helped keep print comics alive, and promote all areas of American popular culture, was the increasing popularity of Comic-Con. Throughout the 2000s, dozens, if not hundreds, of pop culture conventions emerged across the country, but the granddaddy of them all was San Diego Comic-Con (SDCC), which has become the Mecca of pop culture conventions. SDCC began in 1970 as a simple, local comic-book convention, founded by Richard Alf (1952–2012), Shel Dorf (1933–2009), Ken Krueger (1926–2009), and Mike Towry (b. 1955). What started as a simple, local event grew to an annual attendance of over one hundred fifty thousand people by 2010. Today, the SDCC showcases not only the latest in comic books (and a massive offering of past comics for sale) but also the latest in video games, television, and film.

Most pop culture franchises debut their upcoming projects at SDCC because of the event's massive audience and coverage. It is also a place where up-and-coming artists can showcase their work in hopes of achieving contracts with a major publisher. SDCC has also spawned an entirely new job market for cosplayers. Many attendees of 'cons around the nation arrive in costume, many of them homemade and with artistic twists on established pop culture characters. Some cosplayers, however, have proven to be so amazing in their costuming that they are paid to attend. Hundreds, if not thousands, of professional cosplayers now attend conventions around the world as their full-time job. As with all other media of pop culture, however, cosplayers gain considerable access to audiences—and potential clients—through the current king-of-all-media: the internet.

THE INTERNET

In 1993, mainstream America gained access to the World Wide Web through the release of the Mosaic web browser, from the company soon to be known as Netscape. By 1997, every movie, television series, and even commercial products had a ".com" website for audiences and consumers to visit. In 1999, the creators of the film *The Blair Witch Project* were able to utilize Americans' growing fascination with the internet—as well as their relative naivete as to what the Web could do—to package their film as authentic found footage material of three college students suffering a mysterious and deadly fate at the alleged hands of the Blair Witch. By the time audiences discovered that the material on the website was a hoax designed to market the fictional film, they were too impressed by the ingenuity of the idea to be angered by the deception.

The rapid rise of websites like Amazon, eBay, Yahoo!, and others led to an investors' bubble, and, like all such bubbles, it was doomed to eventually burst. By 2000, it was clear that returns on internet start-up investments would be years in the future (if they ever saw returns at all), and from 2000 to 2002, the market experienced what came to be known as the dot-com crash or dot-com bubble. Meanwhile, the company that had started it all, Netscape, became a victim of the crash. In 1998, the company America Online (AOL) began the process of buying out Netscape, which it finally did in 2002. However, when AOL split with Time Warner, the latter received Netscape in the divorce, closing it down in 2003. In 2004, AOL shut down Netscape DevEdge (the portion of the company it kept) and utilized its technology to launch Mozilla Firefox. By 2020, any mention of Netscape is most commonly connected to some joke referring to outdated material.

One site that not only survived the bubble but has gone on to be one of the most important informational resources on the internet is Wikipedia. Launched in 2001 by Larry Sanger (b. 1968) and Jimmy Wales (b. 1966), Wikipedia is, as its name implies, an online encyclopedia. People have long relied on published encyclopedia for guidance in researching every topic imaginable. In the first decade of Wikipedia, anyone could add to or delete from any online entry if they saw material that was wrong or missing. This, however, proved problematic, as literally anyone could alter anything with no factual basis to back up their changes. This made Wikipedia a bit of a joke early on and a source that no respected researcher would completely rely on. Throughout the 2010s, however, stricter controls on changes to Wikipedia entries have been implemented, and most information within entries is clearly and distinctly footnoted, making it more trustworthy than ever before. By 2020, millions around the world utilize Wikipedia as a quick reference on a daily basis, as it is available in 309 languages (according to Wikipedia).

One of the biggest success stories of the internet in the 2000s has been Google. Founded in 1998 by Sergey Brin and Larry Page (both b. 1973), Google was designed as a competitor for Yahoo!, the largest search engine on the internet in the late 1990s. Throughout the 2000s, Google continued to grow, expanding its offerings to users with the inclusion of separate search engines such as Google Images and Google Maps. Like Yahoo!, Google also offered an email service, Gmail. By 2005, Yahoo! had gone the way of Netscape in the American consciousness, though the search engine does still remain active. In the 2010s, Google, along with fellow success stories Amazon, Apple, and Facebook, has become one of the most powerful names on the internet and a corporate force to be reckoned with.

Among the many things that the internet has to offer—information, entertainment, and communication—one of the biggest internet stories to come out of the 2000s was the advent of social media. Through social media, friends and strangers around the world now interconnect on a daily and even hourly basis. The upside of this is that it connects far away family members, long-lost friends, and strangers with similar interests, as well as providing numerous dating platforms for potential couples to meet who, prior to the internet, may have never been able to do so. The unfortunate downside, however, is that it provides platforms for individuals and groups that seek to divide, intimidate, and even harm others. For good or ill, social media has changed America and the world to a deeper degree than perhaps any other media, technology, or movement in human history.

SOCIAL MEDIA

In the 2010s, social media would come to dominate and define American culture. Through social media, political campaigns would change forever. Yard signs and campaign advertisements on television would greatly diminish in their abilities to affect national elections. In 2012 and 2016, President Barack Obama and Republican nominee Donald Trump, respectively, would spend less campaign money than their opponents and yet go on to win their elections. They were able to do this, to a large degree, on their respective uses of social media such as Facebook, YouTube, and Twitter. Meant to unite people around the nation and the world, social media would prove to be as divisive as uniting. Online bullying would become a nightmare for young people across the country. Families and friends would turn against each other based on posts on social media platforms. With the advent of these platforms in the late 2000s, little could anyone in America at the time realize how massive these platforms would become or how they would change the course of history.

As the U.S. government had sole original access to what would become known as the internet, they had the first of what, today, would be called chat rooms. The program was called EMISARI. It went online in 1971 and could allow up to ten offices at a time to have conference chats. The first chat room available for public use came in 1980, created by CompuServe. Throughout the 1990s, internet chat rooms gained in popularity, with most chat rooms dedicated to specific topics: video games, news, pop culture franchises, sports, and so on. By 2000, chat rooms were in slight decline as more Americans were engaging in texting for the first time. The long-distance interconnectivity that chat rooms and texting provided would take a massive leap with the advent of social media websites.

Perhaps the earliest social networking website was theGlobe. In 1995, Stephan Paternot and Todd Krizelman (both b. 1974) created the company WebGenesis. They then developed theGlobe, which first went online that year. The site offered chat rooms and message boards. The company went public in 1998, but as the internet was still in its relative infancy, social media had not yet caught on. By 2008, just as social media was about to take off, the company went essentially defunct. A more successful site launched in 2003: LinkedIn. This site was dedicated more toward professional networking, job searches, and the like. Though still used throughout the 2010s, by 2015, the site became more or less a joke by comparison to the bigger names in social media.

The first truly popular social media site was MySpace. Launched in 2005, within its first year online, MySpace surpassed Google as the most popular site on the Web. Similar in many ways to the later Facebook, MySpace allowed users to essentially tell their story to the world. It allowed users to personalize their pages with background themes of their favorite themes: from franchises such as *Star Wars* or comic books, to guitars, stars, or their own personal artwork. MySpace users could also present their favorite music and chat online with their connections.

Another site that went online in 2005 has gone on to be one of the most viewed websites around the world by 2020: YouTube. Founded by Steve Chen (b. 1978), Chad Hurly (b. 1977), and Jawed Karim (b. 1979), YouTube allows users to upload, view, and comment on video files. By 2006, the potential of YouTube was so apparent that it was bought out by Google. Over time, users could even share YouTube videos on other social media sites. Users could create their own channels, frequently uploading videos, and other users could subscribe to such channels, receiving alerts when their subscribed channels uploaded new material. Some channels uploaded educational material; others created review programs, reviewing the latest in such areas as films, television, music, sports, and fashion. Fans of various franchises could create fan films, taking fan fiction to a whole new level. One of the earliest popular fan films was the *Star Wars*–themed fan film *Troops*. Directed by Kevin Rubio (b. 1967), *Troops* was first filmed in 1997, a mockumentary parody combining the franchises of *Star Wars* and the popular reality television series *COPS* (FOX, 1989–2013; Spike, 2013–2017; Paramount, 2018–present). *Troops* was passed around the internet for years until YouTube allowed the entire world to experience this true masterpiece in early fan filmmaking.

The site that would come to define social media went national (and international) in 2006: Facebook. Created by Mark Zuckerberg (b. 1984), Chris Hughes (b. 1983), Andrew McCollum (b. 1983), Dustin Moskovitz (b. 1984), and Eduardo Saverin (b. 1982), Facebook was initially designed to be a social networking site for student and alumni of major American universities. Controversy hit soon after its launch when Harvard University undergrads Cameron and Tyler Winklevoss (twins, b. 1981) and Divya Narendra (1982) sued Zuckerberg and his team, claiming that the idea for a university-themed social media site was theirs and that Zuckerberg had promised to help them develop it and then stole the idea for himself and his team. The suit was eventually settled in 2008, with the plaintiffs receiving a large sum of Facebook stock.

The concept of connecting with old classmates proved so profitable that Zuckerberg took Facebook international, allowing anyone anywhere (except in countries where internet access is limited or banned outright) to connect with anyone anywhere in the world. The site would all but eliminate all competitors, most notably MySpace, and by 2020, Facebook had nearly 2.5 billion users, essentially, one-third of the world's population. Throughout its popular run as a social media site, however, Facebook has experienced numerous scandals: monopoly charges; accusations of selling user data; inability (or refusal) to monitor hate speech and online bullying; and allowing the posting of misinformation (and outright lies). Most of these issues, however, come down to one basic argument: free speech. If Facebook were to begin limiting speech, for even the most noble of reasons, it would be a slippery slope that could have disastrous results.

The last major social media site to launch in the 2000s went national around the same time as Facebook and has proven to be Facebook's only real competitor in the social media market: Twitter. Founded by Jack Dorsey (b. 1976), Noah Glass (birth year unknown), Biz Stone (b. 1974), and Evan Williams (b. 1972), Twitter possesses far fewer functions than Facebook but has proven to be just as popular throughout the 2010s. Originally, Twitter users could only tweet posts in a maximum of 140 characters (in the 2010s, that would double to 280). Users could also share articles and videos and have private conversations. In the last half of the 2010s, candidate and then president Donald Trump (b. 1946) would further popularize the site, using it as his primary method of communication with followers, both during his candidacy and his presidency.

Social media would continue to expand in the decade that followed. Instagram (2010) and Snapchat (2011) gained a massive, particularly young, following, allowing users to upload quick photographs and short videos that would, initially, disappear soon after viewing. In 2012, the social media app Tinder launched, utilized as a dating app allowing people to meet up for potential dating, romantic, and casual encounters. By 2020, Facebook, Twitter, Instagram, and Snapchat would all but dominate American culture, forever changing how Americans interact and communicate, for better or worse.

Throughout the 2000s, media of all genres transformed in ways never before expected or dreamed. By 2010, cable news, television viewing, print media, and the internet all were completely different media than when the decade and the century began. As the internet continued to grow and become more and more a part of Americans' minute-by-minute lives, these media transformed even more throughout the 2010s, promising to do so even more during the decades beyond. The upside, of course, has been the providing of more interconnectivity than at any prior point in human history. The unfortunate—and unavoidable—downside has been the deepening in the social divide in America that had been growing since the mid-1990s. By 2020, due in very large part by cable news and social media, the United States was a more divided nation than at any point in the nation's history, except, perhaps, the Civil War. The question, then, becomes whether these same media can stem and turn that tide and, if not, what can arise with the ability to do so.

FURTHER READING

Abad-Santos, Alex. 2016. "Marvel's Civil War and Its Politics, Explained." *Vox*, May 3. https://www.vox.com/2016/5/3/11531348/marvel-civil-war-explained. Retrieved January 2, 2020.

Bennett, Jessica. 2019. "This Gen X Mess: The Tech, Music, Style, Books, Trends, Rules, Films and Pills That Made Gen X . . . So So-So." *New York Times*, May 16. https://www.nytimes.com/interactive/2019/05/14/style/generation-xers.html?utm_source=pocket-newtab. Retrieved May 16, 2019.

Bodroghkozy, Aniko. 2018. *A Companion to the History of American Broadcasting*. New York: Wiley-Blackwell.

Brands, H. W. 2011. *American Dreams: The United States since 1945*. New York: Penguin.

Bush, George W. 2001. "Address to the Nation." American Rhetoric, September 11. https://www.americanrhetoric.com/speeches/gwbush911addresstothenation .htm. Retrieved March 31, 2019.

Bush, George W. 2010. *Decision Points*. New York: Crown.

Carr, Nicholas. 2011. *The Shallows: What the Internet Is Doing to Our Brains*. New York: W. W. Norton.

Carter, Bill. 2005. "CNN Will Cancel 'Crossfire' and Cut Ties to Commentator." *New York Times*, January 6. https://www.nytimes.com/2005/01/06/business/media /cnn-will-cancel-crossfire-and-cut-ties-to-commentator.html. Retrieved January 12, 2020.

Carter, Bill. 2011. *The War for Late Night: When Leno Went Early and Television Went Crazy*. New York: Plume.

Castleman, Harry, and Walter J. Podrazik. 2016. *Watching TV: Eight Decades of American Television*. 3rd ed. New York: Syracuse University Press.

Chamberlain, Will. 2019. "Jon Stewart Was Wrong about Crossfire: It's Time to Bring Bombastic, Evenly Matched Debates to Cable TV." Human Events, September 6. https://humanevents.com/2019/09/06/jon-stewart-was-wrong-about-crossfire/. Retrieved January 12, 2020.

Chomsky, Noam. 2005. *Imperial Ambitions: Conversations on the Post-9/11 World*. New York: Metropolitan.

Colbert, Stephen. 2009. *I Am America (and So Can You!)*. New York: Grand Central.

Collins, Scott. 2004. *Crazy Like a Fox: The Inside Story of How FOX News Beat CNN*. New York: Portfolio.

Coontz, Stephanie. 2016. *The Way We Never Were: American Families and the Nostalgia Trap*. New York: Basic.

Crowson, H. Michael, Teresa K. Debacker, and Stephen J. Thoma. 2006. "The Role of Authoritarianism, Perceived Threat, and Need for Closure or Structure in Predicting Post-9/11 Attitudes and Beliefs." *Journal of Social Psychology* 146, no. 6: 733–750.

Cullen, Jim. 2002. *The Art of Democracy: A Concise History of Popular Culture in the United States*. New ed. New York: Monthly Review.

Dittmer, Jason. 2005. "Captain America's Empire: Reflections on Identity, Popular Culture, and Post-9/11 Geopolitics." *Annals of the Association of American Geographers* 95, no. 3: 626–643.

Errico, Marcus. 1996. "Marvel Files for Bankruptcy." *E! News*, December 27. https:// www.eonline.com/news/33907/marvel-files-for-bankruptcy. Retrieved January 14, 2020.

Evans, Jennifer C. 2002. "Hijacking Civil Liberties: The USA PATRIOT Act of 2001." *Loyola University Chicago Law Journal* 33, no. 4: 933–990.

Fahy, Thomas, ed. 2005. *Considering Aaron Sorkin: Essays on the Politics, Poetics and Sleight of Hand in the Films and Television Series*. Jefferson, NC: McFarland.

Faludi, Susan. 2008. *The Terror Dream: Myth and Misogyny in an Insecure America*. London: Picador.

Farris, Scott. 2012. *Almost President: The Men Who Lost the Race but Changed the Nation*. Guilford, CT: Lyons.

Farrow, Ronan. 2018. *War on Peace: The End of Diplomacy and the Decline of American Influence*. New York: W. W. Norton.

Ford, Rebecca. 2013. "Oscars: Ellen DeGeneres's Hosting History." *Hollywood Reporter*, August 2. https://www.hollywoodreporter.com/news/oscars-ellen-degeneres -hosting-history-598767. Retrieved January 13, 2020.

Gournelos, Ted, and Viveca Greene, eds. 2011. *A Decade of Dark Humor: How Comedy, Irony, and Satire Shaped Post-9/11 America*. Jackson: University Press of Mississippi.

Graff, Garrett M. 2019. "Pagers, Pay Phones, and Dialup: How We Communicated on 9/11." *Wired*, September 11. https://www.wired.com/story/pagers-pay-phones-and-dialup-how-we-communicated-on-911/. Retrieved January 10, 2020.

Guerrasio, Jason. 2015. "New 'Saturday Night Live' Documentary Recounts the Emotional First Show after 9/11." *Business Insider*, April 16. https://www.businessinsider.com/saturday-night-live-first-show-after-911-2015-4. Retrieved January 13, 2020.

Handscombe, Claire. 2016. *Walk with Us: How* The West Wing *Changed Our Lives*. New York: CH Books.

Heilemann, John, and Mark Halperin. 2010. *Game Change: Obama and the Clintons, McCain and Palin, and the Race of a Lifetime*. New York: Harper Perennial.

History on the Net. [Posting Date Unknown]. "The 2000 Presidential Election." https://www.historyonthenet.com/authentichistory/1993-2000/3-2000election/2-electionnight/index.html. Retrieved January 12, 2020.

Howe, Sean. 2012. *Marvel Comics: The Untold Story*. New York: Harper Perennial.

Kruse, Kevin M., and Julian E. Zelizer. 2019. *Fault Lines: A History of the United States since 1974*. New York: W. W. Norton.

Letukas, Lynn. 2014. *Primetime Pundits: How Cable News Covers Social Issues*. Washington, DC: Lexington.

Mezrich, Ben. 2009. *The Accidental Billionaires: The Founding of Facebook, a Tale of Sex, Money, Genius, and Betrayal*. New York: Doubleday.

9/11 Commission. 2004. "The 9/11 Commission Report." National Commission on Terrorist Attacks Upon the United States. https://www.9-11commission.gov/report/. Retrieved January 3, 2020.

9/11 Memorial. [Posting Date Unknown]. "September 11 Attack Timeline." https://timeline.911memorial.org/#Timeline/2. Retrieved May 8, 2019.

Obama, Barack. 2009. "First Inaugural Address." Obama White House, January 20. https://obamawhitehouse.archives.gov/blog/2009/01/21/president-barack-obamas-inaugural-address. Retrieved March 31, 2019.

Olbermann, Keith. 2006. *The Worst Person in the World: And 202 Strong Contenders*. Hoboken, NJ: Wiley.

O'Reilly, Bill. 2006. *Culture Warrior*. New York: Crown.

Oswald, Debra L. 2005. "Understanding Anti-Arab Reactions Post-9/11: The Role of Threats, Social Categories, and Personal Ideologies." *Journal of Applied Social Psychology* 35, no. 9: 1775–1799.

Patterson, James T. 2005. *Restless Giant: The United States from Watergate to* Bush v. Gore. Oxford: Oxford University Press.

Rakove, Jack N., ed. 2002. *The Unfinished Election of 2000: Leading Scholars Examine America's Strangest Election*. New York: Basic.

Rogak, Lisa. 2015. *Angry Optimism: The Life and Times of Jon Stewart*. New York: St. Martin's.

Rollins, Peter, and John E. O'Connor. 2003. The West Wing: *The American Presidency as Television Drama*. Syracuse, NY: Syracuse University Press.

Salkowitz, Rob. 2012. *Comic-Con and the Business of Pop Culture: What the World's Wildest Trade Show Can Tell Us about the Future of Entertainment*. New York: McGraw-Hill.

Smith, Chris. 2016. The Daily Show *(The Book): An Oral History as Told by Jon Stewart, the Correspondents, Staff and Guests*. New York: Grand Central.

Staff. 2017. "Watch Jon Stewart Call Tucker Carlson a 'Dick' in Epic 2004 'Crossfire' Takedown." *Hollywood Reporter*, January 5. https://www.hollywoodreporter.com/news/jon-stewart-takes-down-tucker-carlson-crossfire-video-961127. Retrieved January 12, 2020.

Stewart, Jon, et al. 2004. *America (The Book)*. New York: Warner/Grand Central.

Thompson, Derek. 2016. "The Print Apocalypse and How to Survive It." *Atlantic*, November 3. https://www.theatlantic.com/business/archive/2016/11/the-print -apocalypse-and-how-to-survive-it/506429/. Retrieved January 14, 2020.

Toobin, Jeffrey. 2002. *Too Close to Call: The Thirty-Six-Day Battle to Decide the 2000 Election*. New York: Random House.

Tucker, Reed. 2017. *Slugfest: Inside the Epic 50-Year Battle Between Marvel and DC*. New York: Da Capo.

Van Dijck, José. 2013. *The Culture of Connectivity: A Critical History of Social Media*. Oxford: Oxford University Press.

Veloso, Francisco, and John Bateman. 2013. "The Multimodal Construction of Acceptability: Marvel's *Civil War* Comic Books and the PATRIOT Act." *Critical Discourse Studies* 10, no. 4: 427–443.

Von Drehle, David, et al. 2001. *Deadlock: The Inside Story of America's Closest Election*. New York: PublicAffairs.

Watson, Bruce. 2016. *Jon Stewart: Beyond the Moments of Zen*. Scotts Valley, CA: CreateSpace.

Whitehead, John W., and Steven H. Aden. 2002. "Forfeiting 'Enduring Freedom' for 'Homeland Security': A Constitutional Analysis of the USA Patriot Act and the Justice Department's Anti-Terrorism Initiatives." *American University Law Review* 51, no. 6: 1081–1133.

Willis, Susan. 2005. *Portents of the Real: A Primer for Post-9/11 America*. London: Verso.

Wright, Bradford W. 2003. *Comic Book Nation: The Transformation of Youth Culture in America*. Baltimore, MD: Johns Hopkins University Press.

CHAPTER 8

Fashion and Art

As in other areas of pop culture, the 2000s would prove to be a transformative decade for fashion and art. Whereas for the last decades of the twentieth century, fashion models appeared to be getting thinner and thinner, the 2000s would see the rise of the plus-size model. Long-standing stereotypes of beauty and practices of body shaming began to give way to more realistic representations of American women in the field of fashion. As MTV's influence on fashion and pop culture in general waned, pop stars such as Lady Gaga rose to have a profound influence, even combining fashion even more with artistic expression. The internet began to affect fashion as MTV once had with the rise of fashion blogs. In high schools and on college campuses across the country, whereas previous decades' popular fashions helped to define those decades (i.e., hoop skirts and ducktail haircuts in the 1950s, hippie culture in the 1960s, Black is beautiful in the 1970s, baggy clothes and neon colors in the 1980s, and the now deservedly maligned mullet of the 1990s), youth fashions in the 2000s began to lean more toward individualism and a resistance to fads.

The 2000s saw the rise of the mysterious artist known only as Banksy. The art of stand-up comedy, with a long history of political satire and parody, transitioned to actual political commentary and a platform for educating an increasingly divided public. A new generation of filmmakers, such as Bryan Singer and J. J. Abrams, arrived on the scene and broke new ground in film and television. George Lucas's experimentation with CGI effects in film once more proved the already iconic filmmaker to be a groundbreaking artist. Comic books, on verge of collapse by 2000, once more rebounded, again becoming a platform for sociopolitical commentary by decade's end. Like most other areas of pop culture, fashion and art were influenced by the events of September 11, 2001.

9/11

Some of the issues that fundamentalist terrorist organizations such as Al-Qaeda held against the United States were its unbridled freedom, rabid secularism, the power of women's voices, and the nation's seeming preoccupation with sex. In response to the events of 9/11, perhaps subconsciously, the United States appeared to double down in all these areas. President George W. Bush (b. 1946) went out of his way to underscore to the American people that terrorist groups like Al-Qaeda did not represent the religion of Islam, going so far as to begin publicly recognizing the religious holidays of all three of the Abrahamic religions at the White House; in doing so, he attempted to emphasize America's respect of all religions.

At the same time, throngs of Americans across the country did their best to enforce the idea of separation of church and state (something Al-Qaeda and its leader, Osama bin Laden, despised). Women became more prominent voices in politics, and former first lady Hillary Rodham Clinton (b. 1947) was elected to the U.S. Senate in 2000 and became a major contender for the Democratic nomination for president in 2008 and only the third woman to be appointed U.S. secretary of state in 2009. Ironically and simultaneously, oversexualization of women crossed lines unheard of just a decade before. Musical artists such as Jennifer Lopez (b. 1969), Beyoncé (b. 1981), and Lady Gaga (b. 1986) made music videos steamier than ever. Free pornography flooded the internet. While all of this spoke against the fundamentalist criticisms of the United States, however, it also further divided a country already evenly split in the ever-expanding Culture Wars.

In the immediate wake of the attacks, annual awards ceremonies were perplexed about how to proceed. Should the annual self-aggrandizing events of the Grammys, Emmys, and Oscars continue, or should they be set aside out of respect? Even when it was decided to proceed, producers of the programs found it difficult to find comedian hosts, most uncomfortable attempting to be funny so soon after the attacks. The Emmy Awards, scheduled to air November 4, 2001, finally approached stand-up comedian Ellen DeGeneres (b. 1958) to host. A relative outcast in Hollywood after coming out as lesbian in 1997, DeGeneres accepted the challenge. With the country watching to see how she would handle the fine line between respect and comedy, audiences both on television and in the room were floored by DeGeneres's brilliant and adept performance, giving Americans permission to laugh again while simultaneously being highly respectful of the trauma all were still feeling. Her sheer artistry has gone down in television and comedy history, and it made Ellen America's sweetheart overnight. As a result of this comedic artistic mastery, throughout the remainder of the 2000s, 2010s, and beyond, Ellen DeGeneres has become a beloved American icon.

In 2002, iconic cartoonist Art Spiegelman (b. 1948) began publishing a series of newspaper comic strips reflecting his own reactions to 9/11. Though originally appearing in the German newspaper *Die Zeit*, once they were completed in 2004, the strips, titled *In the Shadow of No Towers*, were collected and released as a hardcover book for enthusiasts of Spiegelman's works as well as those wishing to pay tribute to the tragic events. While the strips were not meant as a retelling of events or even an homage to the victims, they did allow the artist an outlet through which he could come to terms with the trauma of that day. The book later inspired composer Mohammed Fairouz (b. 1985) to produce a symphony along the same reflective lines.

Another work of art inspired by 9/11 was the theatrically released documentary *Fahrenheit 9/11* (2004), by acclaimed and controversial documentarian Michael Moore (b. 1954). Hot off the commercial and critical success of his previous documentary, *Bowling for Columbine* (2002), examining American gun culture in the wake of the tragic 1999 high school shooting in Columbine, Colorado, *Fahrenheit 9/11* examined the increasingly controversial war in Iraq, launched in 2003. Though well established as having no part in the 9/11 attacks, Iraqi president Saddam Hussein (1937–2006) became a target of the War on Terror that resulted from 9/11. Viewing Iraq as a threat to allies in the region, Bush administration invaded Iraq in the spring of 2003, quickly ousting Hussein from power. Although the first half of *Fahrenheit 9/11* provided interesting facts and insights into the Bush administration's decisions to invade, the last half quickly devolved into a more radical and less documented attack on President Bush's motives and rationale. Appearing as it did during an election year, the work was immediately disregarded as partisan, unfortunately playing a key role in returning America to the Culture Wars that had raged up till 9/11.

The major comic book publishers, DC and Marvel, were located in New York City and felt the ground shake on 9/11. As a result, both publishers quickly produced 9/11 memorial issues, showing the responses of various superheroes to the day's events. By 9/11, Marvel Comics had decided to cancel its long-running *Captain America* title and was examining how to reboot the series for a new millennium. After 9/11, the Sentinel of Liberty's next step became clear. Giving the book to writer John Ney Rieber and artist John Cassaday, the new *Captain America* opened with Steve Rogers (Captain America) at Ground Zero in New York City sifting through the rubble. He is recruited by Colonel Nick Fury of SHIELD to return to duty and help fight in the new War on Terror. Cap responds to the call (Rieber and Cassaday, *Captain America, Vol. 4, #1*, Marvel Comics, June 2002). However, rather than repeating the strongly patriotic and nationalist adventures of World War II, the War on Terror Cap would delve into the deeper meanings of terrorism as well as the victims of American retaliation, misunderstandings of Islam, and the dangers of overreaction. This run of *Captain America* ran for two-and-a-half years until December 2004, before relaunching once more with a less politicized format in 2005 (to begin with).

The events of 9/11 were so traumatic that a memorial to the victims was a must. Architects Michael Arad (b. 1969), Daniel Libeskind (b. 1946), and Peter Walker (b. 1932) were tasked with creating the 9/11 Memorial at the site of the original Twin Towers of the World Trade Center in New York City. Construction began in 2006, and the memorial was officially opened on the tenth anniversary of the attacks, September 11, 2011. The piece consists of two massive fountains and reflecting pools covering the sites of the bases of the original towers. On the parapets of the pools are engraved the names of all 2,977 people who died in the attacks, as well as the six names of those who died during the first attack on the towers in 1993. The waterfalls that pour from the pools into a central pit in each pool are said to be the largest human-made waterfalls in the United States. Millions of people every year visit the site to pay their respects to those lost.

FASHION ICONS

Several big-name celebrities became fashion icons in the 2000s. At the 2000 Grammy Awards, singer, dancer, and actress Jennifer Lopez (b. 1969) chose to wear what would quickly become the most iconic dress of the decade: a green dress designed by Donatella Versace (b. 1955). Typically, celebrities prefer to debut dresses on the red carpet, wearing pieces never before seen. This dress, however, had already been worn by actress Sandra Bullock (though in a different color), one of the members of the British girl group the Spice Girls, and even Versace herself. Lopez was adamant, however. What made the dress such a big deal at the time was the fact that the front was very low cut (cut to below the navel in fact), widening near the top, nearly exposing the breasts and giving the appearance that the breasts could become completely exposed at any second. The dress quickly became a source of conversation, controversy, parody, and, naturally, internet image searches. Google, in fact, created its Image Search specifically to handle the traffic for the J-Lo pictures (Ginsberg 2020).

Another celebrity fashion icon of the decade was hotel heiress Paris Hilton (b. 1981). In the 1990s, the then-teenager began a modeling career under the management of Trump Model Management, owned by New York real estate mogul and future president of the United States Donald Trump. In 2001, a former boyfriend released a sex tape he had made of Hilton onto the internet; in 2004, he released the video for sale under the title *1 Night in Paris*. This tabloid attention shot Hilton to superstar status, and young women across the country began to look up to the party girl Hilton as a role model. In 2004, the sociopolitical satire comedy series *South Park* (Comedy Central, 1997–present) aired the episode "Stupid Spoiled Whore Video Playset," eviscerating Hilton and her influence on popular culture and ridiculing young women who looked up to the heiress as a role model.

One cannot discuss fashion in the 2000s without mentioning one of the most iconic models of all time: RuPaul (born RuPaul Andre Charles in 1960). RuPaul is, perhaps, the most famous drag queen of all time. With a magnetic personality and a flair for performance, RuPaul played a massive role in the growing acceptance of the LGBTQ+ community in the 2000s. Both in and out of drag, a nod from RuPaul remains a highly desired accolade in the world of fashion throughout the 2000s, the 2010s, and well into the 2020s. Since 2009, RuPaul has been the host and producer of the long-running television series *RuPaul's Drag Race* (Logo, 2009–2016; VH1, 2017–present).

Perhaps the most widely respected fashion critic of the decade was Tim Gunn (b. 1953). From 1982 to 2007, Gunn served as a professor at Parsons School of Design in New York City, spending the last seven years of his tenure as chair of fashion design. He came to national prominence as the primary mentor on the long-running television series *Project Runway* (Bravo, 2004–2008; Lifetime, 2009–2017; Bravo, 2019–present). He is also the author of numerous books on fashion and frequently appears on other television programs as a fashion consultant.

Other than *Drag Race* and *Project Runway*, other reality programs tied to fashion in the 2000s included *America's Top Model* (UPN, 2003–2006; CW, 2006–2015; VH1, 2016–present), created and hosted by supermodel Tyra Banks (b. 1973), and *Queer Eye for the Straight Guy* (Bravo, 2003–2007), where Kyan Douglas (b. 1970) was the "grooming guru," giving straight men advice on personal appearance, and Carson Kressley (b. 1969) was the "fashion savant," giving advice on men's fashions. The rest of *Queer Eye*'s Fab Five consisted of food and wine connoisseur Ted Allen (b. 1965); the design doctor Thom Filicia (b. 1969), expert on home design; and the culture vulture Jai Rodriguez (b. 1979), expert on all things popular culture to prepare men for more interesting conversation on dates. *Queer Eye* succeeded in two major ways: creating new levels of respect and acceptance of gay men and developing the term "metrosexual," referring to straight men who had an appreciation for the finer aspects of food, fashion, and grooming.

Beginning as a presidential candidate's wife in 1960, First Lady Jaqueline Bouvier Kennedy (later Onassis, 1929–1994) became a fashion icon to women across the United States. For the remainder of the twentieth century and into the twenty-first, no first lady had ever achieved her level of iconic status. That changed in 2008, when First Lady Michelle Obama (b. 1964) once more set fashion trends from the White House. Her formfitting long-sleeved and loose-fitting sleeveless tops matched with knee-length skirts exuded class and style for a new generation of American women. Mixing professionalism with a traditional mom look, Michelle Obama took what could be considered a simple or plain look into something fashionable, respectable, and—in its own way—iconic.

Just as J-Lo had brought in the decade with a fashion bang, a new artist would redefine fashion, further combining it with artistic expression by decade's end. In 2008, American audiences were introduced to Lady Gaga (born Stefani Germanotta in 1986). Her debut album, *The Fame*, gained overnight critical and commercial success. On the red carpet as well as on stage, Lady Gaga's fashion's ran the gambit from classic elegance to outlandish eccentricity, and from traditional fashion to avant-garde expressionism. The success of her follow-up album, *The Fame Monster* (2009), led to thirteen MTV Video Music Award nominations. At the 2010 awards ceremony, Lady Gaga wore a dress made entirely of raw meat designed by Franc Fernandez (b. 1986) and Nicola Formichetti (b. 1977). Animal rights groups were outraged. In an interview with Ellen DeGeneres, Lady Gaga stated that the dress was worn in protest of the U.S. military's Don't Ask, Don't Tell policy toward LGBTQ+ servicemembers (Mapes 2010). One year later, on September 20, 2011, Congress repealed DADT, allowing LGBTQ+ servicemembers to serve openly in the military.

In the area of women's fashions, perhaps the greatest influencer of the 2000s was the television series *Sex and the City* (HBO, 1998–2004) and its follow-up feature films, *Sex and the City* (2008) and *Sex and the City 2* (2010). The series centered on the lives and loves of four single New York City professional women: Carrie, played by Sarah Jessica Parker (b. 1965); Samantha, played by Kim Cattrall (b. 1956); Charlotte, played by Kristin Davis (b. 1965); and Miranda, played by Cynthia Nixon (b. 1966). Each character exhibited a specific fashion style, underscoring their distinct personalities. Fans of the series—specifically, female fans—began identifying themselves relative to which character was most like them or which character they would most prefer to be like.

The character admired by most fans was the main character, Parker's Carrie. Carrie dressed in an artistic combination of what would be considered high and low fashion, such as designer tops with off-the-rack skirts, shattering the historic barrier between the two. The shoes worn by the four protagonists made fashion superstars of their designers: Manolo Blahnik (b. 1942) and Jimmy Choo (b. 1948). The series' costume designer, Patricia Field (b. 1942), has been noted for revolutionizing women's everyday fashions throughout the 2000s and beyond. As such, the series contributed to adding fashion as an element of women's agency in the new millennium.

FASHION TRENDS

As with decades past, young people drove the day-to-day fashion trends of the 2000s. Young women began wearing crop tops, which exposed the stomach and upper waist. These were often worn with bell-bottoms and low-ride jeans. The low-ride jeans became somewhat controversial as, for a time, many women began wearing jeans that were so low riding as to expose to tops of their thong underwear. Both men and women wore a tank top (often called a wifebeater) over a T-shirt or a long-sleeved shirt under a T-shirt. The latter fashion trend was prominently featured in the character of Dr. Sheldon Cooper, played by Jim Parsons (b. 1973), on the hit television series *The Big Bang Theory* (CBS, 2007–2019). Another popular fashion trend was wearing hoodie sweatshirts under a traditional suit blazer.

One popular item of clothing since the 1970s, the graphic T-shirt, remained common throughout the 2000s and beyond. Since its inception, this fashion trend has acted as an icebreaker, opening conversations by expressing to the world something in which the wearer is interested (i.e., rock bands, movie or television franchises, sports teams). Both men and women also began raising the collars of their collared shirts, a trend known as popped collars, previously popular in the 1950s and 1980s. Women made the corset look popular again, with designers producing tops that, to one degree or other, resembled the traditional nineteenth-century undergarments of the same name that were designed to emphasize a woman's waist and breasts. Yet another callback to the past was the resurgence in popularity of fishnet stockings.

In the area of popular shoes, Nike continued to dominate shoe sales across the United States By 2000, many consumers, especially men, began collecting Nikes, and pairs with low production numbers brought massive resale prices on the collectors' market. Skate shoes were also popular. Roughly twenty companies, including Nike and Adidas, began producing skate shoes: shoes with wheels embedded in the soles that could quickly turn seemingly ordinary sneakers, tennis shoes, and trainers into working roller skates, or de facto skateboards.

Timberland boots also became wildly popular with both young men and women of all regions and backgrounds. Two types of shoes were simultaneously popular and, oddly, reviled in the 2000s. In the early 2000s, Crocs, brightly colored foam clogs, became hugely popular. In 2003, television talk show icon Oprah Winfrey (b. 1954) declared that UGG boots—fur-lined flat-heeled boots—were one of her "favorite things." They immediately became a phenomenon with celebrities from Jennifer Lopez to supermodel Kate Upton (b. 1992), who were often seen wearing them. UGGs were also frequently worn by Carrie on *Sex and the City*.

Popular fashion accessories from the decade included shutter shades, sunglasses whose lens areas were filled with slanted shutters, similar to window blinds. These glasses were made popular by such hip-hop icons as Sean "Puff Daddy" Combs (b. 1969) and Kanye West (b. 1977). Perhaps the biggest youth fashion fad of the 2000s, however, were the Livestrong bracelets, simple yellow rubber bracelets with "LIVESTRONG" engraved on them. Popular among men and women alike, the original bracelets were sold by the Livestrong Foundation, created in 1997 by famed professional bicyclist Lance Armstrong (b. 1971) to raise money for and bring awareness to cancer research. By the time that Armstrong's reputation took a massive dive after the discovery of his use of performance-enhancing drugs, the concept behind the original Livestrong bracelets had expanded. Companies sold similar rubber bracelets in a wide array of colors, with an equally wide array of messages carved into them, including bracelets that allowed purchasers to have whatever they wanted engraved into them.

FASHION CONTROVERSIES

One of the big fashion controversies of the 2000s was the issue of computer touch-ups. Since the early days of photography, images of models have been professionally tweaked, from airbrushing skin blemishes to shifting clothing or camera angles to hide or manipulate the natural shape of the model's body. With the explosion of CGI in the late 1990s, fashion photographers possessed a vast new array of tools to alter models' images. Computers began to be used to alter photos to make models appear thinner or to make their eyes or lips larger or their hair more lustrous. This was, of course, dishonest, even going so far as to be considered false advertising. Models, themselves, even opposed this practice, as it created an idealized image of them that would prove untrue whenever photographed in public.

Body image had long been an issue in the fashion trade. At one time, models were chosen mostly for facial beauty. Over time, however, models were also chosen based on how thin they were, becoming thinner and thinner over the decades. This created a massive problem in the area of body image, with women judging themselves (and being judged by others) according to how much their build looked like—or did not look like—popular models. Millions of young women suffered from horrible body-image-related psychoses, all too often causing poor health and even death. This problem, of course, only became more exacerbated by computer photoshopping. Most aware of the issue, millennials began embracing plus-size models. Some of the most famous groundbreaking plus-size models of the 2000s included Ashley Graham (b. 1987), Toccara Jones (b. 1981), and Velvet d'Amour (b. 1967).

Another controversy that had been building for decades was fast fashion. This phenomenon occurs when high-end designers create a popular fashion trend and other clothiers begin producing cheap knockoffs of the look, frequently by utilizing cheap labor in underdeveloped countries (in essence, enslaved labor). Though high-end designers such as Gucci and Versace have attempted to stem this tide, they have been largely unsuccessful, often due to the complex issues of import treaties with such developing countries. The most recent case of this was the suit Gucci filed against Forever 21 in 2017. However, as long as consumers desire to appear high end without paying high-end prices, the problem of fast fashion will continue to exploit workers abroad and cheat consumers at home.

FASHION INFLUENCES

Many sources influence fashion in the United States. Magazines, television, film, musical artists, and videos have been influences on fashion for decades. Magazines such as *Vogue* and *Teen Vogue* continued to influence women's fashions coming into the 2000s. Television series such as *Sex and the City*, *Buffy the Vampire Slayer* (WB, 1997–2001; UPN, 2001–2003), *Friends* (NBC, 1994–2004), *Felicity* (WB, 1998–2002), and *Veronica Mars* (UPN, 2004–2006; CW, 2006–2007; Hulu, 2019) had a great influence on young women's hair and fashions throughout the decade. Likewise, musical artists such as Jennifer Lopez, Britney Spears (b. 1981), Christina Aguilera (b. 1980), Beyoncé (b. 1981), Rihanna (b. 1988), and Avril Lavigne (b. 1984) were all huge influencers on fashion at the dawn of the new millennium. With the rise of the internet throughout the 2000s, a new genre of influencer arose: the fashion blog.

One of the first big online fashion bloggers was Tina Craig (b. 1971), who founded BagSnob in 2005. Experienced in media and hosting, Craig turned her passion for handbags into a massively popular and financially successful blog about all things handbags. Early on, designers began sending her bags that they were about to introduce on the market to get her early input and stamp of approval. In 2008, eleven-year-old Tavi Gevinson (b. 1996) started her fashion blog Style Rookie, where she wore various outfits and provided commentary on current fashion trends. Her near-overnight massive following gained the attention of such fashion followers as the *New York Times*, *Harper's Bazaar*, and *Pop* magazine. In 2011, at the age of fifteen, Gevinson founded *Rookie* magazine. Throughout the late 2000s, more and more fashion, hair, and makeup blogs rose from all over the world, making some bloggers immensely influential and wealthy.

Another influencer bridged the small gap between fashion and art throughout the 2000s: San Diego Comic-Con. Founded in 1970 as the Golden State Comic Book Convention by Richard Alf (1952–2012), Shel Dorf (1933–2009), Ken Krueger (1926–2009), and Mike Towry (b. 1956) as a simple, local comic book convention, SDCC, as it has come to be known, emerged as the pop culture Mecca by the end of the twentieth century. Aside from the impressive cosplayers who are rampant throughout the annual crowd of over one hundred thirty thousand people, outfitters also sell pop-culture-related merchandise, from T-shirts to hoodies and jackets, giving pop culture afficionados the opportunity to wear their passions as public displays of their support. Likewise, the latest television and film projects hold panels featuring the major stars of the various franchises, all of whom are fashion influencers themselves.

In the end, as in decades past, fashion influencers of the 2000s were people large numbers of Americans looked up to, either for their talent, their personal stances on social issues, or their basic coolness. Through blogs, Americans who may feel they know little about fashion can turn to individuals that they trust, individuals who, in some form or other, have proven their opinions on fashion to be both professional and contemporary. A cemented facet of American society throughout the last half of the twentieth century and on into the twenty-first is the overwhelming peer pressure to look cool, with one's appearance a major factor on what and how others think of them. The degree to which this is good or bad for society can be—and for decades has been—debated, but its omnipresence in American society cannot be denied.

ARTISTIC ICONS

Probably the biggest name in art in the 2000s was the mysterious, anonymous street artist known only as Banksy. For roughly a quarter-century now, England-based Banksy has managed to produce art—even publishing books and directing documentaries—while remaining completely anonymous. Determining Banksy's true identity has become a global obsession on par with the century-plus guessing game regarding the true identity of infamous serial killer Jack the Ripper (also British). The most suggested name for Banksy is Bristol, England, resident Robin Gunningham (b. 1973). Another name that some believe to be Banksy is Robert Del Naja, also known as 3D, the lead singer of the musical group Massive Attack; in interviews, Banksy has named 3D as an influence. In 2004, Banksy created a large number of counterfeit British ten-pound currency notes, replacing the image of Queen Elizabeth with the late Princess Diana. In 2005, Banksy painted a live elephant pink and gold, raising the ire of animal rights activists. As much of Banksy's work is street art, sometimes entire sections of public walls, benches, and sidewalks are removed to preserve—and sell—the artist's masterpieces.

Comic book art was revolutionized beginning in the mid-1990s by Alex Ross (b. 1970). Rather than drawing comic book superheroes, Ross paints both covers and panels, utilizing live models in superhero costumes as his source material. He rose to fame with back-to-back works in the 1990s: *Marvels* (1994) for Marvel Comics and *Kingdom Come* (1996) for DC Comics. Since then, Ross has gone on to produce art of nearly all of the superheroes from each of the aforementioned comic book publishers as well as numerous works on characters that belong to other franchises (such as *Star Wars*). Prints of his published works are available through his website, and an actual Ross painting can bring five-figures at auctions.

Political comedy was hugely popular in the 1960s, but since 1975, the primary source for live comedic political commentary was *Saturday Night Live* (NBC, 1975–present). In the 1990s, stand-up comedian Bill Maher (b. 1956) took the old premise to a much deeper analytical level with his program *Politically Incorrect* (Comedy Central, 1993–1997; ABC, 1997–2002) and, after *Politically Incorrect* was canceled for his controversial statements following 9/11, his next project, *Real Time with Bill Maher* (HBO, 2003–present). However, it was comedian Jon Stewart (b. 1962) and his team of correspondents—most notably Stephen Colbert (b. 1964), Samantha Bee (b. 1969), and John Oliver (b. 1977)—who mixed the concepts of *Saturday Night Live* and Maher's deeper analysis to create a whole new level of artistry in the arena of comedic political punditry with his tenure on *The Daily Show* (Comedy Central, 1996–present).

In January 1999, Stewart took over the show from previous host Craig Kilborn (b. 1962). To that point, *The Daily Show* had been, simply, a fake news program with celebrity interviews in the final segment. Stewart altered the format to be more focused on comedic takes on the actual news of the day. He also transitioned the interview segment from celebrities to politicians, historians, political scientists, and journalists. During the show's coverage of the 2000 presidential election called Indecision 2000, *The Daily Show* began educating viewers through comedy. With cable news becoming increasingly partisan, by the next presidential election cycle in 2004, *The Daily Show* had become the go-to source for a legitimate take on the day's events. That year, Stewart and company published *America (The Book): A Citizen's Guide to Democracy Inaction*, a mock textbook that simultaneously educates and satirizes American history, government, and institutions.

The massive popularity of Stewart's format and firmly part of the American zeitgeist by 2004 a spin-off series, *The Colbert Report* (Comedy Central, 2005–2014) began to air immediately after Stewart. *The Colbert Report* featured Stephen Colbert as his on-air personality of a radical conservative pundit, adding to the artistry established by Stewart. What *The Daily Show* was to nightly news, *The Colbert Report* was to cable news opinion programs such as *The O'Reilly Factor* (FOX News, 1996–2017). In 2007, Colbert published *I Am America (And So Can You!)* (Grand Central), a faux biography of Colbert's fictional on-air persona, satirizing the conservative take on America and politics.

Stewart and Colbert's partnership became a political powerhouse throughout the 2000s and well into the 2010s. In 2014, Colbert left his show to replace David Letterman (b. 1947) as host of CBS's *The Late Show*. Stewart retired in 2015, turning the reigns of his highly successful program to South African stand-up comedian Trevor Noah (b. 1984). By that time, Stewart's take on political commentary had become a national mainstay that continues to this day, not only with the continuation of *The Daily Show* under Noah's direction but also through programs from former *Daily Show* correspondents, *Last Week Tonight with Jon Oliver* (HBO, 2014–present) and *Full Frontal with Samantha Bee* (TBS, 2016–present).

Another important piece of television sociopolitical art in the 2000s was the animated series *South Park* (Comedy Central, 1997–present), created by Trey Parker (b. 1969) and Matt Stone (b. 1971). The show centers on four foul-mouthed grade schoolers in South Park, Colorado: Stan, Kyle, Kenny, and Cartman. The Cartman character soon emerged as the villain of the show, exhibiting the worst in racism, sexism, homophobia, and so on. Rather than drawn animation, the animation of *South Park* is created through stop-motion, construction-paper-based images. By 2000, the series had begun taking on controversial sociopolitical issues of the day: from child molestation cases within the Catholic Church, to the legitimacy of the Church of Jesus Christ of Latter-Day Saints (Mormons) and the Church of Scientology, to America's compulsive celebrity worship, to the War on Terror and beyond. Another area where *South Park* deviates from other animated programs is that it goes from concept to screen in less than a week, rather than filming an entire season months in advance. This is done to keep the content as up to date as possible.

In the area of television and film, a new visionary artist arose to prominence in the 2000s. J. J. Abrams (b. 1966). Through his production company, Bad Robot (f. 2001), Abrams produced two wildly popular television programs in the 2000s: the spy thriller *Alias* (ABC, 2001–2006) and the mysterious paranor-mal serial *Lost* (ABC, 2004–2010). For both series, Abrams composed the open-ing title theme music for both. In 2006, Abrams rejuvenated the floundering *Mission: Impossible* film franchise with the third installment of the series, which has gone on to be a continuing box-office powerhouse. In 2009, Abrams reinvented the *Star Trek* franchise with a box-office-success soft reboot of the original television series. Abrams is famous for his box of mysteries concept, introducing questions in his narratives, some of which are never answered (for example, the MacGuffin of *Mission: Impossible III* is a device called "the rabbit's foot," and audiences are never informed as to what it is, what it does, or why it is important). In 2013, Disney and Lucasfilm tagged Abrams to relaunch the *Star Wars* franchise; the result, *Star Wars: Episode VII—The Force Awakens* (2015), went on to become the highest-grossing film in American box-office history.

As in all other areas of popular culture, the 2000s were important in many ways. The internet and 9/11 made it also one of the most transformative decades in American history. As with decades past and to come, the decade was largely defined by the fashions of the day and the arts that it produced. As with television, sports, music, film, literature, and media, the fashion and art of the 2000s helped to define who America was at the time, what the nation's concerns were, and how the sociopolitical issues of the day were experienced and absorbed by Americans en masse. As is always the case with history, the 2000s would help to shape and define who America was to be in the 2010s and beyond.

FURTHER READING

Abad-Santos, Alex. 2016. "Marvel's Civil War and Its Politics, Explained." *Vox*, May 3. https://www.vox.com/2016/5/3/11531348/marvel-civil-war-explained. Retrieved January 2, 2020.

Abrams, Loney. 2018. "How Does Banksy Make Money? (Or, a Quick Lesson in Art Market Economics)." Artspace, March 30. https://www.artspace.com/magazine /art_101/close_look/how-does-banksy-make-money-or-a-lesson-in-art-market -economics-55352. Retrieved January 26, 2020.

Armstrong, Jennifer Keishin. 2018. Sex and the City *and Us: How Four Single Women Changed the Way We Think, Live, and Love*. New York: Simon & Schuster.

Banksy. 2005. *Wall and Piece*. London: Random House UK.

Bennett, Jessica. 2019. "This Gen X Mess: The Tech, Music, Style, Books, Trends, Rules, Films and Pills That Made Gen X . . . So So-So." *New York Times*, May 16. https:// www.nytimes.com/interactive/2019/05/14/style/generation-xers.html?utm _source=pocket-newtab. Retrieved May 16, 2019.

Bennetts, Leslie. 2016. *Last Girl Before Freeway: The Life, Loves, Losses, and Liberation of Joan Rivers*. Boston: Little, Brown and Company.

Brands, H. W. 2011. *American Dreams: The United States since 1945*. New York: Penguin.

CBS News. 2018. "Meet the Artist Who Put a Realistic Spin on Comic Book Superheroes." *CBS This Morning*, December 22. https://www.cbsnews.com/news/comic -book-artist-alex-ross/. Retrieved January 26, 2020.

Colbert, Stephen. 2009. *I Am America (and So Can You!)*. New York: Grand Central.

Crowson, H. Michael, Teresa K. Debacker, and Stephen J. Thoma. 2006. "The Role of Authoritarianism, Perceived Threat, and Need for Closure or Structure in Predicting Post-9/11 Attitudes and Beliefs." *Journal of Social Psychology* 146, no. 6: 733–750.

Cullen, Jim. 2002. *The Art of Democracy: A Concise History of Popular Culture in the United States*. New ed. New York: Monthly Review.

Ebner, Mark. 2009. *Six Degrees of Paris Hilton: Inside the Sex Tapes, Scandals, and Shakedowns of the New Hollywood*. New York: Gallery.

Evans, Jennifer C. 2002. "Hijacking Civil Liberties: The USA PATRIOT Act of 2001." *Loyola University Chicago Law Journal* 33, no. 4: 933–990.

Faludi, Susan. 2008. *The Terror Dream: Myth and Misogyny in an Insecure America*. London: Picador.

Ginsberg, Merle. 2020. "All the Ways Jennifer Lopez's Grammys Versace Dress Changed History." *New York Post*, January 18. https://nypost.com/2020/01/18/all -the-ways-jennifer-lopezs-grammys-versace-dress-changed-history/. Retrieved January 19, 2020.

Graham, Ashley, and Rebecca Paley. 2017. *A New Model: What Confidence, Beauty, and Power Really Look Like*. New York: Dey Street.

Guerrasio, Jason. 2015. "New 'Saturday Night Live' Documentary Recounts the Emotional First Show after 9/11." *Business Insider*, April 16. https://www.businessinsider.com /saturday-night-live-first-show-after-911-2015-4. Retrieved January 13, 2020.

Gunn, Tim. 2007. *Tim Gunn: A Guide to Quality, Taste and Style (Tim Gunn's Guide to Style)*. New York: Harry N. Abrams.

Herbert, Emily. 2010. *Lady Gaga: Behind the Fame*. New York: Harry N. Abrams.

Hinton, Rachel, and Helena Hunt, eds. 2020. *RuPaul: In His Own Words*. Evanston, IL: Agate B2.

Howe, Sean. 2012. *Marvel Comics: The Untold Story*. New York: Harper Perennial.

Kruse, Kevin M., and Julian E. Zelizer. 2019. *Fault Lines: A History of the United States since 1974*. New York: W. W. Norton.

Letukas, Lynn. 2014. *Primetime Pundits: How Cable News Covers Social Issues*. Washington, DC: Lexington.

Mapes, Jillian. 2010. "Lady Gaga Explains Her Meat Dress: 'It's No Disrespect.'" *Billboard*, September 13. https://www.billboard.com/articles/news/956399/lady-gaga-explains-her-meat-dress-its-no-disrespect. Retrieved January 25, 2020.

Obama, Michelle. 2018. *Becoming*. New York: Crown.

Oliver, William. 2012. *Style Feed: The World's Top Fashion Blogs*. Munich: Prestel.

Oswald, Debra L. 2005. "Understanding Anti-Arab Reactions Post-9/11: The Role of Threats, Social Categories, and Personal Ideologies." *Journal of Applied Social Psychology* 35, no. 9: 1775–1799.

Paskett, Zoe. 2019. "Who is Banksy?: Best Theories from Robert Del Naja to Robin Gunningham." *Evening Standard*, December 9. https://www.standard.co.uk/go/london/arts/who-is-banksy-identity-street-artist-a4285461.html. Retrieved January 26, 2020.

Potter, Patrick, and Gary Shove. 2019. *Banksy You Are an Acceptable Level of Threat and If You Were Not You Would Know about It*. London: Carpet Bombing Culture.

Ross, Alex. [Posting Date Unknown]. "Alex Ross." Alex Ross Art. https://www.alexrossart.com/. Retrieved January 26, 2020.

Salkowitz, Rob. 2012. *Comic-Con and the Business of Pop Culture: What the World's Wildest Trade Show Can Tell Us about the Future of Entertainment*. New York: McGraw-Hill.

Stewart, Jon, et al. 2004. *America (The Book)*. New York: Warner/Grand Central.

Tapies, Xavier. 2016. *Where's Banksy?: Banksy's Greatest Works in Context*. Berkeley, CA: Gingko.

Tonic, Gina. 2016. "The Plus Size Models Who Were Killing It before the Divine Ashley Graham—PHOTOS." *Bustle*, January 21. https://www.bustle.com/articles/136353-the-plus-size-models-who-were-killing-it-before-the-divine-ashley-graham-photos. Retrieved January 25, 2020.

Veloso, Francisco, and John Bateman. 2013. "The Multimodal Construction of Acceptability: Marvel's *Civil War* Comic Books and the PATRIOT Act." *Critical Discourse Studies* 10, no. 4: 427–443.

Weinstock, Jeffery Andrew, ed. 2008. *Taking* South Park *Seriously*. Albany: State University of New York Press.

Whitehead, John W., and Steven H. Aden. 2002. "Forfeiting 'Enduring Freedom' for 'Homeland Security': A Constitutional Analysis of the USA Patriot Act and the Justice Department's Anti-Terrorism Initiatives." *American University Law Review* 51, no. 6: 1081–1133.

Willis, Susan. 2005. *Portents of the Real: A Primer for Post-9/11 America*. London: Verso.

CHAPTER 9

Controversies in Culture

The 2000s was a decade that began and ended with society-splitting controversies, further dividing a nation that was already increasingly partisan. As the 1990s came to a close, the country was still reeling from the April 20, 1999, school shooting at Columbine High School in Colorado. Two high school seniors killed thirteen people, twelve fellow students and a teacher. At that time, mass shootings were still essentially rare in the United States, and school shootings even more so. Though the event did spark conversations on gun rights versus societal safety, the argument did not reach the fever pitch it would reach in the decades that followed, when events such as Columbine became all too common.

The 2000 presidential election cemented the division between the political left and right. That division would only grow as the decade proceeded, from questioning responses and motivations for the War on Terror following the events of 9/11, to questioning the very citizenship qualifications of America's first Black president. Though all media of popular culture attempted to heal that divide, they ultimately added to it more often than not. By 2010, the United States had devolved to an amalgamation of red states and blue states, with the nation more politically and socially divided than at any point in the country's history since the American Civil War, from 1861 to 1865.

Outside of politics, there were other issues that divided the nation. Steroid use in professional sports appeared to be rampant. The question of whether or not it was legal to freely share music online exposed the fact that the capitalist aspect of music production far outweighed artistic and entertainment aspects. The population even divided over the issue of whether or not pop icon Michael Jackson had acted inappropriately with children. Jackson's sister, Janet, found controversy over a "wardrobe malfunction." Sexuality, long a taboo subject throughout American society, went mainstream as the LGBTQ+ community's

fight for equality and acceptance gained new momentum, and religion, politics, and popular culture were all dragged into the discussion. Americans
could not even agree on whether or not Pluto was a planet. The melting pot of
American society was quickly devolving into an oil-and-water mixture, and
the issues of the day would even divide families.

Some of the controversies of the decade continued into the next. Should
urban police forces be militarized? Will online shopping lead brick-and-
mortar stores to go extinct? Do the health benefits of marijuana outweigh its
perception as a dangerous and addictive drug? Does same-sex marriage erode
the sanctity of the institution, or does it expand love in society? Will social
media bring a divided nation together or more deeply divide the population?
What follows are the controversies that defined twenty-first century America,
the arguments of each side of the debates, and the solutions—though few—
that resulted. The 2000s were a decade that sought not only to define who we
are but also who we will ultimately be.

POLITICS

One of the earliest controversies of the new millennium revolved around a
three-and-a-half-year-old boy, Elian Gonzalez (b. 1996). In November 1999,
Gonzalez's mother died fleeing communist Cuba by raft, but her child survived, making it to Florida. There he was placed in the custody of his father's
relatives (his father still in Cuba). The family attempted to gain asylum status
for the child, but the federal courts ordered that only the boy's biological father
could do so. As a result, federal agents under orders from U.S. attorney general
Janet Reno (1938–2016) stormed the family's home in the dead of night in June
2000, grabbing the terrified child from his hiding spot in a closet. Elian was
then quickly returned to his father in Cuba. The returning of a child to a communist dictatorship against what was clearly his late mother's wishes plus the
Justice Department's heavy-handed tactics the ire of millions of Americans
and opened the conversation about the strict, by-the-book implementation of
undocumented immigrant policies that continues to rage well into the 2020s.

The Gonzalez deportation did not help the presidential campaign of Vice
President Al Gore (b. 1948). Though the economy was still strong and President Bill Clinton (b. 1946) possessed a 65 percent approval rating (higher, still
today, than any outgoing president since World War II), Gore was struggling
in the polls against his opponent, the Republican Texas governor George W.
Bush (b. 1946). The final election results were a dead heat: Gore received 48.4
percent of the popular vote, and Bush received 47.9 percent. Florida became
the deciding factor.

Originally, on election night (November 7, 2000), the major news networks
were calling Florida for Bush, but the Associated Press, the country's premier
news organization, declined to call Florida on hearing of voting irregularities
in some Florida counties. Although Gore had already conceded the election to
Bush by telephone and was about to do so live on television, his staff stopped
him at the last minute, telling him of the reports of irregularities in Florida.
Gore called Bush back to withdraw his concession. Both campaigns then

descended on Florida, along with all the major news outlets, as demands for recounts were implemented. After the first recount on November 10, Bush's initial lead reduced to just over three hundred votes (*Pittsburgh Post-Gazette* 2000). That paper-thin margin immediately kicked in a manual recount. Here is where the controversy grew.

The hand recounts exposed the primary problem with the Florida ballot count. Most districts utilized punch card ballots. Voters place a punch card in a ballot, lining it up with the names of the prospective candidates, and then punch through the card at the spot the corresponds with the candidate of their choosing, Then the holes in the cards are read by machine to determine the election results. The punched-through portion of the card, called a chad, falls into the voting machine. Over time, these chad (the plural of "chad" is "chad") build up, and, unless frequently cleaned out, could prevent future cards from being successfully penetrated; this creates a dimpled ballot rather than a fully punched ballot.

Machines did not count these ballots, as the rollers of the machine would depress the dimple, unable to read the intent of the voter. Another problem was that the puncher devices would dull over time, unable to fully punch through the card, creating "dangling chad," which could also go unread by the machine. Still *another* problem was that if the card was not inserted properly into the ballot, the holes would not line up with the correct candidates, causing voters to accidentally vote for the wrong candidate. All of these problems made the accurate manual recounting of votes difficult, to say the least.

As the Bush's margin of victory continued to decrease, Democrats began demanding more recounts in traditionally liberal districts. This gave rise to accusations that Democrats were not interested in counting all votes, but, rather, only Democrat votes. While the Florida state court system consistently sided with the Democrats, the Florida secretary of state's office, led by Katherine Harris (b. 1957), sided with Republicans. Another controversial factor was that Secretary of State Harris had actively worked for the Bush campaign. The Bush campaign then appealed to the U.S. Supreme Court, arguing that established deadlines were being ignored due to the Florida courts' rulings in favor of the Gore campaign. On December 12, the U.S. Supreme Court ruled in a split 5–4 decision that the recounts must be stopped and the initial recount results confirmed, giving the state and the presidency to Bush (*Pittsburgh Post-Gazette* 2000). This decision, intended to settle the controversy, only added to the divide with the five-member majority all appointed by Republican presidents and the four minority justices all appointed by Democrats. Vice President Gore conceded, and on January 20, 2001, George W. Bush was sworn in as the forty-third president of the United States.

The 2000 election only exacerbated the growing political divide in America. Since 1995, the Republican Party had begun an increasingly radicalized conservative trajectory, which would continue well into the 2020s. Though politically moderate since the early 1990s, the Democrats were painted in conservative media as radically socialist, further enraging the political right (the conservatives) while confounding the political left (the liberals). Up to and including the 2000 election, television news outlets had utilized the colors red, blue, and either yellow or white to keep track of each party's victories on their election-night coverage maps. However, there was no consistency in which colors were used. Some networks used red to identify Republican victories, while others used blue. Yellow or white were used to identify states whose results were not yet confirmed.

With the high voter turnout in 2000, viewers grew confused going from channel to channel seeing different colors representing their candidates. Since 2000, all news outlets (including print and online media) have universally used red to identify Republicans and blue to identify Democrats. This has led states and citizens within states to begin identifying themselves by color as much as by political party. Traditionally conservative states, such as Texas, Alabama, and Mississippi, were now identified as red states, while traditionally liberal states, such as California, New York, and Massachusetts, were now identified as blue states. So-called swing states—states that were more evenly divided, going conservative some years and liberal in others—were identified as purple, a combination of red and blue. This trend, which does more to divide the nation than unite it, continues well into the 2020s.

A certain irony exists in this new red state–blue state political war. In the early 1990s, two rival street gangs, the Crips and the Bloods, had gone national, with chapters in most major cities across the country. Throughout the first half of the 1990s, these gangs were involved in a violent, murderous war. The Crips identified themselves by wearing the color blue, and the Bloods identified themselves by the color red. Wherever blue and red collided, violence ensued. As the tensions between red states and blue states continued to worsen throughout the 2000s, 2010s, and into the 2020s, American politics devolved into a twenty-first century analogy of the Crips and Bloods. Another irony is that during the Cold War, communists were identified as "reds," and Republicans were the party most ardently opposed to them. Yet another irony is that, prior to 2000, conservative Democrats had been given the nickname Blue Dog Democrats. Although, to date, violence between red Republicans and blue Democrats has been rare, it is not unrealistic to foresee that a possible increase is becoming increasingly probable. Unless common ground can be found between Republicans and Democrats, the political division of the United States will eventually become a threat to the nation's very security.

In the immediate wake of the terrorist attacks of September 11, 2001, Americans were terrified of when and where the next attack would occur, many believing that, sooner or later, another attack would, indeed, take place. Those fears seemed confirmed just a week after the attacks with the anthrax scare that occurred from September 18 to October 12, 2001. Someone was sending anthrax-laced letters to politicians and journalists. The FBI eventually concluded that government scientist Bruce Edwards Ivins (1946–2008) was responsible, and his suicide ended the investigation.

In response to Americans' growing fear, Congress passed the Uniting and Strengthening America by Providing Appropriate Tools Required to Intercept and Obstruct Terrorism Act (or, the USA PATRIOT Act) on October 26, 2001, just fifty-five days after the attacks. This act gave government intelligence and investigatory agencies sweeping authority to monitor private cell phone calls, email traffic, and internet search history. At first, Americans embraced the act as a necessary sacrifice to protect the country. Over time, however, as the events of 2001 faded into history and Americans' fears subsided, citizens became angry that the government was free to monitor their private conversations and actions. Though the act was amended to limit the government's powers in these areas, the controversy surrounding the issue of liberty versus security remains.

Just days after the 9/11 attacks, on September 16, 2001, President Bush declared a War on Terror, vowing to go after those responsible for the attacks as well as any nations, governments, or organizations that support them. This began on October 7, 2001, with the NATO invasion of Afghanistan. The Taliban, having ousted the legitimate government of Afghanistan in the 1990s, supported and provided safe haven for Osama bin Laden (1957–2011) and his organization, Al-Qaeda (f. 1988), who were responsible for planning the 9/11 attacks. In President Bush's first post-9/11 State of the Union Address on January 29, 2002, he declared yet another threat to America: the Axis of Evil, consisting of the rogue states of Iran, Iraq, and North Korea. By this time, the War on Terror was further defined by the Bush Doctrine, a doctrine of preemption, attacking potential could act against the United States or its allies. With this doctrine, anyone who so much as threatens the United States or its allies would be considered a threat.

Since the Persian Gulf War (1991), Iraqi president Saddam Hussein (1937–2006) had consistently threatened neighboring countries, including U.S. allies Saudi Arabia and Israel, with what he called "weapons of mass destruction" (WMDs). The United Nations had been unable to prove these claims. In 2002, President Bush claimed to possess intelligence confirming Hussein's claims of WMDs, although the intelligence soon proved faulty and highly questionable. In a televised speech in the fall of 2002, President Bush threatened Hussein to either prove the existence of these weapons and immediately give them up or to risk American intervention. When Hussein failed to comply, Bush authorized the invasion of Iraq on March 19, 2003, opening a new front in the War on Terror. Though no WMDs were found, Hussein was ousted from power and executed by the new Iraqi government on December 30, 2006. Bin Laden was assassinated by U.S. Navy SEAL Team Six on May 2, 2011, under the next U.S. president, Barack Obama (b. 1961).

Both Afghanistan and Iraq soon turned into quagmires, with no clear exit strategy in sight. Though Obama officially declared the War on Terror over on May 23, 2013, combat forces remain in Afghanistan, and logistical military personnel remain in Iraq throughout his presidency and beyond. From 2001 to 2019, approximately seven thousand American troops have died in the two wars. Though Obama sought to bring most American troops home in 2014, a new threat emerged: the radical Islamic State of Iraq and the Levant, sometimes referred to as the Islamic State of Iraq and Syria (ISIL/ISIS). This new threat to the region has required American forces to remain in theater long after official combat operations were declared over. Although Americans continue to stand by the justification of invading Afghanistan, the failure to discover Hussein's WMDs quickly turned Americans against that war, many calling it unjust and illegal. The seemingly never-ending war in the region was a major controversy in the 2016 elections and a factor in the rise of President Trump (b. 1946).

Directly linked to the controversial war in Iraq is the Abu Ghraib prison scandal of 2004. That year, CBS News reported on inhumane treatment of Iraqi prisoners by U.S. armed forces. U.S. servicemembers were accused of torture, rape, and even murder of Iraqi prisoners of war. Abu Ghraib was a maximum-security prison west of Baghdad, Iraq, under the regime of Saddam Hussein. After the American invasion, the U.S. Army utilized the prison for Iraqi war prisoners. The American soldiers involved in the torturous behavior toward their Iraqi prisoners often took photographs of their battered and humiliated victims. Once exposed, the Bush administration assured the public that this was an isolated incident of soldiers under stress going too far. However, investigations by human rights organizations such as Amnesty International and the International Red Cross stated that similar abuses were being conducted at American containment facilities in both Iraq and Afghanistan, as well as the marine base and detention center at Guantanamo Bay, Cuba.

Further investigation exposed that the Bush administration had authorized "enhanced interrogation techniques" (i.e., torture) for prisoners of the War on Terror. Members of Congress from both parties—most notably Republican senator John McCain (1936–2018), himself a victim of torture during his service in the Vietnam War (1955–1973)—came out firmly against the Bush administration's policies. In response to Abu Ghraib specifically, seventeen soldiers were dismissed from duty; eleven were arrested, convicted, and sentenced to prison; and Brigadier General Janis Karpinski (b. 1953), commander of prison facilities in Iraq, was demoted to colonel and retired in 2005. Just a few years removed from 9/11, Americans' fear and anger had subsided enough for more clarity on the issue of "how far is too far" in regard to interrogation.

The technique that gained the most press coverage throughout the scandal was that of waterboarding. This is a method where captives are usually tilted back to one degree or other and have a cloth placed over their eyes, nose, and mouth, and water is poured over the cloth for several seconds or minutes. This experience leads captives to feel the effects of drowning. Under controlled circumstances, death is easily preventable, but if done incorrectly at any one point, captives can experience lung and brain damage, and possibly even die. This was apparently a commonly used tactic during the early years of the War on Terror to extract information from enemy captives.

There were Americans who held little-to-no regard for "enemy" life and who saw no problem with the procedure. Experts on interrogation, however, including future secretary of defense, U.S. Marine Corps general James Mattis (b. 1950), had long ago determined that torture of any kind was an inaccurate form of information gathering, as the tortured individual is willing to say whatever the interrogator wants to hear in order to stop the torture. Although Americans were less evenly divided on this than on other issues of the day, there were still considerably strong opinions on both sides of the debate. *If* torture does manage to gain any information that saves even one American life, is it worth abandoning American ideals of fairness and due process of law?

Through the course of the Abu Ghraib scandal, focus began to center on the detention facility at Guantanamo Bay, Cuba. In order to avoid having to provide due process to prisoners of war held within the United States, the Bush administration chose to use the marine base in Cuba as a detention facility, holding some alleged terrorists and terrorist sympathizers for years and exposing them to enhanced interrogation techniques. The primary reason for this decision appears to be that, in many cases, the evidence against detainees was thin, which would have led to their release under U.S. rules of due process and jurisprudence, and the justification was that the prisoners, of course, were not U.S. citizens and, therefore, possessed no rights under the U.S. Constitution. This opened the argument of the letter of the law versus the spirit of the law. Throughout the 2008 presidential campaign, Democratic nominee Barack Obama promised to close Guantanamo Bay and either release the prisoners or bring them to the United States to stand trial. However, by the end of his two terms of office, President Obama had still not done so, although some detainees were released. To date, President Trump, likewise, has not done so.

After 9/11, Americans were angry and afraid. Those emotions, especially when held en masse, can lead a democracy down a dark road. Did Americans want justice or vengeance? That question becomes all the more important when a country of such superpower status as the United States is fully capable of either. A key role of the president in such circumstances is to lead calmly and rationally, leading the people from a place of fear to one of calm and standing up for the principles that "the land of the free" has claimed to stand for throughout the twentieth century. In this capacity, post-9/11 presidents Bush, Obama, and Trump failed, although, admittedly, in different ways and to different degrees. Unfortunately for President Bush, Abu Ghraib and Guantanamo Bay would be far from the last controversy of his presidency.

On August 25, 2005, Hurricane Katrina hit Florida as a category one storm, cutting a swath of destruction across the state. Though weakening some as it headed to the Gulf of Mexico, once over warm water, it intensified to a category five, slowing to a category three before hitting Louisiana and Mississippi on August 29. The storm destroyed the southern portions of both states before finally moving inland enough to dissipate on August 31. Hardest hit was the coastal city of New Orleans, Louisiana. By the time the storm passed, roughly 80 percent of the city was flooded.

Investigations in the aftermath of the storm exposed that the levee system built by the U.S. Army Corps of Engineers had proven inadequate to protect the city from flooding. Simultaneously, the Federal Emergency Management Agency, tasked with providing assistance in the wake of such natural disasters, proved both inadequate and incompetent in meeting the needs of the people of New Orleans. This left rescue and response efforts largely in the hands of state and local authorities and private citizen assistance. With the largest portion of the affected population of New Orleans being African American, this inadequacy exacerbated the perception that Republicans cared little for the Black community in America. Nearly 1,900 deaths have been connected to Katrina and its aftermath, and the storm caused some $125 billion in damages.

With less than a year left in office, President Bush's problems were not yet over. Beginning in 2007, serious problems became evident in the investment banking industry (i.e., Wall Street). For years, the major Wall Street banks had been gambling with so-called subprime mortgages. In essence, banks would approve home loans for individuals who, on paper, clearly could not afford such loans; knowing that the loans would go into default, the banks then took out insurance policies on each loan, and when the loans did default, the banks, having already taken considerable monies from the original borrowers, could confiscate the homes for resale to other subprime buyers and cash in on their policies, making huge profits on the losses of trusting customers.

In 2008, Lehman Brothers, one of the major Wall Street banks, filed for bankruptcy. Earlier that year, the federal government had already been forced to bail out lending institutions Fannie Mae and Freddie Mac. This led to a collapse of faith in the investment banks, leading several to begin to teeter on the brink of collapse. During the crisis, American Insurance Group, or AIG, the country's largest insurance corporation, nearly collapsed as the Wall Street banks' policies on their defaulting loans were leaving the company cash poor. This placed the federal government and the Bush administration in particular in a quandary. To bail out the banks would be to protect Wall Street from the ramifications of their bad behavior; to refuse to bail out the banks would lead to the complete collapse of the global capitalist market.

The people tasked with finding a solution were Secretary of the Treasury Hank Paulson (b. 1946), Federal Reserve chair Ben Bernanke (b. 1953), and New York Federal Reserve president Timothy Geithner (b. 1961). This proved to be a very adept team, with Paulson's experience coming from his decades on Wall Street, Bernanke's coming from academia, and Geithner's coming from a career in bureaucracy. Their ultimate solution was the Troubled Assets Relief Program (TARP). In a nutshell, this plan was to infuse capital into the major banks in order to provide them with capital they could then loan out, although few chose to do so. After a tough battle in Congress, TARP was passed, and economic collapse was averted. However, the solution was not rapid or expansive enough to completely stave off a major economic downturn. Soon, the auto manufacturers in Michigan announced that they, too, would require a government bailout to avoid collapse. By the time President Obama took office on January 20, 2009, the Great Recession had begun, roughly seven hundred fifty thousand jobs had been lost, and it would take around five years for the nation to recover.

What made the Wall Street crisis even worse was that all of those involved in causing the collapse went unpunished, many escaping with multi-million-dollar parachutes. Meanwhile, millions of people across the country had still lost their homes and businesses, and millions more experienced massive losses to their retirement funds and property values. The Obama administration suggested numerous policies to protect and compensate consumers and to put into place preventions to avoid similar crises in the future, but few of those policies were passed or enacted (and some that were passed were later overturned by the Trump administration). For a country already deeply divided politically, each political party was successful, largely through the equally divisive news media, in blaming the other for the collapse. This exacerbated Americans' trust in the system that they had come, throughout the twentieth century, to depend on to protect them.

The 2008 election of the first Black president of the United States brought America's long history of racism bubbling to the surface once more. A ridiculously large portion of conservatives across the country began to believe a conspiracy theory that President Obama, who was born in Hawaii, was not a "natural-born" U.S. citizen as the Constitution requires for presidents. They believed, and many still do, that the president was born in the African country of Kenya, the birthplace of his father, Barack Obama Sr. (1936–1982). The senior Obama had married the president's mother, Ann Dunham (1942–1995), a native of Kansas in the United States. Divorcing in 1964, Dunham remarried, joining her second husband in Indonesia in 1967, where her young son attended a Muslim madrassa, or religious school. These facts became muddled in the conservative press until a narrative was created that President Obama was not only a native of Kenya but a trained terrorist as well.

The controversy did not go away until President Obama released his birth certificate to prove his American citizenship (the only U.S. president in American history to be asked to do so). Despite all of the evidence, there remains still in 2020 a portion of Americans who believe that President Obama is not a natural-born citizen and, therefore, that his presidency was illegitimate. This controversy brought center stage once more the long-embedded racism in American society and a stark reminder that the United States still has a very long way to go before racism is ended in America . . . if, in fact, it ever can be.

Another aspect of conservative opposition to President Obama was the rise of the Taxed Enough Already Party (TEA Party) in 2009. As President Obama's team began to look into a new health care system to provide insurance for more Americans while, simultaneously, bringing down overall insurance premiums for everyone, radical conservative advocates foresaw (mistakenly) the possibility of a universal, government-based health care system, such as Medicare for All. The result was the TEA Party. This group demanded fiscal responsibility on the part of government through reduced taxes, reducing the government's debt and budget deficits through reducing social welfare programs, and an overall reduction of government in general.

Though initially a grassroots movement, the TEA Party was soon circumvented and taken over by the Koch Brothers, David (1940–2019) and Charles (b. 1935). The two began using the "grassroots" organization to funnel money to conservative politicians. Soon a Tea Party Caucus formed in the halls of Congress, later renaming themselves the Freedom Caucus after the Koch's involvement in the TEA Party became well known. This, then, became the hub of the radical conservative movement that would, by 2016, completely control the Republican Party, forcing old-school moderate Republicans to either join them or leave the party altogether, which many chose to do. In 2010, the TEA Party's primary target became the Affordable Care Act (ACA), or, as the radical right-wing renamed it, Obamacare.

Far from being the socialist universal health care system feared by conservatives, the Affordable Care Act of 2010 was a mishmash of liberal and conservative ideas meant to expand health care coverage in the United States and to lower overall health care costs to consumers. Similar in many ways to a state system enacted by Republican governor Mitt Romney (b. 1947) in Massachusetts between 2003 and 2007, the ACA required all Americans over the age of twenty-six to have health insurance. Those who could not afford private insurance on the open market could find more affordable options through a government website. Those still unable to afford insurance could receive tax rebates to do so. For those *still* unable to afford private insurance, the government program of Medicaid would be expanded to provide free health care.

Requiring everyone to purchase health insurance on the open market would, in theory, bring down overall insurance premiums, as more people would be paying into each company's pool of resources. Additionally, as unemployment was still high in 2010 and the largest number of unemployed was Americans in their early twenties, children could remain on their parents' plans until the age of twenty-six. Perhaps the most appealing portion of the ACA was the elimination of preexisting conditions, a long-standing policy through which insurance companies refused to cover health care costs for any conditions the customer had before joining their insurance plan, which had cost countless lives over the decades. Despite the essentially fifty-fifty conservative-liberal aspect of the law, the far right fought it voraciously simply because President Obama was the progenitor of it, even going so far as to call the law Obamacare so as to turn more conservative voters against it, even though a massive number of conservative voters benefited from the program.

Obamacare divided the country once more along party lines. Red states fought the Medicare expansion, eventually succeeding in the Supreme Court, and President Obama's successor, President Trump, though unsuccessful in overturning the law, has successfully gutted the program to such a degree that it will likely soon fail. As a Democrat president with a Democrat majority in Congress in 2010, Obama could have attempted to push through a more liberal universal program, as President Clinton had attempted to do in the mid-1990s, but being a more moderate Democrat and hoping that a more bipartisan approach might bring Congress and the American people together behind it, Obama chose the middle path. The ACA did succeed in providing health insurance to over twenty million more Americans, but the quality of many of those insurance plans remained a matter of considerable controversy. As a result of all of the controversies listed above, the American body politic by 2010 was more divided than at any point since the American Civil War of 150 years earlier.

SOCIETY

Just a month after the events of 9/11, in October 2001, the Enron Corporation, a Houston, Texas–based energy company, was exposed for having deceived stockholders and auditors by hiding billions of dollars in failed investments throughout the 1990s through an orchestrated series of accounting loopholes and sleights of hand. Additionally, Arthur Andersen, one of the world's most highly regarded auditing firms, was also exposed as having cooperated with Enron in their fraudulent behavior. The news led Enron stock to drop to almost nothing, and shareholders sued the company. Several Enron executives went to jail, and Arthur Andersen was found guilty for their misdeeds, leading to the company's dissolution. Though most Americans' attentions were still glued to cable news for the latest on the War on Terror, the Enron scandal, along with the continuing dot-com crash, caused investors to become even more reluctant to take chances on American stocks. Though the stock market remained considerably stable (especially considering the back-to-back contributing factors of the terror attacks and corporate scandals), it was becoming blatantly clear to many Americans that the high times of the 1990s economy ultimately covered up a multitude of sins.

Along the same time as the Enron scandal was unfolding, the online company Napster also teetered on the verge of ultimate bankruptcy. Launched in 1999, Napster was an online file-sharing website that allowed users to share MP3 music files, creating a massive online music library of copyrighted material that users could download for free. While there were already several file-sharing websites up and running, the fact that Napster was dealing specifically with copyrighted material quickly gained the attention of the music recording industry. From the perspective of Napster and its users, this service was no different from young people in the 1980s and 1990s borrowing their friends' music cassettes and CDs and recording or burning free copies for themselves. While true in principle, the sheer volume of free trading through Napster created a far deeper, and easier to pinpoint as a hit to music industry profits. Just six months after the website's launch, the Recording Industry Association of America filed suit for Napster to terminate its offerings.

In early 2000, the popular heavy-metal band Metallica (f. 1981) discovered that an unreleased song of theirs, "I Disappear," was being circulated on Napster. That spring, Metallica filed suit against Napster. Shortly thereafter, powerful rap mogul Dr. Dre (born Andre Young in 1965) also filed suit when Napster ignored his lawyer's written request that they remove the artist's songs from their library. This led to public outcry. From the perspective of Napster and its millions of users, they were providing free advertising for the music of these various artists, which could inspire untold numbers of record sales that may not otherwise have occurred. From the perspective of Metallica, Dr. Dre, and the music industry, this was piracy, clear and outright. It was difficult for consumers to sympathize with multimillionaire recording artists and production companies. But in reality, the production of music was the work of untold thousands of hardworking people, and if the results of their labor was simply handed around for free, the industry would, in a straw man argument, eventually go out of business.

Ultimately, copyright law prevailed, and Napster was forced to begin charging for the songs in their catalog. This led to an immediate drop in website activity, made even worse by competing iTunes, which launched its for-sale services on January 9, 2001. In 2002, Napster declared bankruptcy and attempted to sell out to German company Bertelsmann, but a bankruptcy court blocked the sale, forcing Napster to sell its assets to cover their bankruptcy. The controversy died down rather quickly as consumers viewed the

$0.99–$1.29 charge for songs on iTunes seemed more than fair, especially considering how much cheaper this was than cassette singles from a decade prior. However, the perception of corporate greed stemming from the Enron and Napster scandals only exacerbated Americans' already strong distrust of Wall Street and the "1 percent."

In the early 2000s, numerous athletes—Olympian Marion Jones (b. 1975), cyclist Lance Armstrong (b. 1971), and baseball greats Mark McGwire (b. 1963) and Alex Rodriguez (b. 1975), to name but a few—were exposed for using performance-enhancing drugs to boost their athletic prowess. In 2002, the federal government began investigating Bay Area Laboratory Co-operative (BALCO) for providing metabolic steroids to professional athletes. In the wake of the scandal, BALCO went out of business, and Major League Baseball implemented harsh penalties for steroid use. Jones was stripped of her two bronze medals for track-and-field won during the 2000 Olympics. Armstrong's career and reputation were destroyed by his own scandals. Both McGwire and Rodriguez (and countless other MLB players) were allowed to continue their careers, though under considerable scrutiny going forward.

The argument used to defend steroid use was primarily fan pressure. By 2000, professional baseball, once America's pastime, had experienced massive drops in attendance and television viewership to far more exciting sports such as football and basketball. In those two sports, something new and exciting could literally happen any second, whereas in baseball, entire games could conclude without anything exciting happening. As such, baseball players were under pressure to make the game more exciting, specifically through more home runs, runs batted in (RBIs), and stolen bases. Some of the MLB's biggest stars, then, chose to experiment with performance enhancers, which, to be fair, did, in fact, create more power hitters and, therefore, more exciting game play. The counterargument, naturally, was that the use of enhancers was cheating, giving some players an unnatural advantage over those who played by the rules. This severely affected the role model status of these athletes.

On February 1, 2004, the nation was shocked by the infamous wardrobe malfunction during the Super Bowl XXXVIII halftime show. The featured artist for the show was the iconic pop star Janet Jackson (b. 1966), the youngest sister of the legendary Jackson Five (f. 1969) and their lead singer, the King of Pop, Michael Jackson (1958–2009). Well into her set, surprise guest star Justin Timberlake (b. 1981) came out to perform his sexually suggestive song "Rock Your Body" as a duet with Jackson. On the song's final line, "I'm gonna have you naked by the end of this song," Timberlake pulled at a portion of Jackson's top, fully exposing her right breast. CBS aired the yearly event live to more than 140 million viewers, and its subsidiary, MTV, produced the halftime set. In the wake of the scandal, the NFL cut all ties to MTV for future halftime shows, and CBS-owned MTV and Infinity Broadcasting Company banned all Janet Jackson songs from television or radio play for some time afterward.

Whether accidental or not, the controversy quickly exhibited the growing divergence in American values across the country. Many viewed the incident as harmless; it was over in an instant, and far worse was already easily available at the touch of a button on the internet. Many others viewed any nonchalance toward the incident to be further proof that American values had severely degraded over the past few decades. By 2004, the unity America had experienced in the wake of 9/11 had already severely dissipated, and the divisive Culture Wars had once more come to the forefront of American society. Nipplegate, as it was quickly dubbed (a play on the infamous Watergate political scandal of the early 1970s), was a clear sign that the divide in American culture was still present, with no sign of abating and, unknown at the time, only to get worse as the following years (and decades) unfolded. Janet Jackson's scandal, however, would soon dissipate into the past when her more famous brother faced a much larger scandal the following year.

In 2005, Michael Jackson went on trial for molesting a then-thirteen-year-old male cancer patient in 2003. Jackson had previously been accused of molesting a teenage boy in 1993, paying a $25 million settlement to make the case go away. A 2002 television interview with controversial British journalist Martin Bashir (b. 1963) featured the young cancer patient and aroused the suspicions of California law enforcement. Jackson was arrested on November 20, 2003, and was officially charged a month later on seven counts of child molesting and two more counts of giving alcohol to a minor. Similar in many ways to the O. J. Simpson trial of a decade earlier, many of Jackson's fans remained loyal to the superstar, even in the face of mounting and damning evidence against him.

The prosecution called numerous witnesses to inappropriate behavior, including the accuser, his younger brother, and several staff members of Jackson's Neverland Ranch. Defense attorneys cast doubt on the staff's testimonies, claiming that, prior to coming forward, they had tried to sell their stories to tabloid media. The defense then called three young men, including child star Macaulay Culkin (b. 1980), all of whom had stayed with Jackson in his bedroom when they were young and testified that they had experienced no inappropriate behavior on the pop star's part. Jackson attorneys then called several other celebrities—stand-up comedian George Lopez (b. 1961), late-night television host Jay Leno (b. 1950), and actor Chris Tucker (b. 1971)—all of whom testified that the family of the accuser were greedy opportunists out to take the wealthy for money off the sympathy toward their sick son. On June 13, 2005, the jury returned a verdict of not guilty on all counts. Despite the outcome, millions around the world would continue to believe the testimonies of the two boys, as well as the accusations from the 1993 case, making Jackson a social pariah in many places throughout the United States for the remainder of his life. Like the O. J. Simpson case, the Michael Jackson trial brought forth the complaint that the wealthy, especially celebrities, can get away with anything in a pop-culture-obsessed nation like the Unites States.

As the LGBTQ+ community gained more and more social acceptance throughout the 2000s, a controversy arose in 2005 that brought to the forefront both America's evolution of thought on the subject as well as the stiff resistance that a considerable portion of the population still held on to. The source of the controversy was the blockbuster feature film *Brokeback Mountain* (River Road Entertainment/Focus Features). Directed by Ang Lee (b. 1954), the film starred Jake Gyllenhaal (b. 1980) and Heath Ledger (1979–2008) as seemingly heterosexual/bicurious cowboys who become first sexually and soon romantically involved. Their continuing relationship destroys their heterosexual marriages, with one of the two cowboys eventually murdered because of his sexuality. The film was masterfully performed, providing a heartrending story of a twist on the star-crossed lovers dynamic.

The film was a box office hit and went on to win three Academy Awards, four Golden Globe Awards, and four British Academy of Film and Television Arts (BAFTA) Awards. It also cemented Heath Ledger as a legitimate dramatic actor. The primary controversy arose both from the idea of a gay couple being the center of a major romantic feature film, as well as from the breaking of the cowboy stereotype of macho, manly, heterosexual icon. Ultimately, however, the film did far more to benefit the LGBTQ+ community in regard to increasing social acceptance than it did the reverse. Showing two men in a deeply loving relationship did much to humanize gay men in a way that did much to break down the stigma of gay sex. All societies are resistant to change, even when change is obviously the right thing to do. The utilization of popular culture in the 2000s to break down stereotypes and taboos was a major factor in the slow-but-steady change in overall American attitudes toward sexual preference and identity.

Pluto was the source of considerable controversy in the 2000s. In 1992, it was discovered that the ninth planet was, in fact, one of many celestial bodies of similar mass that, collectively, constituted what came to be known as the Kuiper Belt. In August 2006, the International Astronomical Union established clear definitions to qualify a body as a planet: it must have its own distinct orbit around the sun; it should have a defined shape created by its own gravity; and it must be the gravitationally dominant body in its immediate vicinity, with no other bodies of similar size, other than its own moon(s), in its immediate gravitational area. By these new standards, Pluto failed on the third, reducing it to a dwarf planet.

This led to massive disagreements throughout the scientific community, even bleeding into the zeitgeist in a reference on the hit television series *The Big Bang Theory* (CBS, 2007–2019). With several astronomers and astrophysicists arguing that the new definitions would bring into question the identification of numerous celestial bodies in the solar system, including Earth, an international conference was called in 2008. Attendees eventually came to the conclusion that no consensus could be reached, instead inventing the word "plutoid" to define Pluto and any similar interstellar bodies (Library of Congress). To a large degree, the nonscientific resistance to the Pluto's downgrading can be attributed to society's overall resistance to change. There had always been nine planets; any change to that model made many outside the scientific community uncomfortable.

CONTINUING CONTROVERSIES

While the above-mentioned controversies were, more or less, exclusive to the decade of the 2000s, some of the bigger issues dividing the nation were inherited from the decades prior and bled into the decades that followed. As the growing divide in American society that has come to be known as the Culture Wars split the nation into the previously mentioned red states and blue states, several issues became deeply important to both sides, with each taking the opposite view. Whereas in 1860 the country became divided over one primary issue—slavery—the United States of the Culture Wars was split over a myriad of topics ranging from religious freedom, abortion rights, immigration, health care, and national security, to the growing power of the internet, the militarization of police, and individual gun rights.

Since the early 1990s, one of the biggest hot-button controversies in American culture has been so-called Second Amendment rights. Gun ownership in the United States surpasses that of any industrialized nation per capita in the world. Americans en masse love guns. They have been prevalent in the most popular video games, movies, and television series for decades. However, there has been considerable debate on several key issues: to what degree should the government be allowed to regulate gun sales; should American civilians have access to the same high-powered weaponry utilized by the military and police; and where should the line be drawn between a private citizen's right to own a gun and the overall safety of society? By 2020, gun rights had become one of the most divisive issues in American society.

In 1994, former U.S. presidents Gerald Ford (1913–2006), Jimmy Carter (b. 1924), and Ronald Reagan (1911–2004) wrote a joint letter to the *Boston Globe*, stating, "While we recognize that assault weapons legislation will not stop assault weapon crime, statistics prove that we can dry up the supply of these guns, making them less accessible to criminals." This letter was in support of an assault weapons ban which was being debated in Congress at the time, a ban that was passed (expiring in 2004). In 2013, President Barack Obama (b. 1961) quoted this letter in support of additional assault weapons restrictions (Mehrotra 2013). The Supreme Court did not declare that the Second Amendment protected the absolute right of gun ownership until the 2008 case *DC v. Heller* (554 U.S. 570).

The Second Amendment reads, "A well regulated Militia, being necessary to the security of a free State, the right of the people to keep and bear Arms, shall not be infringed." The meaning behind the amendment, however, has been completely warped in modern times, by both sides of the issue. The Founding Fathers had just succeeded in gaining their independence from what they viewed as a despotic regime. Their fear was that, with a new, powerful federal government, such despotism might arise again. The term "well regulated" is better interpreted in modern American English as "well trained," and "the right of the people" is better interpreted as "the right of the population." It was important to the Founders that the individual states maintain well-trained state militias, what today would be called the state national guard and reserves, in the event that the federal government or some other external or internal threat should infringe on their liberties. In the late 1700s, it is doubtful that any politicians would have ever considered a need to protect private gun ownership, as private gun ownership was a daily necessity, to hunt for food, kill livestock, and—on the frontiers—protect themselves from possible Native attack. They would likely have considered the need to protect private gun ownership equivalent to needing to protect private rights to own a fishing pole.

On the flip side of the issue, the Ninth Amendment could be interpreted more accurately to protect private gun ownership rights. The Ninth Amendment reads, "The enumeration in the Constitution, of certain rights, shall not be construed to deny or disparage others retained by the people." In this amendment, the Founders, most notably James Madison (1751–1836), wanted to make clear that just because they may have not specified a specific right, such as the twentieth-century concept of the right to privacy, it should not be interpreted to mean that the people do not have such rights. This amendment could be utilized to ensure the rights of citizens to own guns for protection, especially as twentieth- and twenty-first-century America experienced such dramatic rises in violent crime unforeseeable in the eighteenth century. Despite the misuse of the Second Amendment—or ignoring the Ninth—the issue of gun rights versus stricter regulations for societal safety dominated the 2000s and beyond.

Along similar lines was the issue of the militarization of urban police departments. As violent and organized crime increased in the major cities, big city police departments felt increasing pressure to make use of tactics and weapons that would allow them to stay a step ahead of criminals. Special Weapons and Tactics (SWAT) teams, in place already for decades prior to the twenty-first century, became even more militarized. Rather than standard armored police vans, SWAT teams began using military armored personnel carriers. Additionally, SWAT weaponry evolved from 9mm pistols and M-16 rifles to include higher-powered assault rifles, grenade launchers, and long-range sniper rifles. In addition to utilizing "old school" street informants for information on upcoming criminal activity, police departments began to implement intelligence-agency-level methods of interrogation and information gathering.

On the surface, this may appear as a logical step forward in the pledge of police forces to protect and serve the community. As the bad guys improve their weapons and tactics, so, too, must the police. The deeper issue, however, is one primarily of training. Military and intelligence personnel undergo entirely different modes of training than do police departments. Giving police the same tools and methods without changing the methods of training opens the door for corruption and misuse of extremely powerful resources. Additionally, should local communities begin to be looked at like battlegrounds, at what point has society crossed the fine line between security and liberty?

In discussing this issue, many opposed to the militarization of police often quote Founding Father Benjamin Franklin (1706–1790), who during the French and Indian War (1756–1763) wrote, "Those who would give up essential liberty to purchase a little temporary safety deserve neither liberty nor safety." This has been interpreted to mean that anyone who is willing to allow the government to infringe on personal liberties in order to provide security deserves neither. However, according to Dr. Benjamin Wittes of the Brookings Institute, that quote has been completely turned around. According to Wittes, Franklin was actually writing in response to the Penn family of Pennsylvania attempting to buy their way out of increased taxes that were needed to improve security for the colony during the war. As such, the quote actually means the opposite of how it has been utilized in recent years. Franklin was, in fact, supporting the government's right to keep the colony secure (Siegel 2015).

At their cores, the issues of private gun ownership and the militarization of police go very much hand in hand. As the availability of more powerful firearms continue on the open market, it is logical to assume that criminals will have easier access to them. Conversely, if criminals are going to be armed with state-of-the-art weaponry, law enforcement possesses few options other than to respond in kind. Before there can be any solution to either issue, there must be common ground found by the two sides of each issue. However, as the American electorate becomes increasingly divided year by year, such common ground seems equally increasingly unlikely. Eventually, it is logical to assume that either one or both issues will reach a tipping point that could prove devastating to all involved.

In the mid-1990s, the internet took the nation and the world by storm. Coming into the 2000s, the internet was still a new and exciting frontier, but by decade's end, the internet had become a vital day-to-day (actually minute-to-minute) part of American culture, with numerous aspects of daily life becoming increasingly dependent on the 'net and its rapidly increasingly number of interconnecting devices. One of the more controversial subjects in the 2000s was the rapid increase in online shopping. Amazon, in particular, grew rapidly in popularity, quickly putting old-school brick-and-mortar businesses such as Barnes & Noble and Books-A-Million on the ropes. The ease of online shopping and home delivery spoke to Americans' increasing demand for ease and instant gratification. As the decade proceeded, Amazon began offering more and more products outside of books, putting brick-and-mortar titans like Walmart, Target, and Sears in a similar bind to the longtime booksellers. By decade's end, historically brick-and-mortar retailers began offering online services of their own just to keep their companies solvent, still losing market share to Amazon despite their upgrades.

The last half of the 2000s saw the rise of what would come to be known as social media. Since the advent of the internet, chat rooms and email had brought people of similar interests closer together than at any point in human history; but with the rise of MySpace, Facebook, and Twitter, more people than ever before could come together, for better or worse. Social media sites allowed Americans to keep in touch with long-distance relatives, reconnect with long-lost friends and romantic interests, and form communities of like-minded individuals, creating a truly global sense of community. However, very soon the darker, unintended consequences of social media became clear. With people connected on a more-or-less 24-7 basis, people who were online for the purpose of friendly interconnection could find their respite disturbed by individuals with malevolent intent.

Con men, bullies, and even the mentally disturbed could now come directly into one's home, causing emotional pain, anxiety, and even desperation deep in the only safe spaces many possessed. This darker side of social media would only worsen throughout the 2010s. With the postmillennial generation literally growing up in a social media world, never having known what a pre–social media world was like, this latest generation of Americans would reach adulthood with more depression and anxiety than any generation previous. By 2020, there appeared to be no answer to keeping the darker nature of social media in check, and it quickly became a powerful tool in further dividing a nation already on the brink of a new civil war. Do social media's benefits outweigh its downsides? On this point, only time will tell.

From the mundane to issues of literal life and death, the 2000s was a decade of many controversies. While multiple controversies are not unique to the decade, what made the controversies of the first ten years of the twenty-first century different from those prior was the massive advancements in communication: the cell phone and the internet. These devices interconnected American society to a degree never before imagined. As such, the issues that divided the country could be amplified and easily hyperbolized to a previously unimaginable scale. By 2010, not only was American society more divided than ever before; it was able to find massive numbers of like-minded individuals to create large groups on either side of any issue.

Many of the issues mentioned above would evolve or continue as they were into the next decade and beyond. This division would be reflected in the national politics of the 2010s, as the next two U.S. presidents, Barack Obama and Donald Trump, would become two of the most divisive presidents in American history, each with as many ardent defenders as vitriolic opposers. In a nation as diverse as the United States—racially, ethnically, religiously, economically, and educationally—controversy is the unavoidable nature of the beast. However, when the differences that divide the nation outweigh or overpower the issues that should connect it—specifically, "the right to life, liberty, and the pursuit of happiness"—then the divided house becomes increasingly in danger of falling, crushing the hopes and dreams of all.

FURTHER READING

Albergotti, Reed, and Vanessa O'Connell. 2014. *Wheelmen: Lance Armstrong, the Tour de France, and the Greatest Sports Conspiracy Ever.* New York: Penguin/Avery.

Alter, Jonathan. 2010. *The Promise: President Obama, Year One.* New York: Simon & Schuster.

Armstrong, Lance, and Sally Jenkins. 2001. *It's Not about the Bike: My Journey Back to Life.* New York: Berkley Trade.

Balko, Radley. 2014. *Rise of the Warrior Cop: The Militarization of America's Police Forces.* New York: PublicAffairs.

Bennett, Jessica. 2019. "This Gen X Mess: The Tech, Music, Style, Books, Trends, Rules, Films and Pills That Made Gen X . . . So So-So." *New York Times*, May 16. https://www.nytimes.com/interactive/2019/05/14/style/generation-xers.html?utm_source=pocket-newtab. Retrieved May 16, 2019.

Berman, William C. 2001. *From the Center to the Edge: The Politics & Policies of the Clinton Presidency.* Lanham, MD: Rowman & Littlefield.

Bodroghkozy, Aniko. 2018. *A Companion to the History of American Broadcasting.* New York: Wiley-Blackwell.

Brands, H. W. 2011. *American Dreams: The United States since 1945.* New York: Penguin.

Bush, George W. 2001. "Address to the Nation." American Rhetoric, September 11. https://www.americanrhetoric.com/speeches/gwbush911addresstothenation.htm. Retrieved March 31, 2019.

Bush, George W. 2010. *Decision Points*. New York: Crown.

Canseco, José. 2005. *Juiced: Wild Times, Rampant 'Roids, Smash Hits, and How Baseball Got Big*. New York: William Morrow.

Canseco, José. 2009. *Vindicated: Big Names, Big Liars, and the Battle to Save Baseball*. New York: Gallery/Simon & Schuster.

Carr, Nicholas. 2011. *The Shallows: What the Internet Is Doing to Our Brains*. New York: W. W. Norton.

Castleman, Harry, and Walter J. Podrazik. 2016. *Watching TV: Eight Decades of American Television*. 3rd ed. New York: Syracuse University Press.

Chomsky, Noam. 2005. *Imperial Ambitions: Conversations on the Post-9/11 World*. New York: Metropolitan.

Clinton, Hillary Rodham. 2003. *Living History*. New York: Simon & Schuster.

Collins, Scott. 2004. *Crazy Like a Fox: The Inside Story of How FOX News Beat CNN*. New York: Portfolio.

Coontz, Stephanie. 2016. *The Way We Never Were: American Families and the Nostalgia Trap*. New York: Basic.

Crowson, H. Michael, Teresa K. Debacker, and Stephen J. Thoma. 2006. "The Role of Authoritarianism, Perceived Threat, and Need for Closure or Structure in Predicting Post-9/11 Attitudes and Beliefs." *Journal of Social Psychology* 146, no. 6: 733–750.

Cullen, Jim. 2002. *The Art of Democracy: A Concise History of Popular Culture in the United States*. New ed. New York: Monthly Review.

Dittmer, Jason. 2005. "Captain America's Empire: Reflections on Identity, Popular Culture, and Post-9/11 Geopolitics." *Annals of the Association of American Geographers* 95, no. 3: 626–643.

Dominguez, Eddie, Christian Red, and Teri Thompson. 2018. *Baseball Cop: The Dark Side of America's National Pastime*. New York: Hachette.

Elfrink, Tim, and Gus Garcia-Roberts. 2014. *Blood Sport: Alex Rodriguez, Biogenesis, and the Quest to End Baseball's Steroid Era*. New York: Dutton.

Eriksson, Maria, Rasmus Fleischer, Anna Johansson, Pelle Snickars, and Patrick Vonderau. 2019. *Spotify Teardown: Inside the Black Box of Streaming Music*. Cambridge, MA: MIT.

Evans, Jennifer C. 2002. "Hijacking Civil Liberties: The USA PATRIOT Act of 2001." *Loyola University Chicago Law Journal* 33, no. 4: 933–990.

Fahy, Thomas, ed. 2005. *Considering Aaron Sorkin: Essays on the Politics, Poetics and Sleight of Hand in the Films and Television Series*. Jefferson, NC: McFarland.

Fainaru-Wada, Mark, and Lance Williams. 2006. *Game of Shadows: Barry Bonds, BALCO, and the Steroids Scandal that Rocked Professional Sports*. Los Angeles: Gotham.

Faludi, Susan. 2008. *The Terror Dream: Myth and Misogyny in an Insecure America*. London: Picador.

Farris, Scott. 2012. *Almost President: The Men Who Lost the Race but Changed the Nation*. Guilford, CT: Lyons.

Farrow, Ronan. 2018. *War on Peace: The End of Diplomacy and the Decline of American Influence*. New York: W. W. Norton.

Frontline. [Posting Date Unknown]. "A Chronology of the Elian Gonzalez Saga." PBS. https://www.pbs.org/wgbh/pages/frontline/shows/elian/etc/eliancron.html. Retrieved January 30, 2020.

Georgiou, Aristos. 2018. "'Make Pluto a Planet Again' Say Scientists after Controversial Downgrade." *Newsweek*, September 11. https://www.newsweek.com/make -pluto-planet-again-say-scientists-after-controversial-downgrade-1115514. Retrieved February 5, 2020.

Gournelos, Ted, and Viveca Greene, eds. 2011. *A Decade of Dark Humor: How Comedy, Irony, and Satire Shaped Post-9/11 America*. Jackson: University Press of Mississippi.

Grossman, Dave. 2009. *On Killing: The Psychological Cost of Learning to Kill in War and Society, Revised and Updated*. New York: Back Bay.

Handscombe, Claire. 2016. *Walk with Us: How* The West Wing *Changed Our Lives*. New York: CH Books.

Hart, Kylo-Patrick R., ed. 2016. *Queer TV in the 21st Century: Essays on Broadcasting from Taboo to Acceptance*. Jefferson, NC: McFarland.

Healthcare.gov. 2010. "The Affordable Care Act." March 23. https://www.healthcare .gov/where-can-i-read-the-affordable-care-act/. Retrieved February 1, 2020.

Heilemann, John, and Mark Halperin. 2010. *Game Change: Obama and the Clintons, McCain and Palin, and the Race of a Lifetime*. New York: Harper Perennial.

Hilal, Maha. 2017. "Abu Ghraib: The Legacy of Torture in the War on Terror." Al Jazeera, October 1. https://www.aljazeera.com/indepth/opinion/abu-ghraib -legacy-torture-war-terror-170928154012053.html. Retrieved February 1, 2020.

History on the Net. [Posting Date Unknown]. "The 2000 Presidential Election." https:// www.historyonthenet.com/authentichistory/1993-2000/3-2000election/2-election night/index.html. Retrieved January 12, 2020.

Klemens, Guy. 2010. *The Cellphone: The History and Technology of the Gadget That Changed the World*. Jefferson, NC: McFarland.

Kruse, Kevin M., and Julian E. Zelizer. 2019. *Fault Lines: A History of the United States since 1974*. New York: W. W. Norton.

Legal Information Institute. [Posting Date Unknown]. "Supreme Court of the United States: *George W. Bush, et al., Petitioners v. Albert Gore, Jr., et al.*" Cornell Law School. https://www.law.cornell.edu/supct/html/00-949.ZPC.html. Retrieved January 30, 2020.

Letukas, Lynn. 2014. *Primetime Pundits: How Cable News Covers Social Issues*. Washington, DC: Lexington.

Library of Congress. [Posting Date Unknown]. "Why Is Pluto No Longer a Planet?" https://www.loc.gov/everyday-mysteries/item/why-is-pluto-no-longer-a -planet/. Retrieved February 5, 2020.

Linzmayer, Owen W. 2004. *Apple Confidential 2.0: The Definitive History of the World's Most Colorful Company*. San Francisco, CA: No Starch.

Macur, Juliet. 2014. *Cycle of Lies: The Fall of Lance Armstrong*. New York: Harper.

Mehrotra, Karishma. 2013. "Did Reagan Support an Assault-Weapons Ban?" PolitiFact. https://www.politifact.com/factchecks/2013/feb/05/barack-obama/did-reagan -support-assault-weapons-ban/. Retrieved February 6, 2020.

Menn, Joseph. 2003. *All the Rave: The Rise and Fall of Shawn Fanning's Napster*. New York: Crown.

Mezrich, Ben. 2009. *The Accidental Billionaires: The Founding of Facebook, a Tale of Sex, Money, Genius, and Betrayal*. New York: Doubleday.

National Commission on Terrorist Attacks Upon the United States. 2004. *The 9/11 Report*. New York: St. Martin's.

9/11 Commission. 2004. "The 9/11 Commission Report." National Commission on Terrorist Attacks Upon the United States. https://www.9-11commission.gov /report/. Retrieved January 3, 2020.

9/11 Memorial. [Posting Date Unknown]. "September 11 Attack Timeline." https:// timeline.911memorial.org/#Timeline/2. Retrieved May 8, 2019.

Obama, Barack. 2006. *The Audacity of Hope: Thoughts on Reclaiming the American Dream*. New York: Crown.

Obama, Barack. 2009. "First Inaugural Address." Obama White House, January 20. https://obamawhitehouse.archives.gov/blog/2009/01/21/president-barack-obamas-inaugural-address. Retrieved March 31, 2019.

Olbermann, Keith. 2006. *The Worst Person in the World: And 202 Strong Contenders.* Hoboken, NJ: Wiley.

O'Reilly, Bill. 2006. *Culture Warrior.* New York: Crown.

Oswald, Debra L. 2005. "Understanding Anti-Arab Reactions Post-9/11: The Role of Threats, Social Categories, and Personal Ideologies." *Journal of Applied Social Psychology* 35, no. 9: 1775–1799.

Patterson, James T. 2005. *Restless Giant: The United States from Watergate to* Bush v. Gore. Oxford: Oxford University Press.

Pittsburgh Post-Gazette. 2000. "Election 2000 Timeline." December 17. http://old.post-gazette.com/election/20001217pztimeline.asp. Retrieved January 30, 2020.

Radomski, Kirk. 2009. *Bases Loaded: The Inside Story of the Steroid Era in Baseball by the Central Figure in the Mitchell Report.* New York: Hudson Street.

Rakove, Jack N., ed. 2002. *The Unfinished Election of 2000: Leading Scholars Examine America's Strangest Election.* New York: Basic.

Reed, Ryan. 2018. "Metallica's Kirk Hammett: 'We're Still Right' about Suing Napster." *Rolling Stone,* May 14. https://www.rollingstone.com/music/music-news/metallicas-kirk-hammett-were-still-right-about-suing-napster-630185/. Retrieved November 23, 2019.

Rogak, Lisa. 2015. *Angry Optimism: The Life and Times of Jon Stewart.* New York: St. Martin's.

Rollins, Peter, and John E. O'Connor. 2003. The West Wing: *The American Presidency as Television Drama.* Syracuse, NY: Syracuse University Press.

Siegel, Robert. 2015. "Ben Franklin's Famous 'Liberty, Safety' Quote Lost Its Context in 21st Century." *All Things Considered,* March 2. https://www.npr.org/2015/03/02/390245038/ben-franklins-famous-liberty-safety-quote-lost-its-context-in-21st-century. Retrieved February 6, 2020.

Smith, Chris. 2016. The Daily Show *(The Book): An Oral History as Told by Jon Stewart, the Correspondents, Staff and Guests.* New York: Grand Central.

Smith, Michael. 2017. *Streaming, Sharing, Stealing: Big Data and the Future of Entertainment.* Cambridge, MA: MIT.

Sorkin, Andrew Ross. 2009. *Too Big to Fail: The Inside Story of How Wall Street and Washington Fought to Save the Financial System—And Themselves.* New York: Penguin.

Staff. 2017. "Watch Jon Stewart Call Tucker Carlson a 'Dick' in Epic 2004 'Crossfire' Takedown." *Hollywood Reporter,* January 5. https://www.hollywoodreporter.com/news/jon-stewart-takes-down-tucker-carlson-crossfire-video-961127. Retrieved January 12, 2020.

Stone, Brad. 2013. *The Everything Store: Jeff Bezos and the Age of Amazon.* Boston: Little, Brown and Company.

Stratyner, Leslie, and James R. Keller, eds. 2009. *The Deep End of* South Park: *Critical Essays on Television's Shocking Cartoon Series.* Jefferson, NC: McFarland.

Street, John. 2011. *Music and Politics.* Cambridge: Polity.

Sullivan, Randall. 2012. *Untouchable: The Strange Life and Tragic Death of Michael Jackson.* New York: Grove.

Swanson, Jess, and Angel Garcia. 2019. "Why the Elian Gonzalez Saga Resonates 20 Years Later." *Vox,* November 11. https://www.vox.com/the-highlight/2019/11/4/20938885/miami-cuba-elian-gonzalez-castro. Retrieved January 30, 2020.

Taraborrelli, J. Randy. 2010. *Michael Jackson: The Magic, the Madness, the Whole Story, 1958–2009.* New York: Grand Central.

Terry, Josh. 2019. "Sixteen Years Later, Country Radio Is Still Mad at the Dixie Chicks." *Vice*, September 10. https://www.vice.com/en_us/article/evjvqe/sixteen-years -later-country-radio-is-still-mad-at-the-dixie-chicks-taylor-swift-soon-youll -get-better. Retrieved November 23, 2019.

Thompson, Gayle. 2019. "16 Years Ago: Natalie Maines Makes Controversial Comments about President George W. Bush." Boot, March 10. https://theboot.com /natalie-maines-dixie-chicks-controversy/. Retrieved November 28, 2019.

Tsonga, Taj. 2019. "Remembering the Greatest Con in Silicon Valley History." *Wired*, January. https://www.wired.com/wiredinsider/2019/01/remembering-greatest -con-silicon-valley-history/. Retrieved May 16, 2019.

Van Dijck, José. 2013. *The Culture of Connectivity: A Critical History of Social Media*. Oxford: Oxford University Press.

Von Drehle, David, et al. 2001. *Deadlock: The Inside Story of America's Closest Election*. New York: PublicAffairs.

Waldfogel, Joel. 2018. *Digital Renaissance: What Data and Economics Tell Us about the Future of Popular Culture*. Princeton, NJ: Princeton University Press.

Walsh, David. 2015. *Seven Deadly Sins: My Pursuit of Lance Armstrong*. New York: Atria.

Watson, Bruce. 2016. *Jon Stewart: Beyond the Moments of Zen*. Scotts Valley, CA: CreateSpace.

Weinstock, Jeffery Andrew, ed. 2008. *Taking* South Park *Seriously*. Albany: State University of New York Press.

Wheeler, Tom. 2019. *From Gutenberg to Google: The History of Our Future*. Washington, DC: Brookings Institution.

Whitehead, John W., and Steven H. Aden. 2002. "Forfeiting 'Enduring Freedom' for 'Homeland Security': A Constitutional Analysis of the USA Patriot Act and the Justice Department's Anti-Terrorism Initiatives." *American University Law Review* 51, no. 6: 1081–1133.

Willis, Susan. 2005. *Portents of the Real: A Primer for Post-9/11 America*. London: Verso.

Witt, Stephen. 2016. *How Music Got Free: A Story of Obsession and Invention*. New York: Penguin.

CHAPTER 10

Game Changers

The 2000s was a transformative decade, with numerous milestones in American history. The nation elected its first African American president, who, then, appointed the first Hispanic to the U.S. Supreme Court. The 2008 election that gave us that first Black president also saw the first former first lady to run for president, as well as only the second woman to appear on a major party ticket as a vice presidential candidate. Television provided a platform for creating more acceptance of the LGBTQ+ community, and still long before that acceptance would reach a national majority, a lesbian woman brought the nation together in the wake of its most devastating trauma. A group of gay men taught straight men that it was okay to be conscious of style and fashion, and the straight community embraced them for it.

A struggling comic book company ended the decade as a major Hollywood powerhouse. Professional wrestling achieved never-before-dreamed-of heights of popularity thanks to the amazing in-ring talent of their superstars, and African American athletes rose to the top of previously white-dominated sports. Hip-hop music dominated American music, just as country music fans turned on their own. A British single mother dependent on social welfare became one of the wealthiest women in the history of the world. Cable news outlets further divided an already heated society, while more and more Americans turned to television comedians for the truth behind national events. All the while, the nation experienced the most massive technological advancements ever. As all of these milestones unfolded, the United States was recovering from the most game-changing event in its 225-year history.

9/11

The biggest game changer of the 2000s—and perhaps all of American history—was not a person but an event: the terrorist attacks of September 11,

2001. On that cool, clear fall morning, nineteen radicalized Muslim Arab terrorists, belonging to the international terror organization Al-Qaeda, hijacked four American passenger aircraft, crashing two into the Twin Towers of the World Trade Center in New York City, a third into the Pentagon in Washington, DC, and the last into an open field in Pennsylvania after the American passengers attempted to retake the plane to stop the terrorists' nefarious scheme. In all, 2,977 people, not including the terrorists, died on 9/11, six more dying of their injuries in the days that followed. This was the most devastating foreign attack on American soil in U.S. history, surpassing the 2,403 who died during the Japanese attack on Pearl Harbor, Hawaii, nearly sixty years earlier.

Unlike Pearl Harbor, however, the events of 9/11 unfolded for all Americans in real time, with millions around the country watching on live television, helpless as the attacks happened. For the decade leading up to the attacks, Americans had been steeped in the Culture Wars, with the political right and left in an increasing struggle for dominance over American society. The 9/11 attacks brought the nation together, albeit briefly. Still fresh off his controversial win in the 2000 election, President George W. Bush (b. 1946; president, 2001–2009) soon became the most important rallying figure in the country, expected to both calm the public's fears and lead the counterstrike against the nation's new enemy.

In the area of restoring calm, the president and both parties of both houses of Congress rushed through the USA PATRIOT Act. This act placed most American intelligence agencies under the umbrella of the new Department of Homeland Security; it also gave intelligence agencies broad powers to collect the phone, text, and email transcripts of private citizens, something that, once Americans' fears had subsided, would unleash unbridled rage toward the government's infringement on Americans' privacy. In the area of achieving justice and vengeance against the nation's enemies, President Bush invaded the terrorist haven of Afghanistan with the help of NATO allies and the dictatorship of Iraq, with the help of a much smaller coalition. Although both fronts of the new War on Terror were originally supported by both political parties both in and outside of Washington, as years passed, fears subsided, and body counts rose, popular support for both wars dramatically fell before Bush left office.

A key factor in the country's waning support was the bringing to light of the government and military's policy of "enhanced interrogation techniques" (i.e., torture). More conservative Americans were in favor of any tactics that might make their family's safer, while more liberal Americans were disgusted at this clear violation of the ideals of human rights for which the nation had, for so long, stood firm. By mid-decade, the War on Terror became simply one more aspect of society that drove the two political wings further apart, adding to the deep divisions evident on September 10, 2001. Throughout the 2000s, 2010s, and well into the 2020s, the United States and the entire planet lived in a post-9/11 world. Once the foreign threat appeared to be subdued, however, the pent-up fears still felt by a large number of Americans needed a new target on which to focus, and just as after the sudden end of the Cold War, that target quickly became each other. In the first decade of this newer, darker America, however, several individuals in politics and pop culture contributed to American society in (mostly) positive ways, becoming some of the decade's true game changers.

POLITICS

In the realm of politics, the election of 2008 proved a game changer on several levels. To begin with, Senator Hillary Rodham Clinton (D-NY, b. 1947) was the early front-runner for the Democratic nomination, placing her on a very small list of women who have run for president and the first former first lady to do so. Former U.S. congresswoman Shirley Chisholm (1924–2005) had been the first woman to run for the Democratic Party nomination in 2004, and Victoria Woodhull (1838–1927) had been the first woman ever to run for president, on the small Equal Rights Party ticket in 1872. Woodhull had chosen as her vice presidential running mate the former slave Frederick Douglass (c. 1818–1895). Like Chisholm, Clinton failed to achieve the nomination in 2008, coming in second in the delegate count to relative political newcomer Senator Barack Obama (D-IL, b. 1961). She would, however, have a political comeback, finally becoming the first woman to gain the presidential nomination on a major party ticket in 2016.

Obama would not only secure the Democratic nomination in 2008; he would go on to defeat Senator John McCain (R-AZ, 1936–2018) to become the first African American president of the United States on January 20, 2009. Obama had first come on the national scene for his keynote address to the 2004 Democratic National Convention, the year he was running for and won the U.S. Senate seat from Illinois. On becoming president in 2009, Obama inherited the worst economy since the Great Depression, already being called the Great Recession. Despite the challenges, however, Obama accomplished a great deal, mostly in his first term. After completing the bank and automaker bailouts initiated by President Bush, which were repaid by all concerned, Obama passed Wall Street reform to hopefully avoid a similar meltdown in the future.

Obama also passed student loan reform, providing numerous paths to repayment for the more than forty million Americans burdened by student loan debt. One of his first acts as president was to appoint Judge Sonia Sotomayor (b. 1954) as the first Hispanic justice to the U.S. Supreme Court in 2009. In 2010, he appointed another female justice, Elena Kagan (b. 1960). The crowning achievement of his administration, however, was passing the Affordable Care Act (2010), known more popularly as Obamacare. This was the biggest change to the American health care system since the passage of Medicare and Medicaid more than forty years earlier.

The ACA has several game-changing aspects. All Americans over the age of twenty-six were required to have private health insurance, with affordable options open for lower-income families through healthcare.gov. Dependent children could remain on their parents' health insurance until age twenty-six. Anyone who does not purchase health insurance must pay an annual fee, up to roughly $2,000. Insurance companies could not deny coverage for preexisting conditions. People who made too much money to qualify for Medicaid but still not enough to afford health insurance could qualify for tax rebates to assist. States were asked to extend Medicaid benefits.

Many liberal Democrats opposed the act, feeling that it was not liberal enough and would still leave millions of Americans not covered. Though the ACA was roughly a fifty-fifty split of conservative and liberal ideas, conservative Republicans, who dubbed it Obamacare, strongly opposed it, presenting it to their constituents (many of whom benefited from the program) as socialism. By the time President Obama left office, roughly twenty-two million Americans had health insurance who did not before.

President Obama also drew down U.S. military presence in Afghanistan and Iraq, officially calling an end to combat operations in the latter in 2010, due to an agreement made by his predecessor with the Iraqi government. Also, on May 2, 2011, Obama ordered the U.S. Navy SEAL Team Six mission that killed Al-Qaeda leader Osama bin Laden (1957–2011), the mastermind behind the 9/11 attacks. His presidency was, however, plagued by two terrible trends: the growing political division in the country, exacerbated by racist response to a Black president, and the dramatic rise in mass shootings across the country (from 2009 to 2019, nearly 180 mass shootings in the United States occurred just at schools). The political divisions that ripped the nation apart were already evident during Obama's 2008 run.

Since the Democrats were breaking new ground with an African American presidential candidate in 2008, the Republicans, running a traditional older white man, sought out their own game-changing idea. The result was to work for the women's vote, as they believed that Hillary Clinton's loss of the Democratic nomination might throw the women's vote up for grabs. As such, the Republican party chose Alaska governor Sarah Palin (b. 1964) to be McCain's vice presidential running mate. The young, fiery governor appealed not only to soccer moms but also to the radical conservative fringe, soon to be known as the Taxed Enough Already Party, or TEA Party. As Obama was a moderate Democrat, Republicans could see that they were losing both the left and center votes. To remain competitive, they needed to inspire the radical fringe of conservatism in America. Among that fringe, however, included racists, sexists, and homophobes. Unfortunately for the Republican Party, once that fringe gained a political significance, they would come to dominate the party throughout the 2010s and well into the 2020s.

With most of the 2000s relatively politically united in the wake of 9/11, the 2008 election proved the most significant political game changer of the new century. Throughout the 2010s, women and racial and ethnic minorities would gain considerably more representation in government; on the flip side, unfortunately, that also brought with it a rise in radical racist and sexist representation. By 2020, the United States would be more divided than at any point in its history, including the Civil War. Outside of politics, however, many Americans proved to be game changers in all areas of popular culture: from television and movies, to sports and music, and media and technology. America was changing across the board.

POPULAR CULTURE: TELEVISION

The 2000s ushered in what has come to be known as the second golden age of American television. Programming appeared to dumb down in the immediate wake of 9/11 with the rapid and massive production of reality programming—unscripted series that centered on everyday people competing in one fashion or other for various goals. But just as scripted television appeared to be on the way out of the American zeitgeist, a handful of dramas and sitcoms maintained strong audiences, causing both genres to bounce back strong by decade's end. One person responsible for the high-quality programming was screenwriter Aaron Sorkin (b. 1961) with his iconic television series *The West Wing* (NBC, 1999–2006).

Hot off his back-to-back successes of his critically acclaimed feature film *The American President* (1995) and his popular television comedy drama *Sports Night* (ABC, 1998–2000), Sorkin combined the two premises and created a landmark series with *The West Wing*. The series was set around the personal staff of the fictional U.S. president Josiah "Jed" Bartlet, played by Martin Sheen (b. 1940), a liberal Democrat and devout Catholic. Aside from the mind-blowing dialogue written by Sorkin, the series also boasted one of the greatest acting troupes in television history: John Spencer (1946–2005), Allison Janney (b. 1959), Bradley Whitford (b. 1959), Richard Schiff (b. 1955), Rob Lowe (b. 1964), Stockard Channing (b. 1944), and, in one of her earliest roles, Elisabeth Moss (b. 1982).

Despite its strong liberal bias, the series was wildly popular. Sorkin never wrote down to the audience, requiring many to spend some time looking up government jargon, policies, programs, departments, and the like. During the chaotic aftermath of the 2000 presidential election, television ads for the series boasted that *The West Wing* possessed "the one president we can all agree on." Running for seven seasons, the series maintains a strong fan following fifteen years after its cancellation. This series showed that programming could be smart and that audiences would not only follow it but become devoted to it in throngs. The success of *The West Wing* upped Hollywood's game, leading them to produce more and more intelligent programming and raising the bar for television as an entertainment medium, as well as once more being a platform for commentary on social issues of the day. This would lead to more and more big-name Hollywood stars becoming interested in television.

The 2000s were also a transformative decade socially, with mainstream America becoming more open to the LGBTQ+ community than really any decade prior. Twenty years on from the height of the AIDS epidemic that for so long ostracized the gay community, what was for so long considered taboo was now becoming an accepted way of life to a wider swath of American society. Pop culture and television in particular, as usual, was key in greasing the wheels of social movement toward a more diverse and open society. One of the people most responsible for this movement—herself previously ostracized for her sexual orientation—was comedian Ellen DeGeneres (b. 1958). An upcoming comedy superstar in the early 1990s, Ellen experienced massive success with her sitcom *Ellen* (ABC, 1994–1998), until in April 1997, Ellen came out as lesbian, her fictional counterpart following suit on the sitcom. Societal backlash led to her program being cancelled and her career taking a nosedive.

On November 4, 2001, less than two months since the nightmare of 9/11, Ellen accepted the hosting job for the 2001 Emmy Awards. Big-name comedians have always been the first choice for award show hosting duties, but in the wake of 9/11, most comedians were hesitant to take on the daunting responsibility of balancing comedy and respect for recent events. Ellen took the challenge and became America's sweetheart overnight for her brilliant performance. Scholars today remain in awe of how Ellen managed to use this unifying event to transcend what had divided the nation just months before and tread that fine line of laughter and tears. From that night, Ellen DeGeneres has been one of America's most beloved icons.

Shortly after this, the Bravo cable television network launched the series *Queer Eye for the Straight Guy* (Bravo, 2003–2007). This reality series saw five gay men—Ted Allen (b. 1965), Kyan Douglas (b. 1970), Thom Filicia (b. 1969), Carson Kressley (b. 1969), and Jai Rodriguez (b. 1979)—educate straight men on the finer aspects of dating: fashion, hair, dining, dancing, and personal grooming. The show played on the stereotype that straight men avoided these things, considering them to be feminine, and therefore, failed to attract the women they were interested in. Breaking the barriers of stereotypes by, in fact, embracing them, the series built bridges between gay and straight men, allowing them to find commonalities of manhood that had, for centuries, eluded both groups. From the series, the term "metrosexual" a straight man who takes into consideration things that have traditionally been associated with gay men, a part of the American lexicon. In utilizing the gay community to educate the straight community on how to better their romantic endeavors, the series also subtly educated the straight viewing community to see this "other" group as people and not, as before, something other.

POPULAR CULTURE: SPORTS

In the area of sports, perhaps the greatest game changer was Dwayne "the Rock" Johnson (b. 1972). A third-generation professional wrestler, Johnson is the son of Rocky Johnson (born Wayde Bowles, 1944–2020) and the grandson of Peter Maivia (born Fanene Anderson, 1937–1982). Johnson made his professional wrestling debut in the World Wrestling Federation (WWF) in 1996 under the professional name Rocky Maivia. He began referring to himself in the ring as "the Rock" in 1997, and by 1998, he was quickly becoming the biggest name in sports entertainment. By 2000, the Rock gained the nickname "the Most Electrifying Man in Sports Entertainment." Since the 1980s, Vince McMahon's WWF had steadily built a strong and dedicated fan base. The Rock, however, expanded that fan base further by millions. His powerful charisma raised the bar for wrestling fans' expectation, a bar that has not been met since the Rock left the ring for Hollywood. As such, while he took sports entertainment to new heights of popularity, his leaving it also marked another game change in the opposite direction.

Tiger Woods (b. 1975) was the biggest name in golf throughout the 2000s. Throughout his career he was won eighty-two Professional Golf Association (PGA) tours, tying with golf legend Sam Snead (1912–2002) for most PGA Tour victories. From 2000 to 2009, Woods won PGA Player of the Year every year except 2004 and 2008. He also won the Vardon Trophy and Byron Nelson Award each of those same years. He was the leading money winner in the PGA every year of the 2000s, except for 2003, 2004, and 2008. He was out the entire 2008 season recovering from knee surgery. Woods also won the FedEx Championship in 2007 and 2009. Prior to Tiger Woods, professional golf in the United States was an overwhelmingly white man's sport. While there had been pro golfers of color prior to Woods, none were able to break through to the heights Tiger Woods achieved.

Another sport that had been predominantly white for decades was professional tennis. In the 2000s, two sisters changed that: Venus and Serena Williams (b. 1980 and 1981, respectively). As a doubles team, the sisters have won fourteen Grand Slam women's doubles titles from 1999 to 2010. In the 2000 Olympic Games in Sydney, Australia, and the 2008 Olympic Games in Beijing, China, they won the gold medals for doubles competition. Venus also won gold for singles at Sydney, and Serena won gold for singles at the London Olympic Games in 2012. They also won doubles competition at Wimbledon in 2000, 2002, 2008, 2009, 2012, and 2016. Like Tiger Woods—and even the Rock— the Williams sisters shattered the ceiling for athletes of color in their field.

POPULAR CULTURE: FILM

In 1997, legendary sci-fi filmmaker James Cameron (b. 1954) shocked the world when his film *Titanic*, a fictional romance centered on the historic sinking of the titular passenger ship, became the biggest box office success in history. In the early 2000s, the director turned his attentions to documentary filmmaking but did so using new, updated 3D technology. One of these 3D docs, *Ghosts of the Abyss* (2003), took him back to the wreckage of the *RMS Titanic*. He was working with the new 3D technology with a goal in mind. In 1995, Cameron had written a script for the film *Avatar*, but he waited until 2006 to begin work on it as he needed filmmaking technology to catch up with his imagination.

George Lucas (b. 1944) and his team at Industrial Light and Magic had made huge strides in CGI technology for the *Star Wars* prequels (1999–2005), as had Pixar Studios throughout the 1990s and 2000s. Cameron took the technology to the next level, incorporating what he had discovered with 3D, and in 2009, *Avatar* surpassed *Titanic* as the biggest box-office hit in history. The magical splendor of the CGI world created for *Avatar*, enhanced by the audience's ability to enjoy a more interactive experience through 3D, made *Avatar* something that no one had ever seen before. The film also added to the boom of 3D films in the late 2000s that would bleed into the 2010s.

Possibly the biggest game changer in Hollywood in the 2000s was Marvel Comics. Still recovering from bankruptcy when the 2000s began, the company would exit the decade as a groundbreaking motion picture studio, soon to become part of the ever-expanding Disney empire. In the late 1990s, Marvel had been forced to sell the move and television rights to some of their more profitable properties—*Spider-Man* and the *X-Men* in particular—which led to some considerable box-office success for the studios that took them. In 2006, Marvel decided that they were best positioned to make a proper superhero movie, but the company was forced to do so with their lower-tier characters.

The studio chose Iron Man as their first feature film endeavor. Directed by Jon Favreau (b. 1966) and starring Robert Downey Jr. (b. 1965), *Iron Man* (2008) quickly became one of the biggest films of all time, with an initial-run box office of nearly $600 million. Downey was a risk, as his longtime drug habit had all but destroyed his once-promising acting career. Ultimately, the choice proved one of the most brilliant casting decisions in Hollywood history and overnight put Downey's career back on top. It also launched what has become known as the Marvel Cinematic Universe, with over twenty interconnected feature films over the next decade, and made Marvel one of the most profitable companies of the 2010s. The masterful work of all involved with each succeeding film also changed the game for how comic book superheroes are considered in the American zeitgeist. Once the butt of jokes, superheroes became deep, thoughtful analogies of humanity at its best and worst.

POPULAR CULTURE: MUSIC

Rapper Eminem (born Marshall Mathers III in 1972) broke ground for white artists in rap/hip-hop music. Prior to Eminem's massive success, a white rapper conjured images of Vanilla Ice (born Robert Van Winkle in 1967), long considered a joke after his 1989 hit "Ice Ice Baby." Eminem shot to the top of the charts in 2000 with his breakthrough hit, "The Real Slim Shady." In 2002, he starred in the semi-biographical film *8 Mile*, for which he won the Academy Award for Best Song with "Lose Yourself," making him the first hip-hop artist to win that award. Like mainstream Black rappers—and unlike Vanilla Ice—Eminem's songs spoke to his background and the struggles he had overcome in life. Eminem's success broke barriers by showing that this genre of music, born from the predominantly minority inner cities, could also be used to speak of the experiences of people of all races, ethnicities, and backgrounds.

The 2000s also saw the rise of the greatest power couple in music history: Jay-Z (born Shawn Carter in 1969) and Beyoncé Knowles (b. 1981). Jay-Z entered the 2000s as an upcoming rapper and record producer since his debut in 1996. Beyoncé came to national fame as part of the hip-hop group Destiny's Child, also consisting of Kelly Rowland and Michelle Williams (born 1981 and 1979, respectively). Destiny's Child broke through with their 2000 hit, "Say My Name," before going on to have six more Top Five hits over the next five years. Beyoncé and Jay-Z first collaborated on her breakout single hit, "Crazy in Love" (2003). The two married in 2008 and, together, have become the most powerful couple in popular music. The two lent their time for appearances and performances in support of Hillary Clinton's 2016 presidential run, a run in which Clinton would ultimately win the popular vote by 2.9 million votes.

With each at the top of their games in their individual careers, the union of the two proved to be an unstoppable force of nature.

A group less lauded for their impact on pop culture in the 2000s was the country music group the Dixie Chicks, consisting of members Martie Maguire (b. 1969), Natalie Maines (b. 1974), and Emily Strayer (b. 1972). The group shot to the top of country charts beginning with "Wide Open Spaces" (1998) and had a long chain of chart-topping hits through 2002. On March 10, 2003, the band experienced massive controversy when Maines, the band's lead singer, expressed embarrassment for being from the same state as U.S. president George W. Bush (b. 1946) during a concert in London, England. This statement came just as Bush was about to order the U.S.-led coalition invasion of Iraq for their continued violations of UN resolutions.

Maines's statement was met with massive backlash among country fans back in the United States. The group received death threats and were forced to cancel numerous live performances. Additionally, their career took a nosedive. Even after popular support for Bush and the Iraq war waned, country fans were still unwilling to forgive the group for their comment. Though President Bush defended their right to express themselves just a month after the comment, he also defended the rights of their fans to boycott their music. In 2006, the group released the song "Not Ready to Make Nice," defending their prior comment and expressing that they still stood by their criticism despite the backlash. The song did hit number four on the overall U.S. music charts, but it did not fare as well on country charts. The incident did, however, show the growing divisions that would reach nightmare proportions throughout the 2010s.

POPULAR CULTURE: LITERATURE

Without question or compare, the biggest name in literature in the 2000s was British author J. K. Rowling (born Joanne Rowling in 1965). Her 1997 novel *Harry Potter and the Philosopher's Stone* launched the best-selling book series in history, culminating with its seventh installment, *Harry Potter and the Deathly Hallows* (2007). Throughout that ten-year period, audiences around the world— and especially in the United States—lined up around the block at bookstores when each installment was released. The adventures of the young wizard captivated audiences of all ages, and after it seemed that generations of Americans had been reading less and less, *Harry Potter* led to a renaissance of Americans once more turning to the printed page for entertainment. The *Harry Potter* book series also launched a multi-billion-dollar film franchise, an amusement park section at Universal Studios in Florida, and a wildly popular Broadway play, *Harry Potter and the Cursed Child* (2016). The series also made Rowling one of the wealthiest women in the world.

POPULAR CULTURE: MEDIA

In 1996, Fox Corporation owner Rupert Murdoch (b. 1931) and longtime Republican Party media specialist Roger Ailes (1940–2017) launched FOX

News, a twenty-four-hour cable news outlet to compete with CNN and the recently launched MSNBC. Many conservatives had come to feel that CNN had become radically liberal in their news coverage , often referring to CNN as the Clinton News Network and the Communist News Network. FOX, therefore, promised "fair and balanced" news coverage, but coverage soon appeared to be right leaning. Their conservative spin became even more acute after 9/11. Once the United States committed to the War on Terror, FOX became the White House's ardent defender, questioning the loyalties of anyone who disagreed with President Bush. By the end of the decade, spin devolved to outright lies, conspiracy theories, and false narratives, particularly after Barack Obama was elected in 2008. Beginning in 2009, FOX's stance on patriotism shifted from ardently defending the president to just as ardently opposing him. In 2009, the TEA Party began as a grassroots organization that was quickly subverted by conservative billionaires, promoting the growing division between conservative and liberal across the country. Throughout the 2010s, even after Ailes's death, FOX would devolve further, to the point of becoming a key source of disinformation, leading many of its legitimate reporters to leave. Throughout the 2000s, however, FOX News was a massive component in the burgeoning Culture Wars that would rip the nation apart in the decade to come.

On the flip side of FOX's influence was the rise of comedian-turned-pundit Jon Stewart (b. 1962) and his historic tenure as host of *The Daily Show* (Comedy Central, 1996–present). The series began as a simple parody of nightly news broadcasts, hosted by Craig Kilborn (b. 1962). When he left the show at the end of 1998, the show was already very popular, leading Comedy Central to find a new host in Stewart. Jon Stewart had been a popular on-air personality throughout the 1990s but had failed to find an outlet for his talents that struck with audiences. With his takeover of *The Daily Show*, Stewart began the journey from lovable comedian to serious political commentator. Stewart began by slowly altering the program from fake news to comedic takes on the day's actual events. The celebrity interviews that were the staple of the last segment of each show changed to interviews with politicians, professors, scientists, and serious newsmakers who could inform the public on various topics through the comedic format of the show.

Stewart and his team of correspondents provided in-depth coverage of the 2000 presidential election with Indecision 2000. Their coverage made overnight stars of correspondents Steve Carell (b. 1962) and Stephen Colbert (b. 1964). The 2000 coverage gained larger audiences for the show, and by the time of their Indecision 2004 coverage, *The Daily Show* had become the go-to source for news in the coveted demographic of eighteen- to forty-five-year-olds. Unlike the cable news outlets, Stewart and company did not tow any particular party line and made outright fun of any political spin. They presented facts, pointed out the absurdity of politics as usual, and called out both ends of the political spectrum for the damage they were doing to the overall landscape.

Just a month before the 2004 election, Stewart was invited to be a guest on the CNN debate series *Crossfire* (CNN, 1982–2005; 2013–2014). On that episode, Stewart called out hosts Tucker Carlson (b. 1969) and Paul Begala (b. 1961) for allowing the program to devolve from legitimate debate to political theater. A testament to Stewart's growing political influence, his appearance and criticism led CNN to cancel the program shortly after the election. In 2005, *Daily Show* correspondent Colbert—who had made a character of his role, presenting himself as daft, blindly loyal conservative—was given his own program to follow *The Daily Show*, *The Colbert Report* (Comedy Central, 2005–2014). Whereas *The Daily Show* maintained its premise as nightly news parody, *Colbert* was a parody of FOX News commentary programs, most notably *The O'Reilly Factor* (FOX News, 1996–2017). Stewart and Colbert became a political powerhouse throughout the last half of the 2000s and the first half of the 2010s, moving from political commentators to political influencers.

In 2014, Colbert announced he was leaving his program to become the new host of *The Late Show* on CBS. The following year, Stewart announced his own retirement, the weight of the increasingly divided political landscape clearly taking its toll on the once-optimistic host. Their legacy, however, remains well into the 2020s. Hosting duties on *The Daily Show* continued with South African comedian Trevor Noah (b. 1984). Along with continuing Stewart's legacy on the show, Noah has added not only a more youthful take on the day's events but also an outside-looking-in approach of someone not raised in the United States. After a shaky beginning, Colbert slowly transformed *The Late Show* into something more resembling the work he was doing on his Comedy Central program. *Daily Show* correspondents carried on Stewart's legacy with their own programs: *Last Week Tonight with John Oliver* (HBO, 2014–present) and *Full Frontal with Samantha Bee* (TBS, 2014–present). As America became even more divided under the presidency of Donald Trump (b. 1946), Jon Stewart was no longer on the political front lines, but his legacy lives on.

Prior to *The Daily Show*, the biggest name in political satire on television for decades had been *SNL*, or *Saturday Night Live* (NBC, 1975–present). Under the guidance of series creator Lorne Michaels (b. 1944), *SNL* continued to be a strong voice in political satire throughout the 2000s. Cast member Will Ferrell (b. 1967) cemented his legacy on the show with his iconic portrayals of President George W. Bush. In 2002, two years after his razor-thin defeat in the 2000 presidential election, former vice president Al Gore (b. 1948) became the first politician to host the show. This led to several appearances of political figures in the decades since. Leading up to the 2008 elections, Republican nominee Senator John McCain; his running mate, Governor Sarah Palin; and his Democratic rival Senator Barack Obama all made appearances on the show. The trend would continue the following decade, with former secretary of state Hillary Clinton and presidential candidate Trump both making appearances on the series. As ratings of *SNL* have risen and fallen over the decades, depending on the popularity of the cast as well as the quality of the writing, their political sketches have remained a constant source of hilarious and biting comedy centered on the often-ridiculous nature of American politics.

POPULAR CULTURE: TECHNOLOGY

The 2000s saw more technological advancements than perhaps any decade prior. Advancements that would forever change the very core of American society. The first of those being the advent of what has come to be known as social media, and one of the founders of that phenomenon was Mark Zucker-berg (b. 1984). He and his Harvard classmates developed Facebook, which launched initially in 2004. Although internet users were already connecting through MySpace, Facebook quickly took over as the premier social media network, exploding across American society in 2007. The network allows users to make friends with people of common interests anywhere in the world, as well as look up old friends or distant family members, making the world a smaller place than ever before.

The massive popularity of Facebook would launch similar social network-ing sights such as Twitter, YouTube, and Instagram in the months and years that followed. With all the good that social media brought, it brought just as much bad. A new phenomenon was borne from social media: online bullying. Whereas people could previously avoid bullies in the safety of their homes, social media brought bullying directly into the privacy of the bedroom, with no escape from those who would torment, leading to a horrible rise in suicides due to constant bullying. The political divide was likewise worsened by social media, with friends and family members unfriending each other over political differences. As fake news and disinformation rose with the internet, social media provided multiple platforms to spread lies and half-truths. In 2016, social media platforms, and Facebook in particular, became a useful tool for Russian interference in that year's presidential elections. As of 2020, Facebook possessed 2.5 billion users, or over one-third of the planet's population.

Social media might have been something that people could distance them-selves from when it was confined to their computers. That would change with the advent of the smartphone—in particular, the iPhone. Steve Jobs (1955–2011) had cofounded Apple Computers in 1976 with his partner Steve Wozniak (b. 1950). In 1985, Jobs's eccentricities and volatile temper led the company to force him out, after which, Apple took considerable downturns, coming to the brink of bankruptcy in 1997. When Apple acquired Jobs's new company, NeXT, Jobs was quickly placed back on top of the company he'd helped start. Making a devil's bargain with his longtime opponent, Microsoft's Bill Gates (b. 1955), Jobs was able to make a deal where the wildly popular Microsoft software could be installed in the next generation of Apple computers: the iMac (1998). Jobs's greatest role was as a visionary.

In 2001, Apple introduced the iPod, an MP3 audio player, as well as iTunes, an online source for downloading content for the Apple devices, and the com-pany opened a chain of brick-and-mortar Apple Stores to provide not only Apple products but also access to Apple Geniuses, who could help with any malfunctioning devices. Perhaps Jobs's greatest vision and legacy was the iPhone, launched in 2007. This next-generation smartphone gave users a cell phone, an iPod, internet access, and various other helpful apps. Though often outsold by Samsung's Galaxy phones, the term "iPhone" has become synony-mous with cellular smartphones, often the first word that springs to mind when someone refers to a phone. Shortly before his death, Jobs released his latest vision, the iPad, a tablet with all the functions of the iPhone minus the phone. The world of the 2020s was envisioned by Steve Jobs in the early 2000s, and his impact on human civilization cannot be overstated.

The 2000s was one of the most transformative decades in American and world history, for good and bad. From the perspective of 2000, 2010 would look like a science fiction movie. America would become united after the darkest day in its history, only to go on to split in half over every sociopolitical issue by decade's end. America would elect its first Black president, only to expose how deeply racism was still embedded in the system that elected him. The LGBTQ+ community would finally gain widespread acceptance throughout the country, allowing more and more to live openly and be who they are, only to provide outlets through social media by which they could be bullied even more directly than ever before.

American audiences showed that they no longer needed entertainment to be dumbed down for them, following in massive numbers entertainment franchises that offered deep, thoughtful commentary on the events of the day. Black athletes dominated sports that had long been predominantly white, and a white rapper showed how the genre could speak to audiences of all races and socioeconomic backgrounds. A boy wizard would unite the world like nothing before in history. The news media would divide Americans more than ever, and it would become the role of comedians to desperately attempt to repair the damage. Social media brought friends and enemies closer than ever before, and smartphones brought the entire world to every person's fingertips. For good or ill, Americans had more tools in 2010 to unite or divide themselves than ever before. The 2010s would be the most technologically advanced and socially divided decade in American history, and the world of 2020 was born from the ashes of a clear autumn day in 2001.

FURTHER READING

Abad-Santos, Alex. 2016. "Marvel's Civil War and Its Politics, Explained." *Vox*, May 3. https://www.vox.com/2016/5/3/11531348/marvel-civil-war-explained. Retrieved January 2, 2020.

Alter, Jonathan. 2010. *The Promise: President Obama, Year One*. New York: Simon & Schuster.

Assael, Shaun, and Mike Mooneyham. 2004. *Sex, Lies, and Headlocks: The Real Story of Vince McMahon and World Wrestling Entertainment*. Portland, OR: Broadway.

Berman, William C. 2001. *From the Center to the Edge: The Politics & Policies of the Clinton Presidency*. Lanham, MD: Rowman & Littlefield.

Bodroghkozy, Aniko. 2018. *A Companion to the History of American Broadcasting*. New York: Wiley-Blackwell.

Bowen, Michelle. 2018. *J. K. Rowling: From Welfare to Billionaire, a Biography*. Scotts Valley, CA: CreateSpace.

Brands, H. W. 2011. *American Dreams: The United States since 1945*. New York: Penguin.

Bush, George W. 2001. "Address to the Nation." American Rhetoric, September 11. https://www.americanrhetoric.com/speeches/gwbush911addresstothenation.htm. Retrieved March 31, 2019.

Bush, George W. 2010. *Decision Points*. New York: Crown.

Carter, Bill. 2005. "CNN Will Cancel 'Crossfire' and Cut Ties to Commentator." *New York Times*, January 6. https://www.nytimes.com/2005/01/06/business/media/cnn-will-cancel-crossfire-and-cut-ties-to-commentator.html. Retrieved January 12, 2020.

Castleman, Harry, and Walter J. Podrazik. 2016. *Watching TV: Eight Decades of American Television*. 3rd ed. New York: Syracuse University Press.

CBS News. 2018a. "How Sports Helped America Heal after 9/11." September 8. https://www.cbsnews.com/news/how-sports-helped-america-heal-after-911-new-york-city-exhibit/. Retrieved November 14, 2019.

CBS News. 2018b. "Meet the Artist Who Put a Realistic Spin on Comic Book Superheroes." *CBS This Morning*, December 22. https://www.cbsnews.com/news/comic-book-artist-alex-ross/. Retrieved January 26, 2020.

Chamberlain, Will. 2019. "Jon Stewart Was Wrong about Crossfire: It's Time to Bring Bombastic, Evenly Matched Debates to Cable TV." Human Events, September 6. https://humanevents.com/2019/09/06/jon-stewart-was-wrong-about-crossfire/. Retrieved January 12, 2020.

Chambers, Veronica. 2019. *Queen Bey: A Celebration of the Power and Creativity of Beyoncé Knowles-Carter*. New York: St. Martin's.

Chang, Jeff. 2005. *Can't Stop Won't Stop: A History of the Hip-Hop Generation*. London: Picador.

Charnas, Dan. 2011. *The Big Payback: The History of the Business of Hip-Hop*. New York: Berkley.

Chomsky, Noam. 2005. *Imperial Ambitions: Conversations on the Post-9/11 World*. New York: Metropolitan.

Chossudovsky, Michel. 2004. "What Happened on the Planes on September 11, 2001? The 9/11 Cell Phone Calls. The 9/11 Commission 'Script' Was Fabricated." GlobalResearch, August 10. https://www.globalresearch.ca/more-holes-in-the-official-story-the-911-cell-phone-calls/5652872. Retrieved January 10, 2020.

Clinton, Hillary Rodham. 2003. *Living History*. New York: Simon & Schuster.

Colbert, Stephen. 2009. *I Am America (and So Can You!)*. New York: Grand Central.

Collins, Scott. 2004. *Crazy Like a Fox: The Inside Story of How FOX News Beat CNN*. New York: Portfolio.

Dittmer, Jason. 2005. "Captain America's Empire: Reflections on Identity, Popular Culture, and Post-9/11 Geopolitics." *Annals of the Association of American Geographers* 95, no. 3: 626–643.

Edmondson, Jaqueline. 2005. *Venus and Serena Williams: A Biography*. Santa Barbara, CA: Greenwood.

Evans, Jennifer C. 2002. "Hijacking Civil Liberties: The USA PATRIOT Act of 2001." *Loyola University Chicago Law Journal* 33, no. 4: 933–990.

Fahy, Thomas, ed. 2005. *Considering Aaron Sorkin: Essays on the Politics, Poetics and Sleight of Hand in the Films and Television Series*. Jefferson, NC: McFarland.

Faludi, Susan. 2008. *The Terror Dream: Myth and Misogyny in an Insecure America*. London: Picador.

Ford, Rebecca. 2013. "Oscars: Ellen DeGeneres's Hosting History." *Hollywood Reporter*, August 2. https://www.hollywoodreporter.com/news/oscars-ellen-degeneres-hosting-history-598767. Retrieved January 13, 2020.

Glastris, Paul, Ryan Cooper, and Siyu Hu. 2012. "Obama's Top 50 Accomplishments." *Washington Monthly*, March/April. https://washingtonmonthly.com/magazine/marchapril-2012/obamas-top-50-accomplishments/. Retrieved February 9, 2020.

Gournelos, Ted, and Viveca Greene, eds. 2011. *A Decade of Dark Humor: How Comedy, Irony, and Satire Shaped Post-9/11 America*. Jackson: University Press of Mississippi.

Graff, Garrett M. 2019. "Pagers, Pay Phones, and Dialup: How We Communicated on 9/11." *Wired*, September 11. https://www.wired.com/story/pagers-pay-phones-and-dialup-how-we-communicated-on-911/. Retrieved January 10, 2020.

Guerrasio, Jason. 2015. "New 'Saturday Night Live' Documentary Recounts the Emotional First Show after 9/11." *Business Insider*, April 16. https://www.businessinsider.com/saturday-night-live-first-show-after-911-2015-4. Retrieved January 13, 2020.

Handscombe, Claire. 2016. *Walk with Us: How* The West Wing *Changed Our Lives.* New York: CH Books.

Hart, Kylo-Patrick R., ed. 2016. *Queer TV in the 21st Century: Essays on Broadcasting from Taboo to Acceptance.* Jefferson, NC: McFarland.

Healthcare.gov. 2010. "The Affordable Care Act." March 23. https://www.healthcare.gov/where-can-i-read-the-affordable-care-act/. Retrieved February 1, 2020.

Heilemann, John, and Mark Halperin. 2010. *Game Change: Obama and the Clintons, McCain and Palin, and the Race of a Lifetime.* New York: Harper Perennial.

Hodgkinson, Mark. 2019. *Serena: A Graphic Biography of the Greatest Tennis Champion.* London: White Lion.

Howe, Sean. 2012. *Marvel Comics: The Untold Story.* New York: Harper Perennial.

Iannucci, Lisa. 2008. *Ellen DeGeneres: A Biography.* Santa Barbara, CA: Greenwood.

Irwin, William, and Gregory Bassham, eds. 2010. *The Ultimate* Harry Potter *and Philosophy: Hogwarts for Muggles.* Hoboken, NJ: Wiley.

Isaacson, Walter. 2011. *Steve Jobs.* New York: Simon & Schuster.

Jennings, John. 2017. *The Wit and Wisdom of Ellen DeGeneres.* Independently published.

Johnson, Dwayne "the Rock," and Joe Layden. 2000. *The Rock Says . . . : The Most Electrifying Man in Sports Entertainment.* New York: Harper Entertainment.

Klemens, Guy. 2010. *The Cellphone: The History and Technology of the Gadget That Changed the World.* Jefferson, NC: McFarland.

Kruse, Kevin M., and Julian E. Zelizer. 2019. *Fault Lines: A History of the United States since 1974.* New York: W. W. Norton.

Letukas, Lynn. 2014. *Primetime Pundits: How Cable News Covers Social Issues.* Washington, DC: Lexington.

Linzmayer, Owen W. 2004. *Apple Confidential 2.0: The Definitive History of the World's Most Colorful Company.* San Francisco, CA: No Starch.

Mezrich, Ben. 2009. *The Accidental Billionaires: The Founding of Facebook, a Tale of Sex, Money, Genius, and Betrayal.* New York: Doubleday.

Mulholland, Neil. 2007. *The Psychology of Harry Potter: An Unauthorized Examination of the Boy Who Lived.* Dallas, TX: Smart Pop.

National Commission on Terrorist Attacks Upon the United States. 2004. *The 9/11 Report.* New York: St. Martin's.

9/11 Commission. 2004. "The 9/11 Commission Report." National Commission on Terrorist Attacks Upon the United States. https://www.9-11commission.gov/report/. Retrieved January 3, 2020.

9/11 Memorial. [Posting Date Unknown]. "September 11 Attack Timeline." https://timeline.911memorial.org/#Timeline/2. Retrieved May 8, 2019.

9/11 Memorial and Museum. 2019. "Comeback Season: Sports after 9/11." https://www.911memorial.org/visit/museum/exhibitions/comeback-season-sports-after-911. Retrieved November 14, 2019.

Obama, Barack. 2004. "Barack Obama's Remarks to the Democratic National Convention." *New York Times*, July 27. https://www.nytimes.com/2004/07/27/politics/campaign/barack-obamas-remarks-to-the-democratic-national.html. Retrieved February 9, 2020.

Obama, Barack. 2006. *The Audacity of Hope: Thoughts on Reclaiming the American Dream.* New York: Crown.

Obama, Barack. 2009. "First Inaugural Address." Obama White House, January 20. https://obamawhitehouse.archives.gov/blog/2009/01/21/president-barack -obamas-inaugural-address. Retrieved March 31, 2019.

O'Reilly, Bill. 2006. *Culture Warrior.* New York: Crown.

Ritter, Jonathan. 2007. *Music in the Post 9/11 World.* London: Routledge.

Rogak, Lisa. 2015. *Angry Optimism: The Life and Times of Jon Stewart.* New York: St. Martin's.

Rollins, Peter, and John E. O'Connor. 2003. The West Wing: *The American Presidency as Television Drama.* Syracuse, NY: Syracuse University Press.

Smith, Chris. 2016. The Daily Show *(The Book): An Oral History as Told by Jon Stewart, the Correspondents, Staff and Guests.* New York: Grand Central.

Sorkin, Andrew Ross. 2009. *Too Big to Fail: The Inside Story of How Wall Street and Washington Fought to Save the Financial System—And Themselves.* New York: Penguin.

Staff. 2017. "Watch Jon Stewart Call Tucker Carlson a 'Dick' in Epic 2004 'Crossfire' Takedown." *Hollywood Reporter,* January 5. https://www.hollywoodreporter .com/news/jon-stewart-takes-down-tucker-carlson-crossfire-video-961127. Retrieved January 12, 2020.

Stewart, Jon, et al. 2004. *America (The Book).* New York: Warner/Grand Central.

Terry, Josh. 2019. "Sixteen Years Later, Country Radio Is Still Mad at the Dixie Chicks." *Vice,* September 10. https://www.vice.com/en_us/article/evjvqe/sixteen-years -later-country-radio-is-still-mad-at-the-dixie-chicks-taylor-swift-soon-youll -get-better. Retrieved November 23, 2019.

Thompson, Gayle. 2019. "16 Years Ago: Natalie Maines Makes Controversial Comments about President George W. Bush." Boot, March 10. https://theboot.com /natalie-maines-dixie-chicks-controversy/. Retrieved November 28, 2019.

Tinsley, Omise'eke Natasha. 2018. *Beyoncé in Formation: Remixing Black Feminism.* Austin: University of Texas Press.

Tucker, Reed. 2017. *Slugfest: Inside the Epic 50-Year Battle Between Marvel and DC.* New York: Da Capo.

Veloso, Francisco, and John Bateman. 2013. "The Multimodal Construction of Acceptability: Marvel's *Civil War* Comic Books and the PATRIOT Act." *Critical Discourse Studies* 10, no. 4: 427–443.

Watson, Bruce. 2016. *Jon Stewart: Beyond the Moments of Zen.* Scotts Valley, CA: CreateSpace.

Whitehead, John W., and Steven H. Aden. 2002. "Forfeiting 'Enduring Freedom' for 'Homeland Security': A Constitutional Analysis of the USA Patriot Act and the Justice Department's Anti-Terrorism Initiatives." *American University Law Review* 51, no. 6: 1081–1133.

Willis, Susan. 2005. *Portents of the Real: A Primer for Post-9/11 America.* London: Verso.

Conclusion: Legacy of the 2000s

The 2000s was a transformative decade in so many ways. The terror that so many around the world had experienced for decades came to American shores in the most stunning nightmare the country had ever experienced. This led to a two-front War on Terror that would at first unite but eventually divide the nation even more. By mid-decade, the unity brought on by 9/11 had dissipated, and the cultural divide begun in the 1990s resumed. By 2010, the split between conservative and liberal seemed irreparable, and the ensuing decade would see that situation worsen.

Popular culture attempted to salve these wounds, trying to find common ground in the area of entertainment, but more often than not, pop culture tended to side with those of a more liberal bend, only exacerbating the situation more. Cable news became less a media of information and more a contest for presenting the "facts" that each side was most comfortable with. Technology proved it could divide as much as it united. The one group to benefit from the events of the decade was the LGBTQ+ community, as a wider swath of Americans became open to accepting the group and promoting long-denied civil liberties. The 2000s had opened with the worst attack on American soil in the country's history, and as it came to a close, the decade ended with the biggest economic collapse since the Great Depression. Few looked to 2010 with hope for the future.

THE POST-9/11 WORLD

By far the greatest legacy of the 2000s has been 9/11. Since September 11, 2001, the United States and the world have existed in a post-9/11 world. The resulting War on Terror saw American forces entrenched in Afghanistan and Iraq for the remainder of the decade and well into the 2010s (and, in the case of Afghanistan, well into 2020). At home, airport security and the controversial

USA PATRIOT Act created more invasive security measures than had ever been implemented within American boundaries. Fear of Al-Qaeda aroused racial tensions against Arab Americans and raised Islamophobia to its highest levels ever. Abroad, the radical offshoots of Al-Qaeda—ISIS (the Islamic State of Iraq and Syria) and ISIL (the Islamic State of Iraq and the Levant)—led to American involvement in Syria. In 2011, U.S. Navy SEAL Team Six led an assault on the compound of Al-Qaeda leader Osama bin Laden (1957–2011), killing the terrorist leader and providing some sense of justice for Americans at home.

The liberation of Afghanistan from the Taliban regime and Iraq from the dictatorship of Saddam Hussein (1937–2006) led to the Arab Spring of 2011. Prodemocracy movements arose in Egypt, Libya, and Syria. Egypt and Libya ousted their own dictators, Egyptian president Hosni Mubarak (1928–2020) and Libyan dictator Colonel Muammar Gaddafi (1942–2011), while Syria was less successful in their attempt to oust Syrian president Bashar al-Assad (b. 1965). Syria turned into a two-front war: with U.S.-backed Syrian resistance fighting the government forces of al-Assad (himself backed by Russia and Iran) and the combined forces of the United States, the Syrian resistance, al-Assad's government forces, Russia, and Iran fighting another war against the encroaching forces of ISIS. Meanwhile, the United States and Iran were on opposing sides in supporting the civil war in Yemen. Throughout the region, the forces of ISIS/ISIL raised the terror level through their online videos showing them beheading Western citizens.

As stated, Americans at first were united in the immediate wake of 9/11. Vengeance against this new enemy brought Americans of all races, classes, genders, and political persuasion together to a degree not seen since the end of the Cold War. However, as the dust settled, the War on Terror seemed to be more quagmire than quest, and more and more American blood was spilled on foreign battlefields, the political divide once more widened. President Bush (b. 1946) maintained his promised resolve, and his approval ratings fell to a point that, by the time he left office in January 2009, he was the least popular president since World War II.

THE POLITICAL DIVIDE

With political animosities at an all-time high by 2009, the election of America's first Black president, Barack Obama (b. 1961), brought to light levels of racism not publicly seen since the days of the civil rights movement four decades earlier. The political right wing saw the rise of the TEA Party, or Taxed Enough Already Party. This group began as a grassroots organization demanding officially demanding more fiscal responsibility in Washington. The TEA Party was soon infiltrated by the billionaire Koch brothers: Charles (b. 1935) and David (1940–2019). FOX News and politicians such as Congresswoman Michele Bachmann (b. 1956) and the 2008 Republican vice presidential candidate, Alaska governor Sarah Palin (b. 1964), became the mouthpieces for this radical conservative movement, and Bachmann became the head of the TEA Party Caucus in Congress, later dubbed the Freedom Caucus.

On the left, two radical organizations developed: the Occupy Wall Street (OWS) movement and the 99 Percent. Both groups addressed the growing income inequality in the country, made even worse by the government bailing Wall Street banks in the wake of the 2008 economic collapse while doing nothing to help those Americans hurt by Wall Street's unethical actions. The "99 Percent" referenced the fact that most of the nation's wealth was held by a tiny 1 percent of Americans. In the 2010s, these groups would help the rise of democratic socialist Vermont senator Bernie Sanders (b. 1941) as a presidential contender in 2016 and 2020. By the end of the 2010s, this new radical left would also see the rise of upcoming liberal superstar politicians such as New York congresswoman Alexandria Ocasio-Cortez (b. 1989), and her radical environmental package, the Green New Deal.

This division was most manifest in the 2016 presidential election, where many radical liberals boycotted the Democratic Party when the nomination was denied Sanders and given to former secretary of state Hillary Clinton (b. 1947). The far right found their champion in the form of New York real-estate tycoon and reality-show celebrity Donald Trump (b. 1946), who would become the forty-fifth president of the United States with his promise to "make America great again." By 2020, the political divisions begun in 2008 had led to an America more divided than at any point in its history, including the Civil War (1861–1865) and the civil rights movement (1955–1968).

POPULAR CULTURE

The most powerful legacy of popular culture in the 2000s was the expansion of the Disney empire. Founded in 1923 by animator Walt Disney (1901–1966), the Disney empire was already a pop culture icon and powerhouse by the beginning of the 2000s, with decades of animated feature films, theme parks, television programs, and a cable network making them a global pop culture presence. In 2004, Disney began looking outside its own massive library of original intellectual properties and purchased Jim Henson's *Muppet* franchise, bringing Kermit the Frog and Miss Piggy into the Disney fold. This move proved profitable for the company, leading it to look for other intellectual properties to add to the Disney brand.

In 2005, Bob Iger (b. 1951) became the chief executive officer of the Walt Disney Corporation. The following year, Disney purchased Pixar Studios. In the 1980s, Hollywood icon George Lucas (b. 1944) sold off the computer-animation department of his Industrial Light and Magic. Under the guidance of Steve Jobs (1955–2011), Pixar Studios began working on computer animated feature films, culminating with *Toy Story* (1995) and followed by a chain of number-one box-office hits over the next decade. In 2006, Iger made his first big purchase when he acquired Pixar for $7.4 billion. After the massive success of Marvel Studios' film *Iron Man* (2008), Iger/Disney purchased Marvel Enterprises for $4.2 billion in 2009. This gave Disney ownership of the roughly five thousand characters in the Marvel catalog.

Iger sought to expand the Disney brand even more in the 2010s. When George Lucas decided to retire in 2012, Disney purchased Lucasfilm, including the *Star Wars* franchise, for $4.05 billion. Iger's last big acquisition for Disney came in 2019 with his purchase of the entertainment division of 20th Century Fox for $71.3 billion. Aside from its massive movie and television catalog, which included such pop culture icons as *The Simpsons* and *The X-Files*, it also gained total ownership of the original *Star Wars* (1977), the only film in the franchise not owned by Lucasfilm. By 2020, Disney owned roughly 40 percent of the television and movie market. Bob Iger retired in 2020, becoming the most impactful chief executive officer of the Disney Corporation since its founder.

TELEVISION

The biggest legacy of the 2000s on television would be the advent of the reality show. Competition programs such as *Survivor* (CBS, 2000–present), *American Idol* (FOX, 200–2016; ABC, 2018–present), *The Apprentice* (NBC, 2004–2015; 2017), and *RuPaul's Drag Race* (Logo, 2009–2016; VH1, 2017–present) made celebrities of everyday Americans. Celebrity families entered the reality genre with programs such as rock legend Ozzy Osbourne's family in *The Osbournes* (MTV, 2002–2005) and model Kim Kardashian's family in *Keeping Up with the Kardashians* (E!, 2007–present). The History Channel even entered the reality show craze by the end of the decade with their wildly popular series *Pawn Stars* (History, 2009–present), which shows audiences the fascinating historical artifacts that come into a local Las Vegas pawn shop, mixing reality show with educational programming. The popularity of reality shows in the 2000s only expanded in the 2010s, providing commercially successful and cheaply produced programming for network and cable outlets.

MOVIES

Other than the obvious advancements in CGI and 3D technology in the 2000s, the decade's greatest legacy would have to be the superhero movie. Superhero films had always been hit-and-miss for Hollywood. There were massive box-office successes (*Superman: The Movie*, 1978, and *Batman*, 1989) and equally disastrous failures (*Superman IV: The Quest for Peace*, 1987, and *Batman & Robin*, 1997). The 2000s saw a chain of very successful superhero films, due in no small part to the fact that superhero narratives become more popular during times of uncertainty or fear. From the beginning of the decade, 20th Century Fox had success with the first two films of their *X-Men* franchise, and Sony Pictures had equal success with their first two *Spider-Man* films. However, the third films in each of those franchises—as well as other lackluster showings such as *The Hulk* (2003), *Fantastic Four* (2005), and *Ghost Rider* (2007)— showed that the genre was not yet a box office guarantee.

That started to change in 2005 with Warner Brothers' *Batman Begins*. This rebooting of the recently failed *Batman* franchise was directed by Christopher Nolan (b. 1970) and starred Christian Bale (b. 1974) as comics' Dark Knight Detective. The considerable success of this film led to a full trilogy, the next of which, *The Dark Knight* (2008), became one of the highest-grossing films of all time as well as the first superhero film to garner an Academy Award for Best Supporting Actor, given posthumously to Heath Ledger (1979–2008) for his portrayal of iconic villain the Joker. The third film of the franchise, *The Dark Knight Rises* (2012), was another box-office success although it failed to gain the critical acclaim of the second film.

While the gritty realism of the new *Batman* films showed what a superhero movie could be, the genre's enduring success is most accountable to the new Marvel Studios. In the late 1990s, Marvel Comics had been forced to sell the television and movie rights to some of their more lucrative properties in stave off bankruptcy, and though some of the movies produced were popular with fans, many more were not. It was the opinion of the company that they were best suited to bring their properties to the big screen, and, in 2008, the company released its first self-made feature film, *Iron Man*. Robert Downey Jr. (b. 1965) gave an iconic performance of billionaire-turned-superhero Tony Stark, bringing the comic book page to life in a way only seen by Christopher Reeve (1952–2004) in his brilliant portrayal of Superman in the 1970s and 1980s.

Marvel would take the characters of their *Avengers* franchise, the only major characters still in the company's full control, and release a series of films revolving around individual Avengers, building toward a meeting of them all in the 2012 film *Marvel's The Avengers*, which broke opening-weekend box-office records with over $200 million. As of 2020, it remains one of the top ten highest-grossing films of all time. Throughout the 2010s, Marvel would release twenty more films, each one a massive box-office blockbuster. By 2020, superheroes dominated Hollywood and all of popular culture.

A more frightening legacy from Hollywood in the 2000s came from a moderate box-office success but cult classic 2006 film, *Idiocracy*. This film, directed and cowritten by animator Mike Judge (b. 1962), starred Luke Wilson (b. 1971) as a U.S. soldier who volunteers to be placed in cryogenic hibernation and is inadvertently awakened in the twenty-sixth century. In that dystopian future, commercialism has become the only factor in American society. Centuries of dependency on technology have created a generation of idiots, as education has been diluted by generations of anti-intellectualism to the point that no one understands how anything works and Americans put their trust entirely into what they are told by commercial producers, who, themselves, do not understand how anything works. While it was a moderately humorous sci-fi story in 2006, the massive rise of dependence on technology and a frightening rise of anti-intellectualism throughout the 2010s has made the film less sci-fi and comedy and more terrifying cautionary tale.

MEDIA

The news media—heretofore the protector of fact versus fiction in U.S. history—has played a major role in this diminution of intellectual curiosity since the 2000s. As some misinformation from trusted news organizations such as FOX News pushed farther to the political right to gain viewers, MSNBC pushed to the far left to gain viewers, formatting their news coverage to support the preconceived ideas of that audience, vilifying the political right to make their viewers feel all the more correct in their assumptions. As a result, CNN, the self-proclaimed "most trusted name in news," whose leftist bend on the news had led to FOX's rise, attempted to find a spot in the middle politically. Unfortunately, by 2010, left and right were so politically divided that there were few viewers left in the center, and CNN began a long period of third-place finishes in the ratings.

The 2000s also saw the rapid decline of the print media. As more and more Americans turned to television and the internet for up-to-the-minute information, the slower print media of newspapers and magazines began to go out of business. Most major news outlets, such as the *New York Times*, the *Washington Post*, and *Newsweek*—opened online outlets that could prove profitable enough to keep their print division in business. Other periodicals such as comic books saw less success with online and digital products, and their print media was kept alive primarily through the massive economic success of their film and television branches. Many more magazines and newspapers simply went out of business, and such longtime American businesses responsible for informing the public for centuries quickly became a thing of the past.

Perhaps the greatest legacy of media in the 2000s was the rise of Jon Stewart (b. 1962). His takeover of the Comedy Central fake news program *The Daily Show* (1996–present) changed the concept of political satire in America, making it relevant and important social commentary. For his tenure on *The Daily Show*, from 1999 to 2015, Stewart and company became some of the most trusted voices on the political landscape in America. By the time he retired, he and fellow comedian and commentator Stephen Colbert (b. 1964) had become the most trusted source of daily news for millions of Americans. The idea of comedy programs becoming trusted sources for news goes to show the ridiculous nature of the American political landscape by the mid-2010s.

Since leaving *The Daily Show* in 2015, Stewart has been replaced by South African comedian Trevor Noah (b. 1984). His longtime collaborator, Colbert, has changed the face of network late-night television by making politics a key factor of his *Late Show with Stephen Colbert* (CBS, 2015–present). This format shift has also become visible in Colbert's late-night counterparts, *Late Night with Seth Meyers* (NBC, 2014–present) and *Jimmy Kimmel Live!* (ABC, 2003–present). Aside from Colbert, Stewart's other correspondents from *The Daily Show* have also launched their own political programs: *Last Week Tonight with John Oliver* (HBO, 2014–present) and *Full Frontal with Samantha Bee* (TBS, 2016–present). Stewart's show's two important predecessors continue to be of huge relevance well into the 2020s: the "Weekend Update" segment of *Saturday Night Live* (NBC, 1975–present) and comedian Bill Maher (b. 1956) with his two iconic programs, *Politically Incorrect* (ABC, 1993–2002) and *Real Time with Bill Maher* (HBO, 2003–present).

TECHNOLOGY

At no point in human history did society so dramatically change technologically as from 2000 to 2010. By 2000, cellular telephones were just beginning to offer texting services, with many Americans still utilizing pagers to receive contact messages when away from landline telephones. In 2002, the Black-Berry became the portable device of preference and was still used by President Obama when he took office in 2009. The initial BlackBerry allowed phone calls, text messaging, push email, faxing, and Web browsing. With the return of Steve Jobs to Apple in 1998, the country's premier computer hardware company returned to its innovative roots. In 2007, Jobs announced the iPhone, which combined all the benefits of the BlackBerry as well as a built-in iPod. Samsung soon followed in 2009 with the Galaxy. By 2010, smartphone users could talk by phone, text, email, look up information on the internet, and check the hourly weather and their calendar, all the while listening to their favorite music. The future was now, and daily life in America would never be the same as it had been just ten years prior.

In 2005, Steve Chen (b. 1978), Chad Hurley (b. 1977), and Jawed Karim (b. 1979) created YouTube, selling it to Google in 2006. YouTube offered online video sharing and has emerged as one of the most popular sites on the internet, making overnight worldwide celebrities of everyday people around the globe. As the technology and picture quality have improved over the years, video streaming has moved into the entertainment world. Throughout the 2010s, sites like Netflix, Hulu, Amazon Prime, Yahoo!, CBS All Access, HBO GO, and Disney+ have made video streaming the preferred method of video entertainment around the world, quickly replacing television, which had dominated popular culture for over half a century.

Closely connected to video streaming is the various websites of social media. In 2003, MySpace offered users the ability to connect with people across the country. Though popular for its ability to allow users to personalize their pages, the service fell quickly to competitor Facebook in 2007. From Facebook, other social media sites arose, such as Twitter, Snapchat, and Instagram, to name but the most popular. Originating from chat rooms in the early 1990s, social media brought the world closer than ever before. Unfortunately, for all its benefits, social media also opens the door for expanding hate and fear. Cyberbullying brought terrors that had existed largely outside the comfort of home directly into the bedrooms of victims around the world. Social media throughout the 2010s would prove that for all the good it can do, it can do just as much damage. As with all technology, it must be used responsibly and with caution.

Throughout the 2000s, technology slowly but steadily changed the nature of capitalism across the board. For millennia, shopping was done by going outside the home. People had to go to a brick-and-mortar store. That began to change in the late 1990s with the advent of online shopping. Originally an online bookseller, Amazon quickly put pressure on traditional stores such as Barnes & Noble and Books-A-Million, forcing both to open online branches of their stores. As Amazon grew to offer more and more products other than books, other brick-and-mortar stores began to feel the pressure. Some, like superstore Walmart, adapted in the 2010s by developing their own online outlets. Others, like K-Mart, Sears, and Toys "R" Us, lost so much business to Amazon that they were forced to shut down the majority of their stores or, as in the cases of K-Mart and briefly Toys "R" Us, shut down completely. Online shopping possesses far too many benefits to compete with, as people are able to stay at home, save gas and time, and quickly order forgotten items. Online shopping, combined with the luxury of smartphones, allows consumers to purchase whatever they want whenever they want at the touch of a few buttons.

SOCIETY

One of the more positive legacies of the 2000s has been the more widespread social acceptance of the LGBTQ+ (lesbian, gay, bisexual, transgender, queer, questioning, asexual, intersexual, dual spirit, +) community. Long ostracized as "abnormal" and, for a long time, "psychologically disturbed," the community gained acceptance throughout the 2000s as more and more traditionally thinking Americans began to open their minds to the pleas of their fellow citizens. Television programs such as *Will & Grace* (NBC, 1998–2006; 2017–2020) and *Queer Eye for the Straight Guy* (Bravo, 2003–2007), and celebrities such as Ellen DeGeneres (b. 1958) and RuPaul (b. 1960) brought human faces and kind hearts to what heretofore had been identified simply as taboo behavior.

Straight America began seeing the LGBTQ+ community as no different from them, seeking love, acceptance, respect, and to live their lives in peace. Throughout the 2000s, one by one, several states began to end their bans on same-sex marriages, and, in 2015, the U.S. Supreme Court ruled that such bans were unconstitutional, allowing same-sex couples to enjoy, or regret, the bonds of matrimony so long denied them. In 2020, U.S. Navy veteran and mayor of South Bend, Indiana, Pete Buttigieg (b. 1982), became the first openly gay individual to run for president of the United States. Though unable to achieve the Democratic nomination, his widespread national support and strong showing in early caucuses and primaries are, themselves, a testament to how far American society has come in the area of gender and sexual identity acceptance.

THE ECONOMY

As chaotic as the 2000s had been, as America approached the 2008 presidential election, there appeared to be some glimmer of hope that a change of administration, regardless of who won, might usher in a better sociopolitical climate and America could get back to "normal." That, however, was not to be. With only a few months left of President Bush's second term, ending one of the most tumultuous administrations any president had ever endured, the U.S. economy and the global economy along with it dropped off the proverbial cliff. As early as late 2007, there were clear signs in the real estate market that the gambling that Wall Street banks had been doing for the last ten years with subprime mortgages (i.e., approving home loans to individuals who the banks knew could not pay them) was about to cause an economic collapse. As banks gave out loans they knew would default, they also took out insurance policies on those loans. As such, when borrowers defaulted and lost their home, banks recovered their houses to re-sell, kept whatever payments they had collected from borrowers, and were able to cash in their insurance policy for the full amount of the loan. This led to predatory lending: banks actively seeking people they knew would default so that they could make money off the borrower, keep the property, and make more money from the insurance policy.

The collapse began in late summer 2008. During that summer, the U.S. government was forced to bail out lending institutions Fannie Mae and Freddie Mac. Then, in September, the first Wall Street bank, Lehman Brothers, filed for bankruptcy when the government failed to bail them out, with the rationale that bailing out a Wall Street bank would create the precedent of rewarding private corporations for risky behavior and probably exacerbate the practice. Once Lehman collapsed, trust in the other Wall Street banks quickly declined, leading to runs on the banks (investors taking their money out before it was lost). This wave of fear led to the major Wall Street banks falling to the point of collapse, and as the entire global economy was dependent in one way or other on these banks, the entire global economy was threatened. This brought all bank lending to a near halt, freezing credit across the economy.

As the large banks had all insured their loans through AIG, American International Group, the country's largest insurance company, AIG quickly found itself low on capital, which endangered insurance policies and retirement funds for millions of Americans. This had a ripple effect on large companies across the country that depended not only on AIG but also on the lending abilities of the Wall Street banks. Companies such as General Electric, McDonald's, and the Big Three automakers (Ford, General Motors, and Fiat Chrysler) found themselves unable to make future payrolls. At this point, the Bush administration sought a bailout for the investment banks and AIG. What they came up with was TARP, the Tainted Assets Relief Program, injecting billions of dollars into the Wall Street banks so that they could, in turn, lend that money out. However, with the banks now fearful of bad investments, they kept the bailout money to strengthen their capital reserves, and lending remained at an all-time low. By the time President Bush left office in January 2009, more than seven hundred fifty thousand jobs had been lost, and America was in the Great Recession.

President Obama acted quickly to stem the tide of decline. He gave out a bailout to the automakers (approved by Bush before leaving office), and the banks and automakers eventually paid back their bailouts, gaining a profit for taxpayers. He also passed Wall Street reform and opened the Consumer Protection Agency to avoid similar situations in the future. He passed the Affordable Care Act (more commonly known as Obamacare) providing health insurance to more Americans than ever before, thereby bringing down health care costs over time and creating jobs. Despite his actions, the recession continued throughout his first term, and by the time he sought reelection in 2012, unemployment still hovered near 10 percent. By 2014, the Great Recession was over, and America began to rebuild, but the underlying causes of the collapse remain, and the dangers of another collapse are ever present.

The America of 2010 was a completely different world than that of 2000. The enhanced security measures and long-term wars in the wake of 9/11, rapid technological advancements, major shifts in American values, and a collapsed economy made the 2010s impossible to predict. Indeed, the decade that followed did see its own transformations—some for the better, too many for the worse—leaving the predictability of the 2020s equally impossible to foresee. The COVID-19 virus outbreak of 2020 once more caught America—and Americans—off guard. Since 2000, the United States has become a country that far too often has to react to situations rather than taking time to foresee and plan ahead. While, to date, Americans have proven up to the challenge for the most part, continuing to gamble the nation's very existence on this ability is a behavior destined to create more uncertainty, more fear, and possible failure.

FURTHER READING

Abad-Santos, Alex. 2016. "Marvel's Civil War and Its Politics, Explained." *Vox*, May 3. https://www.vox.com/2016/5/3/11531348/marvel-civil-war-explained. Retrieved January 2, 2020.

Alter, Jonathan. 2010. *The Promise: President Obama, Year One.* New York: Simon & Schuster.

Balko, Radley. 2014. *Rise of the Warrior Cop: The Militarization of America's Police Forces.* New York: PublicAffairs.

Bennett, Jessica. 2019. "This Gen X Mess: The Tech, Music, Style, Books, Trends, Rules, Films and Pills That Made Gen X . . . So So-So." *New York Times*, May 16. https://www.nytimes.com/interactive/2019/05/14/style/generation-xers.html?utm_source=pocket-newtab. Retrieved May 16, 2019.

Bodroghkozy, Aniko. 2018. *A Companion to the History of American Broadcasting.* New York: Wiley-Blackwell.

Bush, George W. 2010. *Decision Points.* New York: Crown.

Carr, Nicholas. 2011. *The Shallows: What the Internet Is Doing to Our Brains.* New York: W. W. Norton.

Castleman, Harry, and Walter J. Podrazik. 2016. *Watching TV: Eight Decades of American Television.* 3rd ed. New York: Syracuse University Press.

Chamberlain, Will. 2019. "Jon Stewart Was Wrong about Crossfire: It's Time to Bring Bombastic, Evenly Matched Debates to Cable TV." Human Events, September 6. https://humanevents.com/2019/09/06/jon-stewart-was-wrong-about-crossfire/. Retrieved January 12, 2020.

Charnas, Dan. 2011. *The Big Payback: The History of the Business of Hip-Hop.* New York: Berkley.

Chomsky, Noam. 2005. *Imperial Ambitions: Conversations on the Post-9/11 World.* New York: Metropolitan.

Clinton, Hillary. 2014. *Hard Choices: A Memoir.* New York: Simon & Schuster.

Collins, Scott. 2004. *Crazy Like a Fox: The Inside Story of How FOX News Beat CNN.* New York: Portfolio.

Coontz, Stephanie. 2016. *The Way We Never Were: American Families and the Nostalgia Trap.* New York: Basic.

Crowson, H. Michael, Teresa K. Debacker, and Stephen J. Thoma. 2006. "The Role of Authoritarianism, Perceived Threat, and Need for Closure or Structure in Predicting Post-9/11 Attitudes and Beliefs." *Journal of Social Psychology* 146, no. 6: 733–750.

Danesi, Marcel. 2012. *Popular Culture: Introductory Perspectives.* 2nd ed. Lanham, MD: Rowman & Littlefield.

Essinger, James. 2014. *Ada's Algorithm: How Lord Byron's Daughter Ada Lovelace Launched the Digital Age.* New York: Melville House.

Faludi, Susan. 2008. *The Terror Dream: Myth and Misogyny in an Insecure America.* London: Picador.

Farris, Scott. 2012. *Almost President: The Men Who Lost the Race but Changed the Nation.* Guilford, CT: Lyons.

Farrow, Ronan. 2018. *War on Peace: The End of Diplomacy and the Decline of American Influence.* New York: W. W. Norton.

Fast, Susan, and Kip Pegley, eds. 2012. *Music, Politics, and Violence.* Middletown, CT: Wesleyan University Press.

Ferrence, Matthew J. 2014. *All-American Redneck: Variations on an Icon, from James Fenimore Cooper to the Dixie Chicks.* Knoxville: University of Tennessee Press.

Glastris, Paul, Ryan Cooper, and Siyu Hu. 2012. "Obama's Top 50 Accomplishments." *Washington Monthly,* March/April. https://washingtonmonthly.com/magazine/marchapril-2012/obamas-top-50-accomplishments/. Retrieved February 9, 2020.

Goodman, Lizzy. 2018. *Meet Me in the Bathroom: Rebirth and Rock and Roll in New York City 2001–2011.* New York: Dey Street Books.

Gournelos, Ted, and Viveca Greene, eds. 2011. *A Decade of Dark Humor: How Comedy, Irony, and Satire Shaped Post-9/11 America.* Jackson: University Press of Mississippi.

Graham, Ashley, and Rebecca Paley. 2017. *A New Model: What Confidence, Beauty, and Power Really Look Like.* New York: Dey Street.

Grossman, Dave. 2009. *On Killing: The Psychological Cost of Learning to Kill in War and Society, Revised and Updated.* New York: Back Bay.

Handscombe, Claire. 2016. *Walk with Us: How* The West Wing *Changed Our Lives.* New York: CH Books.

Hart, Kylo-Patrick R., ed. 2016. *Queer TV in the 21st Century: Essays on Broadcasting from Taboo to Acceptance.* Jefferson, NC: McFarland.

Healthcare.gov. 2010. "The Affordable Care Act." March 23. https://www.healthcare.gov/where-can-i-read-the-affordable-care-act/. Retrieved February 1, 2020.

Hilal, Maha. 2017. "Abu Ghraib: The Legacy of Torture in the War on Terror." Al Jazeera, October 1. https://www.aljazeera.com/indepth/opinion/abu-ghraib-legacy-torture-war-terror-170928154012053.html. Retrieved February 1, 2020.

Hinton, Rachel, and Helena Hunt, eds. 2020. *RuPaul: In His Own Words.* Evanston, IL: Agate B2.

Jennings, John. 2017. *The Wit and Wisdom of Ellen DeGeneres.* Independently published.

Kiersz, Andy, and Taylor Nicole Rogers. 2019. "Jeff Bezos Might Lose His Spot as the World's Richest Person as Amazon Shares Tank. Here's How He Makes and Spends His Billions." *Business Insider,* October 25. https://www.businessinsider.com/jeff-bezos-net-worth-life-spending-2018-8. Retrieved January 8, 2020.

Kruse, Kevin M., and Julian E. Zelizer. 2019. *Fault Lines: A History of the United States since 1974.* New York: W. W. Norton.

Letukas, Lynn. 2014. *Primetime Pundits: How Cable News Covers Social Issues.* Washington, DC: Lexington.

Malone, Bill C., and Tracey Laird. 2018. *Country Music USA: 50th Anniversary Edition.* Austin: University of Texas Press.

Manning, Rob, and William L. Simon. 2017. *Mars Rover Curiosity: An Inside Account from Curiosity's Chief Engineer.* Washington, DC: Smithsonian.

Mezrich, Ben. 2009. *The Accidental Billionaires: The Founding of Facebook, a Tale of Sex, Money, Genius, and Betrayal.* New York: Doubleday.

Obama, Barack. 2009. "First Inaugural Address." Obama White House, January 20. https://obamawhitehouse.archives.gov/blog/2009/01/21/president-barack-obamas-inaugural-address. Retrieved March 31, 2019.

Obama, Michelle. 2018. *Becoming.* New York: Crown.

Randolph, Marc. 2019. *That Will Never Work: The Birth of Netflix and the Amazing Life of an Idea.* Boston: Little, Brown and Company.

Rapp, Nicholas, and Krishna Thakker. 2017. "Harry Potter at 20: Billions in Box Office Revenue, Millions of Books Sold." *Fortune*, June 26. https://fortune.com/2017/06/26/harry-potter-20th-anniversary/. Retrieved January 4, 2020.

Redding, Anna Crowley. 2018. *Google It: A History of Google.* New York: Feiwel & Friends.

Richmond, Kia Jane. 2018. *Mental Illness in Young Adult Literature: Exploring Real Struggles through Fictional Characters.* Santa Barbara, CA: Libraries Unlimited.

Rogak, Lisa. 2015. *Angry Optimism: The Life and Times of Jon Stewart.* New York: St. Martin's.

Rolling Stone. 2011. "100 Best Songs of the 2000s." June 17. https://www.rollingstone.com/music/music-lists/100-best-songs-of-the-2000s-153056/damian-marley-welcome-to-jamrock-159253/. Retrieved November 23, 2019.

Salkowitz, Rob. 2012. *Comic-Con and the Business of Pop Culture: What the World's Wildest Trade Show Can Tell Us about the Future of Entertainment.* New York: McGraw-Hill.

Schroeder, Wallace. 2019. *The New York Times Book of Movies: The Essential 1,000 Films to See.* New York: Universe.

Smith, Chris. 2016. The Daily Show *(The Book): An Oral History as Told by Jon Stewart, the Correspondents, Staff and Guests.* New York: Grand Central.

Smith, Michael. 2017. *Streaming, Sharing, Stealing: Big Data and the Future of Entertainment.* Cambridge, MA: MIT.

Sorkin, Andrew Ross. 2009. *Too Big to Fail: The Inside Story of How Wall Street and Washington Fought to Save the Financial System—And Themselves.* New York: Penguin.

Thompson, Derek. 2016. "The Print Apocalypse and How to Survive It." *Atlantic*, November 3. https://www.theatlantic.com/business/archive/2016/11/the-print-apocalypse-and-how-to-survive-it/506429/. Retrieved January 14, 2020.

Tucker, Reed. 2017. *Slugfest: Inside the Epic 50-Year Battle Between Marvel and DC.* New York: Da Capo.

Van Dijck, José. 2013. *The Culture of Connectivity: A Critical History of Social Media.* Oxford: Oxford University Press.

Waldfogel, Joel. 2018. *Digital Renaissance: What Data and Economics Tell Us about the Future of Popular Culture.* Princeton, NJ: Princeton University Press.

Watson, Bruce. 2016. *Jon Stewart: Beyond the Moments of Zen.* Scotts Valley, CA: CreateSpace.

Wheeler, Tom. 2019. *From Gutenberg to Google: The History of Our Future.* Washington, DC: Brookings Institution.

Bibliography

Abad-Santos, Alex. 2016. "Marvel's Civil War and Its Politics, Explained." Vox, May 3. https://www.vox.com/2016/5/3/11531348/marvel-civil-war-explained. Retrieved January 2, 2020.

Abrams, Loney. 2018. "How Does Banksy Make Money? (Or, a Quick Lesson in Art Market Economics)." Artspace, March 30. https://www.artspace.com/magazine /art_101/close_look/how-does-banksy-make-money-or-a-lesson-in-art-market -economics-55352. Retrieved January 26, 2020.

Albergotti, Reed, and Vanessa O'Connell. 2014. *Wheelmen: Lance Armstrong, the Tour de France, and the Greatest Sports Conspiracy Ever.* New York: Penguin/Avery.

Ali, Rahsheeda. 2013. "Top 100 Songs of the '90s." VH1, May 23. https://web.archive .org/web/20120214035830/http://blog.vh1.com/2007-12-13/top-100-songs-of-the -90s. Retrieved May 15, 2019.

Alter, Jonathan. 2010. *The Promise: President Obama, Year One.* New York: Simon & Schuster.

Angelou, Maya. 1978. "Still I Rise." Poets.org. https://poets.org/poem/still-i-rise?gclid =EAIaIQobChMI9cnh2fHn5gIVrP_jBx1BYAPHEAAYASAAEgKFMPD_BwE. Retrieved January 3, 2020.

Armstrong, Jennifer Keishin. 2018. Sex and the City *and Us: How Four Single Women Changed the Way We Think, Live, and Love.* New York: Simon & Schuster.

Armstrong, Lance, and Sally Jenkins. 2001. *It's Not About the Bike: My Journey Back to Life.* New York: Berkley Trade.

Ashby, LeRoy. 2006. *With Amusement for All: A History of American Popular Culture since 1830.* Lexington: University Press of Kentucky.

Assael, Shaun, and Mike Mooneyham. 2004. *Sex, Lies, and Headlocks: The Real Story of Vince McMahon and World Wrestling Entertainment.* Portland, OR: Broadway.

Bailey, Julius, ed. 2015. *The Cultural Impact of Kanye West.* London: Palgrave Macmillan.

Balko, Radley. 2014. *Rise of the Warrior Cop: The Militarization of America's Police Forces.* New York: PublicAffairs.

Banksy. 2005. *Wall and Piece.* London: Random House UK.

Barker, Cory, Chris Ryan, and Myc Wiatrowski, eds. 2014. *Mapping* Smallville: *Critical Essays on the Series and Its Characters.* Jefferson, NC: McFarland.

Beahm, George. 2015. *The Stephen King Companion: Four Decades of Fear from the Master of Horror*. New York: St. Martin's Griffin.

Bennett, Jessica. 2019. "This Gen X Mess: The Tech, Music, Style, Books, Trends, Rules, Films and Pills That Made Gen X . . . So So-So." *New York Times*, May 16. https://www.nytimes.com/interactive/2019/05/14/style/generation-xers.html?utm_source=pocket-newtab. Retrieved May 16, 2019.

Bennetts, Leslie. 2016. *Last Girl Before Freeway: The Life, Loves, Losses, and Liberation of Joan Rivers*. Boston: Little, Brown and Company.

Berman, William C. 2001. *From the Center to the Edge: The Politics & Policies of the Clinton Presidency*. Lanham, MD: Rowman & Littlefield.

Bodroghkozy, Aniko. 2018. *A Companion to the History of American Broadcasting*. New York: Wiley-Blackwell.

Bond, Jeff, and Joe Fordham. 2014. Planet of the Apes: *The Evolution of the Legend*. London: Titan.

Bowen, Michelle. 2018. *J. K. Rowling: From Welfare to Billionaire, a Biography*. Scotts Valley, CA: CreateSpace.

Brands, H. W. 2011. *American Dreams: The United States since 1945*. New York: Penguin.

Breihan, Tom. 2011. "VH1 100 Greatest Songs of the '00s." Stereogum, September 29. https://www.stereogum.com/826992/vh1-100-greatest-songs-of-the-00s/franchises/list/. Retrieved November 23, 2019.

Bryant, Kobe. 2018. *The Mamba Mentality: How I Play*. New York: MCD.

Bush, George W. 2001. "Address to the Nation." American Rhetoric, September 11. https://www.americanrhetoric.com/speeches/gwbush911addresstothenation.htm. Retrieved March 31, 2019.

Bush, George W. 2010. *Decision Points*. New York: Crown.

Cancel, Nola. 2014. *Anne Rice the Interviews: A Compilation of Interviews with the Iconic Author on Everything from the Writing Process to Her Extraordinary Life*. Scotts Valley, CA: CreateSpace.

Canseco, José. 2005. *Juiced: Wild Times, Rampant 'Roids, Smash Hits, and How Baseball Got Big*. New York: William Morrow.

Canseco, José. 2009. *Vindicated: Big Names, Big Liars, and the Battle to Save Baseball*. New York: Gallery/Simon & Schuster.

Carlson, Erin. 2019. *Queen Meryl: The Iconic Roles, Heroic Deeds, and Legendary Life of Meryl Streep*. New York: Hachette.

Carr, Nicholas. 2011. *The Shallows: What the Internet Is Doing to Our Brains*. New York: W. W. Norton.

Carter, Bill. 2005. "CNN Will Cancel 'Crossfire' and Cut Ties to Commentator." *The New York Times*, January 6. https://www.nytimes.com/2005/01/06/business/media/cnn-will-cancel-crossfire-and-cut-ties-to-commentator.html. Retrieved January 12, 2020.

Carter, Bill. 2011. *The War for Late Night: When Leno Went Early and Television Went Crazy*. New York: Plume.

Castleman, Harry, and Walter J. Podrazik. 2016. *Watching TV: Eight Decades of American Television*. 3rd ed. New York: Syracuse University Press.

CBS News. 2018a. "How Sports Helped America Heal after 9/11." September 8. https://www.cbsnews.com/news/how-sports-helped-america-heal-after-911-new-york-city-exhibit/. Retrieved November 14, 2019.

CBS News. 2018b. "Meet the Artist Who Put a Realistic Spin on Comic Book Superheroes." *CBS This Morning*, December 22. https://www.cbsnews.com/news/comic-book-artist-alex-ross/. Retrieved January 26, 2020.

Chamberlain, Will. 2019. "Jon Stewart Was Wrong about Crossfire: It's Time to Bring Bombastic, Evenly Matched Debates to Cable TV." Human Events, September 6.

https://humanevents.com/2019/09/06/jon-stewart-was-wrong-about-crossfire/.
Retrieved January 12, 2020.

Chambers, Veronica. 2019. *Queen Bey: A Celebration of the Power and Creativity of Beyoncé Knowles-Carter*. New York: St. Martin's.

Chang, Jeff. 2005. *Can't Stop Won't Stop: A History of the Hip-Hop Generation*. London: Picador.

Charnas, Dan. 2011. *The Big Payback: The History of the Business of Hip-Hop*. New York: Berkley.

Chomsky, Noam. 2005. *Imperial Ambitions: Conversations on the Post-9/11 World*. New York: Metropolitan.

Chossudovsky, Michel. 2004. "What Happened on the Planes on September 11, 2001? The 9/11 Cell Phone Calls. The 9/11 Commission 'Script' Was Fabricated." GlobalResearch, August 10. https://www.globalresearch.ca/more-holes-in-the-official-story-the-911-cell-phone-calls/5652872. Retrieved January 10, 2020.

Clinton, Hillary Rodham. 2003. *Living History*. New York: Simon & Schuster.

Clinton, Hillary Rodham. 2014. *Hard Choices: A Memoir*. New York: Simon & Schuster.

Colbert, Stephen. 2009. *I Am America (and So Can You!)*. New York: Grand Central.

Collins, Scott. 2004. *Crazy Like a Fox: The Inside Story of How FOX News Beat CNN*. New York: Portfolio.

Conrad, Dean. 2018. *Space Sirens, Scientists and Princesses: The Portrayal of Women in Science Fiction Cinema*. Jefferson, NC: McFarland.

Coontz, Stephanie. 2016. *The Way We Never Were: American Families and the Nostalgia Trap*. New York: Basic.

Crowson, H. Michael, Teresa K. Debacker, and Stephen J. Thoma. 2006. "The Role of Authoritarianism, Perceived Threat, and Need for Closure or Structure in Predicting Post-9/11 Attitudes and Beliefs." *Journal of Social Psychology* 146, no. 6: 733–750.

Cullen, Jim. 2002. *The Art of Democracy: A Concise History of Popular Culture in the United States*. New ed. New York: Monthly Review.

Danesi, Marcel. 2012. *Popular Culture: Introductory Perspectives*. 2nd ed. Lanham, MD: Rowman & Littlefield.

Dennis, Steve. 2010. *Britney: Inside the Dream*. New York: Harper.

Dittmer, Jason. 2005. "Captain America's Empire: Reflections on Identity, Popular Culture, and Post-9/11 Geopolitics." *Annals of the Association of American Geographers* 95, no. 3: 626–643.

Dominguez, Eddie, Christian Red, and Teri Thompson. 2018. *Baseball Cop: The Dark Side of America's National Pastime*. New York: Hachette.

Dominguez, Pier. 2003. *Christina Aguilera: A Star Is Made*. Dubai: Amber.

Ebner, Mark. 2009. *Six Degrees of Paris Hilton: Inside the Sex Tapes, Scandals, and Shakedowns of the New Hollywood*. New York: Gallery.

Edmondson, Jaqueline. 2005. *Venus and Serena Williams: A Biography*. Santa Barbara, CA: Greenwood.

Edwards, Gavin. 2018. *The World According to Tom Hanks: The Life, the Obsessions, the Good Deeds of America's Most Decent Guy*. New York: Grand Central.

Elfrink, Tim, and Gus Garcia-Roberts. 2014. *Blood Sport: Alex Rodriguez, Biogenesis, and the Quest to End Baseball's Steroid Era*. New York: Dutton.

Eriksson, Maria, Rasmus Fleischer, Anna Johansson, Pelle Snickars, and Patrick Vonderau. 2019. *Spotify Teardown: Inside the Black Box of Streaming Music*. Cambridge, MA: MIT.

Errico, Marcus. 1996. "Marvel Files for Bankruptcy." *E! News*, December 27. https://www.eonline.com/news/33907/marvel-files-for-bankruptcy. Retrieved January 14, 2020.

Essinger, James. 2014. *Ada's Algorithm: How Lord Byron's Daughter Ada Lovelace Launched the Digital Age*. New York: Melville House.

Eurodata TV Worldwide. 2009. "'House' Is World's Most Popular TV Show." *Agence France Presse*, June 12. https://web.archive.org/web/20120401043907/https://www.google.com/hostednews/afp/article/ALeqM5gGRhjVWTeAVMws-iEDRJOY3IDH7g. Archived April 1, 2012. Retrieved May 27, 2019.

Evans, Jennifer C. 2002. "Hijacking Civil Liberties: The USA PATRIOT Act of 2001." *Loyola University Chicago Law Journal* 33, no. 4: 933–990.

Fahy, Thomas, ed. 2005. *Considering Aaron Sorkin: Essays on the Politics, Poetics and Sleight of Hand in the Films and Television Series*. Jefferson, NC: McFarland.

Fainaru-Wada, Mark, and Lance Williams. 2006. *Game of Shadows: Barry Bonds, BALCO, and the Steroids Scandal That Rocked Professional Sports*. Los Angeles: Gotham.

Faludi, Susan. 2008. *The Terror Dream: Myth and Misogyny in an Insecure America*. London: Picador.

Farris, Scott. 2012. *Almost President: The Men Who Lost the Race but Changed the Nation*. Guilford, CT: Lyons.

Farrow, Ronan. 2018. *War on Peace: The End of Diplomacy and the Decline of American Influence*. New York: W. W. Norton.

Fast, Susan, and Kip Pegley, eds. 2012. *Music, Politics, and Violence*. Middletown, CT: Wesleyan University Press.

Ferrence, Matthew J. 2014. *All-American Redneck: Variations on an Icon, from James Fenimore Cooper to the Dixie Chicks*. Knoxville: University of Tennessee Press.

Fink, Moritz. 2019. The Simpsons: *A Cultural History*. Lanham, MD: Rowman & Littlefield.

Foley, Mick. 2000. *Have A Nice Day: A Tale of Blood and Sweatsocks*. New York: Harper Entertainment.

Ford, Rebecca. 2013. "Oscars: Ellen DeGeneres's Hosting History." *Hollywood Reporter*, August 2. https://www.hollywoodreporter.com/news/oscars-ellen-degeneres-hosting-history-598767. Retrieved January 13, 2020.

Frontline. [Posting Date Unknown]. "A Chronology of the Elian Gonzalez Saga." PBS. https://www.pbs.org/wgbh/pages/frontline/shows/elian/etc/eliancron.html. Retrieved January 30, 2020.

Gardner, David. 2006. *The Tom Hanks Enigma: The Biography of the World's Most Intriguing Movie Star*. London: John Blake.

Gee, James Paul. 2007. *What Video Games Have to Teach Us about Learning and Literacy*. 2nd ed., revised and updated. New York: St. Martin's Griffin.

Geoffreys, Clayton. 2014. *Kobe Bryant: The Inspiring Story of One of Basketball's Greatest Shooting Guards*. Scotts Valley, CA: CreateSpace.

Georgiou, Aristos. 2018. "'Make Pluto a Planet Again' Say Scientists after Controversial Downgrade." *Newsweek*, September 11. https://www.newsweek.com/make-pluto-planet-again-say-scientists-after-controversial-downgrade-1115514. Retrieved February 5, 2020.

Ginsberg, Merle. 2020. "All the Ways Jennifer Lopez's Grammys Versace Dress Changed History." *New York Post*, January 18. https://nypost.com/2020/01/18/all-the-ways-jennifer-lopezs-grammys-versace-dress-changed-history/. Retrieved January 19, 2020.

Glastris, Paul, Ryan Cooper, and Siyu Hu. 2012. "Obama's Top 50 Accomplishments." *Washington Monthly*, March/April. https://washingtonmonthly.com/magazine/marchapril-2012/obamas-top-50-accomplishments/. Retrieved February 9, 2020.

Goertz, Allie. 2018. *100 Things* The Simpsons *Fans Should Know & Do before They Die*. Chicago: Triumph.

Goodman, Lizzy. 2018. *Meet Me in the Bathroom: Rebirth and Rock and Roll in New York City 2001–2011*. New York: Dey Street Books.

Gournelos, Ted, and Viveca Greene, eds. 2011. *A Decade of Dark Humor: How Comedy, Irony, and Satire Shaped Post-9/11 America*. Jackson: University Press of Mississippi.

Graff, Garrett M. 2019. "Pagers, Pay Phones, and Dialup: How We Communicated on 9/11." *Wired*, September 11. https://www.wired.com/story/pagers-pay-phones -and-dialup-how-we-communicated-on-911/. Retrieved January 10, 2020.

Graham, Ashley, and Rebecca Paley. 2017. *A New Model: What Confidence, Beauty, and Power Really Look Like*. New York: Dey Street.

Gross, Edward, and Mark A. Altman. 2018. *So Say We All: The Complete, Uncensored, Unauthorized Oral History of* Battlestar Galactica. New York: Tor.

Grossman, Dave. 2009. *On Killing: The Psychological Cost of Learning to Kill in War and Society, Revised and Updated*. New York: Back Bay.

Guerrasio, Jason. 2015. "New 'Saturday Night Live' Documentary Recounts the Emotional First Show after 9/11." *Business Insider*, April 16. https://www.busines sinsider.com/saturday-night-live-first-show-after-911-2015-4. Retrieved January 13, 2020.

Gunn, Tim. 2007. *Tim Gunn: A Guide to Quality, Taste and Style (Tim Gunn's Guide to Style)*. New York: Harry N. Abrams.

Hal Leonard Corp. 2010. *#1 Country Hits of the 2000s*. Milwaukee, WI: Hal Leonard.

Handley, Rich, and Lou Tambone, eds. 2018. *Somewhere beyond the Heavens: Exploring Battlestar Galactica*. Edwardsville, IL: Sequart Research and Literacy Organization.

Handscombe, Claire. 2016. *Walk with Us: How* The West Wing *Changed Our Lives*. New York: CH Books.

Hart, Kylo-Patrick R., ed. 2016. *Queer TV in the 21st Century: Essays on Broadcasting from Taboo to Acceptance*. Jefferson, NC: McFarland.

Haskell, Molly. 2017. *Steven Spielberg: A Life in Films*. New Haven, CT: Yale University Press.

Healthcare.gov. 2010. "The Affordable Care Act." March 23. https://www.healthcare .gov/where-can-i-read-the-affordable-care-act/. Retrieved February 1, 2020.

Heilemann, John, and Mark Halperin. 2010. *Game Change: Obama and the Clintons, McCain and Palin, and the Race of a Lifetime*. New York: Harper Perennial.

Herbert, Emily. 2010. *Lady Gaga: Behind the Fame*. New York: Harry N. Abrams.

Hilal, Maha. 2017. "Abu Ghraib: The Legacy of Torture in the War on Terror." Al Jazeera, October 1. https://www.aljazeera.com/indepth/opinion/abu-ghraib -legacy-torture-war-terror-170928154012053.html. Retrieved February 1, 2020.

Hinton, Rachel, and Helena Hunt, eds. 2020. *RuPaul: In His Own Words*. Evanston, IL: Agate B2.

History on the Net. [Posting Date Unknown]. "The 2000 Presidential Election." https:// www.historyonthenet.com/authentichistory/1993-2000/3-2000election/2-elec tionnight/index.html. Retrieved January 12, 2020.

Hodgkinson, Mark. 2019. *Serena: A Graphic Biography of the Greatest Tennis Champion*. London: White Lion.

Holmes, Dave. 2019. "A Decade of Music Is Lost on Your iPod. These Are the Deleted Years. Now Let Us Praise Them: From 2003 to 2012 Music Was Disposable and Nothing Survived." *Esquire*, September 4. https://www.esquire.com/entertain ment/music/a28904211/2003-to-2012-forgotten-music-era/. Retrieved November 23, 2019.

Howe, Sean. 2012. *Marvel Comics: The Untold Story*. New York: Harper Perennial.

Iannucci, Lisa. 2008. *Ellen DeGeneres: A Biography*. Santa Barbara, CA: Greenwood.

Iger, Robert. 2019. *The Ride of a Lifetime: Lessons Learned from 15 Years as CEO of the Walt Disney Company*. New York: Random House.

Irwin, William, and Gregory Bassham, eds. 2010. *The Ultimate* Harry Potter *and Philosophy: Hogwarts for Muggles*. Hoboken, NJ: Wiley.

Isaacson, Walter. 2011. *Steve Jobs*. New York: Simon & Schuster.

Jennings, John. 2017. *The Wit and Wisdom of Ellen DeGeneres*. Independently published.

Johnson, Dwayne "the Rock," and Joe Layden. 2000. *The Rock Says . . . : The Most Electrifying Man in Sports Entertainment*. New York: Harper Entertainment.

Jones, Brian Jay. 2016. *George Lucas: A Life*. New York: Little, Brown and Company.

Kaminski, Michael. 2008. *The Secret History of Star Wars*. Kingston, ON: Legacy Books.

Kiersz, Andy, and Taylor Nicole Rogers. 2019. "Jeff Bezos Might Lose His Spot as the World's Richest Person as Amazon Shares Tank. Here's How He Makes and Spends His Billions." *Business Insider*, October 25. https://www.businessinsider.com/jeff-bezos-net-worth-life-spending-2018-8. Retrieved January 8, 2020.

Kistler, Alan. 2013. Doctor Who: *Celebrating Fifty Years, a History*. Guilford, CT: Lyons.

Klemens, Guy. 2010. *The Cellphone: The History and Technology of the Gadget That Changed the World*. Jefferson, NC: McFarland.

Kranz, Gene. 2009. *Failure Is Not an Option: Mission Control from Mercury to Apollo 13 and Beyond*. New York: Simon & Schuster.

Kruse, Kevin M., and Julian E. Zelizer. 2019. *Fault Lines: A History of the United States since 1974*. New York: W. W. Norton.

Kwon, Amos. 2012. "Life & Limb: The Evolution of Prosthetics." Gear Patrol, August 1. https://gearpatrol.com/2012/08/01/life-limb-the-evolution-of-prosthetics/. Retrieved January 11, 2020.

Lakdawalla, Emily. 2018. *The Design and Engineering of Curiosity: How the Mars Rover Performs Its Job*. New York: Springer.

Legal Information Institute. [Posting Date Unknown]. "Supreme Court of the United States: *George W. Bush, et al., Petitioners v. Albert Gore, Jr., et al.*" Cornell Law School. https://www.law.cornell.edu/supct/html/00-949.ZPC.html. Retrieved January 30, 2020.

Leinbach, Michael, and Jonathan H. Ward. 2018. *Bringing Columbia Home: The Untold Story of a Lost Space Shuttle and Her Crew*. New York: Arcade.

Letukas, Lynn. 2014. *Primetime Pundits: How Cable News Covers Social Issues*. Washington, DC: Lexington.

Levy, Janey. 2019. *The Human Genome Project: History Just before You Were Born*. New York: Gareth Stevens.

Library of Congress. [Posting Date Unknown]. "Why Is Pluto No Longer a Planet?" https://www.loc.gov/everyday-mysteries/item/why-is-pluto-no-longer-a-planet/. Retrieved February 5, 2020.

Linzmayer, Owen W. 2004. *Apple Confidential 2.0: The Definitive History of the World's Most Colorful Company*. San Francisco, CA: No Starch.

Macur, Juliet. 2014. *Cycle of Lies: The Fall of Lance Armstrong*. New York: Harper.

Malone, Bill C., and Tracey Laird. 2018. *Country Music USA: 50th Anniversary Edition*. Austin: University of Texas Press.

Manning, Rob, and William L. Simon. 2017. *Mars Rover Curiosity: An Inside Account from Curiosity's Chief Engineer*. Washington, DC: Smithsonian.

Mapes, Jillian. 2010. "Lady Gaga Explains Her Meat Dress: 'It's No Disrespect.'" *Billboard*, September 13. https://www.billboard.com/articles/news/956399/lady-gaga-explains-her-meat-dress-its-no-disrespect. Retrieved January 25, 2020.

McIlwaine, Catherine. 2018. *Tolkien: Maker of Middle-Earth*. Oxford: University of Oxford.

Meacham, Jon, and Tim McGraw. 2019. *Songs of America: Patriotism, Protest, and the Music That Made a Nation*. New York: Random House.

Mehrotra, Karishma. 2013. "Did Reagan Support an Assault-Weapons Ban?" PolitiFact. https://www.politifact.com/factchecks/2013/feb/05/barack-obama/did-reagan-support-assault-weapons-ban/. Retrieved February 6, 2020.

Menn, Joseph. 2003. *All the Rave: The Rise and Fall of Shawn Fanning's Napster*. New York: Crown.

Mezrich, Ben. 2009. *The Accidental Billionaires: The Founding of Facebook, a Tale of Sex, Money, Genius, and Betrayal*. New York: Doubleday.

Mulholland, Neil. 2007. *The Psychology of Harry Potter: An Unauthorized Examination of the Boy Who Lived*. Dallas, TX: Smart Pop.

National Commission on Terrorist Attacks Upon the United States. 2004. *The 9/11 Report*. New York: St. Martin's.

9/11 Commission. 2004. "The 9/11 Commission Report." National Commission on Terrorist Attacks Upon the United States. https://www.9-11commission.gov/report/. Retrieved January 3, 2020.

9/11 Memorial. [Posting Date Unknown]. "September 11 Attack Timeline." https://timeline.911memorial.org/#Timeline/2. Retrieved May 8, 2019.

9/11 Memorial and Museum. 2019. "Comeback Season: Sports after 9/11." https://www.911memorial.org/visit/museum/exhibitions/comeback-season-sports-after-911. Retrieved November 14, 2019.

Obama, Barack. 2004. "Barack Obama's Remarks to the Democratic National Convention." *New York Times*, July 27. https://www.nytimes.com/2004/07/27/politics/campaign/barack-obamas-remarks-to-the-democratic-national.html. Retrieved February 9, 2020.

Obama, Barack. 2006. *The Audacity of Hope: Thoughts on Reclaiming the American Dream*. New York: Crown.

Obama, Barack. 2009. "First Inaugural Address." Obama White House, January 20. https://obamawhitehouse.archives.gov/blog/2009/01/21/president-barack-obamas-inaugural-address. Retrieved March 31, 2019.

Obama, Michelle. 2018. *Becoming*. New York: Crown.

O'Boyle, Britta. 2019. "The History of BlackBerry: The Best BlackBerry Phones That Changed the World." Pocket-Lint, January 16. https://www.pocket-lint.com/phones/news/137319-farewell-blackberry-os-here-are-the-23-best-blackberry-phones-that-changed-the-world. Retrieved January 8, 2020.

Olbermann, Keith. 2006. *The Worst Person in the World: And 202 Strong Contenders*. Hoboken, NJ: Wiley.

Oliver, William. 2012. *Style Feed: The World's Top Fashion Blogs*. Munich: Prestel.

O'Reilly, Bill. 2006. *Culture Warrior*. New York: Crown.

Oswald, Debra L. 2005. "Understanding Anti-Arab Reactions Post-9/11: The Role of Threats, Social Categories, and Personal Ideologies." *Journal of Applied Social Psychology* 35, no. 9: 1775–1799.

Paskett, Zoe. 2019. "Who Is Banksy? Best Theories from Robert Del Naja to Robin Gunningham." *Evening Standard*, December 9. https://www.standard.co.uk/go/london/arts/who-is-banksy-identity-street-artist-a4285461.html. Retrieved January 26, 2020.

Pate, Nancy. 2003. "Lord of the Rings Films Work Magic on Tolkien Book Sales." *South Florida Sun-Sentinel*, August 20. https://www.sun-sentinel.com/news/fl-xpm-2003-08-20-0308190249-story.html. Retrieved January 4, 2020.

Patterson, James T. 2005. *Restless Giant: The United States from Watergate to* Bush v. Gore. Oxford: Oxford University Press.

Pearlman, Robert Z. 2011. "NASA's Space Shuttle Program Officially Ends after Final Celebration." Space.com, September 1. https://www.space.com/12804-nasa-space -shuttle-program-officially-ends.html. Retrieved January 10, 2020.

Pittsburgh Post-Gazette. 2000. "Election 2000 Timeline." December 17. http://old.post -gazette.com/election/20001217pztimeline.asp. Retrieved January 30, 2020.

Potter, Patrick, and Gary Shove. 2019. *Banksy You Are an Acceptable Level of Threat and If You Were Not You Would Know about It.* London: Carpet Bombing Culture.

Price, David A. 2009. *The Pixar Touch: The Making of a Company.* New York: Vintage.

Radomski, Kirk. 2009. *Bases Loaded: The Inside Story of the Steroid Era in Baseball by the Central Figure in the Mitchell Report.* New York: Hudson Street.

Rakove, Jack N., ed. 2002. *The Unfinished Election of 2000: Leading Scholars Examine America's Strangest Election.* New York: Basic.

Ramsay, Randolph. 2008. "Blu-Ray vs. HD DVD: Which Video Format Is for You?" C-Net, August 14. https://www.cnet.com/news/blu-ray-vs-hd-dvd-which-video -format-is-for-you/. Retrieved January 9, 2020.

Randolph, Marc. 2019. *That Will Never Work: The Birth of Netflix and the Amazing Life of an Idea.* Boston: Little, Brown and Company.

Rapp, Nicholas, and Krishna Thakker. 2017. "Harry Potter at 20: Billions in Box Office Revenue, Millions of Books Sold." *Fortune,* June 26. https://fortune.com /2017/06/26/harry-potter-20th-anniversary/. Retrieved January 4, 2020.

Redding, Anna Crowley. 2018. *Google It: A History of Google.* New York: Feiwel & Friends.

Reed, Ryan. 2018. "Metallica's Kirk Hammett: 'We're Still Right' about Suing Napster." *Rolling Stone,* May 14. https://www.rollingstone.com/music/music-news /metallicas-kirk-hammett-were-still-right-about-suing-napster-630185/. Retrieved November 23, 2019.

Rice, Anne. 2010. *Called out of Darkness: A Spiritual Confession.* New York: Anchor.

Richmond, Kia Jane. 2018. *Mental Illness in Young Adult Literature: Exploring Real Struggles through Fictional Characters.* Santa Barbara, CA: Libraries Unlimited.

Ridley, Matt. 2006. *Genome: The Autobiography of a Species in 23 Chapters.* New York: Harper Perennial.

Ritter, Jonathan. 2007. *Music in the Post 9/11 World.* London: Routledge.

Rogak, Lisa. 2015. *Angry Optimism: The Life and Times of Jon Stewart.* New York: St. Martin's.

Rolling Stone. 2011. "100 Best Songs of the 2000s." June 17. https://www.rollingstone .com/music/music-lists/100-best-songs-of-the-2000s-153056/damian-marley -welcome-to-jamrock-159253/. Retrieved November 23, 2019.

Rollins, Peter, and John E. O'Connor. 2003. The West Wing: *The American Presidency as Television Drama.* Syracuse, NY: Syracuse University Press.

Ross, Alex. [Posting Date Unknown.] "Alex Ross." Alex Ross Art. https://www .alexrossart.com/. Retrieved January 26, 2020.

Salkowitz, Rob. 2012. *Comic-Con and the Business of Pop Culture: What the World's Wildest Trade Show Can Tell Us about the Future of Entertainment.* New York: McGraw-Hill.

Schroeder, Wallace. 2019. *The New York Times Book of Movies: The Essential 1,000 Films to See.* New York: Universe.

Siegel, Robert. 2015. "Ben Franklin's Famous 'Liberty, Safety' Quote Lost Its Context in 21st Century." *All Things Considered,* March 2. https://www.npr.org/2015 /03/02/390245038/ben-franklins-famous-liberty-safety-quote-lost-its-context -in-21st-century. Retrieved February 6, 2020.

Simons, Iain, and James Newman. 2019. *A History of Videogames: In 14 Consoles, 5 Computers, 2 Arcade Cabinets . . . and an Ocarina of Time.* London: Carlton.

Sivolella, Davide. 2017. *The Space Shuttle Program: Technologies and Accomplishments.* Cham, Switzerland: Springer Praxis.

Smith, Chris. 2016. The Daily Show *(The Book): An Oral History as Told by Jon Stewart, the Correspondents, Staff and Guests.* New York: Grand Central.

Smith, Michael. 2017. *Streaming, Sharing, Stealing: Big Data and the Future of Entertainment.* Cambridge, MA: MIT.

Sorkin, Andrew Ross. 2009. *Too Big to Fail: The Inside Story of How Wall Street and Washington Fought to Save the Financial System—And Themselves.* New York: Penguin.

Spears, Britney. 2000. *Britney Spears' Heart to Heart.* New York: Three Rivers.

Spitzmiller, Ted. 2017. *The History of Human Space Flight.* Gainesville: University Press of Florida.

Staff. 2017. "Watch Jon Stewart Call Tucker Carlson a 'Dick' in Epic 2004 'Crossfire' Takedown." *Hollywood Reporter,* January 5. https://www.hollywoodreporter.com /news/jon-stewart-takes-down-tucker-carlson-crossfire-video-961127. Retrieved January 12, 2020.

Starr, Larry, and Christopher Waterman. 2017. *American Popular Music: From Minstrelsy to MP3.* New York: Oxford University Press.

Stewart, Jon, et al. 2004. *America (The Book).* New York: Warner/Grand Central.

Stone, Brad. 2013. *The Everything Store: Jeff Bezos and the Age of Amazon.* Boston: Little, Brown and Company.

Stratyner, Leslie, and James R. Keller, eds. 2009. *The Deep End of* South Park: *Critical Essays on Television's Shocking Cartoon Series.* Jefferson, NC: McFarland.

Street, John. 2011. *Music and Politics.* Cambridge: Polity.

Stuller, Jennifer K. 2010. *Ink-Stained Amazons and Cinematic Warriors: Superwomen in Modern Mythology.* London: I. B. Tauris.

Sullivan, Randall. 2012. *Untouchable: The Strange Life and Tragic Death of Michael Jackson.* New York: Grove.

Swanson, Jess, and Angel Garcia. 2019. "Why the Elian Gonzalez Saga Resonates 20 Years Later." *Vox,* November 11. https://www.vox.com/the-highlight/2019/11/4 /20938885/miami-cuba-elian-gonzalez-castro. Retrieved January 30, 2020.

Tapies, Xavier. 2016. *Where's Banksy?: Banksy's Greatest Works in Context.* Berkeley, CA: Gingko.

Taraborrelli, J. Randy. 2010. *Michael Jackson: The Magic, the Madness, the Whole Story, 1958–2009.* New York: Grand Central.

Taylor, Chris. 2015. *How* Star Wars *Conquered the Universe: The Past, Present, and Future of a Multibillion Dollar Franchise.* New York: Basic.

Terry, Josh. 2019. "Sixteen Years Later, Country Radio Is Still Mad at the Dixie Chicks." *Vice,* September 10. https://www.vice.com/en_us/article/evjvqe/sixteen-years -later-country-radio-is-still-mad-at-the-dixie-chicks-taylor-swift-soon-youll-get -better. Retrieved November 23, 2019.

Thompson, Derek. 2016. "The Print Apocalypse and How to Survive It." *Atlantic,* November 3. https://www.theatlantic.com/business/archive/2016/11/the-print -apocalypse-and-how-to-survive-it/506429/. Retrieved January 14, 2020.

Thompson, Gayle. 2019. "16 Years Ago: Natalie Maines Makes Controversial Comments about President George W. Bush." Boot, March 10. https://theboot.com /natalie-maines-dixie-chicks-controversy/. Retrieved November 28, 2019.

Tinsley, Omise'eke Natasha. 2018. *Beyoncé in Formation: Remixing Black Feminism.* Austin: University of Texas Press.

Tonic, Gina. 2016. "The Plus Size Models Who Were Killing It before the Divine Ashley Graham—PHOTOS." *Bustle,* January 21. https://www.bustle.com/articles

/136353-the-plus-size-models-who-were-killing-it-before-the-divine-ashley
-graham-photos. Retrieved January 25, 2020.

Toobin, Jeffrey. 2002. *Too Close to Call: The Thirty-Six-Day Battle to Decide the 2000 Election*. New York: Random House.

Topping, Seymore, and Sig Gissler. [Posting Date Unknown]. "History of the Pulitzer Prizes." Pulitzer Prizes. https://www.pulitzer.org/page/history-pulitzer-prizes. Retrieved January 2, 2020.

Tsonga, Taj. 2019. "Remembering the Greatest Con in Silicon Valley History." *Wired*, January. https://www.wired.com/wiredinsider/2019/01/remembering-greatest -con-silicon-valley-history/. Retrieved May 16, 2019.

Tucker, Reed. 2017. *Slugfest: Inside the Epic 50-Year Battle Between Marvel and DC*. New York: Da Capo.

TV Guide Editors. 2002. TV Guide: *Fifty Years of Television*. New York: Crown.

"TV Guide Picks TV's 60 Nastiest Villains." 2013. Wordsmithonia, April 22. http:// wordsmithonia.blogspot.com/2013/04/tv-guide-picks-tvs-60-nastiest-villains .html. Retrieved August 24, 2018.

Tye, Larry. 2013. *Superman: The High-Flying History of America's Most Enduring Hero*. New York: Random House.

Van Dijck, José. 2013. *The Culture of Connectivity: A Critical History of Social Media*. Oxford: Oxford University Press.

Vance, Ashlee. 2015. *Elon Musk: Tesla, SpaceX, and the Quest for a Fantastic Future*. New York: Ecco.

Veloso, Francisco, and John Bateman. 2013. "The Multimodal Construction of Acceptability: Marvel's *Civil War* Comic Books and the PATRIOT Act." *Critical Discourse Studies* 10, no. 4: 427–443.

Von Drehle, David, et al. 2001. *Deadlock: The Inside Story of America's Closest Election*. New York: PublicAffairs.

Waldfogel, Joel. 2018. *Digital Renaissance: What Data and Economics Tell Us about the Future of Popular Culture*. Princeton, NJ: Princeton University Press.

Walsh, David. 2015. *Seven Deadly Sins: My Pursuit of Lance Armstrong*. New York: Atria.

Watson, Bruce. 2016. *Jon Stewart: Beyond the Moments of Zen*. Scotts Valley, CA: CreateSpace.

Weinstein, Deena. 2015. *Rock'n America: A Social and Cultural History*. Toronto, ON: University of Toronto Press.

Weinstock, Jeffrey Andrew, ed. 2008. *Taking* South Park *Seriously*. Albany: State University of New York Press.

Wheeler, Tom. 2019. *From Gutenberg to Google: The History of Our Future*. Washington, DC: Brookings Institution.

Whitehead, John W., and Steven H. Aden. 2002. "Forfeiting 'Enduring Freedom' for 'Homeland Security': A Constitutional Analysis of the USA Patriot Act and the Justice Department's Anti-Terrorism Initiatives." *American University Law Review* 51, no. 6: 1081–1133.

Willis, Susan. 2005. *Portents of the Real: A Primer for Post-9/11 America*. London: Verso.

Witt, Stephen. 2016. *How Music Got Free: A Story of Obsession and Invention*. New York: Penguin.

Wright, Bradford W. 2003. *Comic Book Nation: The Transformation of Youth Culture in America*. Baltimore, MD: Johns Hopkins University Press.

Index

About the Author

Richard A. Hall resides in Laredo, Texas. After serving four years in the U.S. Army, he attended Texas A&M International, finishing his BA and MA before receiving his PhD in history from Auburn University in Auburn, Alabama. He is the author of *The American Superhero: Encyclopedia of Caped Crusaders in History*; *Pop Goes the Decade: The Seventies*; and *The American Villain: Encyclopedia of Bad Guys in Comics, Film, and Television* (all from ABC-CLIO/Greenwood Press). He is a contributor and member of the board of advisors for the online pop-culture database Pop Culture Universe: Icons, Idols, and Ideas (also from ABC-CLIO). He is also a contributor to *The Supervillain Reader*, a reader on villains in popular culture from University of Mississippi Press. His upcoming projects include *Robots in Popular Culture: Androids and Cyborgs in the American Imagination* from ABC-CLIO/Greenwood and *Gotham, USA: Critical Essays on Ethics, American Society, and the Batman Universe of Television's* Gotham (both due in 2021).

A father of five and grandfather of five, he lives in Laredo, Texas, with the youngest of his children and his wife, best friend, fellow former soldier, coworker, and frequent collaborator, Dr. Maria A. Reyes. This project would not have been possible without the valuable contributions of his research assistants Anahi Montelongo, Mireya Montes, and Pamela Wallace (all undergraduates at Texas A&M International at the time of writing); Rebekah Rodriguez, his Graduate Teaching Assistant; and his daughters, Blanca Hall and Samantha Eachus.